METALWORKING TECHNOLOGY

METALWORKING TECHNOLOGY

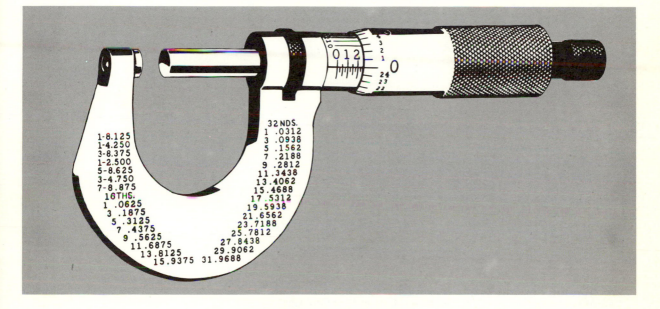

RICHARD L. LITTLE
Southern Illinois University
Carbondale, Illinois

Gregg Division
McGRAW-HILL BOOK COMPANY
New York • St. Louis • Dallas • San Francisco • Auckland • Bogotá • Düsseldorf
Johannesburg • London • Madrid • Mexico • Montreal • New Delhi
Panama • Paris • São Paulo • Singapore • Sydney • Tokyo • Toronto

Library of Congress Cataloging in Publication Data

Little, Richard L.
  Metalworking technology.

  Includes index.
  1. Metal-work. I. Title.
TS205.L59   671   76-856
ISBN 0-07-038097-X

Photo Credits, part- and chapter-opening art.
Part One: Caterpillar Tractor Co. **Part Two:** L. S. Starrett Company.
Part Three: Pyrometer Instrument Company. **Part Four:** Stanley
Tools. **Part Five:** Cincinnati Milacron Company. **Part Six:** Victor
Equipment Company.

Metalworking Technology

1 2 3 4 5 6 7 8 9 0   V H V H   7 8 3 2 1 0 9 8 7 6

The **editors** for this book were Don Helpler and Susan L. Schwartz,
the **designer** was Dennis G. Purdy, the **art supervisor** was George
T. Resch, and the **production supervisor** was Regina R. Malone.
It was set in Caledonia by Progressive Typographers.
Printed and bound by Von Hoffman Press, Inc.

For my students—those past, present, and future

Contents

Preface

Technological demands have created a field for which study materials either are constantly going out of date or are simply inapplicable. *Metalworking Technology* bridges the gap between the materials that are currently available and those that are actually needed.

A technical student today occupies a position with its own peculiar requirements. Besides the extreme importance of being aware of the new processes developed by industry, he or she must also understand the theoretical principles on which the processes are based. Instructors must encourage their students to apply the principles to the general process rather than have them just memorize the steps in operating particular machines. If this is done, updating equipment will not make what has been learned obsolete. A change in operations does not need to mean retraining as long as the process is understood in its theoretical as well as its practical aspects. Consequently, this text presents the scientific principles necessary to explain the theories behind the processes in the metalworking industry.

The first part of the book, "Metals," is designed to acquaint students with the physical properties and structure of metal. The second part, "Quality Control," identifies the means by which metals are tested. The rest of the book is divided into four main metalworking areas, the major manufacturing processes. Each of these four parts contains the theories behind the processes, as well as the application of these theories to specific problems. Every chapter ends with questions that will help to emphasize the major points within that chapter.

Metalworking Technology is designed as an introductory text at a college level. The theoretical principles are presented in such a manner that a scientific background is not mandatory, although students will learn to apply a certain amount of mathematics and science in metalworking technology. They will learn not only the concepts of the process but also the operation. When they finish, they should be able to operate any machine whether they have operated it before or not, and they should also know why it does what it does.

Richard L. Little

METALWORKING TECHNOLOGY

Part One

Metals

Extraction of Metals

The study of metals, called metallurgy, encompasses extractive metallurgy and physical metallurgy. *Physical* metallurgy studies the mechanical treatments, the chemical composition, and the manufacturing processing of metals, as well as how to use metals. *Extractive*, or process, metallurgy, on the other hand, deals solely with how ores are mined and processed into metals.

All metals are extracted either from the sea or from the crust of the earth. So far, our deepest penetration into the crust of the earth has been approximately 10 mi. From the study of these 10 miles, the basic elements which compose the crust have been identified. Table 1-1 presents the percentage by weight in which these basic elements occur. All the elements on the periodic table are present in the earth's crust in varying amounts. Not all these elements are readily available; many can only be derived by means of some processing. Slightly more than 46 percent of the crust is oxygen with oxygen, silicon, and alumina making up 74 percent of the total composition of the crust. All other elements exist only in small percentages by weight. For example, iron makes up 5 percent of the crust, whereas molybdenum makes up only 0.0006 percent by weight (weight percent).

Few metallic or nonmetallic elements are found in their natural, or free, state. A few metals that are available without processing include gold, silver, and small amounts of copper and iron. Most metals must be extracted from the minerals that are found in the ore. The substance for which the ore is mined is called the *value*. Ore is also composed of the *gangue*, which is its waste material. A large part of extractive metallurgy is the process of separating the values from the gangues. The minerals extracted from the ores are either oxides or sulfides. *Oxides* are minerals that have combined with oxygen, and *sulfides* are minerals that have combined with sulfur. Typical minerals containing metallic oxides are iron, chromium, aluminum, and magnesium. Minerals containing metallic sulfides are copper, lead, and zinc.

Metals are extracted from the crust of the earth by two types of mines: the open-pit mine and the underground, or shaft, mine (Figs. 1-1 and 1-2). The open-pit mine is used when deposits are within 300 or 400 ft of the earth's surface. First, the overburden, the material above the mineral, is removed. Sometimes it takes earth-moving equipment working 24 hours a day for 1 year to remove this overburden. If a vein is discovered deep underground, a vertical shaft is dug alongside the vein with tunnels shooting off from the shaft into the vein. Underground

TABLE 1-1. METALS IN THE CRUST OF THE EARTH

METAL	WEIGHT, %
Aluminum	8.1
Copper	0.01
Chromium	0.037
Iron	5.0
Lead	0.002
Magnesium	2.1
Manganese	0.1
Molybdenum	0.0006
Nickel	0.02
Tin	0.0005
Titanium	0.6
Tungsten	0.005
Vanadium	0.017
Zinc	0.004
Zirconium	0.026

work is more hazardous, naturally, than open-pit work, and also more expensive.

Ore may be found with an infinite variety of values. This variation makes the extraction of a value from an ore a complex process. In fact, the specific process of extracting copper from sulfide ore differs from one ore to the next because of the varying amounts of extraneous values and gangues in the different ores.

PROCESS OF EXTRACTING

Flowcharts help to explain the complex and varying procedures of extraction. Figure 1-3 explains the basic procedure used for extracting metals and follows the process through physical metallurgy to the use of the metal in manufactured goods. A typical flowchart for the milling of sulfide copper ores

Fig. 1-1. Open-pit mine. (*Courtesy of Don Green, Kennecott Copper Corporation.*)

Fig. 1-2. Underground mine. *(Courtesy of Don Green, Kennecott Copper Corporation.)*

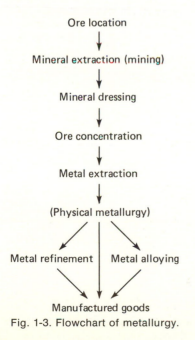

Ore location

↓

Mineral extraction (mining)

↓

Mineral dressing

↓

Ore concentration

↓

Metal extraction

↓

(Physical metallurgy)

↙ ↘

Metal refinement | Metal alloying

↘ ↙

Manufactured goods

Fig. 1-3. Flowchart of metallurgy.

identifies the steps from the removal of the ore from the open-pit mine by shovels through the crushing, grinding, and flotation stages, and then through the separation of the ore concentrate in the tailings. This flow of mineral from the mine to the final concentrate (Fig. 1-4) is typical of most metals.

Ore Dressing

The pulverizing of the mineral so that it can be further treated is called *ore dressing*. Ore dressing involves three steps: primary crushing, secondary crushing, and grinding. Primary and secondary crushing are accomplished with the same equipment but with different settings on the crushing jaws. Primary crushing brings the ore down to 2- to 3-in.-diameter pieces. These minerals will then go through one, two, or three stages of secondary crushing, reducing the diameter of the mineral pieces to approximately ¼ in.

The crushers that perform the primary

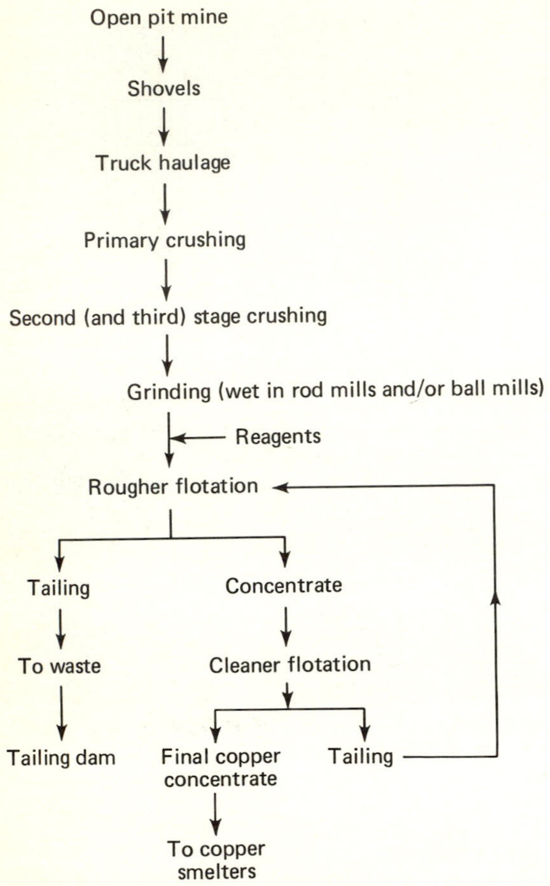

Open pit mine
↓
Shovels
↓
Truck haulage
↓
Primary crushing
↓
Second (and third) stage crushing
↓
Grinding (wet in rod mills and/or ball mills)
↓ ← Reagents
Rougher flotation ←
↓   ↓
Tailing   Concentrate
↓   ↓
To waste   Cleaner flotation
↓   ↓   ↓
Tailing dam   Final copper   Tailing
              concentrate
                   ↓
              To copper
              smelters

Fig. 1-4. Milling of sulfide copper ores. (*American Smelting and Refining Company.*)

and secondary crushing may be jaw crushers, cone crushers, and hammer, or drum, mills. Jaw crushers have a stationary jaw and a movable jaw that moves 1 to 2 in. This small amount of movement is sufficient to crush most minerals (Fig. 1-5a). Cone crushers, used for both primary and secondary ore dressing, have one cone inverted into another. The distance between the vibrating cone and the stationary cone determines the size of the material that will pass through the crusher. Generally, the cone moves 1 or 2 in. in a circular motion to crush the mineral (Fig. 1-5b).

Drum mills are rotating drums. The ore is introduced into one section of the drum, and the drum revolves, allowing the ore to

tumble (Fig. 1-5c). The ore is then forced out the other end of the drum. If the mineral being ground does not have sufficient weight to allow a grinding action, or if it is desirable to reduce the grinding time, the drum mill can be charged with either round steel balls or rounded rods made out of flint or metal, usually a heat-treated metal. As the drum mill rotates, these metal balls fall upon the ore, grinding it further. Drum mills that use balls as a grinding media are called *ball mills*, and those that use rods are called *rod mills*. Drum mills can produce mineral pieces with 0.0006-in. diameter. The longer the mineral

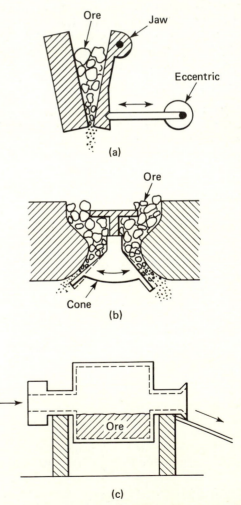

Fig. 1-5. Ore dressing. (a) Jaw crusher; (b) cone crusher; (c) drum mill.

stays within the rotating drum mill, the smaller the particles will be.

Concentration

Concentration separates the value from the gangue. It takes place after the crushing and grinding stages. Generally, the metal concentrate is separated by means of gravity, flotation, or magnetism.

GRAVITY. The gravity system relies on the difference in specific gravity between the ore and the gangue for separating the gangue from the mineral. The basic types of gravity concentration systems are the sink system, the sink-float system, and the jigging system. The *sink system* dumps the mineral that has been ground to the same size and roughly the same shape into still water. The value, having a higher specific gravity, will sink more rapidly than the gangue. As the gangue floats, a stream of water bears it away, and thus only the ore falls to the bottom. The *sink-float system* works in the same manner except that water is not used as the floating solution. The floating solution used will have a specific gravity between the specific gravities of the values and the gangues. Consequently, the gangue will be suspended in, or will float to the surface of, the solution and the values will fall to the bottom of the solution. The major problem with the sink-float method for the separation of most minerals is that solutions with exact specific gravities must be used and these solutions are not readily available.

The *jig plunger gravity system* of concentration is a variation of the other two systems. Water is used as a flotation device, and a plunger is used to agitate the water to wet the mineral. The mineral is fed into the water, and the plunger, as it moves up and down, increases and decreases the water level, forcing water up through a screen. A separation begins because the specific gravities of the gangue and the ore differ. The gangue, because it is lighter, tends to remain at the top of the water level, while the ore sinks onto the screen. A stream of water is

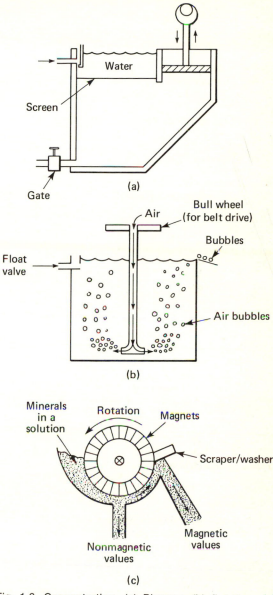

Fig. 1-6. Concentration. (a) Plunger; (b) flotation; (c) magnetism.

directed across the top of the water, removing the gangue and leaving the ore to collect on the screen (Fig. 1-6a).

FLOTATION. The flotation process of separating the gangue from the ore, probably the most used method in extractive metallurgy, mainly uses water as the flotation medium. Chemicals are added to the water to act as either collectors or frothers. The ground mineral is placed in the flotation cell and air is injected through the water. The air, with the frothing element, creates air bubbles, which have an oil coating resulting from the collector chemical. The bubbles attach themselves to the ore and float it to the surface. The ore-carrying air bubbles then are forced out of the flotation cell (Fig. 1-6b).

The apparatus that injects the air into the flotation cell rotates at high speed, further mixing the water. The gangue, wetted by the water, becomes heavy and sinks to the bottom of the cell, while the ore attached to the oil-coated air bubbles rises to the surface to be processed further. The surface area of the air bubbles determines the amount of ore

that each bubble can pick up. Groups of small bubbles have a larger surface area than do large bubbles, making it possible for the small bubbles to remove more ore.

MAGNETISM. A magnetic separator separates magnetic from nonmagnetic values, or values with high conductivity from those with low conductivity. Minerals in a solution are exposed to a set of magnets mounted on a drum. As the minerals pass the magnets, the magnetic minerals are attracted to the magnets. The nonmagnetic minerals are routed away from the magnetic drum for further processing. The magnetic values that are attached to the drum rotate around until they bump into a scraping, washing device that cleanses the drum and removes all values

Fig. 1-7. Tailings dump. (*Courtesy of Don Green, Kennecott Copper Corporation.*)

from it. Directly below the scraper, ductwork routes the values toward further metallurgical processes (Fig. 1-6c).

Tailings

Even though most of the value has been separated from the gangue, it is a common practice to store the gangue resulting from concentration. This gangue, known as *tailings*, is stored in tailings dumps (Fig. 1-7). The tailings are not dispersed because it may someday be possible to extract the values that have been impossible to extract with current processes. For example, not too many years ago only high-grade copper ore could be processed through extractive metallurgy. Today it is possible to extract extremely low-yield ore profitably so that material from the old tailings dumps is being recycled and values are being separated from them.

Refining

Refining is a final process in extractive metallurgy. It is the process by which the metal is extracted from the ore concentrate. Refining is accomplished by three processes: pyrometallurgical, hydrometallurgical, or electrometallurgical extraction. The pyrometallurgical extraction process uses heat from the burning of fuels for extracting the ore. The hydrometallurgical extraction process depends on a solvent to precipitate the metal from the ore. The electrometallurgical extraction process uses electrolysis or a form of electrolytic deposition, such as is used in plating, for the separation of the metal from the ore.

PYROMETALLURGICAL EXTRACTION. *Smelting*, the major method of pyrometallurgical extraction, is used for more than 95 percent of all pyro processing. Smelting reduces the ore to a metal. Reduction involves reducing the oxygen content of a compound. The ore previously has either had an oxide or a sulfide introduced into it. Now reduction lowers this oxygen or sulfide content and helps recover (*win*) the metal from the ore. The major types of smelting furnaces are the

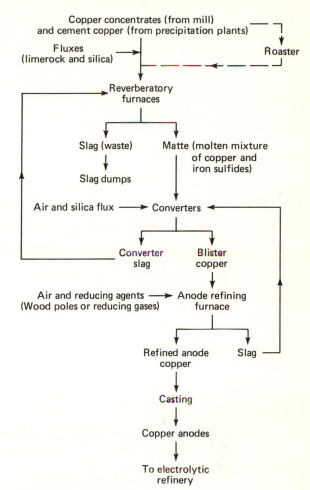

Fig. 1-8. Pyrometallurgical extraction. Smelting of copper concentrates. (*American Smelting and Refining Company.*)

reverberatory furnace, used mainly for the smelting of nonferrous metals, and the blast furnace, used mainly for the smelting of ferrous metals.

Sintering, calcination, and roasting are other pyro processes that may be used prior to the actual smelting of the metal. The *sintering* process is used to increase the particle, or mass, size of the ore. Sintering heats the concentrated ore until it balls together into clinkers. Sintering generally is used because the concentrated ore is in a powdered or ground form, and if the metal were introduced

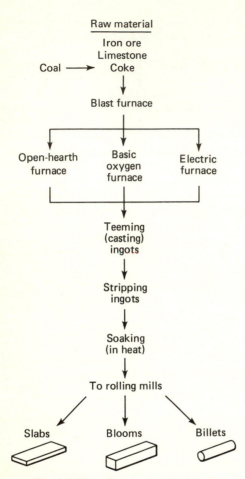

Fig. 1-9. Flow line on steel making.

transferred directly to the smelter for further winning of the ore.

The smelting of copper is an example of pyrometallurgical extraction. When the copper concentrate comes from the concentration cells, it is roasted or sometimes it goes straight to the reverberatory furnace. There it is mixed with lime and silicon. The furnace produces a matte of copper, a molten mixture of copper and iron sulfides. A matte metal is always a sulfide metal. The slag is removed

into a smelting furnace in this form, much of the metal would go up the flue.

Calcination is used when the ore concentrate is a compound of a gas and a solid. The calcination process separates the solids from the gas. For example, bauxite, an aluminum ore, is mixed with lime and soda ash; the mixture, when heated, produces a hydrated aluminum. This hydrated aluminum is then reheated to produce alumina. The alumina changes from hydrated alumina to aluminum in the calcination process.

Roasting forms oxides and sulfides in the ore. Roasting is exactly what the name implies: the ore is simply heated until the oxide or sulfide coating is present. The ore is then

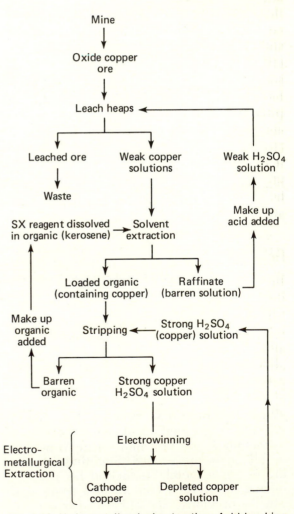

Fig. 1-10. Hydrometallurgical extraction. Acid leaching oxide copper ores with solvent extraction and electrowinning of copper. (*American Smelting and Refining Company.*)

from the melt and transported to the slag dumps. The smelted copper then proceeds for further refinement (Fig. 1-8).

The conversion of iron ore, limestone, and coal into iron is the basis of 90 percent of all metal winning. The blast furnace is the basic pyrometallurgical process used in making iron. The process involves crushing, washing, and sizing iron ore and crushing and sizing limestone. Also necessary is coke, a product of coal that has been burnt in a relatively oxygen-free atmosphere. The iron ore, limestone, and coke are placed in a blast furnace (Fig. 1-9) and put through the smelting operation. The blast furnace generates 3000°F, producing a pig iron and a slag. The pig iron is placed in mixing furnaces or in molten-iron transfer cars for further refining. The further refinement of iron into steel lies

within the realm of physical metallurgy, discussed in later chapters.

HYDROMETALLURGICAL EXTRACTION. The major method used in the hydrometallurgical process of winning ore is *leaching*. Leaching is often done in conjunction with some other extraction process. Figure 1-10 illustrates the acid leaching of oxide copper ores with the solvent extraction and electrowinning of copper. A sulfuric acid solution is used as a solvent with the ore, suspending the copper in the solution. The solution then goes through an electrowinning process, which is a basic electroplating process, and the copper that is held in the solution is attracted to copper cathodes. Cathodic copper is then refined, going on into its commercial shapes (Fig. 1-11). Hydrometallurgical metal extraction is

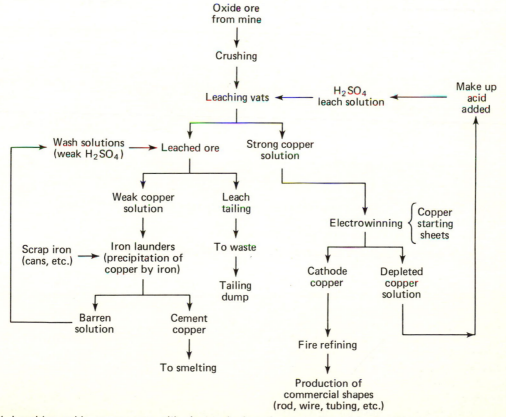

Fig. 1-11. Leaching oxide copper ores with electrowinning of copper. (*American Smelting and Refining Company.*)

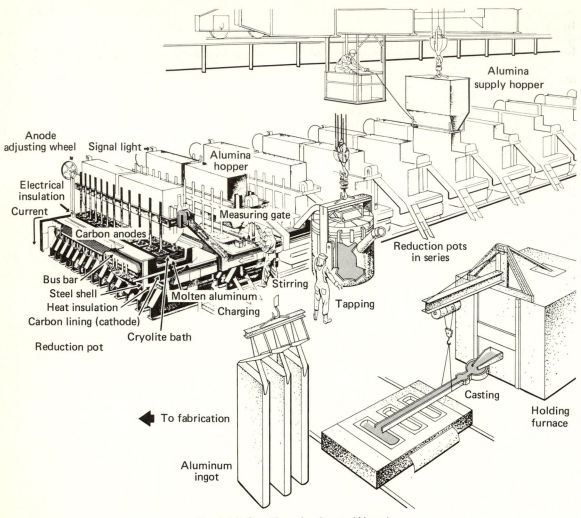

Anode adjusting wheel

Signal light

Alumina hopper

Electrical insulation

Current

Carbon anodes

Bus bar

Steel shell

Heat insulation

Carbon lining (cathode)

Cryolite bath

Reduction pot

Measuring gate

Stirring

Molten aluminum

Charging

Tapping

Alumina supply hopper

Reduction pots in series

Casting

Holding furnace

To fabrication

Aluminum ingot

Fig. 1-12. Smelting aluminum. (*Alcoa.*)

used for deriving aluminum, silver, zinc, oxided copper, gold, and magnesium.

ELECTROMETALLURGICAL EXTRACTION. In the electrometallurgical extraction of metal, electrolysis is used to win the metal from the ore. One of the two major processes is *electrowinning*, used with copper. This process works on the same principle as electroplating. The second process wins the metal from a chemical compound that usually separates the metal from the oxygen in a reduction cell. The aluminum reduction cell is a typical cell in which the aluminum itself plays the role of the cathode and the anodes are composed of carbon. The aluminum is also surrounded by a carbon-walled furnace. The electrical action between the cathode and the anode separates the oxygen in the aluminum bath from the electrolyte, which is usually sodium aluminum fluoride and molten cryolite. This separation produces a molten aluminum. All of this action takes place under a seal of frozen aluminum and electrolyte, a crust that fully protects the molten aluminum (Fig. 1-12).

QUESTIONS

1. What elements compose approximately three-quarters of the earth's crust?
2. What is physical metallurgy?
3. What is extractive metallurgy?
4. Explain the difference between a value and a gangue.
5. What are the two major ways to mine metals?
6. Explain ore dressing.
7. How is the concept of specific gravity used in ore concentration?
8. Explain the flotation process.
9. Compare and contrast pyrometallurgical, electrometallurgical, and hydrometallurgical refining of metals.
10. What is a tailings dump?

Structure of Metals

2

Metallurgy, the study of metal, includes process, or extractive, metallurgy and physical metallurgy. After the metal-bearing ore has been extracted and refined, the extractive process is ended. The pure metal is then further refined, or further processed. It can be used in its pure state or combined with other metals to form alloys. Physical metallurgy studies the structure of metals, the properties of metals, and the influence of fabrication methods on the properties and structure of metals.

Exceptions to this definition are hydrogen and metalloids. Hydrogen collects at the negative pole (cathode), but it is a nonmetallic element. Metalloids also are elements that are attracted to the cathode although they too are nonmetallic. Metalloids do not have all the characteristics of a metal. Although they have some conductivity, they have little or no ability to be deformed. Many metalloids (such as carbon, boron, and silicon) can be combined readily with metals.

CHARACTERISTICS OF METALS

Most metals may be described as having the following characteristics: They are usually opaque and solid at room temperature. They are thermal (heat) and electrical conductors. They are reflectors when polished. They expand when heated and contract, or shrink, when cooled. These characteristics describe the apparent aspects of metals, but a metal can be identified in a different, more exact manner. A *metal* is an element that is, when immersed in a caustic acid solution, attracted to a cathode when a small current is passed through the solution (Fig. 2-1). Elements that are not attracted to the cathode but are attracted to the anode are scientifically called nonmetallic elements.

ATOMIC STRUCTURE AND BONDS

Metals are composed of separate atoms, just like all substances. All atoms have the same basic structure (Fig. 2-2). An atom consists of a nucleus, with positively charged protons and uncharged neutrons. The nucleus makes up the major portion of the mass of the atom. Surrounding the nucleus in orbits or shells are electrons. Electrons, having relatively small mass and a negative charge, balance the charge of the protons. The maximum number of electrons that exist in any orbit is represented by the symbol $2N^2$, where N represents the shell, or orbit, number. Therefore, the first orbit or first shell surrounding the nucleus is composed of 2×1^2 electrons, or 2 electrons. The second shell has

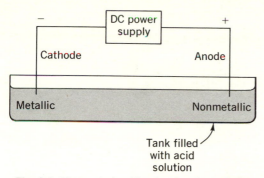

Fig. 2-1. Element classification by electrolysis.

2×2^2, or 8 electrons, and so on. A characteristic of all metallic elements is that there are always free electrons in the outer shell of the atomic structure. This means that the outer shell will not be completely filled with electrons no matter how many shells the metal has. These outer electrons are released readily from the atomic structure, a characteristic called *thermionic emission*. This characteristic can be used in joining one atom to another or for precipitating electrons from the metal, as in the case of the arc column when arc welding. The electrons in the outer shell that can be released readily are known as *valence electrons*.

There are several theories that explain how atomic structures are bonded. One such theory describes an ionic bond, a bond that is typical of many gases or liquids. In the *ionic bond* theory the valence electron in the outer shell is attracted to an element whose outer shell has a deficiency of electrons instead of

an overabundance of electrons. The valence electron balances the two shells when they are placed in close proximity. Another theory describes the *covalent bond*, in which electrons are shared in the outer shell, a sharing that completes the number of electrons in each individual shell. The covalent bond is a

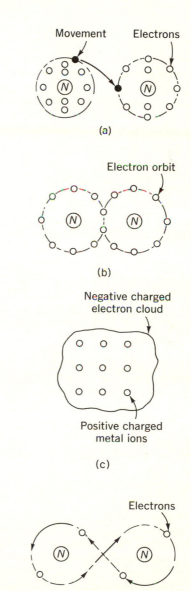

Fig. 2-3. Atomic bonds. (a) Ionic bond; (b) covalent bond; (c) metallic bond; (d) van der Waals force.

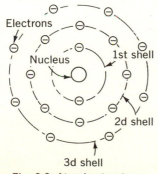

Fig. 2-2. Atomic structure.

strong bond because of the attraction, or the tie-in force, of these shared electrons.

The *metallic bond* theory explains the chief way that the atoms within metals are bonded. The metallic bond may be thought of as a negatively charged electron cloud that completely surrounds the positively charged metal ions or metal nuclei. This electron cloud is composed entirely of the valence electrons of the metallic element. Still another theory explains the *van der Waals forces*, weak attraction forces that are caused by the separation of the electrons from the nucleus. The electrons often interchange from one nucleus to another. The van der Waals bonding forces are characteristic of inert gases (Fig. 2-3).

SPACE LATTICES

Metals in a liquid state have no crystalline structure, a state called *amorphic*. When the free-moving atoms within a liquid metal begin to freeze or solidify, they attach themselves to each other in an orderly, well-defined system. This pattern is called the *space lattice system,* and it is the basis for the crystalline form of metal. A metal arranges its crystallinity during solidification the same way every time. The most common space lattice systems in which metal crystals usually arrange themselves are face-centered cubic (fcc), body-centered cubic (bcc), and hexagonal close-packed (hcp) (Figs. 2-4 to 2-6). There are five other crystalline systems besides the cubic and the hexagonal: triclinic, monoclinic, orthorhombic, rhombohedral (a

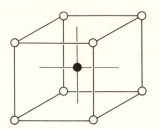

Fig. 2-5. Body-centered cubic space lattice unit cell.

triangular design), and tetragonal. These seven space lattice systems can produce 14 possible types of crystalline structures.

Iron is the best known metallic element that has a bcc space lattice system. Iron, however, changes its bcc system to an fcc system at elevated temperatures. This change in space lattice systems is known as *allotropism*. The change from a bc to an fcc lattice allows carbon to move through the fcc system. Because the atoms are far apart in the bcc system, carbon cannot rearrange itself; however, the carbon can and does change position in the fcc system. Common metals that have bcc space lattices at room temperature are tungsten, molybdenum, vanadium, columbium (niobium), and iron. The bcc metals are generally extremely hard and have little ductility; however, the bcc metals rate high in strength when compared to fcc metals. Also, bcc metals are not easily cold-worked.

Common fcc metals are aluminum, copper, gold, lead, and nickel. In their pure form, fcc metals are soft and ductile. Generally, fcc metals are easily cold-worked and are low in strength.

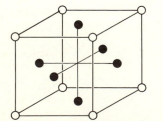

Fig. 2-4. Face-centered cubic.

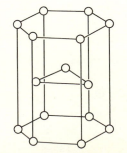

Fig. 2-6. Hexagonal close-packed.

The hcp system is present in cobalt, cadmium, magnesium, titanium, and zinc. The hcp system is found in metals that cannot be cold-worked because cold-working will lead to immediate failure of the metallic structure. The strength of these metals varies; some are weak and some are strong.

DENDRITES

Basically, most metals solidify in a set sequence established by the temperature loss. They progress from a liquid state, in which individual atoms of metal exhibit extremely free movement, to a state of complete rigidity. The metal passes through three crystalline forms during this sequence. These three forms are based on dendrite growth.

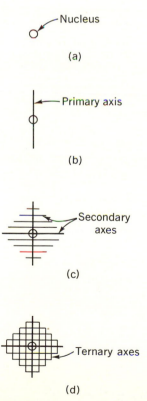

(a) Nucleus

(b) Primary axis

(c) Secondary axes

(d) Ternary axes

Fig. 2-7. Dendrite growth (crystal).

Dendritic growth begins with a nucleus which proceeds to grow a skeletal form that fills in with additional metal until the crystal is completely filled (Fig. 2-7). The only interference that stops the crystal from continuing to flow is the lack of space caused by the growth of surrounding crystals. As the metal cools slightly, a nucleus, sometimes called a *seed crystal*, is formed in the metal bath. This nucleus begins a crystalline growth. A primary axis is the first portion to form as the temperature of the bath decreases. The primary axis extends for a distance and then the limbs, or the secondary axes, grow. The secondary axes, upon further heat loss, develop a third axis, or a ternary axis. At this point, the skeletal structure is complete, expanding and filling in until a solid dendrite is formed.

The physical solidification process goes through three changes in structural rigidity: liquidus, liquidus-solidus, and solidus. *Liquidus* is the point at which the first crystalline structure begins to form. *Liquidus-solidus* is the point in time and the temperature at which the metal is in a mushy state. The *solidus* is the point at which the grain formation is complete and the metal is a solid even though it is still hot. Graphically, these three characteristics can be represented as a time-temperature function (Fig. 2-8). The mushy state, or the liquidus-solidus point, is indicated graphically by a change in the direction of the line.

The time-temperature studies of metals have led to the plotting of a collection of

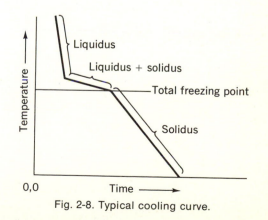

Fig. 2-8. Typical cooling curve.

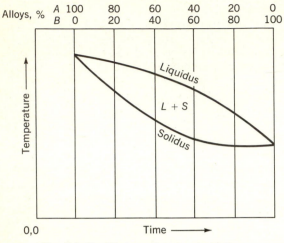

Alloys, %
A 100   80   60   40   20   0
B   0   20   40   60   80   100

Fig. 2-9. Equilibrium diagram derivation.

time-temperature graphs called *equilibrium diagrams*. These diagrams indicate the liquidus point and the solidus point of metals and their alloys (Fig. 2-9). For example, if two metals were mixed, there would be a different time-temperature graph for each of the two metals in the alloy. If an alloy is composed of 60 percent of alloy *B* and 40 percent of alloy *A*, its liquidus and solidus points will be different from those of other possible mixtures (Fig. 2-10). In equilibrium diagrams, a line connects the liquidus points and the solidus points of the possible alloys, making it unnecessary to use separate time and temperature graphs for each metal in the alloy.

Many times two metals that are alloyed have different melting points. These two metals can be mixed together in such a combination that there will be a point at which both are in their liquid state. The point at which the two metals are in balance, the melting of the combined metals (which can be lower than the melting point of either metal) is called the *eutectic point* (Fig. 2-10). The eutectic point illustrated in Fig. 2-10 represents this point of balance for a mixture of 60 percent of alloy *A* and 40 percent of alloy *B*.

The eutectic point is helpful in defining various alloys. A hypoeutectic metal, or below-eutectic-point alloy, is a mixture that has more of alloy *A* plus a eutectic mixture, while a *hypereutectic alloy* has more of the solid *B* metal plus a eutectic mixture. Therefore, the characteristics of a hypoeutectic metal are different from those of a hypereutectic alloy. The hypoeutectic alloy would exhibit many of the physical and mechanical characteristics of alloy *A*, while the hypereutectic alloy would exhibit many of the characteristics of alloy *B*.

An alloy that is represented by the eutectic point is said to be in solid solution. The phrase *in solid solution* describes something dissolved in a liquid or an intermingling of one substance in another so closely that the dissolved substance cannot be distinguished or separated from the dissolver. An example would be a homogeneous mixture of alloy *Z* and alloy *B* (Fig. 2-11*a*). However, most

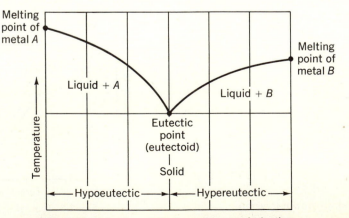

Fig. 2-10. Eutectic equilibrium diagram derivation.

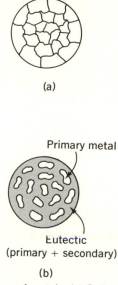

(a)

Primary metal

Eutectic
(primary + secondary)

(b)

Fig. 2-11. Solutions of metals. (a) Solid solution (eutectoid metal); (b) primary metal plus eutectic mixture.

metals and their alloys represent a different case under most applications. If two metals are mixed together, alloy A and alloy B, one alloy, supposedly the primary alloy, is the dominant alloy. It will not be able to absorb all of alloy B, nor will alloy B be able to absorb all of alloy A. An alloy can absorb only a certain amount of an alloy substance, and then it cannot absorb any more.

When a metal has absorbed its maximum amount, it has reached its eutectic point, or its maximum saturation point. The rest of the primary metal will remain in its primary state so that in the crystalline form of the alloy there will be grains of primary metal surrounded by the eutectic mixture (Fig. 2-11b). The most frequently used eutectic point is the iron-iron carbide equilibrium diagram (Fig. 2-12).

The rate of crystalline growth in a metal, the *nucleation rate,* is proportional to the lapse in time and temperature loss. This determines the size and the shape of the crystals. The size and shape of the crystals, in turn, determine the strength of the metal. Retarding the nucleation rate causes an excess of new nuclei to develop in the interior of the metal, resulting in extremely large dendritic

structures. These large grains may cause a metal to be physically weaker than if it had solidified at its normal rate (Fig. 2-13).

Three shapes of grain structure result during the normal solidification of a metal or an alloyed metal. The outer layer next to the surface of the metal cools most rapidly. For example, in a weld bead, the fluid metal that comes into contact with the slag facing cools most rapidly. This rapid cooling creates small equiaxed crystals called *chill crystals.* The chill crystal encircles the edges of the weld bead. As the metal cools, progressively long, thin *columnar crystals* begin to grow at right angles to the bead interface or surface. These columnar crystals extend to the center of a metal and are at right angles to the surface interface. The growth of the crystals increases the distance between the internal liquid metal and the interface of the weld bead base metal. As a result, heat dissipation is lessened, retarding the rate of nucleation and causing the production of large equiaxed crystals in the center of large weld beads (Fig. 2-14). Many times, because of the size of the weld bead and because of the metal alloys used for the welding electrode, the only two crystalline shapes represented in a weld bead are the chill crystals and the columnar crystals.

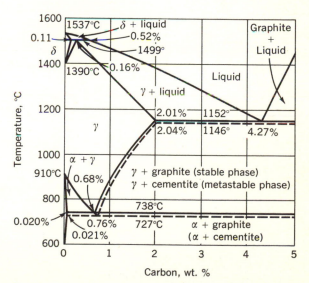

Fig. 2-12. Iron–iron carbide equilibrium diagram. (*U.S. Steel Corporation.*)

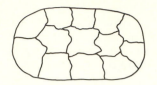

All large crystals (dendrites)

Fig. 2-13. Results of a retarded rate of heat loss.

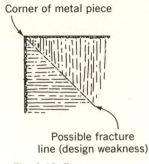

Corner of metal piece

Possible fracture
line (design weakness)

Fig. 2-15. Fracture zones.

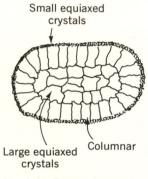

Small equiaxed
crystals

Large equiaxed   Columnar
crystals

Fig. 2-14. Types of crystals.

A pure metal usually has only chill and columnar crystals because a pure metal has an extremely wide mushy zone. This solidification zone often extends into the center of the casting or weld bead and allows a more even heat loss, prolonging the growth time for the columnar crystals. One function of welding flux is to control the solidification rate, which helps to control the growth of co-lumnar crystals. These columnar crystals extend to the center and at right angles to the surface interface of a metal.

Cooling may be used to control interior crystalline growth. For example, in welding, lightly dusted electrodes allow a faster heat loss than semicoated electrodes. While the crystalline shape yielded with both electrodes is generally a columnar configuration, the faster heat loss results in smaller grain size. The smaller the grain size, the stronger the metal. Most weld beads yield a columnar crystal in the interiors of the weld zone and the base metal. While column-shaped crystals are associated with metal strength, possible planes of weakness in sharp corner designs can result because of their angle of growth. These planes of weakness (*fracture zones*) appear as dark lines when the microstructure of the metal is studied (Fig. 2-15).

QUESTIONS

1. What is a metal?
2. What is an atomic shell?
3. What are some of the theories that explain atomic bonding?
4. What is a space lattice?
5. How does atomic arrangement determine the hardness of a metal?
6. How is the arrangement of atomic structure in a metal studied and recorded?
7. What are the major types of crystals?
8. What is liquidus?

9. What is a eutectic point?
10. How are equilibrium diagrams derived?
11. What is the importance of the equilibrium diagram?
12. What does *in solid solution* refer to in a metal?
13. Why are small equiaxed crystals the hardest type of crystals?
14. How do sharp edges affect the strength of a metal part?

Properties of Metals

The properties of metals are divided into three major categories: chemical, physical, and mechanical. Chemical properties determine whether or not metallic elements will combine with each other, and they help to classify possible reactions and interactions of metals in combination. The physical properties of metals are those that are inherent in the metal such as electrical conductivity, thermal conductivity, melting point, and density. The mechanical properties of metals are those that indicate the strength of the metal or the reaction of the metal to an applied external force.

CHEMICAL PROPERTIES

Associated with the chemical properties of a metal are its chemical symbol, its crystalline form, its atomic weight, its atomic number, and its level of electron energy, also referred to as the *quantum number*.

Metals can be separated into the *rare-earth metals*, such as uranium; the *transition metals*, such as nickel and iron; the *noble metals*, such as silver, copper, and gold; the *semiconductor metals*, such as tin and germanium; and the *semimetals*, such as bismuth and antimony. The semimetals have complex crystallographic structures, as in the salt-forming halogens, such as fluorine.

The symbols for all elements, metallic or nonmetallic, are abbreviations of their Latin or English names. The crystalline structure, the atomic number, and the atomic weight have been determined as a result of patient and methodical research. All elements are currently placed on a periodic table, which arranges them in the order of the atomic numbers. The first table was derived by D. I. Mendeleev in 1869, and since then many elements have been added to his original table (Fig. 3-1).

The first element in the periodic table is hydrogen, which has an atomic number of 1 and an atomic weight of 1.008. The *atomic number* of an element is determined by the number of protons in the nucleus. This number is the same as the number of electrons in the shells that surround the nucleus. The atomic number describes the chemical properties of the atom. The *atomic weight* of an element is determined by the total number of protons and neutrons within the nucleus, and it is derived by comparing the weight of the element to the atomic weight of carbon. The atomic weight of carbon has been established as 12.01 atomic mass units (amu). This figure is the basis for establishing the atomic weight for all other elements.

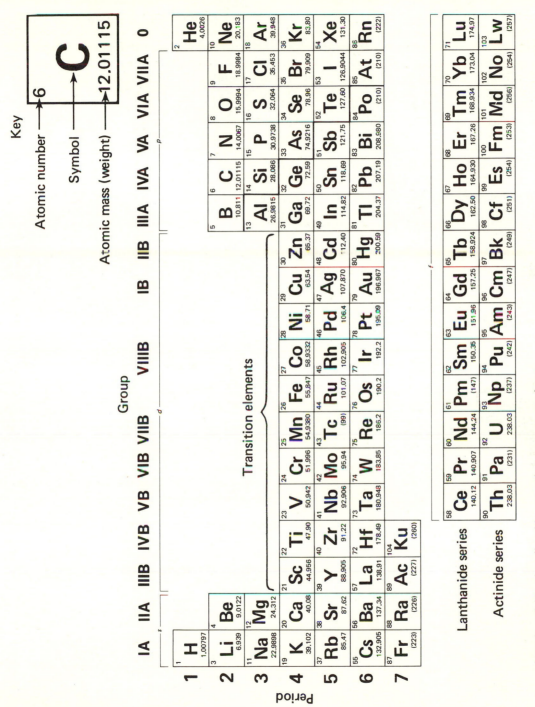

Fig. 3-1. The periodic table. (*Adapted from* General Chemistry *by Frederick Longo. Copyright 1974 by McGraw-Hill, Inc. Used with permission of McGraw-Hill Book Company.*)

Atomic weight values listed in parentheses are approximate.

Key

Atomic number ──→ 6

Symbol ──→ **C**

Atomic mass (weight) ──→ 12.01115

Transition elements

Lanthanide series

Actinide series

A working knowledge of the periodic table of elements has a practical use for the metalworker because the periodic table often leads to an understanding of why a certain element is alloyed to another element. For example, the transitional elements, known as group VIB, are shown in Fig. 3-1. The VIB elements are chromium, Cr, molybdenum, Mo, and tungsten, W. These three elements constitute a group in the fourth, fifth, and sixth periods. Because these elements exist in a group, any one of them can replace another in an alloy and a metal of similar quality will be the product. Chromium, for example, can be used as a substitute for tungsten or molybdenum.

The transitional elements are the elements that are used most by the metalworker. Their name is derived from the fact that all elements within the group have variable valences. Iron, Fe, is a good example of an element with variable valences. As the temperature of iron is increased, the bcc space lattice system changes to an fcc space lattice system, resulting in a change in the valence value of iron. Many elements possess this characteristic change. It is called *allotropism.*

The metals in group VIB are used sometimes to improve red shortness or softening resistance in metals at elevated temperatures. An element used many times to improve the machinability of steel is sulfur, from group VIA. Selenium and tellurium can also be used to improve the machinability of steel, but since they both cost much more than sulfur and since sulfur achieves practically the same results in the alloyed metal, sulfur is used. However, sulfur does have certain reactions in stainless steel so that when a sulfur-free stainless steel with good machinability is desired, selenium and tellurium are used as the alloying elements.

These transitional elements can be substituted for each other because they have similar electron configurations. All groupings in the periodic table are based on the similarity of electron configurations. For example, group IA is composed of hydrogen, lithium, sodium, potassium, rubidium, cesium, and francium. All of these elements have similar electron configurations, and any one element of this group can replace any other element in the group. Understanding the use of the periodic table of elements in identifying this relationship among metals makes the table a tool of significant value to a metalworker.

PHYSICAL PROPERTIES

The physical properties of a metal are those that are inherent to the metal and which remain unchanged regardless of any force applied to the metal. They remain fairly constant, accurate characteristics. For example, the melting point of aluminum remains at 1220°F regardless of what type of heat energy is used to melt it. Some physical properties include melting point, boiling point, density, thermal conductivity, electrical resistivity, coefficient of thermal expansion, volumetric shrinkage, magnetic properties, and specific heat. Other physical properties include resistance to corrosion, color, nuclear radiation characteristics, and reflectivity.

The physical properties most important for the metalworker to know are the melting point, density, thermal conductivity, electrical resistivity, coefficient of thermal expansion, and volumetric shrinkage (Table 3-1).

Specific Gravity

Classifying these properties depends on establishing arbitrary standards of comparison. The density of a metal is determined by using the weight of 1 in.³ of that metal. The specific gravity of a metal is the weight of the metal when compared to the weight of an equal volume of water; or, specific gravity is the ratio between the density of a metal and the density of water. Knowing the density of a metal is important because the metalworker must know and understand what will happen when two dissimilar metals are mixed. If one metal has a higher density than another, then the lighter, or the less dense, metal may float on the surface of the heavier metal and not mix homogeneously.

TABLE 3-1. PHYSICAL PROPERTIES OF SELECTED METALS

ELEMENT	MELTING POINT, °F	BOILING POINT, °F	DENSITY AT 68°F, PSI	THERMAL CONDUCTIVITY AT 68°F, cal/(cm²)(cm)(s)(°C)	ELECTRICAL RESIS-TIVITY, $\mu\Omega$/cm	COEFFICIENT OF THERMAL EXPANSION AT 68°F, in./(in.)(°F)	VOLU-METRIC SHRINKAGE, %
Aluminum	1220	4442	0.0975	0.53	2.7	13.1	−6.4
Copper	1981	4703	0.324	0.94	1.7	9.2	−4.2
Gold	1945	5380	0.698	0.71	2.4	7.9	−5.2
Iron	2798	5430	0.284	0.18	9.7	6.5	−2.8
Lead	621	3137	0.4097	0.08	20.6	16.3	−3.5
Nickel	2647	4950	0.3220	0.22	6.8	7.4	NA
Silver	1761	4010	0.379	1.00	1.6	10.9	−5.0
Tin	449	4120	0.2637	0.15	11.0	13.0	−2.8
Tungsten	6170	10,706	0.697	0.40	5.6	2.6	NA
Zinc	787	1663	0.258	0.27	5.9	22.0	−4.2

NA = not available.

Thermal Conductivity

The rate at which heat is transmitted by conduction through a piece of metal is called *thermal conductivity.* For example, the amount of thermal conductivity in a metal determines the amount of heat needed in order to weld a particular metal. Copper has high thermal conductivity, which necessitates the use of a large heat source in order to bring copper-based metals to a molten stage. The thermal conductivity of a metal is derived from a comparison with silver, which has been given a rating of 1.00. Three theories have been developed to explain the phenomenon of conductivity: the electron transfer theory, the molecular transfer theory, and the space lattice vibration theory. Thermal conductivity is always high in pure metals, so alloying a metal will lower its conductivity. Also, thermal conductivity is inversely proportional to temperature so that as the temperature of a metal increases, its thermal conductivity decreases.

Electrical Resistivity

The electrical conductivity of a metal is also affected by its temperature. The lower the temperature of a metal, the greater its electrical conductivity. Metals at extremely low temperatures, approximately 0 K ("K" stands for "kelvins"), become superconductors, because the valence electrons flow much more easily in cold metal. Electrons, once they are accelerated in a particular direction by an electromotive force (emf) in a conductor, have been found to flow constantly if no resistance to the flow is offered; it is a force that will stay in motion until acted upon by another force. This other force is called *electrical resistivity.* Electrical conduction is based on electron flow. As the metal atoms lose their valence electrons, the atoms change into positive metal ions. These metal ions interfere with electron flow and cause a decrease in electron motion which in turn causes a resistance in the conductor. Although there is an electron flow and an ion resistance to an electron flow, there is no change in the mass in the base metal. The flow can be measured by the standard measurement for electrical resistivity, microhms per centimeter ($\mu\Omega$/cm).

Coefficient of Thermal Expansion

Knowing the coefficient of thermal expansion for a metal is extremely important for metal-workers because this information indicates the amount of expansion or contraction to expect in a metal when heat is applied to it or extracted from it. The hotter the metal, the more it expands at a given rate. Also, metal contraction, which occurs when a metal is going through a cooling process, is indicated by the coefficient of thermal expansion. Giving the linear coefficient of thermal expansion is more informative than telling the volume of thermal expansion. For example, aluminum has a linear thermal expansion of 13.1. This means that aluminum expands at the rate of 13.1 millionths of an inch for each inch in length for each Fahrenheit degree above 68°F. The expansion and contraction of a metal can be determined, then, by the amount of heat applied to the metal. The thermal expansion and contraction of the metal are responsible for many of the locked-in stresses in the base metal after welding, stresses that result in distortion of the base metal. As the linear coefficient of thermal expansion increases, more care is required by the welder.

Corrosion Resistance

The corrosion resistance properties of metals have never been defined clearly or identified numerically; however, materials that are extremely susceptible to corrosion are the most active, such as magnesium, zinc, and aluminum. Those least susceptible are the least active, such as platinum. Ferrous metals corrode readily and nickel-based alloys have a higher corrosion resistance than silver, gold, and platinum. We can say that platinum offers the most resistance to corrosion or that it is the least active metal. All the noble metals are anodic and provide protection for cathodic metals, exhibiting a galvanic protection. If iron or another cathodic metal is submerged in a salt solution, for example, it must be protected from the solution in order to maintain itself, but noble metals do not need this protection. Industry spends much money to overcome corrosion through various protective devices such as painting. (See Chap. 6 for more detailed information.)

MECHANICAL PROPERTIES

The mechanical properties of a metal usually indicate its strength, hardness, ductility, or toughness. The mechanical properties of a metal are directly related to its crystalline structure. As long as a metal has a polycrystalline structure, its mechanical properties are fairly reliable. If a metal has a single-crystal structure (*anisotropic*), the reliability of the mechanical properties of the metal depends on the direction of the primary axis of the crystalline structure. Metals that are *isotropic* are those that do not depend on a single crystal or the rotation of a single crystal for strength but rely instead on a multiaxis polycrystalline structure. In most metals, there is no preferred orientation of the primary axis. Generally speaking, all transition metals are isotropic, even though individual grains within the structure may be anisotropic.

Strength

Robert Hooke discovered that if the strains placed on a metal are strong enough, a simple relationship will exist between the strains, or the force, applied to the metal and the corresponding stress within the metal. This stress-strain relationship is directly associated with the interatomic spacing of the atoms within the metal (Fig. 3-2). *Hooke's law* states that in an elastic material the stress is proportional to the strain. In other words, when a metal is placed under tension, it increases in length as, in a proportionate ratio, it decreases in width (Fig. 3-2*a*). If the metal is elastic, the metal resumes its original shape when the tension is removed (Fig. 3-2*b*). Also according to Hooke's observations, the reverse is true. When a metal is compressed under a force, the length of the metal is reduced, and the width of the metal increases. Again, if the metal is elastic, it resumes its original shape.

Elasticity is defined as the ability of a substance to return to its original size and shape when external stresses are removed. Steel has this property. Materials that retain the deformation caused by the external forces

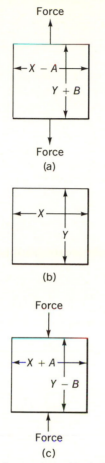

Force

←X − A→

Y + B

Force

(a)

←X→

Y

(b)

Force

←X + A→

Y − B

Force

(c)

Fig. 3-2. Interatomic spacing—Hooke's law. (a) Under tension; (b) at rest; (c) under compression.

are called *plastic*. Such metals are the alkali metals (lithium, sodium, potassium, rubidium, and cesium). For a certain range of stress, a metal may be elastic; but, if that range of force or limit of force is exceeded, the metal will become plastic.

The extension, compression, or bending of a bar will accumulate *potential energy* due to the elastic properties and resultant molecular atomic action within the metal. This potential can be determined mathematically. If a bar has length L and cross-sectional area A and a force is exerted on the bar that either stretches or compresses it by a small length, the potential energy is the average force mul-

tiplied by the displacement in length. An example of this storage of potential energy is a springboard depressed by a diver to the greatest bend of the board. As the diver springs downward, the diver loses potential energy and the board stores an equal amount of potential energy in compliance with the law of conservation of energy and in order for the board to resume its original position.

Hardness

Hardness can be thought of as the resistance of a metal to scratching, denting, drilling, filing, or other deformation. The hardness of metal has been placed on arbitrary scales. The first hardness scale developed compared metals to organic materials and is called *Mohs' scale*. Mohs' scale is commonly used to determine the hardness of rocks and minerals. On this scale 1 is talc, 2 is gypsum, 7 is quartz, 8 is topaz, 9 is sapphire, and 10 is diamond.

The hardness of a metal may be changed by heat treating. For example, a chisel may be made out of a medium-carbon steel and then heat treated. In its heat-treated condition, the chisel can cut the very metal from which it was made. The amount of hardness in a metal also indicates its brittleness. Generally, as the hardness of a metal increases, its brittleness increases proportionately.

The hardness of the metal, however, does not relate directly to the hardenability of the metal. The *hardenability* of a metal is determined by a Jominy test that determines how well a metal hardens from its center to its interface. Many metals can be hardened only on the surface, while the interior remains unhardened. These metals are said to have low hardenability. A metal that is capable of being hardened throughout its structure is said to have high hardenability.

Ductility

Ductile metals can be formed without failure, that is, their shapes can be changed without breaking or cracking. They can be drawn through a die, shaped by cold-working, or have their shapes changed without early failure in the metal. Ductility is determined by a standard stress-strain curve and is represented by the percentage of elongation of a metal coupled with its reduction in area (Fig. 3-3). This information is derived from the standard tensile tests for metals. Usually, ductile metals have an fcc structure. Metals that do not have a great amount of ductility have bcc structures. Brittle metals have hcp or tetragonal space lattice systems.

Machinability

The machinability of a metal is indicated by percentages. All machinable metals are compared to a basic standard, and the comparison yields a percentage rating which indicates the ease of cutting each metal. The standard metal used for the 100 percent machinability rating is a steel, coded by the American Iron and Steel Institute (AISI) Index as B1112 steel. The Society of Automotive Engineers (SAE) has coded this steel as no. 1112. Machinability ratings result when metals are compared to this free-machining steel. For example, aluminum has a machinability rating that ranges between 300 and 2,000 percent greater than free-machining steel, and the rating for nickel steels ranges from 40 to 50 percent when compared with the free-machining steel. Carbon steels generally range from 40 to 60 percent, and cast iron from 50 to 80 percent.

Toughness

Toughness is an important mechanical property that indicates the resistance of a metal to impact; it is sometimes called *impact toughness.* Impact toughness measures the amount of force that is required to fracture completely a test specimen with one sharp blow. The impact toughness of a metal is expressed in foot-pound-force (ft-lb). The most common tool used for testing impact toughness is a hammer.

Fatigue

Metal fatigue is perhaps the most important factor determined through the testing of the mechanical properties of a metal. Hooke's law, standard stress-strain diagrams, and the tensile, bending, and compression test yield the results that indicate when a metal will fail or pull apart. However, metals are exposed to more than one type of force and are subjected to reverse or alternating stresses. These stresses eventually cause failure, indicated by the cracks that form at stress levels. These levels would not be noticeable if force were applied in only one direction. *Metal fatigue* is defined as the deformation or failure of metals due to repeated stresses.

If a metal is subjected to completely reversed stresses of sufficient magnitude, a crack eventually appears and will grow until sudden failure of the cross section occurs. Physically, a minute crack originates at a point of high stress. This point may be a surface scratch, an oxident occlusion, or some other imperfection in the metal. The crack enlarges during continued repetitive loading until there is insufficient material left to support the load.

Fatigue failures are generally determined by subjecting a metal to a given stress or force that is repeatedly applied to a particular portion of the metal (Fig. 3-4). The basic fatigue cycle includes the following steps: First, the test specimen is supported from either one end or two, a force (in psi) is applied to a location that will deflect the test specimen. Then, the force is released and the test specimen is allowed to return to its origi-

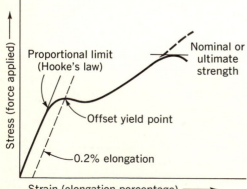
Fig. 3-3. Stress-strain diagram.

No force

Test specimen

Supports

(a)

Force applied, psi

Deflection

(b)

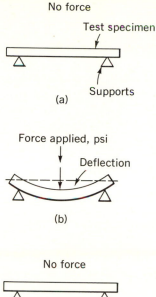

No force

(c)

Fig. 3-4. Fatigue cycle.

Crystals
(dendrites)

(a)

Crystals
(dendrites)

Slip bands

(b)

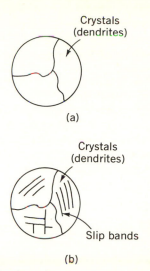

Fig. 3-5. Mechanism of slip. (a) Elastic range; (b) plastic range.

nal position. Fatigue cycle testing is done within the elastic limit of a metal. If enough force is applied to overcome the elastic limit of the metal, permanent deflection will result. The fatigue cycles range from 2 or 3 cycles for a brittle metal to as high as 20 or 30 million cycles for an extremely elastic metal. The number of cycles until ultimate failure occurs is referred to as the *endurance limit of the metal*.

Most of the mechanical properties of a metal are directly concerned with the mechanism of failure, or the mechanism of slip. The mechanism of failure, or slip, results from two possibilities. If a force applied to a metal is within the elastic range, the crystals, or dendrites, will not be affected by the force; therefore, the crystals will maintain their original shape and form. However, if enough force is applied, the crystals can no longer maintain their form and are said to be plastic (Fig. 3-5).

The mechanism of slip and the ultimate failure of a metal are based on what happens within each individual crystal and the location of each crystal relative to the next crystal.

When the force is applied, the primary and secondary axes will be disrupted or broken, or the crystal may move in relationship to the next crystal. When a crystal moves, it creates a small void between the crystals, and fragments a small portion of each adjoining crystal. These fragments are called crystallites. When crystallites are formed, *slip bands*, which indicate the disruption of the primary and secondary axes of a crystal, can be observed by microscope examination. These slip bands are indicators that a metal has been deformed permanently and that it is

(a)

(b)

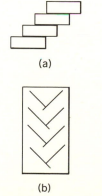

Fig. 3-6. (a) Slipping. (b) Twinning.

in the first stage of failure. The last stage of failure is the ultimate separation of the metal.

An example of the formation of crystallites can be observed by twisting a common paper clip until it fails. First to appear are minute ridges, resulting from the twisting motion. These ridges are minute dislocations and deformations of the metal. As the twisting of the metal continues, the formations of these voids become larger and larger until the ultimate failure of the paper clip. The mechanism of slip moves atoms through complete interatomic spacings, slightly distorting the lattice orientation of the metal.

Another mechanism of failure is *twinning*. Twinning occurs when the atoms are not moved one or more complete spaces in their atomic bonding but are moved just a portion of the way. The effects of slipping can be removed by polishing the specimen, but the mechanism of twinning cannot be removed by polishing the surface of the metal (Fig. 3-6).

QUESTIONS

1. Into what three categories can the properties of metals be classified? What do these categories explain about a metal?
2. Which of the three is the most important in the study and practice of metalworking? Why?
3. What is an atomic number?
4. Why is the knowledge of the coefficient of thermal expansion necessary to the metalworker?
5. What does Fe stand for? How are the symbolic notations for metals determined?
6. What is volumetric shrinkage?
7. What is a valence electron?
8. How is the toughness of a metal measured?
9. What is a fatigue cycle?
10. What is the difference between slipping and twinning?

Classification of Metals

The periodic table of elements identifies all natural elements in the universe. Three-fourths of these are metallic. The one element people use more than all others is iron. All other metallic elements on the periodic table are known as *nonferrous* elements. All metallic elements then are classified into two categories, ferrous, or iron-based elements, and nonferrous elements.

FERROUS METALS

Iron ore is iron as it is removed from the earth, but this ore is not pure iron. The largest deposits of iron ore in the United States, located in the Lake Superior region and the Duluth region, contain beds of hematite, which is Fe_2O_3, or ferrous oxide. These two iron deposits have supplied over 2 billion tons of high-grade iron ore for smelting. The smelting process converts iron oxide into pig iron by heating the oxide with coke and flux. The proportions used are 1 ton of carbon (or coke) and flux mixed with 2 tons of iron ore. When the impurities are burned out of the iron ore in a blast furnace, it becomes pig iron. The grade of the pig iron is determined largely by the amount of phosphorus and silicon present in the ore. A good grade of iron ore is low in phosphorus and high in silicon, a grade of ore that produces hematite iron.

Cool pig iron still contains a certain amount of impurities, such as silicon, carbon, phosphorus, sulfur, and manganese. These impurities must be removed before pig iron is of any use. They can either be burned out or the pig iron can be combined with purifying agents for their removal. The iron is then ready to be used for cast iron, wrought iron, and steel.

Cast Iron

Cast iron is a complex alloy of six or more elements combined in *approximately* these proportions: 96 percent iron, 3 percent carbon, and 1 percent comprised of silicon, sulfur, phosphorus, and manganese. Cast iron is used for many machine parts. Among these parts are automobile blocks, automobile cylinder heads, water pump bodies, pipe fittings, and machinery tool frames. There are three broad categories of cast iron: white cast iron, grey cast iron, and malleable iron. Usually pig iron, the product of the blast furnace, is remelted into one of these types of cast iron or into wrought iron.

White cast iron is hard, brittle, and magnetic. It is broken readily by sharp blows with a hammer and, when broken, will appear silvery and white. White cast iron is produced by cooling molten iron so rapidly that the iron carbide compound does not separate from the carbon. Many times a softer than normal white cast iron is made by allowing the molten iron to cool at a slower rate. White cast iron can be so hard that it is nonmachinable. It is used for plowshares, ball mill agitators, stamping shoes, wear plates, and sometimes railroad car wheels.

Grey cast iron, the most machinable form of cast iron, is also the most common form of cast iron. It is used extensively in machinery castings. When it is broken, the break appears dark grey. Grey cast iron is made by allowing molten iron to cool slowly, separating the iron and carbon. The carbon separates out as tiny flakes of graphite that are scattered homogeneously throughout the grey cast iron, a carbon sometimes called *free*, or *graphite, carbon*. Since graphite is an excellent lubricant, grey cast iron is used for such things as automobile cylinders and blocks that require lubrication. Because of the presence of the scattered flakes of graphite throughout the metal, grey cast iron is more easily machined than the other types of cast iron and it needs little or no lubrication when being machined.

Grey cast iron is classified as either pearlitic, austenitic, alloy, or Meehanite cast iron. Pearlitic cast iron combines the carbon in a pearlite matrix. Generally, pearlitic cast irons contain from 0.60 to 0.90 percent combined carbon. Austenitic cast irons are those in which the grains, or the flakes, of graphite are interspersed with austenitic structures. Cast iron of this type includes such alloying elements as aluminum, nickel, chromium, vanadium, titanium, or zirconium. Meehanite cast iron is a trade name applied to a group of grey cast irons. Cast iron of this type is produced by adding calcium silicide to the molten metal, resulting in a grey iron with characteristics somewhere between a grey cast iron and a white cast iron. Meehanite cast irons have very high strength.

Malleable cast iron withstands great strains and rough usage. It will deform before breaking. When malleable cast iron is broken, a white steely skin extends from the surface to the usually dark and dull center. Malleable iron is made by heat treating white cast iron. The heat treatment consists of reheating the iron under closely controlled conditions to about 1400°F for a certain length of time. The heat acts on the graphite carbon crystals, or flakes, so that they separate out not as flakes but as round particles of carbon. Malleable cast iron is tougher than the other irons and has a higher resistance to shock loads.

Wrought Iron

Wrought iron was used before recorded history and was the first and only basic iron used until the invention of the steelmaking process. Today steel, ferrous alloys, and nonferrous metals have replaced most wrought iron. Wrought iron is composed of a high-purity iron and an iron silicate slag. The properties of wrought iron are determined by its carbon and manganese content. The manganese is usually below 0.06 percent and the carbon ranges from 0.02 to 0.05 percent. Other elements present in wrought iron include phosphorus, 0.10 to 0.5 percent (a higher percentage than found in steel) and silicon (a derivative of silicate slag), 10 percent. This silicate slag is usually distributed throughout the iron in fibers, but the slag is not mixed homogeneously, or fused, with the iron, so that the wrought iron and the slag exist together but are not fused together. This distribution of slag and iron creates a fibrous composition in the wrought iron. It is this fibrous composition that gives the iron its ductility and strength, allowing it to be bent or twisted whether it is hot or cold. Wrought iron currently is used for barbed wire, pipe, nails, plates, and other structural forms.

Steel

Pure iron is not strong enough to be used for tools, machines, or structural shapes, but with a small amount of carbon added to it, it becomes extremely tough. When small amounts of carbon are added, the iron is known as *carbon steel*. If other elements are

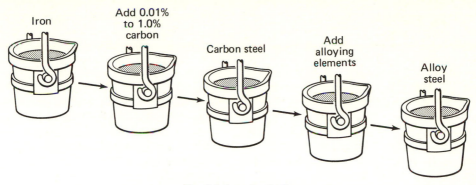

Fig. 4-1. Iron to steel.

added to the carbon steel, the resultant material is called *alloy steel* (Fig. 4-1).

Carbon steels contain less than 1 percent carbon and small amounts of silicon, manganese, phosphorus, sulfur, and copper. Other elements are present in carbon steel but only in residual quantities. Carbon steel can be classified according to the amount of deoxidation that is performed during the production of the steel. The classifications are: rimmed, killed, semikilled, or capped.

Rimmed steels have only a small amount of oxygen removed during the solidification process, leaving an outer layer, or rim, relatively free of carbon with the center of the ingot higher in carbon than the exterior of the ingot. This extremely low-carbon surface is very ductile, has excellent surface qualities and coldforming characteristics.

Killed steels are the opposite of rimmed steels; they have had extreme amounts of oxygen removed, resulting in a relatively carbon-free steel. Killed steels are useful when severe forming techniques are required, but they always require heat treatment when the manufacturing forming technique is completed.

Semikilled steels have composition and mechanical properties which lie between the rimmed and killed steels. *Capped steels* combine the characteristics of the rimmed and semikilled steels, that is, the carbon rim is formed at the surface of the steel, while the bulk of the interior cross section of the steel has the characteristics of semikilled steel.

Carbon steel may also be classified ac-cording to the amount of carbon present in the finished steel. These major classifications are: low-carbon, medium-carbon, and high-carbon steels. *Low-carbon steels* contain up to 0.30 percent carbon. They usually are used for structural shapes, plates, and bars. The carbon content in *medium-carbon steels* ranges from 0.30 to 0.5 percent. These steels usually require some method of heat treating and are used for a large variety of hand tools (such as chisels, punches, and drills). *High-carbon steels* range in carbon content from 0.6 to 1.0 percent. They always require heat treatment before use. High-carbon steels are highly susceptible to cracking when formed but are resistant to wear and offer some of the highest mechanical strengths obtainable in the carbon steels. High-carbon steels are used for springs, sharp cutting devices, and any part of a machine that requires high strength and resistance to wear.

Alloy Steel

Elements that are added to steel are known as *alloy elements*. These special elements greatly change the chemical and physical properties of steel. Elements are of either metallic or nonmetallic material. They can be added to steel as pure elements, either as a pure nonmetal or as a pure metal, or they can be added as a ferroalloy. Ferroalloys are solid mixtures of iron with an alloying element, such as chromium, magnesium, or silicon. Table 4-1 lists several common alloying elements.

TABLE 4-1. ALLOYING ELEMENTS OF IRON (Fe)

METAL	SYMBOL	NONMETAL	SYMBOL
Aluminum	Al	Boron	B
Chromium	Cr	Carbon	C
Cobalt	Co	Hydrogen	H
Columbium (niobium)	Cb (Nb)	Nitrogen	N
		Oxygen	O
Copper	Cu	Phosphorus	P
Manganese	Mn	Selenium	Se
Molybdenum	Mo	Silicon	Si
Nickel	Ni	Sulfur	S
Titanium	Ti	Telerium	Te
Tungsten	W		
Vanadium	V		
Zirconium	Zr		

TABLE 4-2. 12 MAJOR ALLOYING ELEMENTS OF STEEL

ELEMENT	EFFECTS
Boron	Increases depth of hardness by heat treating
Chromium	Heat- and acid-resisting steels
Cobalt	High-temperature service and cutting edges
Columbium (also called Niobium)	Increases high-temperature strength
Copper	Retards rusting
Manganese	Increases strength and toughness
Molybdenum	Improves hardening qualities and resistance to shock
Nickel	Increases strength, ductility, toughness, and resistance to heat and acids
Silicon	Improves magnetic qualities
Titanium	Metallic structure control and high-temperature strength
Tungsten	Increases high-temperature hardness and strength
Vanadium	Improves heat treating and mechanical properties

MAJOR ALLOYING ELEMENTS. Although many traces of elements can be found in alloy steel and many alloys are used for making special types of steel, there are 12 major alloying elements of steel (Table 4-2). Each of the major alloys greatly changes the mechanical properties of the steel. The United States supplies the raw materials of iron ore, coke, and limestone to produce carbon steel; but the major alloying elements of steel must be imported from other countries.

Adding the alloying elements to the steel changes the physical properties of the alloy steel. The amount of alloy added varies from as little as 0.0005 percent to as much as 27 percent. More than one alloying element may be used. For example, boron is used many times with nickel, chromium, and molybdenum. Boron is available in the United States and is less expensive than nickel, chromium, and molybdenum. It produces the same basic results as the more expensive alloying metals (i.e., increases the depth of hardness by heat treating), but it also increases the strength and toughness of the alloyed steel. Of all the major alloying elements only cobalt, copper, and nickel are added as pure metals.

Stainless steel falls into the category of an alloyed steel, but because the AISI recognizes more than 40 types of stainless steel, a special category has been made classifying stainless steel into three broad divisions based on their predominant crystalline structures: ferritic, martensitic, and austenitic (Table 4-3). These three categories of stainless steel describe the different properties which determine the use of the stainless steel. *Ferritic* stainless steels are nonhardenable and magnetic. *Martensitic* steel is hardenable by heat treating and is also magnetic. *Austenitic* stainless steels are extremely tough and ductile in the welded state. Strictly

TABLE 4-3. COMPOSITION RANGE OF STAINLESS STEEL

CLASS	CARBON, %	CHROMIUM, %	NICKEL, %
Ferritic	0.35 max.	16–30	
Martensitic	0.05–0.50	4–18	
Austenitic	0.30–0.25	14–30	6–36

speaking, stainless steel should contain a minimum of 11 percent chromium. Chromium forms a thin, passive, slightly adherent surface layer of chromium oxide that gives the stainless steel its corrosion resistance.

SAE-AISI CODING. The Society of Automotive Engineers, in conjunction with the American Iron and Steel Institute, has adopted a steel classification system that is used by most of the steel-producing industries. The coding or classification system contains a four- or five-digit number with a letter prefix. The prefix indicates the type of furnace in which the steel was produced, and also whether it is basic or acid. The prefix letters are B, acid bessemer; C, basic open hearth; D, acid open-hearth; and E, electric. The interpretation of the digits in the coding system is presented in Table 4-4. For example, a 1XXX series steel indicates a carbon steel. The coded number 1005 indicates a plain low-carbon steel with 0.05 percent carbon. A steel with a number of 1230 is a free-machining resulfurized, rephosphorized, low-carbon steel that will respond to heat treating.

The first digit in the classification system identifies the major alloying ingredient. The second digit identifies the approximate percentage of that alloying ingredient. The last two or three digits generally indicate the carbon content by percentage or in points, where 100 points equal 1 percent. For example, low-carbon steels are designated from 1005 to 130, which means that the carbon content ranges from 0.05 to 0.3 percent. Medium-carbon steels have an SAE-AISI code indicating 0.3 to 0.55 percent carbon, and the numbering system for a plain carbon steel is 1030 to 1055.

NONFERROUS METALS

Nonferrous metals are all metals that are not iron based—a large number of metals. The more common nonferrous metallic elements are aluminum, copper, lead, magnesium, nickel, tin, titanium, and zinc.

TABLE 4-4. SAE-AISI CODING FOR STEEL

TYPE OF STEEL	SERIES DESIGNATION
Carbon steels	1XXX
Plain carbon	10XX
Free-machining, resulfurized (screw stock)	11XX
Free-machining, resulfurized, rephosphorized	12XX
Manganese steels	13XX
High-manganese carburizing steels	15XX
Nickel steels	2XXX
3.50% nickel	23XX
5.00% nickel	25XX
Nickel-chromium steels	3XXX
1.25% nickel, 0.60% chromium	31XX
1.75% nickel, 1.00% chromium	32XX
3.50% nickel, 1.50% chromium	33XX
Corrosion- and heat-resisting steels	30XXX
Molybdenum steels	4XXX
Carbon-molybdenum	40XX
Chromium-molybdenum	41XX
Chromium-nickel-molybdenum	43XX
Nickel-molybdenum	46XX and 48XX
Chromium steels	5XXX
Low chromium	51XX
Medium chromium	52XXX
Corrosion and heat resisting	51XXX
Chromium-vanadium steels	6XXX
Chromium 1.0%	61XX
Nickel-chromium-molybdenum	86XX and 87XX
Manganese-silicon	92XX
Nickel-chromium-molybdenum	93XX
Manganese-nickel-chromium-molybdenum	94XX
Nickel-chromium-molybdenum	97XX
Nickel-chromium-molybdenum	98XX
Boron (0.0005% boron minimum)	XXBXX

Aluminum

Aluminum, chemical symbol Al, is a slightly magnetic, ductile, malleable metal that resembles tin. Aluminum is not found in a metallic state but must be processed through electrolysis from bauxite ore. Aluminum has approximately 60 percent of the electrical conductivity of copper. It is a strongly electropositive metal that corrodes rapidly. In fact, aluminum corrodes so rapidly that an oxide is formed on its surface by simply exposing it to the oxygen in the atmosphere. The oxide melts at approximately 3600°F; thus, if the oxide is heated until it is molten, the base metal will almost boil since aluminum boils at a temperature a little over 4000°F. Aluminum is used in the production of steel as a deoxidizer, removing oxygen from the steel. Aluminum is also used to control the ring growth in steels by forming nucleation points from which the crystals of steels may grow.

Aluminum may be classified into three main groups: commercially pure aluminum, wrought aluminum, and casting aluminum. The Aluminum Association has devised a four-digit numbering system for the identification of aluminum (Table 4-5). This system assigns index numbers that identify aluminum alloys, including such alloys as 99 percent pure aluminum, copper, manganese, and silicon magnesium. The system also has unassigned numbers for further alloying elements.

The first digit of the number always indicates the major alloying element of the aluminum. The second digit ranges from 0 through 9. The zero indicates that no special control has been maintained in the alloying constituents. The numbers 1 through 9 indicate special controls which depend on the manufacturer of the aluminum. The last two digits in the series indicate the minimum amount of

TABLE 4-5. ALUMINUM ASSOCIATION INDEX SYSTEM

ALUMINUM ALLOY	NUMBER
Aluminum, 99.00% pure	1XXX
Copper	2XXX
Manganese	3XXX
Silicon	4XXX
Magnesium	5XXX
Magnesium and silicon	6XXX
Zinc	7XXX
Other element	8XXX
Unused index	9XXX

aluminum not under special control. For example, 1075 aluminum indicates an aluminum that has 99.75 percent controlled aluminum, or pure aluminum with 0.25 percent without any control. The no. 1180 aluminum indicates an alloy that is 99.80 percent pure aluminum; the remaining 0.20 percent has had some kind of special control over it. The 1 as the second digit signifies what kind of control, but what the 1 in this case means depends on which manufacturer is producing the aluminum.

In the 2XXX series through the 9XXX series, the last two digits do not have any special meaning except the meanings assigned by the manufacturers. The last three digits serve to identify the various alloying ingredients added by the manufacturer. For example, 3003 aluminum, or an aluminum-manganese alloy, contains about 1.2 percent manganese and a minimum of 90 percent aluminum. Another example is 6151 aluminum, an aluminum-silicon-magnesium-chromium alloy; here the number 6 is the designation for the magnesium and the silicon, and the numbers 151 indicate the special alloying ingredient and the percentage of the alloy. If the 1 as the second digit signifies chromium, then this code number indicates that 0.49 percent of the uncontrolled impurities is chromium, with 99.51 percent being aluminum, magnesium, and silicon.

Aluminum may be categorized further according to whether or not it is heat treatable. Aluminum that is not heat treatable includes pure aluminum, or the 1000 series; manganese, or the 3000 series; and magnesium, or the 5000 series. In heat-treatable aluminum alloys the principal alloying ingredient is either copper, magnesium, silicon, or zinc. The 4000 series is the silicon series of aluminum alloys, those that are used mainly for welding purposes and for filler materials in weld joints.

The temper designation of a heat-treatable alloy is sometimes indicated by a symbol after the four-digit number for the alloy. Some of these symbols are: F, which means as-fabricated; O, annealed; H, strain hardened, or cold-work hardening. The symbol H can be further subdivided into

H1X, strain hardened only; H2X, strain hardened and partially annealed; and H3X, strain hardened and stabilized. These H designations correspond to and have replaced the older designations of half-hard, three-quarters-hard, and full-hard. The H designations go up to the number 8, indicating full-hard temper, allowing a wider range of hardness values than the older designations.

Other temper designations include: W, which stands for solution heat treated, and T, which means heat-treat temper. The symbol T is always followed by one or more digits, denoting basic heat treatments. The symbol T3 means solution heat treated, cold-worked; T4, solution heat treated and naturally aged; T5, artificially aged; T6, solution heat treated, then artificially aged; T8, solution heat treated, cold worked, then artificially aged; T9, solution heat treated, artificially aged, and then cold-worked; and T10, artificially aged, and then cold-worked.

Aluminum alloys that are not heat treatable are the easiest to weld. These alloys are usually welded with a no. 1100, no. 4043, or no. 4047 welding rod, all of which require flux. Heat-treatable aluminum alloys, especially those alloys that contain copper and zinc (such as alloys 2024 and 7075), generally are not fusion welded because of the difficulty in tracking encountered during the solidification of the weld zone.

Copper

Copper is one of the oldest metals known. Records indicate that copper was worked successfully as early as approximately 4500 B.C. Today, copper, one of the most used commercially available metals, is used in wiring, sheets, rods, tubes, and castings. When it is mixed with silver, it is the most electrically conductive metal known. Silver is rated 100 on the conductivity scale; copper has a rating of 93. Pure coppers melt at 1981°F, and copper alloys melt at temperatures that range from 1800 to 2100°F. The major alloying elements used with copper include aluminum, lead, manganese, silicon, tin, and zinc. Copper, with its extremely high coefficient of expansion, expands more during heating than steel does. As a result, during the cooling process, the copper locks in stresses and tends to crack if precautions are not taken before, during, and after any manufacturing process applied to it. Heat-treat stress relieving is usually used to overcome this great expansion factor.

Copper is classified into two major groups: electrolytic copper and deoxidized copper. *Electrolytic copper* is 99 percent pure and contains only from 0.01 to 0.08 percent oxygen, which is scattered homogeneously throughout the metal. When electrolytic copper is heated, the oxygen in the copper is dispersed around the grain boundaries, developing cuprous oxide, Cu_2O. This cuprous oxide coats each grain or crystal and acts as a chill on the crystal, breaking down the bonding between the grains and causing a reduction in the strength of the copper, a reduction that may be as high as 60 percent of the copper's nominal strength. *Oxidized copper* has had the oxygen extracted from it. The oxygen-free copper is commercially available in many structural shapes and can readily be welded; electrolytic copper cannot be welded.

Lead

Lead, or plumbus (Pb), perhaps the oldest metal known, is derived from the ore galena, which is highly toxic. Miners of lead at one time had greatly shortened life spans because of lead poisoning. Lead is used mainly for storage batteries, solder, bearings, and type metal.

The major alloying metals for lead are bismuth, cadmium, antimony, and tin. Antimony increases the brittleness in lead as well as its hardness. Tin increases the hardness of lead without causing an increase in brittleness. The lead-tin alloys are probably the most common soldering alloys used. Tin has a relatively low melting point, 621°F, and an extremely low recrystallization point. Lead recrystallizes below room temperature, therefore it is always a ductile material and is extremely hard to work harden.

Magnesium

Seawater is the principal source of magnesium, a light, hard metal not found in nature. Magnesium is extracted from seawater in the form of magnesium chloride. The chloride is subjected to electrolysis and pure magnesium collects on the cathode. Magnesium does not have sufficient mechanical properties to be used in its pure state, so it is usually alloyed with aluminum, manganese, silicon, tin, or zinc. When alloyed, it exhibits qualities comparable to aluminum, while weighing only about 75 percent as much as aluminum. Magnesium is subject to hot shortness below its melting point, restricting it to low-temperature use. Its coefficient of thermal expansion is 15.0, which when compared to 6.5 for iron and 13.1 for aluminum, is high, making it necessary for magnesium products to be designed to avoid high stresses or distortions. Magnesium alloys usually have a melting range of 1200 to 1500°F.

A problem encountered in manufacturing with magnesium is that machine shavings of molten magnesium do not require an oxidizing element to catch fire, therefore, a fire hazard *always* exists when magnesium is undergoing one of the manufacturing processes and special fire precautions are always required.

Nickel

Nickel is a commercially available metal that compares with stainless steel in its corrosion properties. The mechanical properties of nickel can exceed those of low-carbon steel. It is available in both structural shapes and casting ingots. Pure nickel is usually composed of 99.5 percent nickel, with traces of copper, silicon, carbon, iron, and manganese. Casting nickel is composed of approximately 96 percent nickel with the remainder alloying elements.

Nickel is alloyed with copper, molybdenum, chromium, iron, silicon, and manganese. If any sulfur or phosphorus elements are alloyed into nickel, the resultant alloy will be brittle. Lead and zinc are also poor nickel alloys and should never be used. The nickel-copper alloy is known as *Monel*, renowned for its corrosion resistance and high strength. The nickel-iron-chromium alloy is called *Inconel*, and it is also known for its heat and corrosion resistance as well as for its nonmagnetic qualities. *Hastelloy* is the name for the nickel alloy containing molybdenum and iron. Hastelloy has excellent heat and corrosion resistance at temperatures that may range up to 2000°F. Nickel has over 40 commercially available alloys, all of which maintain its characteristic of resistance to heat and acid as well as its excellent high-strength and high-temperature characteristics.

Tin

Tin, produced from the ore cassiterite, is a bright silvery metal that is used mainly as an alloying element. The tin alloys, with a melting range of 700 to 900°F, include babbitt, an alloy of lead and tin; pewter, or britannia, used for housewares; type metal; foil; and solders. Major alloy elements used with tin are copper, antimony, silver, and lead.

Pure tin also has a vital use in the production of tin-plated, low-carbon steel. A thin electrolytic coating of tin, approximately 0.000015 in. thick, is applied to the surface of the low-carbon steel used in the production of food containers, or "tin" cans. This very thin tin coating on the low-carbon steel enables foods to remain in the can without becoming contaminated.

Zinc

The two major uses of zinc are for galvanized coatings and die casting. Zinc coatings can prevent the corrosion of steel because the zinc is more susceptible to corrosion than steel. Since zinc is anodic, it succumbs to corrosion and attracts the corrosion away from the steel. The corrosion destroys the zinc coating, thus, the thickness of the zinc coating determines its life. Galvanized coatings can be applied by dipping, electroplating, flame spraying, or mechanical plating. Zinc coatings are popular. For example, all kinds of sheet metal ductwork that are exposed to some corrosive atmosphere, such as the cooling and heating ductwork in a house, are zinc coated.

Zinc-alloy die castings comprise a significant percentage of all die castings produced. Zinc die castings are used in office equipment, toys, novelties, household utensils, automotive parts, as well as in die-cast furniture.

Zinc alloys have a melting range of 730 to 930°F. The major elements alloyed with zinc are aluminum, copper, magnesium, titanium, and cadmium.

METAL IDENTIFICATION

Usually, a metalworker can quickly identify major types of metals by a visual inspection and by a test of the weight of the metal. However, sometimes the main element of a metal is difficult to identify. The density or the specific gravity method of metal identification is one that can be used fairly accurately. The visual inspection together with the spark test and the specific gravity test generally yield an accurate identification of a metal.

Density

Both the density and the specific gravity of a metal are related to the weight of the material. The specific gravity of a substance is an abstract number; the density is usually expressed in pounds per cubic foot (lb/ft³) or in grams per cubic centimeter (g/cm³). Density can readily be converted into specific gravity. The formula for this conversion is that density when expressed in g/cm³ is equal to specific gravity. If the density is given in lb/ft³, it is equal to 62.4 times the specific gravity. The weight of 1 ft³ of water is 62.4 lb. Specific gravity or specific density is the weight of the material when it is compared to the weight of an equal volume of water. Water is always the base element used when determining specific gravity because 1 cm³ of water weighs 1 g. For example, the specific gravity of mercury is 13.6 so that mercury is 13.6 times as heavy as an equal volume of water. Aluminum has a specific gravity, or specific density, of 2.70 so that 1 cm³ of aluminum weighs 2.7 times the weight of the same volume of water. Table 4-6 identifies the density and specific gravity of many of the common metals used in manufacturing. Specific gravity is much easier to compute in g/cm³ than in lb/ft³.

An easy method for determining specific gravity is to measure the weight of the material and divide by the loss of weight of the material when it is submerged in water. Of course, this method can only be applied to materials that will not dissolve when submerged in water. A piece of copper weighs 178 g in air, and when submerged in water the same piece of copper weighs 158 g. The loss of 20 g is the weight of an equal volume of water. The specific gravity of copper, then,

TABLE 4-6. DENSITY AND SPECIFIC GRAVITY

METAL	DENSITY, lb/ft³	SPECIFIC GRAVITY
Aluminum	168.5	2.70
Antimony	413.0	6.618
Bismuth	610.3	9.781
Boron	158.2	2.535
Cadmium	539.6	8.648
Chromium	432.4	6.93
Cobalt	543.5	8.71
Copper	554.7	8.89
Gold	1,204.3	19.3
Iron	491.0	7.86
Lead	707.7	11.342
Magnesium	108.6	1.741
Manganese	455.5	7.3
Molybdenum	636.5	10.2
Nickel	549.1	8.8
Platinum	1,333.5	21.37
Silver	657.1	10.53
Tantalum	1,035.8	16.6
Tellurium	390.0	6.25
Tin	454.9	7.29
Titanium	280.1	4.5
Tungsten	1,192.0	19.1
Vanadium	394.4	5.6
Zinc	446.8	7.16

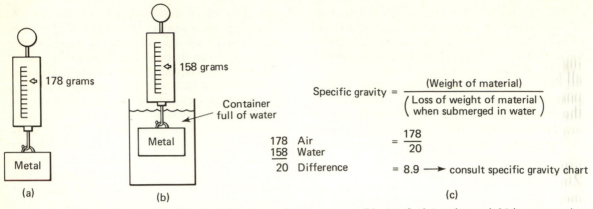

$$\text{Specific gravity} = \frac{(\text{Weight of material})}{\left(\begin{array}{c}\text{Loss of weight of material}\\ \text{when submerged in water}\end{array}\right)}$$

178	Air
158	Water
20	Difference

$$= \frac{178}{20}$$

$$= 8.9 \longrightarrow \text{consult specific gravity chart}$$

Fig. 4-2. Specific gravity test. (a) Step 1, determine weight in grams; (b) step 2, determine weight in grams when submerged in water; (c) step 3, the specific gravity chart reveals that the metal is copper.

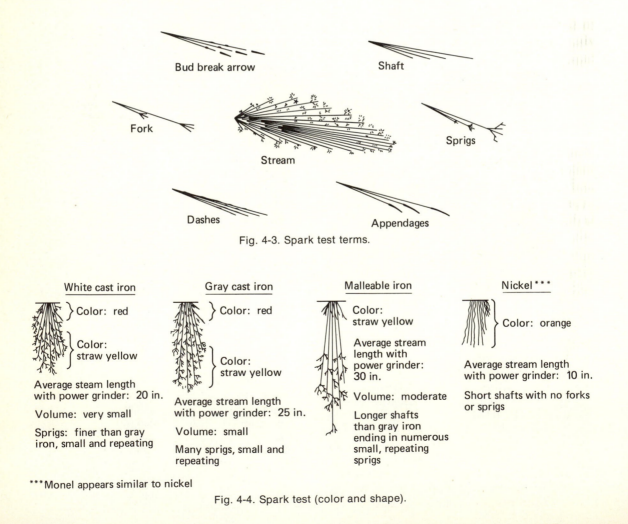

Fig. 4-3. Spark test terms.

Bud break arrow

Shaft

Fork

Stream

Sprigs

Dashes

Appendages

White cast iron

Color: red

Color: straw yellow

Average steam length with power grinder: 20 in.

Volume: very small

Sprigs: finer than gray iron, small and repeating

Gray cast iron

Color: red

Color: straw yellow

Average stream length with power grinder: 25 in.

Volume: small

Many sprigs, small and repeating

Malleable iron

Color: straw yellow

Average stream length with power grinder: 30 in.

Volume: moderate

Longer shafts than gray iron ending in numerous small, repeating sprigs

Nickel***

Color: orange

Average stream length with power grinder: 10 in.

Short shafts with no forks or sprigs

***Monel appears similar to nickel

Fig. 4-4. Spark test (color and shape).

is 178 divided by 20 which equals 8.9 (Fig. 4-2). If the person performing the test did not know the metal was copper, the 8.9 could be checked on a chart and the metal that was discovered to have this specific gravity could then be identified. Many times metals that are alloyed will have varying specific gravity according to the amount of alloying elements within them. Thus, iron and steel have specific gravities covering a particular range rather than one particular number.

Spark Test

The spark test is probably one of the most used methods for identifying metals. Spark tests rely on the perception of the metal-worker to distinguish the color, the shape, the average length, and the activity of the sparks to determine the material being tested. Spark testing is an accurate method of identifying metals, but it is a method that requires considerable practice in order for the metals to be identified correctly. Spark tests should always be performed with a high-speed power grinder, and the metal being tested should always be held so that the sparks will escape from the grinding wheel horizontally. The sparks should be looked at against a common dark background.

The major types of sparks given off by metals are: fork, bud, break arrow, shaft,

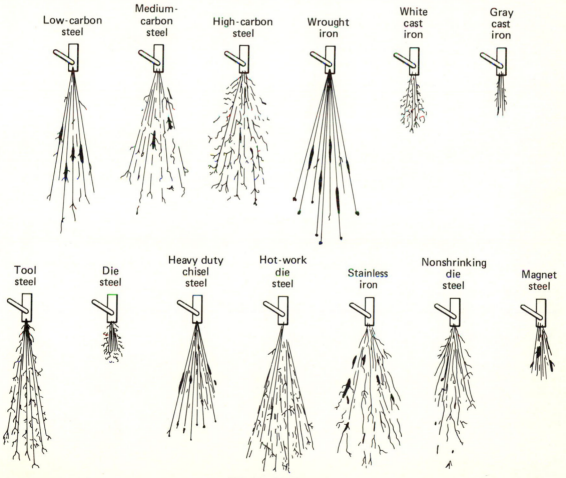

Fig. 4-5. Spark tests.

sprig, stream, dash, and appendage (Fig. 4-3). The color of the sparks coming from the grinding wheel usually will be red, orange, white, and yellow. Plain carbon steels are characterized by forked rays, which are yellow with white stars at the end. The carbon content of the carbon steels can be estimated by the number of white stars given off. Pure iron will show only forked rays with a yellow color. If iron is alloyed with tungsten, the sparks will be bright red. If steel is alloyed to nickel, the sparks will range, according to the alloy content, from an intense white to orange. The initial rays coming off white cast iron will have a red stream that slowly turns to a straw yellow. The average stream length will be approximately 20 in. with a small volume in the stream, and the sprigs will be small and repeating (Fig. 4-4).

The characteristics of several different types of iron and steel are shown with their spark test results in Fig. 4-5.

QUESTIONS

1. How does grey cast iron differ from white cast iron?
2. What is the carbon content of low-carbon steel, medium-carbon steel, and high-carbon steel?
3. What is an alloy steel?
4. Explain how steel is classified by the amount of oxygen in it.
5. What is a ferroalloy?
6. What are the effects of boron on steel, on chromium, and on titanium?
7. Explain the SAE-AISI coding system.
8. Explain the differences between deoxidized and electrolytic copper.
9. Explain the specific gravity method of metal identification.
10. Identify the major types of sparks in the spark testing of metals.
11. How do spark test stars help to determine the carbon content of steel?
12. What are the categories of stainless steel?
13. Explain the aluminum classification system.

5

Heat Treatment of Metals

Heat treating is the heating and cooling of a metal in its solid state under controlled conditions in order to improve its mechanical properties. There are many reasons for heat treating metal. It is used to increase hardness and strength; to remove internal stresses; to increase ductility, toughness, and softness; to refine the grain structure; and to obtain a variety of other physical and mechanical properties.

Heat treating can be either surface hardening or true hardening. Surface hardening of metal may loosely be thought of as changing the properties of only the immediate surface or exterior of the metal. In true heat treating, or interior heat treating, the properties of the metal have been altered completely throughout the metal.

SURFACE HARDENING

Surface hardening is sometimes called *case hardening* because it forms a hardened case around the softer, underlying metal. Many steel objects require a hard outer surface to resist wear and a tough inner core to absorb shocks, such as for a hammer or a crankshaft.

There are two types of surface hardening, depending on the carbon content of the steel. First, the composition of the outer surface in a low-carbon steel can be changed, a process called case hardening; and second, the surface of a medium- or high-carbon steel can be heat treated, as in flame hardening. These two processes can be accomplished by using many different procedures. The major methods used include carburizing, nitriding, cyaniding, chromizing, siliconizing, flame hardening, and induction hardening.

Carburizing

The oldest known method of producing a hard surface on low-carbon steel is carburizing. In carburizing, a steel of a low-carbon content, usually below 0.25 percent, is heated to a red heat while in contact with some carbon material, which can be a solid, liquid, or gas. Iron, for example, has an attraction for carbon at a temperature close to and above its transformation temperature. As iron changes from a bcc to an fcc structure, carbon is allowed to precipitate through the iron because of the fcc arrangement. The carbon enters the surface of the metal to form a solid solution with the iron, converting the outer surface of the metal to a high-carbon steel. As the operation continues, the carbon is gradually diffused into the interior of the part. The depth of the case depends on the length of

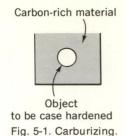

Carbon-rich material

Object
to be case hardened
Fig. 5-1. Carburizing.

time and the temperature used in the treatment. It also depends on the type of carbon-rich material in which the object is suspended for the heating (Fig. 5-1).

Nitriding

Nitriding uses the nitrogen in ammonia gas as a hardening agent. The part to be nitrided is placed in a special furnace, heated to a temperature between 900 and 1000°F, and held there for a period of time varying from 10 to 72 h. A nitrided case that averages a thickness between 0.012 and 0.018 in. usually requires between 35 and 72 h in the furnace. The furnace has a special atmosphere of ammonia gas, and the nitrogen from the ammonia combines with the steel to form an extremely hard case between 0.005 and 0.02 in. thick.

Nitriding, unlike carburizing, does not require quenching to obtain hardness. Nitriding also does not require as high as temperature as carburizing. Because of these two factors, it does not distort, crack, or change any condition of the metal, and because of the relatively low temperatures used, there is little or no loss in core toughness.

Cyaniding

Cyaniding is a case-hardening process that utilizes the absorption of carbon and nitrogen. The part to be cyanide case hardened is immersed in a bath of molten sodium cyanide (a salt containing both carbon and nitrogen) at a temperature of approximately 1550°F. A cyaniding treatment, lasting from 30 to 45 min, yields an increase of 2 percent in the carbon content of the case with a case

thickness of about 0.005 in. Cyaniding is useful when a thin hard case, between 0.001 and 0.015 in., is required in a short period of time.

The cyanide-casing operation is the fastest type of casing that can be applied to a mild steel core; however, its disadvantages are that the cyanide salts are extremely toxic and the process is messy. Special protective equipment must be worn by personnel operating in the vicinity of the cyanide salts. Parts must also be limited to a size that can be handled by one or two people.

Chromizing

Chromizing differs from the more standard case-hardening procedures in that a chromium carbide is diffused into the metal, converting the surface of the metal into a stainless steel case. This stainless steel case has a high hardness and a low coefficient of friction. Chromizing is applied to hydraulic rams, pump shafts, die tools, and dies, such as drop-forging dies. It is used to improve the corrosion resistance and the heat resistance of a metal. The process is not limited to ferrous metals but may be applied to many nonferrous metals, such as cobalt, molybdenum, nickel, and tungsten.

The major use of chromizing, however, is in the case hardening of ferrous metals that contain more than 0.60 percent, or 60 points, of carbon. The steel must contain this percentage of carbon in order for the chromium carbides to precipitate through the carbon, turning the surface of the metal into a stainless steel. The process is usually carried out at an elevated temperature ranging from 1650 to 2000°F. The application of the chromium at this temperature resembles to some extent the application of the ammonia gas in nitriding. The chromium is in a chromium-rich gas that the metal is exposed to while the metal is at an elevated temperature. In the nitriding process, the ammonia breaks down into nitrogen; but in chromizing, the chromium-rich gas is injected onto the surface of the medium- or high-carbon steel, changing it through diffusion to a stainless, case-hardened steel.

Siliconizing

Siliconizing, or ihrigizing, is the diffusion of silicon into the surface of a ferrous-based metal. This silicon creates a case that ranges in depth from 0.005 to 0.1 in. thick, depending on the carbon content of the ferrous material and on the length of time that the material is in contact with a silicon carbide and chlorine gas mixture.

Siliconizing, or ihrigizing, readily lends itself to automation. Common practice is to place the silicon carbide and chlorine gas in a liquid mixture and to bring this mixture to a temperature between 1700 and 1850°F. The mixture is contained in a tank with appropriate heaters to maintain this temperature. The items to be case hardened are placed on a conveyor track that simply runs through this tank of liquid silicon, carbide, and chlorine gas. The depth of the case of the part is controlled by the length of time the part is in the hot solution (Fig. 5-2). Often this conveyor track, prior to ihrigizing, goes through a cleaning tank which cleanses the part before the case is applied. The conveyor also can go through a rinse tank that will cleanse the part again after the case has been applied. A further change in the basic system can be made by using two tanks, one filled with silicon carbide floating in a liquid and the other, heated, containing chlorine. The part is moved from one tank to the next.

Flame Hardening

Flame hardening is a surface-hardening method that uses an oxyacetylene flame to heat treat the surface of the metal. Flame hardening can be performed on only medium- or high-carbon steel. When flame hardening is applied to steels with over 70 points of carbon, extra care must be used in order to prevent surface cracking of the high-carbon steel.

The process is based on the rapid heating of the outer surface of a ferrous metal to or above its transformation temperature. The minimum distance that the oxyacetylene flame must be held from the base metal is approximately $9/16$ in. If the oxyacetylene

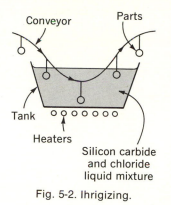

Fig. 5-2. Ihrigizing.

flame is closer than $9/16$ in., the base metal will be deformed by the flame. The metal is moved rapidly under the flame, allowing the flame to heat the base metal only on the surface. This surface heating creates two heat-affected zones, a primary heat-affected zone, where the transformation of the metal has taken place, and a secondary heat-affected zone, where grain growth has been developed or where the grains have been enlarged or decreased by the application of heat to the base metal. Immediately after it is heated, the metal is subjected to a quenching spray, generally water, that hardens the metal area that has undergone transformation.

The depth of hardness depends entirely on the hardenability of the material being treated since no other elements are being added or diffused, as in case hardening. With proper control, the interior of the metal will not be affected by this process. Often an average application of this process involves heat treating a complete piece to a certain specified softness or toughness. The exterior then may be flame hardened so that the finished piece resembles an item that has been case hardened (Fig. 5-3).

Induction Hardening

Induction hardening is a method similar to flame hardening, with the exception that the heat is generated in the metal by an induced electric alternating current. The only metals

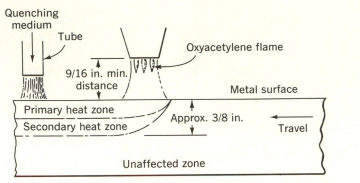

Fig. 5-3. Flame-hardening effects.

that can be induction hardened are those that are conductors or semiconductors. The ACHF (alternating current high frequency) obtained from a pulsating magnetic field about a wire produces the heat in induction hardening. The heat results from molecular agitation induced by the electricity. The high-frequency, low-voltage, high-amperage current produces a great number of eddy currents which are primarily responsible for the heating of the metal, although hysteresis is another source of heating (Fig. 5-4).

An inductor block, similar to a primary coil in a transformer, is placed around the part to be hardened. This coil does not touch the metal. A high-frequency current is passed through the block or the coil and induces a sympathetic current in the surface of the metal, creating heat, a process called *hysteresis*. As the temperature of the metal reached the transformation range, the power is turned off, the heat source is removed, and the area is quenched, usually by a spray. The most important aspect of induction heating is its rapid action. For example, it requires only a few seconds to heat steel to a depth of $1/8$ in. (Fig. 5-5).

The heat produced by induction is the result of both current and frequency. Higher currents produce stronger magnetic fields, while higher frequencies produce more pulsations of the field within a given time. A specific degree of heating can be obtained either by using high current at low frequencies or low current at high frequencies. However, high-frequency induction heating of metals requires a device that can convert 60 hertz (Hz) power to a high frequency of several hundred or more cycles per second. The frequency most used for metal treating applications is 450 kilohertz per second (kHz/s).

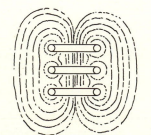

Fig. 5-4. Induction heating—magnetic lines of force (flux).

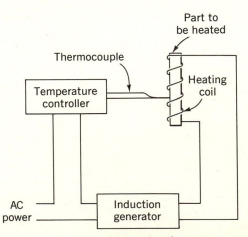

Fig. 5-5. Induction heating.

HEAT TREATING

Heat treating gives a metal greater versatility as a structural material because heat treating can change the mechanical properties of metal. The purpose of heat treating is to harden or soften a metal. The first step toward either softening, also called *annealing,* or hardening, is to elevate the temperature of the metal to a transformation state or the point at which the atoms in the structure either transform the structure from one pattern to another (such as in allotropism) or the point at which the crystals in the solution begin to realign themselves. The second step in hardening, but not in annealing, is to remove some of the hardness, a process called *tempering.*

Softening, or annealing, a metal increases its machinability rating so that such operations as rolling, drawing, and forging can be done more easily. The annealing process is no more than heating a metal until it is above the transformation range and then cooling it slowly to stop hard types of crystalline structures from forming in the metal. Heat treating to harden metals involves heating a metal to a high temperature and then cooling it at a faster rate than when annealing. Tempering follows the hardening process. The comparatively faster cooling allows a different type of crystalline structure to be formed in the metal. This structure is hard and many times internally strained because of the crystal types.

All heat treating, whether for softening or hardening, affects the microstructure of the metal. The types of crystals that are formed as a result of the cooling, or quenching, stage determine the hardness or softness of the metal. The study of the behavior of steel at different stages of heat treating is accomplished by a specific diagram, called variously an S curve, a time-temperature transformation (TTT) diagram, an isothermal transformation diagram, or, more precisely, a graph of isothermal transformation (IT) on cooling (Fig. 5-6).

Isothermal transformation diagrams are derived by cutting large numbers of small samples from a bar of steel. The pieces have homogeneous structures. These small samples are hung on wires and placed in a furnace where they are heated to the proper temperature for complete austenitizing, or

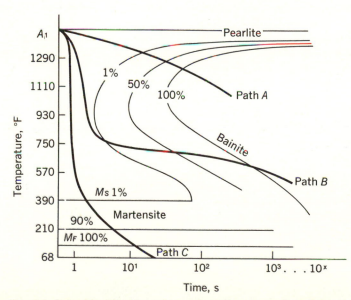

Fig. 5-6. Subcritical isothermal transformation on cooling diagram.

until they have gone completely through transformation. After all the samples have gone through transformation, they are placed immediately in a second furnace, or a holding furnace, which has been preheated to a set temperature below the transformation temperature. These samples are then removed individually and cooled in a progressive cycle in an ice-brine or ice-water quenching medium. The cooling is controlled precisely and the length of time from their removal from the furnace and their introduction into the quenching medium is controlled to a geometric progression of time, such as 1, 5, 10, 20, 40, 80 s, and so on. Each sample is then tested for hardness and also checked microscopically for the type of crystalline structures that are present. From this information the isothermal diagram is derived. Each steel has its own IT diagram. With this information, then, the results of any heat-treating operation can be predicted with a steel of known transformation qualities.

All metals, whether they are to be softened or hardened, should be brought into or above their transformation range. After this step, the hardening or the softening of the metal is accomplished by the amount of heat used and the rate at which the heat is extracted from the metal. The subcritical isothermal transformation on the cooling diagram indicates how quickly heat should be withdrawn (Fig. 5-6). Knowing each crystalline type is a prerequisite for determining what heat treating should be done and what method should be used.

Grain Types

Metal, upon reaching an austenitic temperature, transforms into austenite with three major grain types: pearlite, bainite, or martensite. The development of these three crystalline types depends on the temperature loss imposed on the austenite in the ferrous metal. The first decomposing of austenite yields a pearlite structure. *Pearlite* is the softest crystalline form in ferrous metal and is formed by retarding the cooling rate significantly. If the cooling rate is accelerated, bainite structure is formed from the decom-

posing austenite. If the austenite is quenched as quickly as possible, it completely decomposes into martensite, the hardest form of ferrous metal.

All of the groups are comprised of a mixture of cementite and ferrite. Cementite is a compound of iron and carbon that contains 6.68 percent carbon and 93.32 percent iron. The amount of cementite separating the ferrite determines the hardness and strength of the complete structure.

Cementite and ferrite appear in pearlite as plates (Fig. 5-7). Cementite plates are extremely hard; ferrite plates are soft. A number of these plates make up one crystal. The formation of lamellar pearlite can be coarse, medium, or fine (Fig. 5-8). The coarser the pearlite, the softer the pearlite. Fine pearlite is formed close to the temperature at which upper or feathery bainite is formed. Pearlite is formed by heating a steel to an austenitic temperature and then quenching it, approximately along path A in Fig. 5-6.

Bainite is created in a metal by decom-

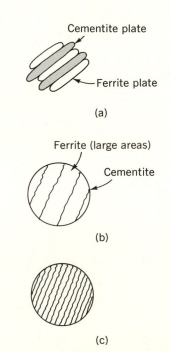

Fig. 5-7. Pearlite. (a) Lamellar; (b) coarse lamellar; (c) fine lamellar.

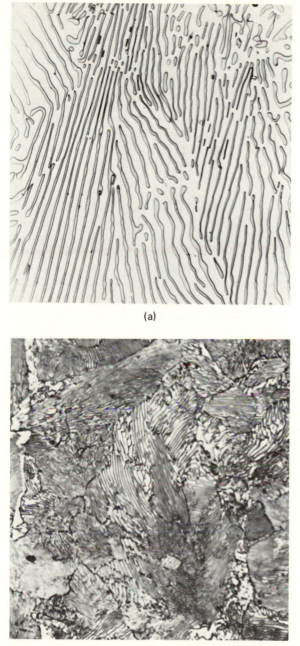

(a)

(b)

Fig. 5-8. Pearlite. (a) Coarse, 2500X. (*U.S. Steel Corporation.*) (b) Fine, 2500X. (*U.S. Steel Corporation.*)

posing the austenite at a fixed rate. The nose, or the knee, of the IT diagram is ignored and the austenite is cooled approximately on path *B* in Fig. 5-6. Whether path *B* is close to either the pearlite ranges or the martensite ranges determines whether or not feathery bainite or acicular bainite is formed from the austenite (Fig. 5-9).

Feather bainite results at the point at which cementite disperses. This feathery bainite consists of the broken-up cementite plates which have assumed a new axis and are no longer lamellar in structure.

Acicular bainite occurs when the cementite plates that have been broken up in the upper bainite ranges have been reduced

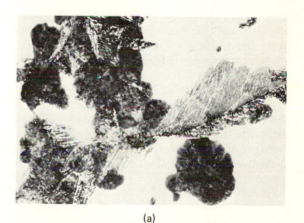

(a)

(b)

Fig. 5-9. Bainite. (a) Feathery (upper), 2500X. (*U.S. Steel Corporation.*) (b) acicular (lower), 2500X. (*U.S. Steel Corporation.*)

in size but increased in strength to produce a stronger structure. The cementite plates are now apparent as small, needlelike plates. The cementite can be thought of as having fine grains. These fine grains are the result of the precipitation of the cementite from austenite by diffusion, the physical movement of the atoms. The cementite requires a concentration of carbon atoms to form the cementite lamina, and time is the basic requirement for this formation.

Martensite, the hardest substance found in a hardened steel, is formed by extracting the heat from a ferrous metal at an extremely fast rate (path *C* in Fig. 5-6). Martensite begins forming at an M_s line, or the start of the martensite line. Approximately 1 percent of martensite will be formed at this temperature, approximately 390°F. If the temperature of the steel continues to fall at a fast rate, it is possible to form a structure of nearly 100 percent martensite, which will be very brittle (Fig. 5-10).

It is difficult to obtain 100 percent martensite because there is usually an amount of retained austenite that remains untransformed. It will transform eventually, but uncontrollably, into untempered martensite. Martensite left in this condition will cause the ferrous metal to crack because of the extreme stresses set up by the martensite crystals. The martensite crystals will have enough energy so that the standard bcc system is distorted and internally distressed. This stress must be relieved if the martensite is to be maintained.

Pearlite is formed at about 930°F (Fig. 5-6). Bainite results from the decomposing of austenite between the temperatures of 930 and 390°F. Martensite is decomposed from austenite between 390°F and ambient, or room, temperature.

Quenching

Cooling has the effect of freezing the mixture of austenite, cementite, and ferrite. If austenite is allowed to cool slowly, the grain formation will be uniform and the austenite will decompose into the cementite and ferrite layers called pearlite. If the austenite is quenched rapidly, the austenite will not have a chance to separate into other components and the iron carbide, or cementite, will be dispersed at a different level. The rate at which metal is cooled depends on the type of coolant used and whether or not the coolant is agitated or heated.

(a)

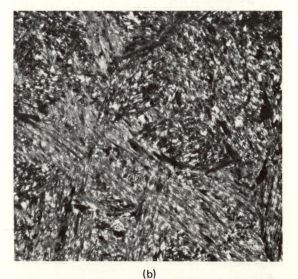
(b)

Fig. 5-10. Martensite. (a) 1 percent, 500X. (*U.S. Steel Corporation.*) (b) 99 percent, 500X. (*U.S. Steel Corporation.*)

The major media used for quenching are water, brine, oil, air, and metal. The major quenchers used commercially include oil, liquid, molten salts, and molten metals. Water is generally used at room temperature. Brine is a solution of salt and water that has the fastest cooling rate of any quenching medium because the salt in the water disperses heat faster than pure water. Oil and low-temperature metal in a liquid state are used for some types of martensitic tempering. Oil has a more even temperature gradient than water. The more the quenching medium can control the temperature loss of the metal, the more efficient it is. Air, either still air or forced air, is used for cooling many metals.

Cracking and warping of steel during the quenching operation can be avoided by a method of *interrupted quenching*. In this operation, the steel is heated to the transformation range and is then cooled to below 1000°F but above 400°F. The traditional heat-treating operation is then performed on the metal. The final heat treatment in interrupted quenching depends on the type of steel being treated and the mechanical properties desired.

Annealing

Annealing is the process of softening metal for further working. Annealing is accomplished by heating the metal to approximately 50°F above the upper critical temperature for hypoeutectoid steel and approximately 50°F above the lower critical temperature for hypereutectic steels. The metal is held at these heating zones until the carbide disperses in the solid solution and austenite is completely formed. The metal is then cooled slowly; usually the temperature loss is between 15 and 30°F/h until the metal is at room temperature.

When ferrous metal is allowed to cool down to room temperature in the furnace at this extremely slow rate, the process is called *full annealing*. However, the process can be speeded up by using isothermal annealing. *Isothermal annealing* occurs when the steel is allowed to cool down so that either medium or coarse pearlite is formed. The

steel is held at the appropriate temperature for a certain length of time so that coarse or medium pearlite is formed completely throughout the volume of the metal, and then it is cooled to room temperature in still air.

The microstructure of fully annealed hypereutectic steel consists of coarse lamellar pearlite with a network of cementite surrounding it. This cementite surrounding the pearlite in a hypereutectic fully annealed steel is brittle, generating planes of weakness. This network, or coring, of cementite also creates a thick, hard, grain boundary, causing poor machinability. For these reasons, hypereutectic steels are annealed by using isothermal annealing so that cementite coring of the grains does not occur.

Normalizing, another type of annealing, consists of heating the steel to approximately 100°F above its critical temperature and holding the steel at this transformation temperature until transformation is complete. The steel is removed from the furnace and allowed to cool in motionless room-temperature air. Normalizing is employed after steel has been cold-worked or has been unevenly heated or cooled, as when it is cast or welded. Normalizing removes the built-up stresses that are present in the metal as a result of these operations, giving the metal ductility and toughness. Normalizing produces a steel with a finer pearlite structure and greater hardness and strength than are obtained by full annealing.

Spheroidizing is also incorporated in the annealing processes. In spheroidizing, the steel is heated for a prolonged time below its transformation range, usually from 1250°F to the lower transformation range of 1333°F, until the carbon-containing cementite gathers into globular form. This transformation of cementite from a plate or needlelike structure into a round ball shape makes it easier for a cutting tool to sheer through it. This process is usually applied to high-carbon steels with 0.75 percent or more carbon. Spheroidizing produces the softest, most ductile, hypereutectoid steels possible but at the expense of strength.

Stress-relief annealing (also called *stress relieving*, and *process annealing*) is also performed below the subcritical annealing temperatures. Stress annealing is similar to spheroidizing except that the temperature used ranges from 1000 to 1200°F. Stress relieving simply unlocks the built-in stress within the grain structure, removing the residual stresses caused by working the metal such as in welding or machining. The stresses are simply dissipated by the extremely slow temperature loss of the metal. This process annealing is accomplished by heating the metal in a furnace to an appropriate temperature and then turning the furnace off, leaving the metal in the furnace to cool off at a slow rate until it reaches room temperature.

Tempering

In the process of hardening, the metal is reheated to a set temperature slightly above the transformation range so that austenite is allowed to form. The metal is then cooled at a controlled rate to form one of the three major types of crystalline structures: pearlite, bainite, or martensite. The formation of pearlite results in a soft structure, generally known as annealed structure. Hardening, on the other hand, involves the bainite and martensite structures. The three basic hardening procedures for the development of martensite, tempered martensite, and bainite are: conventional hardening and tempering (Fig. 5-11), martempering (Fig. 5-12), and austempering (Fig. 5-13). Austempering is sometimes known as bainite tempering because bainite is formed in the metal.

CONVENTIONAL HARDENING AND MARTEMPERING. Conventional hardening and martemperature hardening are related, with the exception that the quenching medium is controlled more closely in martempering than in conventional hardening and tempering. If the ferrous metal is brought up to an austenitic temperature and cooled in a cold-water solution, the difference between the core and surface temperatures creates heat-treating cracks in the metal, and there is a high probability of distortion in the metal to be treated. Martempering (also known as *marquenching*) is one means that stops this distortion and keeps the heat-treating cracks from forming.

Martempering is similar to conventional hardening, except that in quenching the tem-

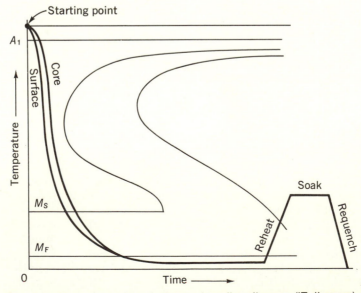

Fig. 5-11. Conventional hardening and cooling diagram (IT diagram).

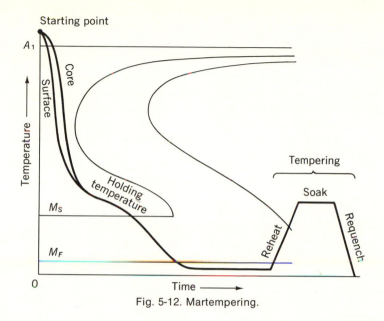

Fig. 5-12. Martempering.

perature of the metal is reduced to approximately 400°F, or slightly above the beginning of the martensite line, the M_s line. This temperature is held until the core and surface temperatures are the same, and then the metal is cooled to room temperature. Martempering of steel involves quenching the steel, which is at the austenitizing temperature, in hot oil, molten salt, or molten metal that is at a temperature at the upper part of, or above, the M_s temperature range.

The steel is kept in the quenching medium until the temperature throughout the steel is uniform, and then it is cooled at a

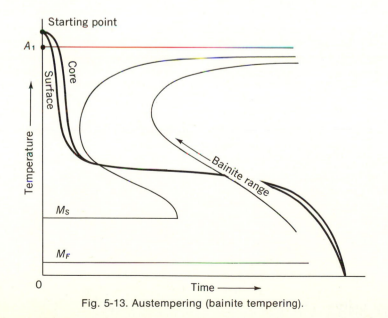

Fig. 5-13. Austempering (bainite tempering).

moderate rate, usually in air. The formation of martensite occurs fairly uniformly through the workpiece during the cooling in the room temperature air. This uniform cooling helps to avoid the formation of excessive amounts of residual stresses. After the martempered parts have cooled to room temperature, they are tempered as though they had been quenched conventionally. Because the final phase of cooling during martempering is relatively slow, light and heavy sections transform from the surface to the center in about the same time, thus minimizing or eliminating the distortion that results from unequal transformation rates present in the conventional hardening of metal.

The main factor in determining the temperature of the martempering bath is the alloying content of the metal. When the steel is cooled quickly from the austenitic state, the carbon simply does not have time to disperse. It is literally frozen in or near its original position in the austenite, preventing the segregation that is required to make cementite or pearlite, resulting instead in martensite. The formulas that have been developed to calculate the M_s temperature for various alloys are as follows: The M_s temperature in Fahrenheit is equal to 1,000 minus 650 times the percentage of carbon; minus 70 times the percentage of manganese; minus 35 times the percentage of nickel; minus 70 times the percentage of chromium; and minus 50 times the percentage of molybdenum in the steel, or

$$M_s = 1,000 - (650\% \ C + 70\% \ Mn + 35\% \ Ni + 70\% \ Cr + 50\% \ Mo)$$

Time in the martempering bath depends on the thickness of the metal, the temperature, the quenching medium, and the degree of agitation in the quenching medium. Because the purpose of martempering is to develop martensitic structure with low thermal and transformational stresses, there is no need to hold the steel in the martempering bath for extended periods of time. Excessive holding time lowers the final hardness because it permits transformation to structures other than martensite. In addition, stabilization of austenite may occur in moderately alloyed steels that are held for an extended period of time at the martempering temperature. The martempering time for temperature equalization is about four to five times the time required for quenching in anhydrous salt at the same temperature.

If the martempering salt or oil is agitated, the degree of hardness obtainable in comparison to the hardness obtainable in still quenching is considerably increased. In some instances, the rapid cooling produced by the most vigorous agitation increases distortion; thus mild agitation is often used to obtain minimum distortion at the sacrifice of some hardness.

Cooling from the martempering bath ordinarily is done in still air to avoid large differences of temperature between the surface and the interior of the steel. Forced-air cooling with a fan is occasionally used if the cross-sectional area is more than $3/4$ in. thick. Cooling steel in cool oil or water after removing it from the martempering bath is considered undesirable because thermal gradients cause unequal stress patterns to be formed, increasing the distortion and destroying the advantages of the martempering procedure.

After the part has been either conventionally hardened or martemper hardened, the piece must be tempered, or some of the hardness must be withdrawn from the piece in order to eliminate cracking during the storage period. The storage period can be overnight with martempered items and a matter of just a few hours with conventionally hardened items. The extreme hardness is withdrawn by the tempering process, a process of reheating the metal to a set temperature below the transformation range for a period of time until the desired mechanical properties are attained (Table 5-1).

AUSTEMPERING. Austempering converts austenite into a hard structure called bainite. In austempering, the steel is quenched in molten salts at a temperature that ranges from 450 to 800°F. This temperature produces a structure having the desired degree of toughness and ductility. When a constant

TABLE 5-1. TEMPERING TEMPERATURES

TEMPER-ATURE, °F	TEMPER COLOR	APPLICATION
590	Pale blue	Hammers, screwdrivers
545	Violet	Axes, chisels, knives
525	Purple	Center punches, scribes, awls
490	Yellow brown	Wood chisels, shearing blades, hammer faces
465	Straw	Dies, taps, punches
425	Light straw	Drills, reamers, milling cutters
380	Light yellow	Lathe tools, shaper tools

temperature is maintained for sufficient time to complete the transformation from austenite, the resulting structure is bainite. Bainite is tougher than tempered martensite. Cracking and warping are less likely to occur because the temperature drop in austempering is less severe than in ordinary quenching or martempering. A disadvantage of austempering is that only metal with thin cross-sectional areas can be austempered; for example, knife blades, razor blades, and wires. Steels containing 0.6 percent or more carbon are easily austempered.

Austempering is a function of the quenching bath temperature and the length of time that the austenitic metal is in the bath. Austempering baths are generally molten salt mixtures that contain sodium carbonate and barium chloride. This salt bath is usually held at a specified temperature by a thermostatically controlled heater. For example, if a particular steel is to be quenched at 650°F, the bath temperature will be 650°F. The steel is submerged in the molten salt and will remain in this molten salt quenching bath for a specified number of seconds. The metal is then removed from the salt bath and the part is allowed to cool in still air. The amount of time and the temperature of the bath are important because the metal has to be in the bath long enough for the bainite to form completely and the temperature must be hot enough to control the type of bainite formed. Austempering is capable of creating a tougher article than one that has been either conventionally hardened and tempered or martempered.

QUESTIONS

1. What are the differences between surface hardening and heat treating and between hardening and tempering?
2. What are the major types of case hardening?
3. How does flame hardening differ from induction hardening?
4. How does an induction coil induce heat into a metal?
5. What is ihrigizing?
6. What is hysteresis?
7. How does martempering differ from austempering and conventional tempering?
8. What are the limitations of austempering and conventional tempering?
9. How is the IT diagram used?
10. How are the crystalline structures of bainite, martensite, and pearlite derived?
11. What are the major quenching media?
12. How does the quenching medium help determine the hardness of a heat-treated metal?
13. What are the differences between annealing and normalizing?
14. What practical uses does knowledge of heat treating have for the metalworker?

6

Coatings of Metals

Metals possess the characteristic of disintegrating back to their natural states. One example of this disintegration process is rust, or iron oxide. Since iron ore is also iron oxide in its natural state, corrosion of iron is a natural process in the disintegration of this metal back to its natural state. Corrosive forces cost industries approximately $6 billion per year. They can be witnessed in the car junkyards and metal scrap yards across the nation. Corrosion is the cause of many accidents and many equipment failures.

Basically, corrosion is an electrochemical reaction between two areas called an anode and cathode. The *anode* is a positively charged area, and the *cathode* is a negatively charged area. The three basic components of corrosion include an anode, a cathode, and an electrolyte bath. The electrolyte bath might be plain water (as in ordinary moisture) or the strongest acid or alkali. The corrosion may be explained as the movement of electrons and ions from the anode to the cathode (Fig. 6-1). A basic electrical difference must exist between the anode and the cathode for corrosion to take place. However, even in one piece of metal the anode and cathode areas are poorly defined and may shift quickly from time to time, resulting in uniform corrosion.

The ever-present prospect of metal cor-

rosion has resulted in the development of the metal coating industries. The purpose of all of the basic processes (electroplating, metalliding, anodizing, and galvanizing) is to prevent corrosion of the metal product, to beautify the metal product, and in some cases to harden the surface of the product.

CORROSION TESTING

In order to understand corrosion and to test the corrosion resistance of various metal and chemical coatings, tests have been devised for the analytical study of corrosion. Three of the most popular corrosion tests are the salt-spray test, the humidity (or tropical) test, and the sulfur dioxide test.

Salt-Spray Test

The salt-spray test consists of exposing the metal to be tested to the salt spray along an oceanfront or to a mist of a sodium chloride solution. In both these atmospheres, the porosity of a test piece can be assessed, and its resistance to oceanfront atmospheric corrosion can be studied. The salt test can be accomplished either by constructing a test apparatus along the beach or by constructing

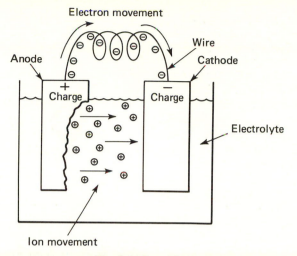

Fig. 6-1. Corrosion.

a chamber that will have a saltwater mist forced through it, saturating the atmosphere of the chamber with a saltwater solution. The sample metal in either case must be thoroughly degreased, suspended by nonmetallic hooks, and exposed to the salt atmosphere for a controlled length of time. Often testing will last as long as 2 or 3 years.

The Humidity or Tropical Test

The humidity test is also designed to assess the resistance of a test piece to a wet, salt-filled atmosphere. The test is carried out either in a highly humid area or in a special

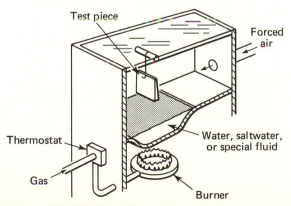

Fig. 6-2. Humidity test for corrosion.

test chamber. A reservoir at the bottom of one end of the test chamber contains water, salt-water, or some special fluid, which is heated by a gas burner causing moisture to rise. A forced-air duct moves air around the test piece in most chambers (Fig. 6-2). The test pieces must be degreased carefully and are always suspended in the chamber by nonmetallic hooks. Again, as in the salt-spray test, the test piece (or pieces) remains in this atmosphere until corrosion begins. A common practice is to check the test piece every 8 hours.

Sulfur Dioxide Test

The sulfur dioxide test is becoming more popular because it causes metal to corrode more quickly than the salt-spray test does. Also, the test piece is visible at all times and is dry so that the pores and the cracks in the corrosion deposits are easily visible (Fig. 6-3). Nickel-plated products, for example, that are in a sulfur dioxide atmosphere quickly show the effects of corrosion in cracks and pits.

There are many other tests for corrosion, but most are variations of these three tests.

CATHODIC PROTECTION

Cathodic protection relies on the thermionic emission of metal ions for electromotive force (emf). For example, zinc is a metal that corrodes rapidly, or loses ions rapidly. A small amount of emf is released during the ion loss, enough emf to direct the ions toward the nearest cathode. If a piece of zinc is

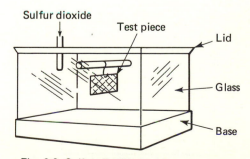

Fig. 6-3. Sulfur dioxide test for corrosion.

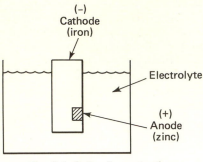

Fig. 6-4. Cathodic protection.

joined to a piece of iron and the product is immersed in an electroyte (such as the ocean), the zinc anode corrodes, providing a path of least resistance for the corrosion. This zinc path protects the iron cathode. If the zinc anode is allowed to disintegrate completely, the iron will corrode because of the anode spots created within it. When a cathodic protection device is used (such as a zinc or magnesium plate), the plate needs to be checked periodically to ensure that it has not been completely corroded (Fig. 6-4).

ELECTROPLATING

In electroplating an electric current is passed through a solution between metals or other conducting materials which act as positive and negative terminals of a direct-current (dc) circuit (Fig. 6-5). Metal deposits

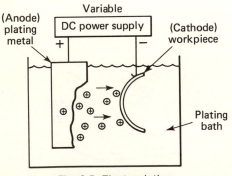

Fig. 6-5. Electroplating.

itself on the negative terminal or electrode. For example, if the ends of two copper wires connected to a dc source are immersed in a solution of copper sulfate and water, the current will flow. After the end of the copper wire connected to the positive end of the terminal power source has been in the solution for a while, it will become thin, while the other wire will grow in size. The loss of weight in one wire is equal to the gain in weight of the other. The amount of copper sulfate in the plating bath remains the same.

Electroplating is lattice building. Grain boundaries on the base metal can be continued in the electrode deposits since all electrode deposits are crystalline in structure. The nature and strength of the crystals determine the quality and the effectiveness of the plate coating. The reason for the adhesion of the electrode deposits is not fully understood, but the adhesion is thought to be a result of interatomic attraction and mechanical keying, or locking, of particles.

The plating process depends on the existence of metal ions in the plating solution or the plating bath. After the ions carry the positive electric charge through the solution, they come to a ground state at the negative electrode, which is also the workpiece, to form the plate. The two metal plates that constitute the anode and cathode must be connected to the positive and negative terminals of a battery, and only direct current should be used so that current will flow in only one direction.

Plating Baths

There are three types of aqueous solutions used in electroplating. They are designated as acid, neutral, and alkaline baths. The *acid bath* is used extensively for low-cost plating in which heavy deposits and bright finishes are the desired end product. One chief disadvantage of the acid bath is that the plating usually has to be polished or buffed. Another distinct disadvantage of the acid bath is that it cannot be used for depositing directly onto iron, steel, or zinc. Acid bath plating may be accomplished with iron, its products, and zinc by first flashing (or exposing) them in a cyanide bath, producing a *flash plate,* or a *flashing.* This flashing is a thin electrode coating that is produced in a short time. The coating acts as a buffer between the acid bath plating and the iron or zinc.

The *neutral bath* is used primarily in the plating of nickel. It will withstand high temperatures and high current densities, but it has a tendency to pit the cathode, or workpiece, so that it must be used with a wetting agent, or an organic addition, in the plating bath.

The *alkaline bath* transmits a dense, fine-grain deposit that may be made highly reflective and smooth. It also has good covering power and the ability to coat deep recesses in the workpiece.

All three of these plating solutions are called *electrolytes* because they conduct the electric current. The presence of water causes these solutions to be broken into ion particles. When a flow of current is created, the charged particles are carried through the electrolyte from one electrode to the other where the ion particles are then neutralized. When the voltage is applied to the electrolyte, the positively charged ions in the solution always move toward the cathode. Those ions which move toward the cathode are called *cations.* Negatively charged ions that move toward the anode are called *anions.*

The primary electrolytic reaction in electroplating is always the depositing of metal ions in a solution or bath. There are two ways to control this concentration of ions: by adding a metal salt to the electrolyte or by using a metal that continuously dissolves in the electrolyte.

Metal Preparation

In order to begin the plating process, the metal must be thoroughly cleansed. There are two general steps in this preparation: degreasing and descaling. *Degreasing* may be done with an alkaline solution, caustic soda, soda ash, phosphates, alkali silicates, soap, or synthetic detergents. Solvent degreasing is also used. *Descaling* can be accomplished with either chemical or mechanical means. After these two primary processes, the work-

piece must then be polished and buffed to ensure adhesion or to obtain the desired appearance. Polishing is accomplished by mechanical polishing, electropolishing, chemical polishing, or by dipping. Plating will not cover up the mistakes or errors in the workpiece.

ANODIZING

Anodic oxidizing, or *anodizing,* creates a stable oxide film on a metal. A natural form of anodizing occurs when aluminum is exposed to the atmosphere. A thin oxide film is formed on the surface of the aluminum, a film which eventually is the same as that produced in the anodizing process. Anodizing protects and beautifies aluminum surfaces, and converts the aluminum surface into a nonconductor.

Anodizing requires the presence of an electrolyte that allows the flow of electrons between the two electrodes. The cathode is made of either lead or graphite. The anode is the aluminum workpiece to be coated. The system uses a dc power source to complete the electrical flow.

The coating, or oxide film, formed on the surface of aluminum is caused by the reaction of the anode and the electrolyte. The anode reaction is the same as that in corrosion, the oxidation of metal. When current is applied through the electrolyte, oxygen is liberated at the surface of the anode and bubbles up to the surface of the electrolyte. During this release of oxygen, the oxygen impinges on the aluminum and causes an oxide formation. During the time of the oxidation process, the oxide coating thickens, or grows, into the metal. The growth can be identified as a cellular structure created as a direct result of the oxidation process. The cellular structure is a porous surface which requires sealing.

The second procedure used in anodizing is the sealing process. Hot water or a steam bath seals the porous surface by increasing the number of the pores mechanically. The sealed layer acts as a barrier layer for the anodized coating.

Two important factors controlling cellular growth and the depth of the oxide penetration are the amount of current flow and the type of power supply. A general rule is that the higher the current flow, the larger the pores. Low current densities create slow reaction rates, producing a dense but porous surface. High current densities cause rapid deep pores to grow in small areas. The commercially available power sources use both alternating and direct current or a combination of the two. Different cellular growth patterns are created according to the type of power supply and the alloy of aluminum. However, a thin anodizing layer is usually generated by alternating current, whereas direct current generates a coating that has a deeper penetration.

The number of steps necessary to complete an anodizing process will vary according to the aluminum to be finished, the texture of the finish, the contaminations on the metal, the previous corrosion of the metal, the heat treatment of the metal, and the color of the finish of the final product. The anodizing process can be accomplished in as few as 13 steps, using fire tanks and a sink with hot and cold water; or the process can take as many as 19 steps, using nine tanks and seven separate hot- and cold-water dips.

GALVANIZING

The word *galvanizing* is derived from *galvanic* and refers to producing an electric current by chemical action. Galvanizing is a process that uses an electrochemical action to produce a thin coat of a highly corrosion-resistant material on the surface of another metal. The galvanizing process mainly uses zinc which is applied to iron and steel. Zinc is one of the most corrosion-resistant metals on the periodic table that can be used as a plating material. Cost of the galvanizing process is low. It is used for coatings on such items as sheet metal, wire, tanks, bridges, ships, bolts, buckets, tubs, and all sorts of containers. The galvanizing of sheet metal is probably the foremost application of zinc as a coating. The annual worldwide production of zinc is approximately 1,300,000 tons. Of this total production, approximately one-half is used for preventing corrosion.

The galvanization of zinc to the surface of metal may be accomplished by four different processes: sherardizing, electrolytic plating (or electroplating), schoop (or spraying), and the hot dipping process.

Sherardizing is the most popular process for use with small intricately designed parts. The parts are placed in a box of zinc powder dust; then the box is placed in a furnace and heated until the zinc dust becomes a vapor. The zinc vapor forms a coating of zinc sulfide on the surface of the parts. When the parts are cooled, a galvanized surface is produced.

The *electrolytic,* or the *electroplating, process* was developed during World War II because zinc was scarce. The electrolytic process is economical, both in the use of power and the use of zinc, but electroplating still is not used for mass production in industry because too much time is required to do the plating and too much zinc is used for galvanizing. The process electroplates the base metal with a layer of zinc. Because the base metal is subjected to little stress, few distortions result. A disadvantage of electroplating is that the resultant plate is too thin to withstand corrosion. Also, the final zinc electroplate has a dull, drab look; whereas other types of galvanizing, like hot dipping, have a bright, shiny look.

The *schoop process* uses basic metal spraying to spray a wire that converts to a molten metal. It is used to coat products that are too large to be dipped into a molten bath of zinc. Such items as water tanks, bridges, and ship hulls are usually metal sprayed. The zinc is in the form of a wire which is loaded into a metal spraying gun. The zinc is then sprayed on the object. It usually is melted by an oxygen fuel source and forced out of the gun onto the workpiece by air pressure.

The *hot dip process* is probably the most economical of all the galvanizing processes for mass production. Hot dipping was the originally developed zinc coating process, although the basic process has been refined and adapted to specific applications. The

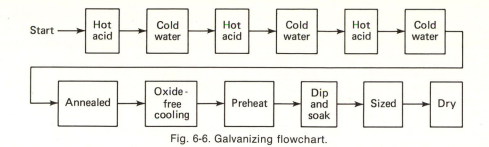

Fig. 6-6. Galvanizing flowchart.

flowchart in Fig. 6-6 presents the steps in the hot dip process. When sheet steel arrives to be galvanized, the first step is to submerge it in an acid bath of hot sulfuric acid. This step is followed immediately by a cold water rinse. The acid bath and cold water rinse are performed three or four times to ensure a clean surface. After the surface of the steel is clean, the steel is annealed and allowed to cool in an oxide-free atmosphere. The oxide-free atmosphere assures protection against the formation of oxides on the hot metal surface. The metal is not allowed to cool completely but is brought down to the temperature of the molten zinc bath, sometimes going through a preheat stage to ensure that it is exactly the bath temperature. The metal is then dipped into the bath. Often the zinc bath will contain 0.02 percent aluminum to increase the fluidity of the molten bath, producing a more uniform and thinner coating. The metal is then pulled through the zinc bath between two sizing rollers which control the amount of zinc that remains on the sheet. The amount on the sheets usually ranges from 0.04 to 1.5 oz zinc/ft².

The final step in the galvanizing process is to allow the sheet to cool and dry. As the hot zinc dries, or solidifies, the spangles appear. The thickness of the galvanized sheet metal is measured by a wire gage. The size of the iron in the sheet metal is one size smaller than the number read on the gage because the zinc coating takes up one number size. Galvanized metals will undoubtedly continue to be popular because corrosion control is becoming more important as the amount of manufactured goods increases. The zinc galvanizing process is the most economical coating process available to modern manufacturing.

AEROSOL PLATING

Aerosol plating started as a method of silvering mirrors. Currently, aerosol plating is used to deposit thin films of gold, copper, and other metals on any metallic or nonmetallic surface. The equipment commonly used for aerosol plating is a double-headed spray gun. The aerosol-plating spray gun sprays two solutions at the same time. One solution contains a complex metallic salt, and the other, a reducing agent. When the two sprays meet and mix on the surface of the object, a metal film is deposited. Excess solution and metal simply drain off. This excess residue can sometimes be filtered and reused. After the complete object is sprayed, it is rinsed and dried, the final step in the spray plating process.

Most surfaces can be plated without any pretreatment other than cleansing the surface. If the plating will not adhere to a surface, a monoatomic layer of a metal, such as a layer of silver or platinum salts, is deposited. An object is dipped into the metallic salt solution, or the solution is sprayed on the object, to create a flash of metallic salts on the object to be surface plated. The aerosol plating is then sprayed on this prepared surface. The plating film itself has very slow buildup rates, but it produces smooth, dense surfaces. Because of the slow buildup rates, most aerosol plating thicknesses are kept to a minimum.

PAINTING

Spray painting is the most common process used to finish manufactured goods. Both organic and inorganic painting materials can be spray painted. Some of the basic materials sprayed include oil-based paints, shellac, lacquer, varnish, enamels, rubber-based paints, primer coatings, bituminous coatings, and many types of paint, such as silicon, vinyl, and acrylic paints. Paints are also available in an almost unlimited number of types and colors. Paints are applied by four basic methods: air paint spraying, airless paint spraying, electrostatic painting, and dip painting.

Air Paint Spraying

The air paint spraying process operates on the Venturi principle (Fig. 6-7). Air pressure, passing by a siphon tube, draws the paint into the nozzle of the spray gun. The nozzle then controls the shape and the density of the spray. The basic components of an air paint spraying system include an air pump with an air storage container, suitable flexible piping, the paint container, and the spray gun. Many times the paint container will be incorporated directly into the spray gun which can hold from 1 pt to 1 qt of paint. Larger reservoirs of paint, as much as 55 gal, can be made available by extending an extra siphoning tube into the paint container. The quality of the finished surface depends on the ability of the operator. Paint spraying is a simple process, but it does require practice to pro-

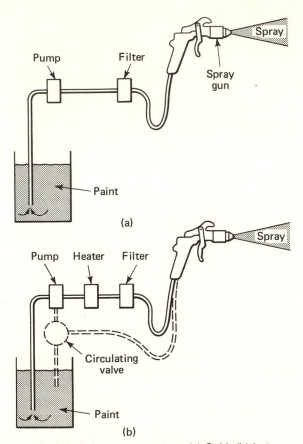

Fig. 6-8. Airless spray system. (a) Cold; (b) hot.

duce an acceptable finish. The novice paint sprayer usually sprays a coating that is too heavy, resulting in runs and drips.

Airless Paint Spraying

Airless paint spraying does not use air pressure as the medium that forces the paint through the spray gun onto the article to be painted. Instead, a hydraulic pump is located in the line that produces a pressurized paint to the spray gun (Fig. 6-8a). The pressure that the pump delivers can vary according to the paint, the material to be sprayed, and the item to be coated. The pressure ranges from 300 to 2,500 psi. The paint spray is atomized as it exits from the spray gun nozzle.

An advantage of the airless method is

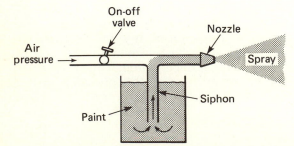

Fig. 6-7. Air paint spraying (venturi principle).

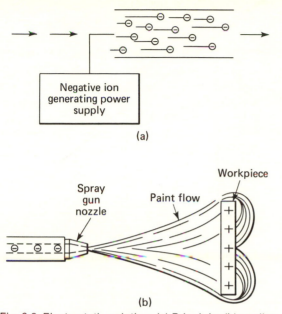

(a)

Fig. 6-9. Electrostatic painting. (a) Principle; (b) application.

Electrostatic Painting

Electrostatic painting uses a positive and negative electrostatic field. The system can be adapted easily to the painting of metals because all metals have a positive charge. If the paint is negatively charged, the spray paint will automatically be attracted to the metal. The negative charge is created by a negative-ion-generating power supply that usually is located in the spray gun. As the paint passes through the spray gun, negative ions are generated into the paint. The spray atomizes as it leaves the nozzle, and the paint is then drawn by an electrostatic force to the material to be painted (Fig. 6-9). This electrostatic painting system is so successful that the spray gun nozzle does not have to be pointing directly at the workpiece. The flow of paint can go completely around an object until the object is covered.

Dip Painting

The dip painting process uses a paint vat into which the article to be painted is dipped. Generally, the dip coating process is incorporated into a conveyor system so that the article to be painted goes through a cleaning and degreasing station, through the dipping in the vat, and then directly to a bake oven. Dip coating also can use the electrostatic principle of painting (Fig. 6-10).

The equipment for electrodip coating is similar to that used in electroplating. The application of electric current causes electrically charged particles to migrate through a conductive aqueous medium, the paint,

that less overspray and paint rebound result because of the lower turbulence in the spray stream. Airless spray guns can also be adapted so that either cold or hot paint can be sprayed by installing a paint heating system between the pump and the filter (Fig. 6-8b). Whenever hot airless spraying is done, a recirculating apparatus is installed from the gun through the pump to the paint to ensure an adequate delivery of hot paint to the spray gun at all times. The airless spraying system has also been adapted to airless electrostatic spraying.

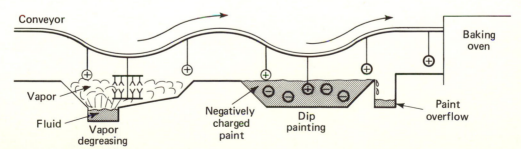

Fig. 6-10. Dip painting. *Note:* The paint is negatively charged (−), and the object is positively charged (+).

TABLE 6-1. CHEMICAL COLORING OF SELECTED METALS

COLOR	MATERIAL APPLIED	COLOR	MATERIAL APPLIED
		BRASS	
Dark antique	Butter of antimony	Old apple green	2 lb arsenious oxide

Slate black	a. 16 oz copper nitrate
	   1 gal water
	b. 1 oz potassium sulfide
	   4 oz hydrochloric acid
	   1 gal water
			12 lb ammonium chloride
			12 lb verdigris
			4 lb copper carbonate
			1 gal hydrochloric acid

		Bluish green	1 oz sodium thiosulfate 8 oz pernitrate of iron 1 gal water
Steel bronze	13 oz white arsenic 1 gal hydrochloric acid	Dull green	2 oz copper sulfate 1 qt boiling water (Immerse articles and allow to dry.)
River clay yellow	16 fl oz ammonium sulfide 1 gal water		
Umber brown	2 oz barium sulfide 1 gal water at 120°F	Olive green	8 oz nickel ammonium sulfate 8 oz sodium thiosulfate 1 gal water
Barbedine bronze	1 oz antimony sulfide 3½ drams red oxide of iron at 180°F		
Flemish bronze	1 to 2 drams arsenious oxide 2 fl oz hydrochloric acid ½ dram potassium sulfide 1 gal water	Antiquate green	1 part acetic acid 30 parts ammonium carbo- nate at 80 to 100°F

Oak bronze	2 oz antimony sulfide
	4 oz caustic soda
	¼ fl oz ammonia
	1 gal water at 160°F
	(Toning solution: 1 oz
	   hydrochloric acid to 1 gal
	   water)
		Antique green	½ oz copper sulfate
			2 oz ammonium chlorate
			1 gal water

		Variegated	(Dip in acetic acid, then ex-
			   pose to ammonia fumes
			   for a few hours.)

		Fern green	1 part copper sulfate 1 part ammonium chloride 1 part lead acetate at 98°F
Chocolate	4 oz copper sulfate 4 oz double nickel salts 4 oz potassium chlorate	Orange	4 oz caustic soda 8 oz copper carbonate 1 gal water
Yellowish green	3½ oz ammonium chloride 2 lb copper acetate 1 gal water	Greenish brown	½ oz potassium sulfide 1 fl oz ammonium sulfide 1 gal water at 80°F
Apple green	10 oz sodium chloride 16 fl oz ammonium chloride 1 gal vinegar		
		ALUMINUM	
Black	½ lb zinc chloride ½ oz copper sulfate 1 qt hot water	Black (a second method)	1 lb zinc chloride 1 oz copper sulfate 2 qt hot water

Copper	30 parts copper sulfate
	30 parts cream of tartar
	25 parts soda
	1,000 parts water
	(Clean article, then plunge it
	   into this bath.)
		Black (a third
		method)
			1 oz white arsenic (arsenious
			   oxide)
			1 oz iron sulfate (ferrous
			   sulfate)
			12 oz hydrochloric acid
			12 oz water

Frost	2 oz caustic soda 1 pt water		

under the influence of a dc field. The article to be painted is positively charged and the paint is negatively charged. The product to be coated acts as the anode, and the cathodes are built within the sidewall of the tank. The articles to be coated are immersed from 1½ to 2 min yielding a 1.0-mil organic coating in the first 15 s. The longer the paint vat time, the thicker the coating. A major requirement of either standard dip coating or electrodip coating is that a large number of parts must be available for painting. Dip coating is usually used only on a production line. After parts have been electrocoated they are rinsed with freshwater and then with deionized water to remove any nondeposited paint particles.

CHEMICAL COLORING

The metals that are most often colored chemically are brass, aluminum, and iron. The chemical coloring of metals involves cleaning the metal by degreasing and descaling and then placing the metal in a chemical solution. Table 6-1 identifies some of the solutions used for coloring brass and aluminum.

QUESTIONS

1. What is corrosion?
2. Explain the salt-spray corrosion test, the tropical test, and the sulfur dioxide test.
3. How does cathodic protection work?
4. What are the major types of electroplating baths?
5. Explain anodic oxidizing.
6. What are the basic types of zinc coatings?
7. Explain the sherardizing process.
8. Compare and contrast electroplating and electrostatic painting.
9. What are the differences in the processes of air, airless, and electrostatic spray painting?

Part Two

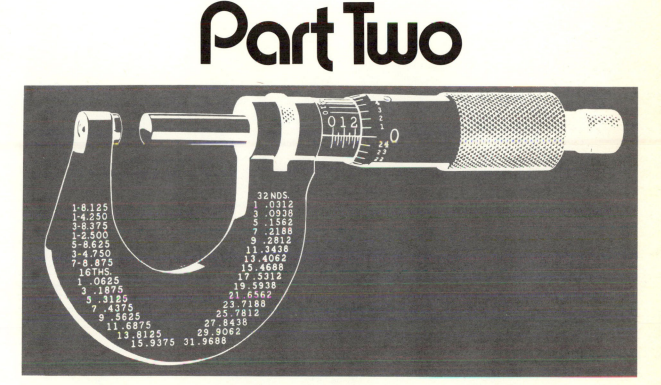

Quality Control

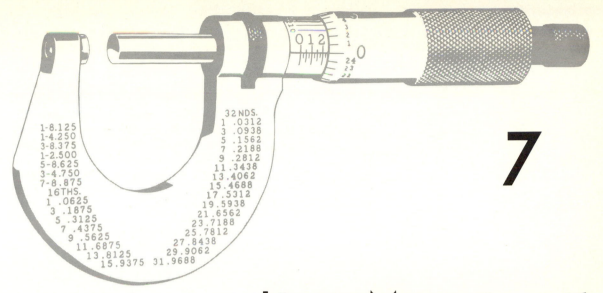

Linear Measurement

7

All measurement ultimately depends on certain basic forms, such as length, time, mass, or potential difference in electrical resistance, but all of these concepts are too abstract to have any practical meaning unless they are defined in terms of a standard.

STANDARDS

Standard rules and tapes are very useful for general layout, but precise accuracy cannot be derived from a rule that only measures to 1/64 in. when specifications demand 0.001 in.

The system of linear measurement depends on standards that have been adopted by the National Bureau of Standards. These standards, when applied to production processes, rely mainly on the gage block, or Johannson block, optical flat, and surface plate as the standards for checking all other gages and instruments. Figure 7-1 illustrates how gage blocks are used as a standard for gages and instruments.

Gage Blocks

Gage block standards were established by the National Bureau of Standards in 1956 and the standards of quality stated in federal specifications are used throughout industry today. These gage block specifications include the tolerances for flatness, parallelism, and finish, as well as a Rockwell C scale of hardness of 65. At the present time, the National Bureau of Standards calibrates 5,000 to 6,000 gage blocks per year. These are mostly master blocks that are used to gage other blocks in various companies.

Gage block are classified according to grades. Grade AA blocks are the most precise of all. Grade A+ blocks are usually used under laboratory conditions. These blocks are used when tolerances of 0.000050 in. or less are desired. Grade A blocks are used for inspection purposes. The grade B block, called a *shop block* or *working block,* is the most common block used for measuring in industry. Gage blocks are also available in three styles or shapes: rectangular, square, or round. The rectangular block is the most popular because it costs less than the round or square blocks. Also the amount of warpage that occurs on a thin rectangular block is less serious than in a round or square block.

A standard set of 81 gage blocks is capable of creating several thousand possible link combinations. This standard set includes a 0.0001-in. series with 9 pieces ranging from 0.1001 to 0.1009 in., a 0.001-in. series with 49 pieces ranging from 0.101 to 0.149 in., a 0.50-in. series with 19 pieces ranging from 0.05 to 0.95 in., and a 1-in. series with 4 pieces

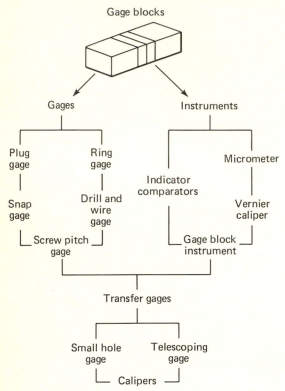

Fig. 7-1. Gage blocks as a standard for gages and instruments.

that are 1, 2, 3, and 4 in. long. Gage blocks are also available for angular measurement in sets that measure from 1 s.

The five major materials used in the manufacture of gage blocks include tool steel, chrome-plated steel, stainless steel, chrome carbide steel, and tungsten carbide. However, the laboratories of the National Bureau of Standards are working on approximately 20 different types of materials to use in the manufacture of better gage blocks.

Cleaning with solvents will remove most contaminants from gage blocks. Scratches and burrs may be removed by wringing the surface of the gage block on a conditioning stone. The blocks should be kept as accurate as possible. The abuse most often found is not maintaining the blocks at an even temperature. Gage blocks should be maintained at 20°C or 68°F. A tool steel block 1 in. in size will expand 0.000006 in. for every degree above 68°F.

WRINGING. For proper wringing to occur gage blocks must be cleaned and oiled with a light film. The cementing action, the adhesion force that holds two or more blocks together, is thought to result from a combination of the molecular attraction of the metal, as in solid-state bonding, and the cementing action of the oil or moisture film on the surface of the block. Properly wrung blocks will support over 250 lb pressure. Perfectly dried blocks will seldom cling together. Attaching or wringing the blocks is accomplished by a sliding, circular motion. There are three basic steps to be followed when wringing gage blocks. First, the gage blocks are picked up, one in each hand. They are held by the sides. Second, one end of the gage block is placed across the end of the other block, keeping the mating surfaces parallel. Last, with a slight pressure, one block is rotated onto the other until the sides of the two blocks are aligned, then one block is slid forward until the ends of the blocks are aligned. Gage blocks can be disengaged by following the wringing process in reverse order. Gage blocks should never be forced apart; the wringing technique should always be used (Fig. 7-2).

Optical Flats

The optical flat uses the theory of light interference as a measuring device. Optical flats are transparent disks of clear fused quartz lapped within a few millionths of an inch of

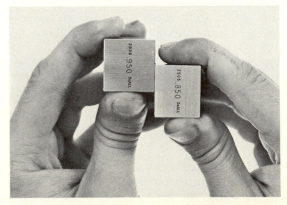

Fig. 7-2. Wringing gage blocks. (*DoAll Company.*)

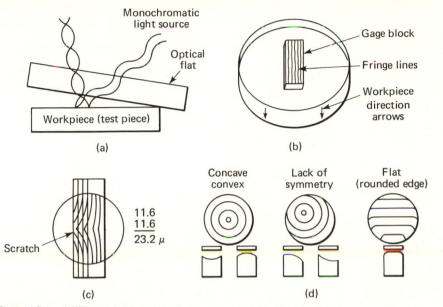

Fig. 7-3. Optical flats. (a) Theory of light interference; (b) application; (c) fringe lines; (d) common tests.

flatness. They are generally used with a helium light source which produces a greenish yellow monochromatic light with a wavelength of 23.1323 microinches (μin.), or 23.1323 millionths of an inch.

The optical flat is placed on the surface of the work to be checked. The monochromatic light passes through the optical flat striking the workpiece. The light wave is then reflected back onto the lower surface of the flat. Because a single color or chroma light is used, the back reflections of the light cancel out a portion of the incoming light, yielding dark interference bands, or *fringe lines*. The fringe lines are a function of the monochromatic light. In other words, the helium monochromatic light of 23 μin. will yield half of a full 23-μin. wavelength, or 11.6 μin. of the wavelength. Each dark interference fringe band, then, represents a progression of 11.6 μin. above the point of contact between the workpiece and the optical flat (Fig. 7-3a and b). For example, if a piece of metal being tested had a scratch, the depth of the scratch could be estimated visually to the nearest millionth of an inch by checking the depth of the waves. Figure 7-3c shows a scratch that is two fringe lines deep, that is, a

scratch 23.2 millionths of an inch deep. The width of the scratch may also be measured by the same method.

In theory, each straight band between flat surfaces represents a region of uniform height or separation. Straight bands typify the flat surface, and equal band spacing is characteristic (Fig. 7-3d). It is advisable to rotate the optical flat 90° for a check by creating a second fringe pattern. If the second fringe pattern shows the same results as the first one, then the accuracy of the measurements seems highly probable.

Surface Plates

Surface plates, related in principle to gage blocks, are much larger than gage blocks. They may range from 3½ to 4 in. square to 48 × 144 in., an area 4 × 12 ft. A surface plate is an extremely smooth flat plate that yields a definite reference point for both laying out and checking material. They are invaluable aids in inspection when a definite reference line or reference surface is needed to measure from.

Surface plates are available in grades just like gage blocks. The grade *AA* plates are

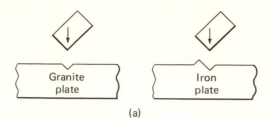

(a)

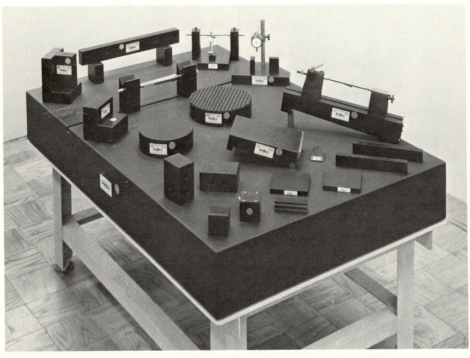

(b)

Fig. 7-4. Surface plate. (a) Granite versus iron; (b) black granite surface plate with accessories. (*DoAll Company*.)

used exclusively for laboratory work where accuracy must be maintained. The grade *AA* plate is usually guaranteed to a surface flatness tolerance of 0.0000025 in./2 ft² area. The grade *A* plate is considered the inspection plate. It has a flatness tolerance of 0.000050 in./2 ft² area. The grade *B* plate is the shop plate with an accuracy of flatness of 0.000100 in./2 ft² area.

Surface plates are available in granite or iron. Iron surface plates are not as reliable as granite because as the temperature increases or decreases from 68°F, the iron plate distorts according to the coefficient of linear expan-

sion for that particular iron alloy. Also, if a sharp object is dropped on an iron plate, the indentation will create a small mountain on the plate ruining the tolerance of the plate (Fig. 7-4a). When accuracy is very important, black granite plates are purchased. Granite has a low coefficient of linear expansion, and if a sharp-cornered object is dropped on a granite plate, the plate will not be distorted. The area struck by the piece will break into fine particles, leaving an indentation in the surface of the plate but not destroying the accuracy of the surface.

Surface plates are so accurate that they

can have gage blocks wring directly to them. The plates also come with a wide variety of accessories such as angle blocks, T slots, box parallels, V blocks, universal right angles, parallels, and sine plates (Fig. 7-4*b*).

MEASURING DEVICES

Production shops in the United States measure in inches or in parts of inches. Measurement devices can be separated into three distinct categories: instruments, gages, and transfer gages.

Instruments

Instruments are those devices, such as the gage block, micrometer, and linear caliper, that can measure workpieces with virtually no limit to size and accuracy.

MICROMETER. The micrometer caliper is by far the most commonly used precision measuring instrument in a machine shop. A micrometer works on the principle of the relation of the circular movement of a screw to its axial movement. The amount of axial movement of a screw per unit of revolution depends on the thread and is known as the *lead*. The lead is the forward distance the thread moves in one full revolution. Micrometers come in various shapes and sizes according to the size of the stock to be measured and according to the primary measuring function. For example, a 1-in. standard micrometer measures from 0.001 to 1.000 in. outside diameter (OD). The major types of micrometers are the standard micrometer caliper, the inside micrometer, the jaw type, the thread micrometer, the depth micrometer, and micrometers with linear scales (Fig. 7-5*a* to *d*).

The micrometer resembles a C clamp. The basis of the tool is an accurate screw which can be revolved in a fixed nut to vary the opening between the two measuring faces, called the *anvil* and the *spindle end*. The barrel end of the spindle is threaded with a pitch of 40 threads per inch. The spindle is then attached directly to a thimble so that every time the thimble is rotated one complete revolution, the thimble advances 0.025 in. This figure, 0.025, is then divided into the 25 equal parts which are marked on the thimble. The $1/25$ or $1/40$ of a revolution equals a $1/1,000$ in. advancement of the spindle.

The barrel of the micrometer is divided into 40 equal parts which total 1 in. The parts are expressed in decimal values starting at zero and then advancing to 0.1, 0.2, 0.3, up to 1 in. (Fig. 7-5). The beveled end of the thimble nearest the barrel is divided into 25 gradations of 0.001 in. each around the circumference of the thimble. One complete turn of the thimble will equal 0.025 in. on the barrel of the micrometer. Each five gradations on the thimble are numbered, 0, 5, 10, 15, 20.

The correct method for using the micrometer is to hold the thimble between the thumb and the forefinger, letting the back of the C frame rest in the palm of the hand. The work to be measured is inserted between the anvil and the spindle with the other hand. The micrometer is closed until a slight drag is felt between the micrometer faces and the work. When the proper tension is attained, the measurement indicated on the micrometer barrel is *added* to the reading on the thimble. For example, if the barrel reading is 0.450 and the thimble reading is 0.003, the full proper measurement is 0.453 (Fig. 7-6).

The *vernier scale* on a micrometer is an additional scale on the barrel that enables the micrometer to measure to 0.0001 in., rather than the usual 0.001 in. The vernier scale is 9 marks long on the thimble. This distance of 9 marks has been separated into 10 spaces, leaving a $1/10$ difference. The vernier scale is read by checking to see which mark on the thimble aligns with a mark on the barrel. Only one mark will align perfectly. This mark is the setting. For example, if 0.075 were visible on the barrel and 0.006 were visible on the thimble plus a slight bit more, in order to read to the nearest 0.0001 in., the distance between the 0.006 and the 0.007 mark on the thimble could be guessed at or the witness

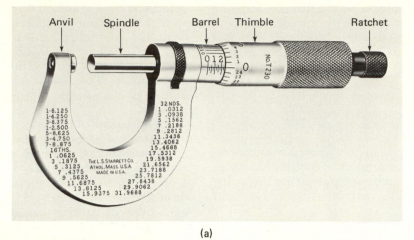

Anvil   Spindle   Barrel   Thimble   Ratchet

(a)

(b)

(c)

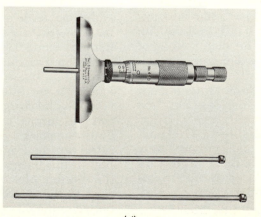

(d)

Fig. 7-5. Some micrometers. (a) 0 to 1 in. standard; (b) inside; (c) thread; (d) depth.

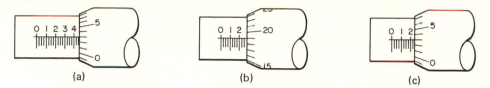

Fig. 7-6. Reading a micrometer caliper. (a) reading 0.453; (b) reading 0.269; (c) reading 0.228.

marks could be checked to see which thimble mark aligns perfectly. In the case shown in Fig. 7-7, it would be the 0.0001 mark. The total reading of the vernier micrometer would be 0.0811.

VERNIER CALIPER. Vernier calipers are used in the same manner as micrometers with the exception that the vernier scale can be adapted to protractors for radial measurements (Fig. 7-8a to c). The vernier caliper can measure up to 0.001 in., and requires the same kind of touch or "feel" for the tension of the workpiece between the caliper nibs as does the micrometer. Although the vernier caliper differs greatly in appearance from the micrometer caliper, each instrument should yield the same result. Most vernier calipers can measure inside and outside an object. Caliper size is generally indicated by the length of the standard scale on the beam of the caliper.

The caliper is used by setting the vernier slide at a close distance to the object to be measured. The slide is locked with the slide setscrew, and the fine adjustment nut is turned until the correct pressure is exerted on the test piece by the nibs. The scale is then read. The accuracy of the vernier caliper can always be checked by closing the two nibs and checking to see if the zeroing is set properly. If the zero is not set properly, there are adjustment screws on the vernier scale on the slide.

The vernier scale has not only been applied to the vernier caliper but also to the dial caliper, the vernier protractor, and to an assortment of height gages that generally are used with surface plates or machine beds to check the height of workpieces. Scribes are incorporated with height gages so that accurate, precise heights can be inscribed on workpieces from a given surface.

The scale on the vernier caliper is read in the same manner as the scale on the vernier micrometer. The scale on the beam of the vernier caliper is divided into 0.025 in. sections. The vernier scale works again on the difference between the true distance and a distance that is 0.001 in. smaller than the true distance. In this case the beam scale is a true 0.025 and the distance of the vernier scale is 0.024, or a 0.001-in. difference, thereby enabling the vernier scale to measure to the nearest 0.001 in. The first step in reading the scale is to determine the number in front of the zero on the vernier scale (Fig. 7-9). The number shown in Fig. 7-9 is 2 in., and the numbers completely in front of the scale are 2.650. The vernier scale reading is then added to this number. The index mark 9 on the vernier scale aligns perfectly with an index mark on the beam, yielding a reading of 2.659.

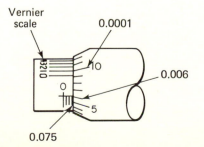

Fig. 7-7. Reading a vernier micrometer. 0.075 + 0.006 + 0.0001 = 0.0811.

ANGULAR MEASUREMENT. An angle can be measured in degrees, radians, or mils. The dominant system of angular measurement is in degrees, where 360° equals a complete circle. The 360° are broken down to minutes and seconds so that 1° is equal to 60 min and 1 min is equal to 60 s. A complete circle con-

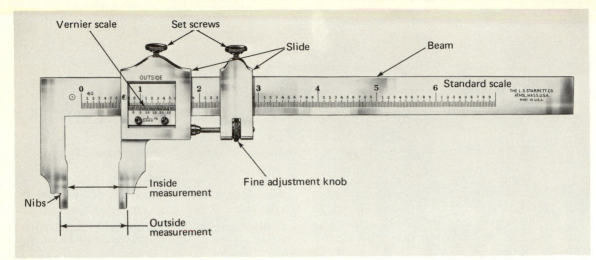

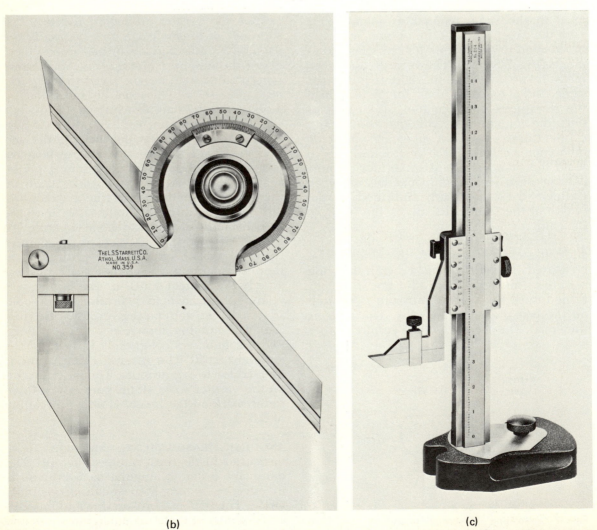

Fig. 7-8. The vernier scale. (a) Vernier caliper; (b) vernier protractor; (c) height gage. (*L. S. Starrett Company.*)

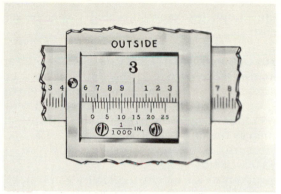

Fig. 7-9. Vernier caliper, reading 2.659. (*L. S. Starrett Company.*)

four quadrants each from 0 to 90°. The scale is further subdivided into numbered degrees between each 10° setting, and each 5° mark is a little bit longer than the others. The vernier scale generally goes from 0 to +60 and 0 to −60 so that the vernier scale can be read in either direction. The vernier protractor scale is read by first determining the greatest number of degrees that can be read before the zero. In Fig. 7-10 the setting is 79°. The number of minutes is then determined by checking to see which number on the vernier scale aligns exactly with a witness or index mark on the standard scale. In the example in Fig. 7-10, it is 30 min. The reading is then read as 79°30′.

tains 1,296,000 s. Such accuracy is not called for in most metalworking situations but is required in inspection or in laboratories. Most angular checking is done in either the degree or the minute range.

The vernier protractor is capable of an accuracy of 5 min of angular measurement. The vernier protractor is read in the same manner as the vernier scale is read except it reads in degrees and minutes (Fig. 7-10). The vernier beveled protractor is the device most commonly used in small machine shops for determining angular measurement. Other devices used include the sine bar and the optical comparer. Seldom are angled gage blocks available in a small shop.

The vernier beveled protractor standard scale is graduated into 360° markings and into

DIAL INDICATORS. The dial indicator directly measures to 0.001 of an inch. Dial indicators are currently being adapted to vernier calipers so that the dial indicator is mounted directly on the vernier slide and replaces the vernier scale. Dial indicators are also used independently. There are two basic designs for dial indicators: balanced and continuous (Fig. 7-11a and b).

With the balanced dial indicator, the plunger is capable of moving in two directions, yielding either a plus or a minus reading to the nearest 0.001. Frequently the center alignment of lathe centers is checked with a balanced line indicator by placing a test bar between the two centers. The dial indicator is slid across the surface and indicates the amount that the lathe tail stock is offset. First the dial indicator is set onto the lathe and a slight pressure is placed on the plunger by its contact with the work. The dial face of the indicator is rotated until the dial is zeroed on the arrow. The dial indicator is then moved the length of the test piece, and it will indicate how many thousandths of an inch the test piece is out.

The continuous dial indicator can perform the same tasks, but it can only generate measurement in one direction. The continuous dial indicator can measure a greater range of variation than the balanced indicator.

Dial indicators are available in a wide

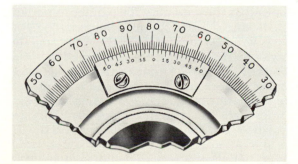

Fig. 7-10. Reading 79°30′ on a vernier protractor. (*L. S. Starrett Company.*)

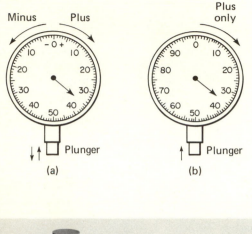

Fig. 7-11. Dial indicators. (a) Balanced; (b) continuous; (c) application. (*L. S. Starrett Company.*)

range of sizes and degrees of accuracy. The accuracy of the dial indicator can be from 0.0001 to 0.001. The travel range of the plunger also varies with dials available that travel a distance from as small as 0.0001 up to 5 in. Of course, the larger and more accurate the range, the more the dial indicator will cost.

ELECTRONIC COMPARATORS. The production of more parts and the demand for more accurate parts have created a demand for measuring instruments that are faster and more accurate. Electronic measuring instruments, such as the microcomparator (Fig. 7-12a), can measure accurately and quickly up to 0.000010 in.

Almost all electronic gages work on the same principle. The movement of an armature that is attached to a spindle is sensed by induction coils that keep the armature at zero. Any movement in the spindle, therefore the armature, is sensed as a movement in the electric current flow. This current flow is measured and represented on the scale of the electronic gage. Many times the spindle end of the gage can be replaced with specially shaped devices that measure specific things. The basic electronic measuring instruments are available either as devices for linear measurement or as devices for surface measurements. The devices that measure the size of a test piece have an anvil incorporated into the machine to ensure a common reference point for measuring the height. Surface testing machines do not have an anvil incorporated within them.

Electronic gages have made it possible to measure surfaces so accurately that various characteristics about a surface are now standard. For example, all flat surfaces are known to have waves, like ocean waves, across them. These waves can have their lengths defined as well as their heights. Two other important characteristics are the roughness of the surface, which is the surface of the wave, and the lay of the finish, which is the direction of the finish (Fig. 7-13a). Surface finish is designated by roughness and waviness and is expressed in millionths of an inch. For example, the cylinder walls of an engine block generally are finished to 0.000030 in., or 30 μin., and the lay is at a 30° angle to the cylinder walls. However, not all products demand such an accurate finish; consequently, other devices, such as visual surface measurement devices, are

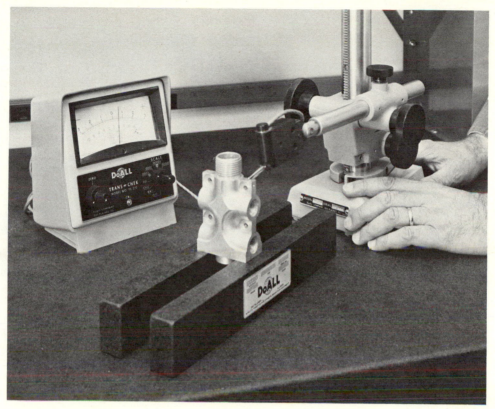

(a)

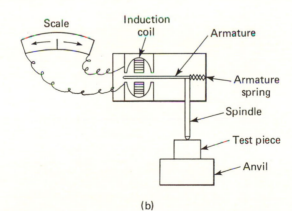

(b)

Fig. 7-12. Electronic measuring instruments. (a) Microcomparator (*DoAll Company*); (b) operation principle.

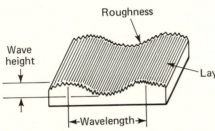

Roughness

Wave height

Lay

Wavelength

(a)

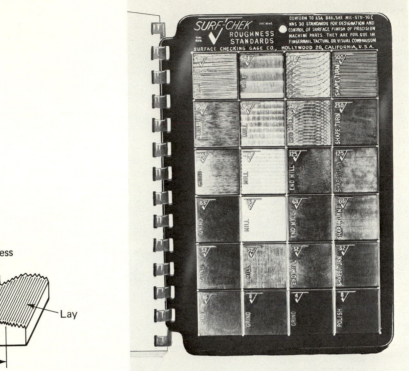

(b)

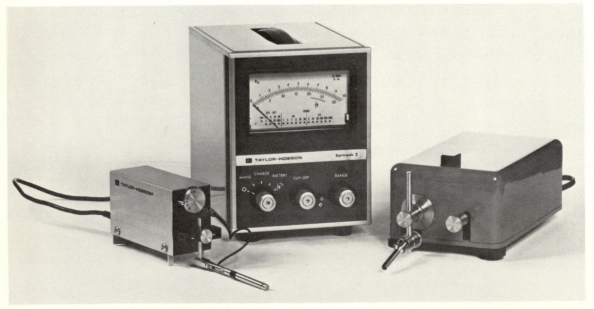

(c)

Fig. 7-13. Surface indicators. (a) The surface; (b) visual surface comparator card (*Surface Checking Gage Company*); (c) profilometer (*Bank Precision Industries.*)

available from most toolmaking companies. Some typical visual surface measurement devices are illustrated in Fig. 7-13b. A profilometer is an electronic gage used when the surface accuracy must be extremely precise (see Fig. 7-13c).

PNEUMATIC COMPARATORS. Pneumatic gaging is becoming more popular because of the accuracy and long life of the gages. The pneumatic gage is based on Bernoulli's theory that pressure decreases as volume increases. The working principle of the gage is

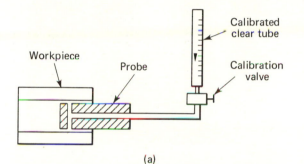

(a)

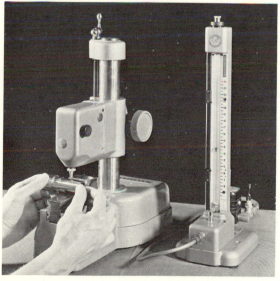

(b)

Fig. 7-14. Pneumatic comparators. (a) Theory; (b) application. (*Bendix, Automation and Measurement Division.*)

that air pressure from 60 to 125 psi entering a calibration valve is reduced from 10 to 20 lb, yielding an even supply of air pressure. The air pressure is then ducted through orifices in the workpiece that allow the air to strike the test piece. The air pressure is set by a standard test piece and all other test pieces are checked against the standard. A variance in size results in a difference in air pressure. These differences in air pressure are indicated by a float in a glass tube that is sealed in the low-pressure side of the pneumatic comparator (Fig. 7-14). A float position below the standard position indicates an undersized workpiece, and a high float setting indicates an oversized workpiece; but when external checking is done, the reverse is true. A high float position indicates an undersized piece and a low float position indicates an oversized piece. An advantage of a pneumatic comparator is that the gating head does not have to be accurately machined although the holes where air escapes must be the same size. Some things that can be checked by pneumatic comparators are true dimensions out of round, bell mouthing, papering, concentricity, camber, parallelism, and flatness.

GAGE BLOCK INSTRUMENTS. Gage block instruments frequently are used to check on machines that are set up for inspection of finished products. Very seldom will gage blocks be used on this line inspection, but the accuracy of gage block instruments depends on the accuracy and care of the gage blocks. Basic gage block instruments are in use for either angular or linear measurement, such as with the ball ends and the center points of linear measurements (Fig. 7-15a and b). The angular measurement device most used by metalworking shops is the sine bar. It is used in conjunction with the surface plate and gage blocks.

The *sine bar* derives its name from the trigonometric function, the sine, because the sine bar always has two knowns which yield a third unknown. The sine of an angle is equal to the gage blocks divided by the sine bar length. The sine bar length is always known and gage blocks are renowned for

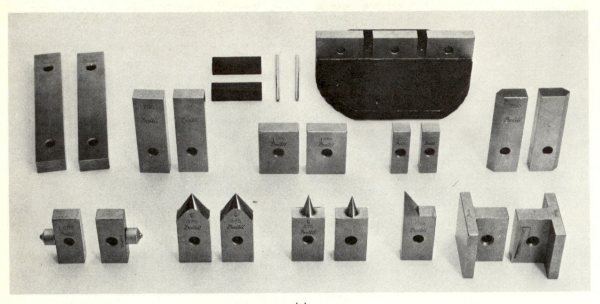

(a)

(b)

Fig. 7-15. Gage block instruments. (a) Gage block parts; (b) application. (*DoAll Company.*)

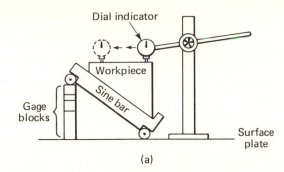

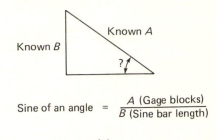

$$\text{Sine of an angle} = \frac{A \text{ (Gage blocks)}}{B \text{ (Sine bar length)}}$$

(a) (b)

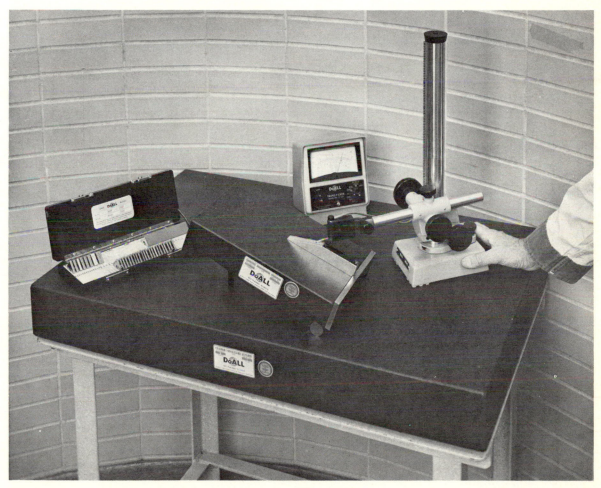

(c)

Fig. 7-16. (a) Sine bar setup for checking an angle; (b) equation; (c) application. (*DoAll Company.*)

their accuracy. A typical test is to check with the use of gage blocks, surface plate, sine bar, and a dial indicator whether a workpiece is parallel to the surface plate (Fig. 7-16). When the dial indicator shows that the workpiece is parallel to the surface plate, the length of the gage blocks then becomes a known value, and both the sine of the angle and the angle can be computed. Standard sine tables are available for computing the angle.

Gages

Gages are measurement tools that can measure only within certain limits. These limits must be set by a standard or measurement instrument. Some common types of gages include the flood gage, the ring gage, the snap gage, the drill and wire gage, and the screw pitch gage. Gages test large numbers of articles without requiring a great deal of operator skill. They can only be used with hard metals; they would scratch or mar soft metal surfaces since they generally are made of tool steel.

PLUG GAGES. Plug gages are used to measure holes in metals on an accept or reject basis. Some types of plug gages are: single-end; double-end; progressive, step, or go–no-go; and thread plug (Fig. 7-17). The two most popular plug gages are the progressive gage and the thread plug gage. The progressive plug gage is designed so that a smaller diameter, for example 0.5000, is the acceptable diameter of the workpiece. The gage is then inserted into the work. The gage should shoulder against the 0.5005 section of the gage, indicating that the hole is the correct size. If the 0.5005 plug gage enters the hole, then the hole is too large for the acceptable standard. As in most measurement, the "feel" of the plug gage in the hole is of prime importance. The usual diameter between the progressive steps on the go–no-go gage range from 0.005 to 0.010 in. However, this can be varied on special plug gages according to the manufacturing standards desired.

RING GAGE. Whereas the plug gage is designed to check holes, the ring gage is de-

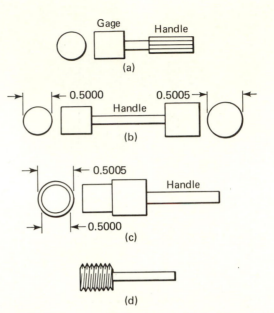

Fig. 7-17. Plug gages. (a) Single end; (b) double end; (c) progressive, or step; (d) thread plug gage.

signed to check rods. Ring gages are used in the same manner as plug gages. They must also be set to a standard. Ring gages, unlike plug gages, can be adjusted over a small range to various sizes (Fig. 7-18). However, some gage manufacturers incorporate two or more adjusting screws in ring gages to offset the possibility that the gage will become out of round. Thus the adjusting screws usually are used only as a device to offset wear of the gage surface.

SNAP GAGE. Snap gages are a special set of linear measurement gages that come either as an adjustable gage or as a solid gage (Fig. 7-19). Snap gages can be set up as go–no-go gages or as a caliper type of gage. An example of a snap gage is that of a type-high gage used in a print shop to measure the height of type. Because the type height is always one measurement, a solid snap gage is ideal. The printer is not required to know the height of the type, only that it meets the standard of passing through the snap gage with little resistance.

The major types of snap gages are: the adjustable, the combination, and the double-

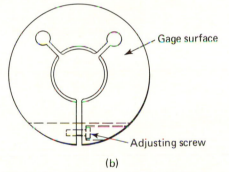

(a)

(b)

Fig. 7-18. (a) Threaded ring gage (*DoAll Company*); (b) ring gage adjustment.

end snap gage (Fig. 7-19). Snap gages are like all other gages in that they are not capable of direct measurement but can only measure those things that they have been standardized to measure.

SPECIAL GAGES. Special gages include a large number of gages that have standard limits. One example is the "feeler" gage that measures the opening between metals (such as in setting the valve lash on a solid lifter automobile engine). Other special types of gages are the screw pitch gage, the drill and wire gage, and the radius gage (Fig. 7-20). Screw pitch gages are designed to determine the pitch or the number of teeth per inch of

screws. Drill and wire gages determine the diameter of the drill or the diameter of the wire. Radius gages are of two types. They measure either the inside or the outside radius and are designed to determine the fairly exact radius of a part. Most special gages are hand held and are considered to be only accurate enough for general shop use, not for major inspection.

Transfer Gages

Transfer gages are those gages that are set to the length desired and then have to be placed in a measuring device (such as a micrometer caliper) in order to determine that length. Major types of transfer gages include small-hole gages, which come in sets (Fig. 7-21), telescoping gages, and calipers (Fig. 7-22).

SMALL-HOLE GAGES. Small-hole gages come in sets, usually of four gages, that are

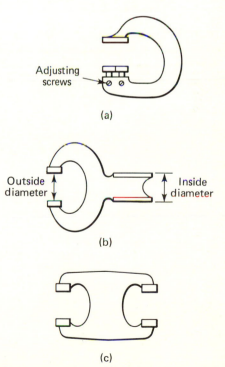

(a)

(b)

(c)

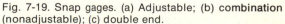

Fig. 7-19. Snap gages. (a) Adjustable; (b) **combination** (nonadjustable); (c) double end.

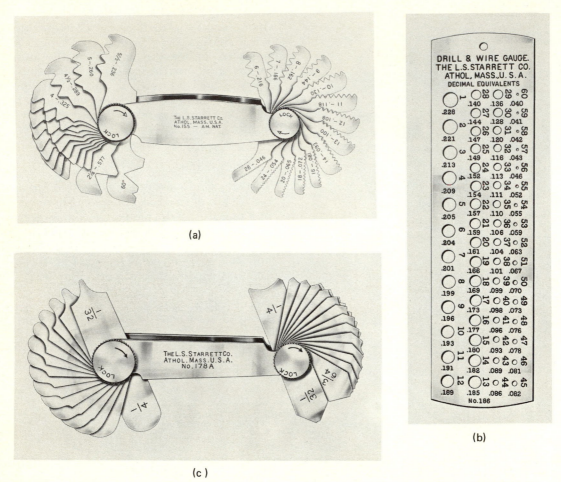

Fig. 7-20. Gages. (a) Screw pitch; (b) drill and wire; (c) radius. (*L. S. Starrett Company.*)

capable of measuring from ⅛ to ½ in. Small-hole gages work on the principle of a split nut with a wedge between the two split halves. A screw is tightened pulling the wedge up between the split halves and expanding them. Extreme care must be taken when using small-hole gages to ensure an accurate measurement to be transferred. The measurement depends entirely on the "feel" of the measurement by the operator using the small-hole gages.

TELESCOPING GAGES. Telescoping gages come in a set of six basic gages which are ca-

pable of measuring from ½ to 6 in. An advantage of the telescoping gage over the small-hole gage is that it does not rely on "feel" or operator touch for proper use. The telescoping gage has a spring behind the telescoping spindles that pushes the spindles out to contact the workpiece surfaces. When releasing the spindle returning screw, care must be used not to snap the spindles out against the areas being measured. Rather, the gage should be set approximately prior to its insertion into the pieces being tested. Telescoping gages are made either with only one movable spindle or with both spindles activated by the spring (Fig. 7-23).

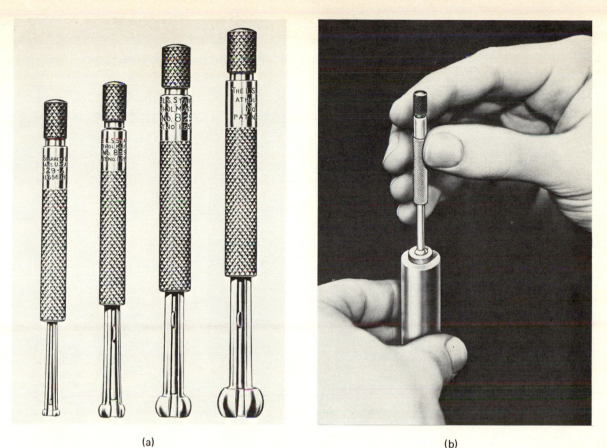

(a)

(b)

Fig. 7-21. Small-hole gages. (a) Set; (b) application. (*L. S. Starrett Company.*)

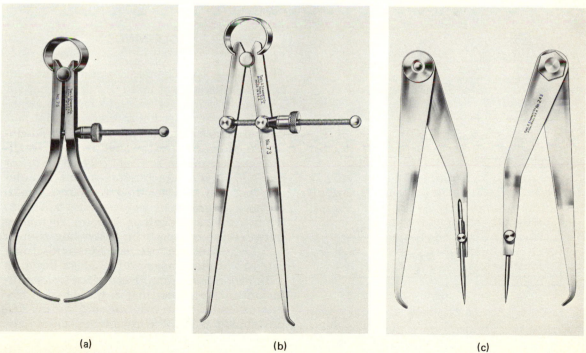

(a)

(b)

(c)

Fig. 7-22. Calipers. (a) Outside; (b) inside; (c) hermaphrodite. (*L. S. Starrett Company.*)

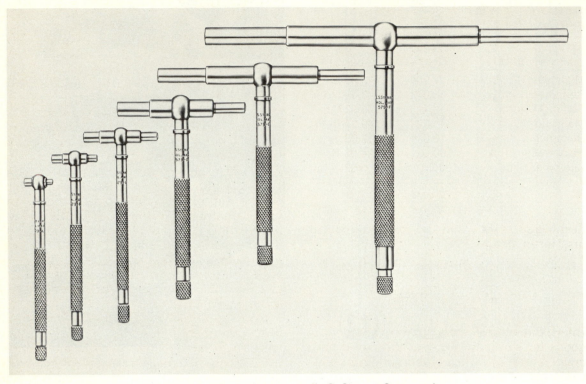

Fig. 7-23. Telescoping gages. (*L. S. Starrett Company.*)

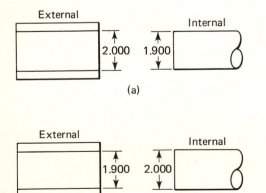

Fig. 7-24. Tolerance. (a) Clearance fit; (b) interference fit.

TOLERANCE

There are two general classifications of fits: the clearance fit and the interference fit. The *clearance fit* is characterized by an internal member that fits into an external part with air space between the two that provides the clearance. The allowance is always positive in a clearance fit (Fig. 7-24). The *interference fit* is characterized by an internal member that is larger than the external part, creating interference between the two parts when mated together. The allowance between the two parts is always negative.

The American National Standards Institute (ANSI) has classified five major fit types, with each major group having several subdivisions. The three major fits of the five groups include the running and sliding fits, designated as RC; the clearance location fits,

TABLE 7-1. U.S. AND METRIC UNITS COMPARED

METRIC UNIT	METRIC LENGTH	U.S. LENGTH
Millimeter (mm)	0.001	0.03937 in.
Centimeter (cm)	0.01	0.3937 in.
Decimeter (dm)	0.1	3.937 in.
Meter (m)	1.0	39.37 in.
Dekameter (dkm)	10.0	10.93 yd
Hectometer (hm)	100.0	328.08 ft
Kilometer (km)	1000.0	0.6214 mi

designated as LC; and the force and shrink fits, designated as FN.

METRIC SYSTEM

International trade and the production of goods for shipment all over the world have created a need for a unified system of measurement. This need has led to an international agreement to adopt the metric system as the standard measurement system. Also, in the United States, the requirements for components in the space program demanded the use of the metric system. The metric system is based on a unit length that is multiplied by 10. For example, 10 millimeters (mm) equal 1 centimeter (cm), 10 centimeters equal 1 decimeter (dm), and 10 decimeters equal 1 meter (m). The meter is approximately as long as a yard, i.e., 1 meter is 39.37 in.; the kilometer (km) is approximately ⅝ mi (Table 7-1).

People in metalworking frequently must transfer from the American system to the metric system. A conversion table or chart is helpful in making this transfer easier (Table 7-2). For example, if inches are to be converted to millimeters, the number of inches can be multiplied by 25 to yield the appropriate number of millimeters. Or, if a blueprint calls for a rod to be a certain number of millimeters long and measurement tools are not available, all that needs to be done is to multiply the number of millimeters by 0.04 to derive the necessary length of the workpiece in inches.

The International System of Units (SI units), the metric system, is quickly gaining world-wide acceptance. For the first time a precise international measurement has been defined as 1,650,763.73 wavelengths in the vacuum of the orange red line in the spectrum of crypton 86, setting a world standard for the length of the meter bar. The United States is now in the process of converting from the American system to the metric system.

TABLE 7-2. APPROXIMATE CONVERSIONS FOR LENGTH AND AREA

SYMBOL	UNIT	MULTIPLIER	SYMBOL	UNIT	MULTIPLIER
	LENGTH, AMERICAN SYSTEM			LENGTH, METRIC SYSTEM	
in.	Inch	25	mm	Millimeter	0.04
in.	Inch	2.5	cm	Centimeter	0.4
ft	Foot	30	m	Meter	3.3
yd	Yard	1.1	m	Meter	0.9
mi	Mile	1.6	km	Kilometer	0.6
	AREA, AMERICAN SYSTEM			AREA, AMERICAN SYSTEM	
in.^{2}	Square inch	6.5	cm^2	Square centimeter	0.16
ft^2	Square foot	0.09	m^2	Square meter	10.8
yd^2	Square yard	0.8	m^2	Square meter	1.2
mi^2	Square mile	2.6	km^2	Square kilometer	0.4
A	Acre	0.4	ha	Hectare	2.5

QUESTIONS

1. What are the differences between gages and instruments?
2. How are gage blocks graded?
3. How many blocks are in a standard gage block set?
4. Explain the wringing process.
5. What is a fringe line?
6. Why are granite surface plates superior to iron surface plates?
7. Why does the micrometer have 40 threads per inch on the spindle?
8. Explain how the vernier caliper is operated.
9. What are the major ways that an angle can be measured?
10. What are the advantages of pneumatic comparators?
11. Explain how the sine bar measures angles.
12. What are the major types of transfer gages? How are they used?
13. What is a go–no-go snap gage?
14. What is the greatest advantage of the SI system of measurement?

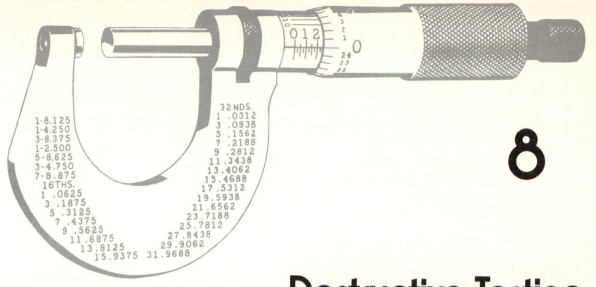

Destructive Testing

Destructive testing uses various types of mechanical tests to derive information concerning the mechanical properties of materials. The mechanical tests either totally destroy the sample or impair its surface. The most common destructive mechanical tests are the tensile test, compression test, torsion test, fatigue test, bending test, and hardness test.

TENSILE TESTING

A tensile-testing machine consists of a mechanism for exerting a pull on a test piece coupled to a device which measures the load or stress. The stressing mechanism may be hydraulic (a cylinder with a piston carrying one of the test pieces); or it may consist of a screw driven in an axial direction by the rotation of a nut; or it may be a simple fulcrum and beam device.

More popular nowadays is the self-indicating machine in which the load is applied to the test piece by a hydraulic force. This force is balanced by a secondary hydraulic force that has a pendulum attached to it. This pendulum controls an indicator dial from which instantaneous values of load can be read (Fig. 8-1).

The universal testing machine is an example of a self-indicating machine that can be used for measuring tensile strength as well as percentage of elongation, elastic limit, yield point, and reduction of area. With this machine, as in all tensile testing machines, the test specimen size is important. The tensile strength of many metals is high; for example, mild steel has a tensile strength of 62,000 psi, but a machine to test this would have to be large. However, mechanical properties remain true for the whole piece even if only a portion of the cross-sectional area is tested and the results are multiplied by a size ratio. For example, a 505 bar (no. 1 in Table 8-1) has a cross-sectional area of 0.2 in.^{2}; therefore the testing may be done on this bar and then the results multiplied by 5 to determine the tensile strength for 1 in.^{2} of metal. The tensile strength specimens that are used for the testing of a weld, for example, come in two full sample sections and two reduced sample sections. The reduced-section tensile test reduces the sample to approximately 0.2 in.^{2} The full-section tests are based on 1 in.^{2} of metal (Fig. 8-2).

With the universal testing machine, before the test piece is inserted into the jaws that clamp it into the machine, the gage length is marked along the parallel length. The gage length for a standard 505 tensile

Fig. 8-1. Universal tester. (*Ametek/Testing Equipment.*)

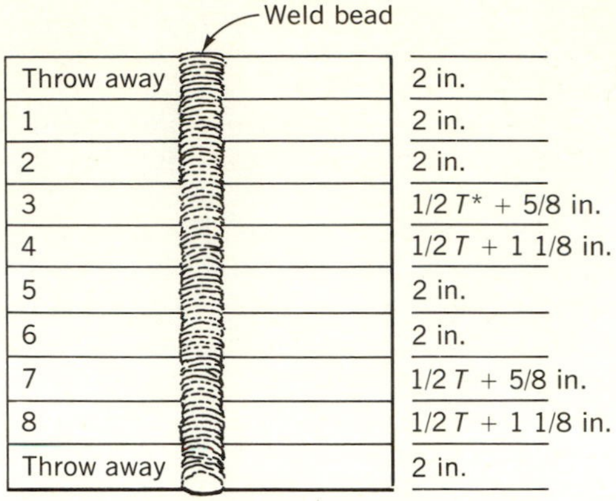

Throw away		2 in.
1		2 in.
2		2 in.
3		1/2 T^* + 5/8 in.
4		1/2 T + 1 1/8 in.
5		2 in.
6		2 in.
7		1/2 T + 5/8 in.
8		1/2 T + 1 1/8 in.
Throw away		2 in.

— Weld bead

1 and 5	Full-section tensile test
2 and 6	Reduced-section tensile test
3 and 7	Nick-break test
4 and 8	Free bend test

$^*T$ = plate thickness, in.

Fig. 8-2. Standard weld specimen (coupon).

test bar is 2 in. The gage length is marked at each end of the bar and the test piece is mounted in the machine. The load is applied and steadily increased until yield occurs. One method of observing is to hold one point of a pair of dividers at one of the gage length marks and lightly scribe across the other end. When a sudden elongation occurs, it will be both seen and felt. At the same time, the

TABLE 8-1. TENSILE TEST SPECIMEN DIMENSIONS

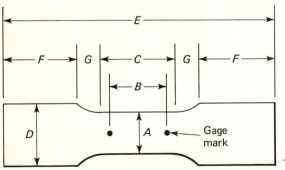

SPECIMEN NUMBER	DIMENSIONS, in.						
	A	B	C	D	E	F	G
1	0.500:0.01	2	2½	¾ D	4¼	¾	⅜
2	0.437:0.01	1.75	2	⅝ D	4	¾	⅜
3	0.357:0.007	1.4	1¾	½ D	3½	⅝	⅜
4	0.252:0.005	1.0	1¼	⅜ D	2½	½	¼
5	0.126:0.003	0.5	¾	¼ D	1¾	⅜	⅛

operator of the universal testing machine can observe when the load indicator stops and falls back. The load at this point should be recorded before forward motion is arrested.

When yielding is complete, the load starts to rise. The beginning of this yielding is the elastic limit. The metal is now in the plastic state and the deformation of the test piece is permanent. The rate of straining will not need to be increased and by the time the maximum load is reached, the gage length will have undergone a uniform extension if the material being tested has any ductility. If the material is brittle, the piece will not elongate but will break or fracture. The maximum load should be noted and the breaking load should also be noted. The maximum load is the ultimate strength of the metal. The test piece is then brought back together while still clamped into the machine, and the gage length is remeasured. The gage length of the test piece is compared to the original gage length of the test piece. For example, if the test piece was 2 in. prior to testing and 2.185 after testing, the elongation would be 9 percent.

Finally, the test pieces are removed from the universal testing machine and each end of the fractured piece is measured with a micrometer. An average of these two measurements is computed and this measurement is compared to the original diameter of the test bar. For instance, if the original diameter of the test bar was 0.505 in. and the diameter of the bar after fracture was 0.405 in., the reduction in area would be 0.100 or about 19.8 percent (Fig. 8-3).

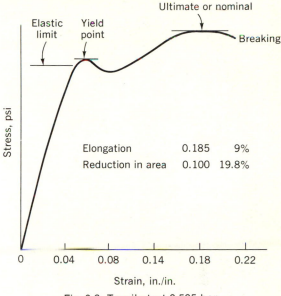

Fig. 8-3. Tensile test 0.505 bar.

lel, the piece may slip from between the platens and cause damage.

Though the compression test ranks low on the list of routine acceptance tests for metals, it can be used to obtain useful data in such fields as plastics and ceramics. The compression test is not used for most metals because it is not as reliable an indicator of ductility as are the tensile test and the reduction of area test. A test piece in tension being tested for tensile strength may break after a 20 percent reduction in area. An identical test piece might be compressed to 80 percent reduction without failure, making compression tests ineffective indicators of a metal's ductility.

COMPRESSION TESTING

A great many of the machines used for tensile testing are universal testing machines. These machines also can be used for compression testing with the special fittings or shackles that are part of the original equipment of the machine. The compression load is applied axially if the parts to be compression tested have parallel ends. If the ends are not paral-

TORSION TESTING

A torsion testing machine applies a twisting action to one end of a test piece while the other end of the test piece is held stationary. A turning or twisting movement at the fixed end of the test piece is registered by a weighing system similar to that on the tensile testing machine (Fig. 8-4).

Fig. 8-4. Torsion testing machine. (*Tinius Olsen Testing Machine Company.*)

Small, hand-operated machines are used for tests on small-diameter wires or small test pieces. When materials in larger sizes are tested, a motor-driven test machine is used. Often the torsion testing of wires is used as an acceptance test for wire products, but usually such an acceptance test uses simple testing devices and specialized machines. A simple wire-testing machine has grips on each end with one of the grips in a fixed position and the other able to be rotated. The wire to be tested is placed in the grips and the end that can be rotated is turned. The number of rotations until fracture of the wire is noted and compared to the specified number of rotations. The specifications for wire testing state that a given length of wire will withstand a certain degree of twisting without fracturing.

Most torsion testing machines are designed so that the test piece can contract in size as it is being twisted. If the test piece is not allowed to contract, another factor will be introduced into the testing that is difficult to measure.

Torsion testing commonly measures five properties: the modulus of rigidity, the limit of proportionality, the maximum torque, the modulus of rupture, and the total twist to fracture. The *modulus of rigidity* is the ratio of the shear stress to the shear strain while the material is in the elastic state. The *limit of proportionality* is determined by plotting a torque twist curve, which is similar to the stress-strain curve in tensile testing, and noting where this curve departs from a straight line. The *maximum torque* is the greatest force used to twist the object before the proportional limit is reached. It occurs well before the fracture point. The *modulus of rupture* is the point at which nominal surface stress occurs. It is calculated from the normal elastic formula as though all the material being tested remained elastic throughout the test. The *total twist to fracture* is a simple test in which the total number of twists or parts of a twist are recorded on a scale. Usually no specific gage length on the test piece is used.

FATIGUE TESTING

Fatigue testing is a study of the phenomena of decreased resistance of a material to repeated stress. When a material is subjected to complete reversed stresses of sufficient magnitude, a crack will eventually start and grow until a sudden failure of the remaining cross section of the test piece occurs.

Physically, a minute crack originates at the point of highest stress and fatigue. This point may be a surface scratch, some imperfection in the metal, or a design weakness of the test piece. The crack enlarges during the continued, repetitive loading and unloading until there is insufficient material left to support the load. This crack decreases the original cross-sectional area of the test piece and the remaining cross-sectional area will generally be too small to carry the load so the piece fails in an ordinary manner. It is extremely difficult to detect progressive changes in test pieces prior to failure. Many times a test piece will give little warning before complete failure. Also fatigue damage is cumulative—that is, periods of rest do not lead to recovery from the effects of the stress even though the piece goes through the stress-rest-stress cycle.

BENDING TEST

Bend testing is conducted to test the bond between materials, such as in welding or in the use of exotic glues like epoxy. It can be accomplished with two types of tests: the free bend test and the guided bend test. Bend tests of ductile metals are usually conducted with no attention paid to the initial stages of bending or the amount of force employed in bending. Bending is continued far beyond the limit of elastic properties of metal and into the plastic zone.

The failure of the weld bead in the free bend test means that the bead does not have the strength that is equal to the base metal. For example, in mild steel the tensile strength of the base metal is approximately 60,000 psi. If the weld were to rupture during the free bend test, the logical conclusion would be that the weld bead is not strong enough for that particular base metal. A few cracks and checks may become apparent during and after the free bend test has been made. Corner cracks are thought to be negligible as long as they do not extend more than $1/16$ in. into the base metal. Any surface defect, any crack or depression, or a slag inclusion, may not be over $1/16$ in. or the weld bead is considered a failure.

The elongation of a piece may also be measured by placing gage lines on each side of the test specimen. This distance is measured to the nearest hundredth of an inch, 0.01 in. After the bend test, the gage lines are remeasured and a percentage of elongation can be equated. If for some reason, the elongation of the test specimen cannot be measured, the elongation can be calculated by the formula

$$elongation = \frac{100T}{2R}$$

where T = thickness of the specimen
R = radius of the piece

The test specimens for the free bend test range between 6 and 21 in. long. The thickness ranges from $1/4$ to $2\frac{1}{2}$ in. The width of test specimens depends on the thickness of the piece; generally it is equal to $1\frac{1}{2}$ times the thickness of the specimens. The fixture for applying force to the test specimens is de-

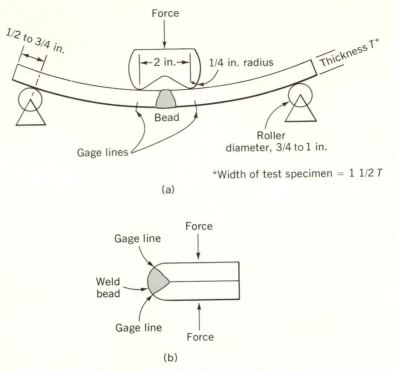

Fig. 8-5. Free bend test. (a) Initial bend; (b) close bend.

termined also by the thickness of the piece. If the piece is small, between ¼ and ½ in., the gage lines should be approximately 1¼ in.; however, for all other tests, the gage length is usually 2 in. (Fig. 8-5).

The guided bend test is designed to show surface imperfections near and in the bonding area. The guided bend tester is designed around a certain thickness of plate. For example, in Fig. 8-6a, the numbers that are shown are multiplied by the thickness of the plate. The width of the mandrel is 4 times the thickness of the plate and the length of the mandrel is 18 times the thickness of the plate. The radius of its corners is twice the thickness of the plate plus ⅛ in. If the radius on the mandrel were designed for ½-in. plate, the radius would be 1⅛ in.

If the guided bend test is conducted on the standard weld specimen shown in Fig. 8-2, no. 4 and no. 8, no. 4 specimen is tested with the face of the bead out or the face of the bead toward the mandrel, and specimen no. 8 is tested with the root of the bead toward the

mandrel. After the piece is tested, the outside of the bend is checked for surface discontinuances. If an occlusion or tear is greater than ¹/₁₆ in., the specimen has failed the test. The test will also show if there is any lack of penetration in a weld bead in the area where it fuses to the work.

NICK-BREAK TEST

The nick-break test is designed to show if interior inclusions exist in any type of bonded joint. For example, in a weld bead, the test would reveal any gas pockets or slag pockets and would show the degree of porosity in the weld bead. The nick-break test is a simple test in which the force may be applied by a press or the sharp blow of a hammer. The intensity or the swiftness of the force to break the piece is not important. A visual inspection of the piece is the test. If the inclusions or discontinuances in the bonded

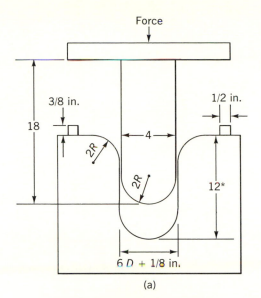

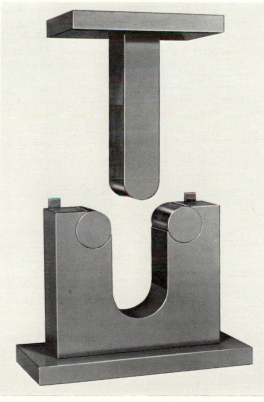

Fig. 8-6. Guided bend tester. (a) Whole numbers are multiplying factors for the plate thickness. *"12" indicates 12 times the specimen thickness. (b) Commercial test device. (*Ametek/Testing Equipment.*)

joint are over ⅛ in. long, the piece will have failed the test.

The standard nick-break test specimens for testing a welded joint are indicated in Fig. 8-2, nos. 3 and 7. The width of the specimen is usually 1½ times the thickness, plus ½ in. The slots for the nick-break test are put in with a saw to a depth of ¼ in. on each side. One of the nick-break test specimen pieces is broken from one side and the other nick-break specimen is broken from the other side (Fig. 8-7).

An adaptation of the standard nick-break test is the fillet nick-break test. The standard length for a welded specimen in the fillet nick-break test is from 4 to 6 in. The test is made by simply applying force in the back of the fillet to crush the angle flat. One requirement of the fillet nick-break test is that there be no tack welds on the other side of the fillet weld. One small tack weld will have enough holding power to invalidate the test.

IMPACT TESTING

Impact testing determines the relative toughness of a material. *Toughness* is defined as the resistance of a metal to fracture after plastic deformation has begun. Plastic deformation is begun and finished by a weighted pendulum which swings down to strike the

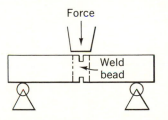

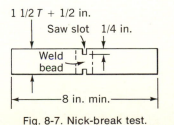

Fig. 8-7. Nick-break test.

test piece as the pendulum swings through its arc. The energy that is required to fracture the test piece is recorded in foot-pound force (ft-lb) on the scale. The tougher the material, the higher the energy absorbed by the test piece. Unalloyed metals are rated in the order of their toughness as follows: copper, nickel, iron, magnesium, zinc, aluminum, lead, tin, cobalt, and bismuth. Bismuth is rated 10, indicating that it can absorb a small amount of energy before plastic deformation and fracture, while copper is highly ductile and can withstand a great deal of plastic deformation.

Two major tests for determining impact toughness are the Izod test and the Charpy test. Both of these methods use the same type of machine and both yield a quantitative value in foot-pound force. The major difference between these methods is in the length of the test specimen and where the pendulum strikes on the test specimen. The Izod test specimen is generally 2.952 in. long with a small V notch in the test bar (Fig. 8-8). The Charpy method of impact toughness testing uses two different test specimens, the V

bar and the keyhole bar (Fig. 8-9). Both the test specimens for the Charpy and the Izod methods are square bars 3.94 in., or 10 mm, on a side.

HARDNESS TESTING

Hardness is sometimes thought to be measured by nondestructive testing, but since testing does deform the surface of the metal slightly, it must be considered destructive testing. Hardness is the ability of a metal to resist penetration, to resist abrasive wear, or to resist the absorption of energy under impact loads. These definitions can be thought of as penetration, wear hardness, and rebound hardness.

The Rockwell hardness tester and the Brinell hardness tester are two means to determine the resistance of a metal to penetration. The scleroscope is an instrument to test the rebound hardness of a metal. The scale for any one of the hardness testing methods

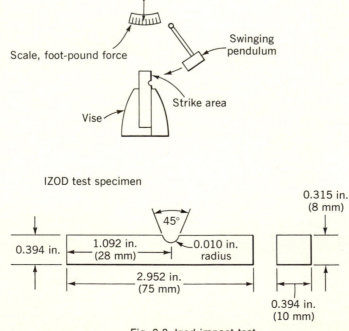

Fig. 8-8. Izod impact test.

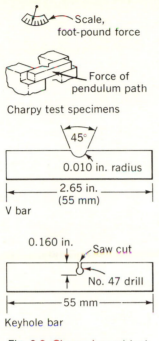

Fig. 8-9. Charpy impact test.

Rockwell Hardness Test

The Rockwell hardness tester is a machine that measures hardness by determining the depth of penetration of a penetrator into the specimen under certain fixed conditions of testing. The penetrator may be either a steel ball (the B scale) or a diamond penetrator (the C scale). The hardness number is related to the depth of indentation. The higher the number on the scale, the harder the material.

The letters B and C were adopted to differentiate between the two Rockwell methods. The letter B applies to tests with a ball penetrator of $1/16$-in. diameter and 100-kilogram (kg) major load. (A kilogram is approximately 2.2 lb.) A Rockwell C test is designed for testing hard materials with a diamond penetrator having a slightly rounded point and a major load of 150 kg. There are other special tests that can be made with the Rockwell test machine, including the A test, the D test, and the E test, depending on the type and the thickness of the material being tested.

The machine is operated by placing the specimen on the platen of the machine. A minor load of 10 kilograms (kg) is first applied causing an initial penetration. This is the beginning point of the hardness test. The minor load is applied to force the penetrator through any scale or other surface hindrance that may be present on the material. After the minor load has been applied, the read-out

can be converted to any other scale: a Rockwell B value of 100 is equal to a Rockwell C value of 24, which is equal to a Brinell value of 245 and a scleroscope value of 34. There are standard tables available from the manufacturers of hardness testing equipment that compute these comparisons (Table 8-2).

TABLE 8-2. HARDNESS COMPARISON

ROCKWELL B	VICKERS PYRAMID	ROCKWELL C	BRINELL	SCLEROSCOPE
	944	69	755	98
	737	60	631	84
	503	50	497	68
	394	40	380	53
	294	30	288	41
100	248	24	245	34
98	229	20	224	32
89	179	10	179	25
78	143	0	143	21
.	.	—	.	.
.	.		.	.
.	.		.	.

dial is reset to zero, and then the major load is applied. The major load is 60 or 100 kg when the steel ball (B scale) is used as a penetrator, and 150 kg when the diamond penetrator (C scale) is used. The 1/16-in.-diameter ball is used for material that is medium hard and the 1/8-in. penetrator may be used for soft metals such as lead, bismuth, antimony, and tin. The diamond penetrator is used for the hard metals such as iron. The 1/16-in.-diameter ball is used for the copper-based metals and other medium-hard metals. After the major load is applied and then removed, the reading is taken while the minor load is still being applied (Fig. 8-10).

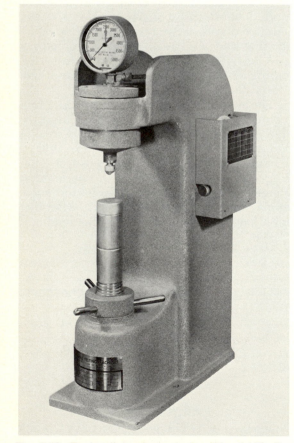

Fig. 8-10. Rockwell hardness tester. (*Ametek/Testing Equipment.*)

Brinell Test

The Brinell hardness test uses a hardened steel ball of 10-mm diameter (0.3937-in. diameter) which is forced, under a pressure of 3,000 kg for hard metals and 500 kg for soft metals, into a flat surface on the test specimen. The ball is allowed to remain there for a minimum of 10 s for iron and ferrous materials or for at least 30 s for nonferrous metals. Then the hardened steel ball is removed, leaving a slight spherical impression. The diameter of this impression is then measured with a special microscope. The hardness of the specimen is defined as the quotient of the pressure divided by the area of the surface of the impression, which is assumed to be spherical. From this measurement, the Brinell hardness number is calculated (Fig. 8-11). The following formula is used to determine the hardness number:

$$B = \frac{P}{\left(\frac{\pi D}{2}\right)(D - \sqrt{D^2 - d^2})}$$

where B = Brinell hardness number
   P = 3,000- or 500-kg load
   D = diameter of the ball
   d = diameter of the impression
   π = 3.141592653580793

Scleroscope

The scleroscope is an instrument that determines the rebound hardness of metals. It consists of a vertical glass tube in which a hammer slides freely (Fig. 8-12). This hammer is pointed at the lower end and is allowed to fall about 10 in. onto the sample being tested. The distance the hammer rebounds back up the vertical glass tube, or slide, is a measure of the rebound hardness of the specimen.

The scale on the tube is divided into 140 equal parts. The hardness is expressed as the number on the scale to which the hammer rebounds. Measured in this way, the hardness of different substances is as follows: glass, 130; porcelain, 120; the hardest steel, 110;

Fig. 8-11. Brinell hardness tester. (*Tinius Olsen Testing Machine Company.*)

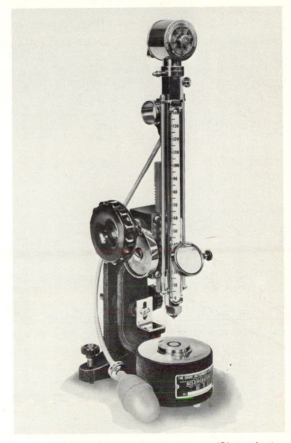

Fig. 8-12. Scleroscope hardness tester. (*Shore Instrument and Manufacturing Company.*)

mild steel, 25 to 30; grey iron, 39; babbitt, 4 to 10; brass, 12; zinc, 8; copper, 6; and lead, 2.

The relationship between the scleroscope and the ultimate strength is given by the following equation: ultimate strength is equal to 4.1 times the scleroscope number minus 15. A simple estimate of ultimate strength can also be derived from a Brinell hardness number: Divide the Brinell hard- ness number by 2, then multiply by 1,000. The result is tensile strength in pounds per square inch. For example, if a Brinell number of 140 were observed on the Brinell hardness tester, the ultimate strength could be calculated by dividing 140 by 2, which equals 70, and multiplying by 1,000, which yields a 70,000-psi tensile strength for the material.

QUESTIONS

1. What does a destructive tensile test reveal about a metal?
2. What are the different types of tensile testing machines?
3. Why are reduced section test specimens used?

4. What are four common tests used for testing weld coupons?
5. What information results from the free bend tests? From the guided bend tests?
6. What is the difference between the Izod and the Charpy impact tests?
7. What is hardness?
8. Why are there different methods to determine the hardness of a metal?
9. What are the principles of the Rockwell hardness tester, the Brinell hardness tester, and the scleroscope hardness tester?
10. What is destructive testing of materials?

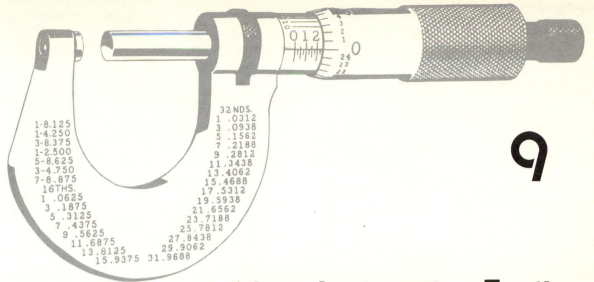

Nondestructive Testing

In today's advanced technology, many things are built that need to be 100 percent reliable. This demand for high reliability has created the field of nondestructive testing. Nondestructive testing defines and locates flaws within a material or a product without destroying or defacing the product. There are many means of testing materials nondestructively. Some of the major tests used to locate flaws, defects, cracks, and discontinuances include ultrasonic testing, radiographic testing, liquid penetrant testing, and magnetic particle testing. Of course, there is always the original type of nondestructive testing available to the metalworker—visual inspection.

ULTRASONIC TESTING

The elastic property of metal can be described as the displacement of metal particles, or molecules, in that metal after it has been struck by another object. If the surface of a metal is displaced, the displacement occurs inward, moving the molecules of the metal inward. As long as the molecules are still elastic, they return to their original position after the force of the blow has been dissipated.

A further application of this concept is that energy is transmitted through a solid portion of material by a series of small displacements or molecular movements. Each molecule displaces the next one in line with it, until a total displacement has occurred. The first displacement is caused by the initial impact of a force, and the second major displacement is caused by the return of the molecules to their original position. A total displacement of these molecules can be expressed as a cycle made up of the two opposing movements. The length of time it takes the cycle to progress through one complete movement is the *frequency of the cycle*. For example, if six cycles are occurring in 1 s, the frequency would be 6 cycles per second (Hz).

Any void within a metal disrupts this cyclic movement of molecules, and this disruption could be portrayed on some type of readout device. Ultrasonics, in the testing of materials, uses waves that reach a frequency range of 200,000 to 25,000,000 Hz.

Several types of waves that pass through solid matter can be used. Longitudinal, or compression, waves are those in which the particle vibrations continue in the same direction as the sound waves. Particle vibrations or shear waves, or transverse waves, are at right angles to the wave motion. With some degree of success, shear waves can be produced along a free surface so that they ripple across the surface, checking for deflection just below the surface. These sound waves have properties similar to those exhibited by light waves; they can be reflected, focused, or refracted. The major characteristic of sound waves is that they can pass through a solid object with little absorption.

Generation of wavelengths through a solid is usually accomplished with a device called a *transducer*, which changes electric energy into sound energy, or sound waves, by utilizing piezoelectric principles. For example, a paddle pushed through the water by some mechanical force produces a wave in the water. A similar type of change can be produced by transducers, creating waves of sound. Transducers operate at frequencies well above 20,000 Hz. There are two types: the sending transducer and the receiving transducer. The sending transducer converts mechanical energy to sound energy; the receiving transducer converts the sound energy to electric energy. These are the input and the output of the energy source for the ultrasonic testing device. Many times the same transducer used to generate the mechanical energy also acts as a receiver, recovering the mechanical energy or the sound waves.

When sound waves vibrate through the medium to be tested, the process of attenuation occurs. *Attenuation* is a loss in the wave form and results from the density of the material. It can be thought of as internal friction in the object being tested. A compensation for the difference in the measurements from the input pulse and the output pulse is provided for in most transducers.

In ultrasonic testing, transducers are placed on the surface of the article that is going to be tested. A *couplant* (a thin layer of fluid) is used to help make contact between the transducer and the surface of the material. The couplant is an oily, glycerine-based substance which performs two major functions; it removes the air between the transducer and the test specimen and provides a medium for the transfer of the sound vibrations.

Testing Devices

Three types of ultrasonic test devices are commercially available: the pulse-echo system, the through-transmission system, and the resonance system.

THE PULSE-ECHO SYSTEM. The *pulse-echo system* is the most widely used ultrasonic test (Fig. 9-1). It generates an ultrasonic wave that passes through the material from the transducer. The wave is returned through the same transducer. The signal is then displayed on the cathode-ray tube (CRT). The pulse-echo system has evenly timed pulses of ultrasonic sound waves which are transmitted into the material being tested. The pulses reflect from the discontinuances in their path or from any boundary of the material being tested. As the waves pass through the top surface of the material being tested, there will be a pip on the CRT indicating the beginning of the test specimen, labeled *A* in Fig. 9-1. If the test specimen has a flaw within it, the wave will bounce off, indicating the distance of this flaw from the surface of the test material, as shown by the letter *B* in Fig. 9-1. The specimen will also be tested through its entire thickness as indicated by the letter *C*

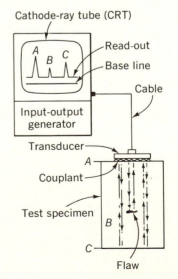

Fig. 9-1. Pulse-echo ultrasonic system.

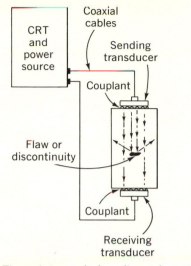

Fig. 9-2. Through-transmission ultrasonic system.

in Fig. 9-1. The pulse-echo ultrasonic system can also be thought of as a measurement device, or a one-sided micrometer, with which the thickness of materials can be measured. The pulse-echo system relies entirely on reflected energy reaching the receiver-sender transducer for any information as to the thickness of the test specimen.

THROUGH-TRANSMISSION SYSTEM. The *through-transmission system* requires the use of two transducers, one for transmitting or sending the sound waves, and the other for receiving the sound waves. As in the pulse-echo system, short pulses of ultrasonic sound are transmitted into and through the material. In a few applications, a continuous sound wave could be used but very seldom is used. Unlike the pulse-echo system, the echoes returning to the sending or transmitting transducer are ignored. However, the receiving transducer, which is aligned with the sending transducer, conveys information in the form of a sound wave, and then in the form of electric energy, to the CRT. The soundness or quality of the material being tested is measured in terms of the energy lost by the sound beam as it travels through the material. A limitation on the use of this

system is that it can only be applied to items whose sides are relative or parallel to each other (Fig. 9-2).

ULTRASONIC RESONANCE SYSTEM. The *resonance system* makes use of resonance phenomena to measure the thickness of material and to determine the quality of bonded materials. It is also used, but to a lesser degree, to detect gross discontinuities. The resonance system transmits ultrasonic sound waves into the material, making this system similar to the pulse-echo system, except that the waves are always continuous longitudinal waves (Fig. 9-3). Wave frequency is varied until standing waves are set up in the system, causing the item to resonate or to vibrate at a greater amplitude. A difference in vibration resonance is then sensed by the transducer acting as the generator indicator instrument, and this information is displayed on the CRT screen. A change in the resonant frequency that cannot be accounted for as a change in the material thickness is usually a discontinuance or a flaw in the test material.

Testing Methods

Two testing methods are used in all ultrasonic testing: a contact testing method and an immersion testing method. The *contact method* involves placing the transducer directly on the test material. The transducer is coupled to the test material through a thin layer of fluid known as a couplant. Contact

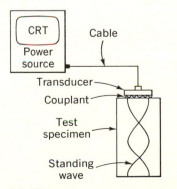

Fig. 9-3. Ultrasonic resonance system.

testing is most frequently used in field and shop locations because the equipment usually can be moved easily, and the only requirement is that there be a 110-V, ac power supply. In *immersion testing* both the test material and the transducer are immersed in a liquid couplant, sending the ultrasonic waves through the liquid into the test specimen. The transducer in this case does not touch the object but is simply immersed in the couplant fluid, usually water. The one major requirement for immersion testing is that the back surface of the test specimen be supported so that total contact is avoided.

Visual Display Units

Three basic types of visual display units show the qualities or soundness of an object being tested: the A, B, and C scan (Fig. 9-4).

The *A scan* display is a presentation of time versus amplitude on the CRT. Time versus amplitude is the most efficient way of revealing the existence of discontinuities. From the location of the pips, the relative depth and size of a flaw in the material can be determined. The interpretation of the A scan is easy. The first pulse, indication, or pip appears at the left of the CRT screen and the back surface reflection is on the right-hand

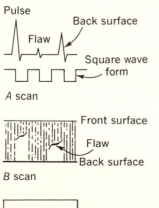

A scan

B scan

C scan

Fig. 9-4. CRT display types.

side of the screen. The discontinuities are shown somewhere between the initial pulse, indicating the front surface, and the back surface reflection pip. The height of the pip on the screen represents the amplitude of the wave reflection coming from the material being tested. Comparing the height of the flaw pip with known discontinuity pips from a material can establish the size of the discontinuity. The distance from the pulse to the flaw pip and the distance from the flaw pip to the back surface reflection are proportional to the elapsed time it takes the pulse to travel through the material. During the initial pulse, the reflection of the sound wave may be blocked by a discontinuity directly under the transducer, which can cause a dead zone at the front edge of the test specimen. Therefore, the flaw pip is determined from the reflected back surface of the specimen.

The *B scan unit* is used mostly in the medical applications of ultrasonic testing and is generally not used for nondestructive testing. But when used, it is capable of yielding a cross-sectional view of the material being tested. The B scan shows the reflection of the front and back surfaces of the test material and any flaws that lie between these two surfaces.

The *C scan* display unit gives a plain view similar to an x-ray picture. The external details on the test specimen are projected onto a plane that is the CRT screen. The reflection from the discontinuity is the only one that is presented. The presentation shows the shape of a discontinuity as viewed from the surface of the test material.

The only other display on the CRT screen is the square wave markers located below the horizontal sweep on all visual display scans. The square wave markers are used as units of time or as units of distance to relate the scan to some increment of time or distance.

RADIOGRAPHIC TESTING

In the radiographic process, a ray is emitted from a controllable source, and this ray penetrates a test specimen film (Fig. 9-5). The errors or flaws in the test specimen are superimposed on the film, providing a visual record of the analysis for future reference.

X-ray analysis can be used to reveal the internal structure of most materials and will reveal errors in fabrication and assembly. Also gas bubbles, fractures, and other weld imperfections and base-metal imperfections can be identified in the x-ray analysis. X-ray radiographic testing is most effective in discerning or identifying small defects. It is not too practical a method for use with complex shapes but is satisfactory for simple shapes. X-ray is also an expensive nondestructive testing method because of the high cost of equipment and the extreme safety precautions that must be taken to ensure operator safety.

Continuous x-rays are produced when a high-energy electron collides with the nucleus of an atom (Fig. 9-6). An x-ray source must be able to produce free electrons and direct them at a target with sufficient velocity so that they reach the nucleus of the constituent atoms of the target. Also, the source must provide for a uniform distribution of the resulting beam of x-rays into a desired pattern. A filament (similar to that in an incandescent light) can be placed near a highly charged cathode, causing the electrons freed by the heating of the filament to be repelled toward and attracted by an anode. The collision of the electrons with the anode produces x-rays of a continuous nature if the potential difference between the anode and the cathode is high. The shape of the anode target determines the

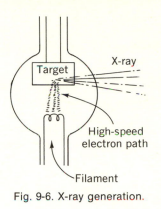

Fig. 9-6. X-ray generation.

pattern of the emitted x-rays. The intensity of the x-rays produced is directly related to the number of electrons freed at the filament. Freeing electrons increases the filament temperature, which is proportional to the current passing through it. Therefore, the logical criterion for rating x-ray machines is the number of milliamperes (mA) the filament draws. The intensity of the x-ray varies according to the inverse of the square of the distance from the source. Doubling the distance between the filament and the target quarters the intensity of the x-ray beam, a factor true with any source of electromagnetic radiation.

Gamma Rays

Gamma rays are also used as a power source in the exact manner that x-rays are used. Some elements used for the radioactive isotopes include cesium 137, cobalt 60, iridium 192, and samorium 153. Radium was the first radioactive isotope to be used for the production of gamma rays in a testing device. Gamma rays penetrate thick sections of metal far more easily than x-rays. Gamma rays are used when x-rays of high power must be used since the radioisotope producing gamma rays does not require an external power source and is small. Gamma-ray exposure time is generally longer than the exposure time for the corresponding x-ray radiographs. However, radiographs that use gamma rays as a wave ray power supply lack the definition or

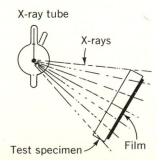

Fig. 9-5. X-ray radiographic process.

sharpness of character that x-rays produce. Generally, a person who is skilled in the use of x-ray equipment is also skilled in the use of gamma-ray radiography.

Gamma rays do not require any external power source. The gamma rays given off by the radioactive isotopes are independent of any electrical source. The x-ray, however, depends directly on electrical power sources. The power requirements for x-ray machines range from 50 to 24,000 kilovolts (kV). A 24,000-kV x-ray machine is capable of photographing approximately 20 in. of steel.

LIQUID PENETRANT TESTING

Liquid penetrant testing, one of the simplest nondestructive tests that can be applied to a metal, is a chemical means of detecting cracks, seams, porosity, folds, inclusions, and any other surface defect that may occur in a metal. It is not limited to ferrous metal but can be applied successfully to nonferrous, nonmagnetic metals. Liquid penetrant testing is an excellent means of testing for porosity and weld inclusions in stainless steel, magnesium, aluminum, brass, and many more nonferrous metals.

Liquid penetrant testing requires six basic steps. Each must be carefully performed in order to achieve the proper results. The six basic steps are: surface preparation, application of penetrant, removal of excess penetrant, developing, inspection, and cleaning.

Surface Preparation

The preparation of the metallic surface is one of the most important steps in the liquid penetrant testing procedure. If the metal to be tested inhibits the penetrant from entering the metal, the metal cannot be tested. Such inhibiting contaminants as dirt, grease, scale, acids, chromates, and other types of contaminants must be removed from the surface of the metal. Of the many possible cleaning methods, solvent cleaning is most popular.

The solvent that cleans the metal must be capable of removing the many contaminants from the components to be tested, and it must also be volatile so that it will evaporate out of the defects in the metal. If the solvent used to clean the metal is not one that vaporizes readily, the solvent will dilute or prevent the liquid penetrant from entering the surface flaws. Solvents currently used for cleaning metallic surfaces are acetone, isopropyl alcohol, methylene chloride, and perchlorethylene.

Penetrant Application

All liquids can be considered penetrants because their penetrating capability is a natural force resulting from capillary action. However, liquid penetrants used for tests have a greater number of demands on them that must coincide with their natural capillary force. These demands are higher fluidity, lower viscosity, and higher wetability. Besides these qualities, a liquid penetrant must also be able to carry a dye that will mark the metal. The dye floated within the liquid penetrant solution can be either a fluorescent or a visible dye. The dye is applied by dipping, immersing, pouring, spraying, or brushing. After the liquid penetrant with the dye has been applied to the surface, there is a waiting period, the length of which depends on the type of penetrant used and the type of metal being tested. After this waiting period, the excess penetrant must be removed.

Removal

The excess penetrant must still be liquid during the removal process. Extreme care should be taken not to remove the penetrant from the possible defective openings in the metal. If the penetrant has dried, then the cycle must be restarted by recleaning the metal and reapplying the penetrant. The three types of penetrants are categorized by the solutions used to remove them: water washable, solvent removable, and postemulsification.

Developing

After the excess penetrant has been removed, the developer is applied in order to make the discontinuities readily visible. The two major types of developers are the wet and the dry. Wet developers can be either solvent-based or water-based; generally both are applied with a pressurized spray. The dry developer differs only in the fact that it is not carried in a liquid and is applied in a powder form. The wet developer can be applied while the surface is still damp to the touch, but the dry developer must be applied only to surfaces that are thoroughly dry.

Inspection

Inspection is the next step in the liquid penetrant test. The inspection can be done either with a normal light and visible-type dyes or with a black light and fluorescent dye penetrants. With either method, two types of indications are revealed: true and false. True indications are caused by penetrants bleeding out from actual discontinuities in the metal. The standard true flaws that are indicated are the large cracks; cold-shut cracks; fatigue cracks, which greatly resemble the cold-shut cracks; pits; and porosities (Fig. 9-7). The large crack is represented by a line and becomes apparent quickly after the developer is applied. The cold-shut crack, which is an undersurface crack that is bleeding through the surface, is represented by a line of dots and dashes and requires a few minutes after the developer has been added to come to the surface. Porosity is noticeable quickly because

an indication of porosity comes to the surface almost immediately, as do indications of the large crack. The area of porosity is generally indicated by dots.

The false or nonrelevant indications are not caused by flaws at the surface of the metal. The major reasons for false indications include failure to follow the correct liquid penetrant application or rough, irregular surfaces on the test metal.

MAGNETIC PARTICLE TESTING

Magnetic particle inspection is based on the magnetic lines of flux, or force lines, that can be generated within the test specimen. These force lines are parallel to each other while traveling through the test specimen if there are no surface or subsurface defects in the piece (Fig. 9-8). In the top half of Fig. 9-8, the force lines are going through the piece without any deviation. However, if there is a surface defect, the magnetic lines of force, or the flux lines, will create a small north-south hole area at the location of the surface defect, causing the iron powder that is used in magnetic particle inspection to collect around the surface defect. This surface defect is called *a magnetic leakage*, or *an indication*.

There are two types of power supplies that can be used to develop the magnetic lines of force in the test specimen: a permanent magnet or an electromagnet. No matter which power source is used, the magnetic lines of force will be the same; however, the electromagnet is capable of producing a stronger force field than the permanent magnet. After the magnetic force lines have

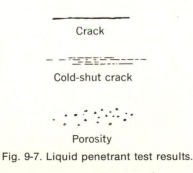

Crack

Cold-shut crack

Porosity

Fig. 9-7. Liquid penetrant test results.

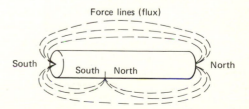

Fig. 9-8. Surface defects—magnetic lines of flux.

been generated in the test specimen, a finely grained iron powder is sprayed or blown over the surface of the test specimen. This powder either may be suspended in a liquid or may be dry. The liquid is applied to the test specimen by blowing it on with some kind of spray device, or the test specimen is immersed completely in a bath in which the particles are suspended in a light or medium oil. If the test specimen is too large to be immersed, portable prods can be used to establish the magnetic field in it. Another way to establish a magnetic field in a large test specimen is to wrap it with arc welding cables.

Magnetic particle inspection can also indicate subsurface defects if these defects are close to the surface. These subsurface defects disrupt the magnetic lines of force and bend them around the defect (Fig. 9-9). A subsurface defect is indicated by the magnetic powder collecting around the broken lines of force at the surface of the test specimen.

Two types of surface defects can be detected by magnetic particle inspection: defects that are parallel to the interface of the workpiece and defects that are perpendicular to the interface, or sides, of the test specimen. Longitudinal, or parallel, defects are indicated because the electric current flow sets up magnetic flux lines at a 90° angle to the current flow, following the right-hand rule of current flow. These magnetic lines of force must cross the defect in a perpendicular line in order to derive the full benefit from magnetic particle inspection. If the defect is parallel to the lines of force, there is a possibility that the indication of a surface or a subsurface flaw in the test specimen would not be noticeable (Fig. 9-10a).

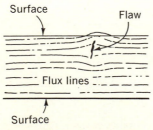

Fig. 9-9. Subsurface defects.

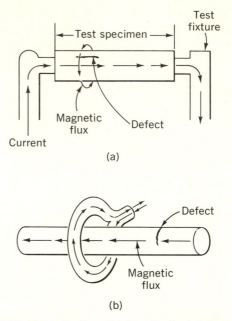

Fig. 9-10. Magnetization. (a) Longitudinal defects; (b) perpendicular defects.

In order to check a test specimen fully, both longitudinal and perpendicular indications must be checked. The perpendicular indications are inspected by using a circular coil which has current flowing through it in one direction. This coil will set up magnetic flux lines that are traveling through the test specimen longitudinally. Any defect that is perpendicular to these magnetic lines of flux will show an indication (Fig. 9-10b). Used together, the longitudinal test and the circular test complete the testing of metal by magnetic particle inspection.

The power requirements for electromagnets are high amperage and low voltage. These are supplied either by direct current or rectified alternating current, both of which will produce a current flowing in only one direction. The particles that are applied to the test specimen can be of different colors according to the color of the specimen. Some colors used for magnetic particles are yellow, red, green, and brown.

For most applications, the test specimen need not be demagnetized; however, the test specimen needs to be restored to its non-magnetic or paramagnetic state, it can be passed through a high field intensity ac coil, which will sufficiently demagnetize the part so that it will resume its original state.

QUESTIONS

1. What defects can ultrasonic testing discover?
2. How do ultrasonic waves indicate where these defects are in material?
3. How is electric energy converted into sound energy?
4. What three types of testing devices are commercially available with ultrasonic equipment?
5. What does CRT stand for?
6. How are x-rays generated?
7. What other power sources are capable of replacing the x-ray power source?
8. How is the test by liquid penetrants conducted?
9. Why are clean surfaces important when using liquid penetrants to test metals for surface and subsurface defects?
10. How does the right-hand rule of current flow apply to the magnetic particle testing method?
11. How are the iron powder particles applied to the test specimen in magnetic particle testing?

Part Three

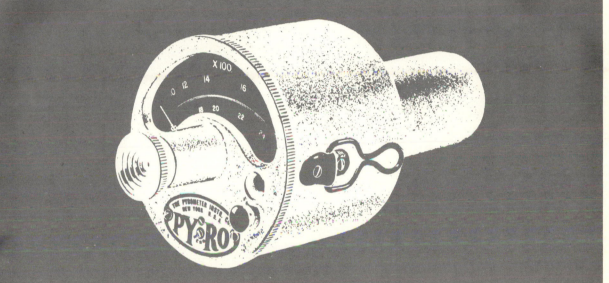

Hot Metalworking

10

Patterns

Essential to the production of high-quality castings is the foundry pattern. The accuracy of the pattern determines the accuracy of the casting. For usable castings to be produced consistently, a thorough knowledge of pattern design is essential to the foundryworker. A preliminary study of such principles as ramming a mold, draft shrinkage, and solidification is helpful in understanding the part the pattern plays in the casting of metal.

RAMMING A MOLD

Ramming a simple solid pattern is accomplished by following the procedures described below. First, the pattern is positioned on the turnover, or molding, board with a minimum of 1 in. clearance between the pattern and the sides of the drag section of the flask. The pattern is placed on the turnover board with the draft, or taper, up (Fig. 10-1). Next, the drag section of the flask is placed in position on the molding board with the flask aligning pins pointing down, and then the pattern is lightly dusted with a parting agent. Facing sand is then riddled, or sieved, over the pattern and the mold board to a minimum depth of 1 in. (Fig. 10-2). Sand from the main pile, heap sand, can then be shoveled into

the drag until the sand overflows the edges of the flask section.

The next step is to ram the drag section of the flask with a rammer (Fig. 10-3). First, the edges of the mold are rammed with the cross peen at an angle of approximately 15°. Then the rammer is reversed and the butt end is used to pack the molding sand. The drag is then leveled with a strike-off bar. The strike-off bar is a straight edge used to level sand to a uniform surface that is even with the edge of the flask section (Fig. 10-4). The best movement for striking off the molding material is to work the bar back and forth as it is pushed across the drag.

When the drag is complete, the next step is to place a bottom board on the top of the drag, grasp it firmly, and turn the drag over. The aligning pins for the cope should now be pointing up (Fig. 10-5). Now the cope is placed in position on top of the drag, and the sprue and riser pins are inserted approximately ½ in. into the rammed sand. Parting compound is dusted over the pattern and the parting area, and then the cope is rammed in the same manner as the drag. However, extra care must be taken not to damage or displace the sprue and riser pins (Fig. 10-6).

After the cope is struck off, the sprue and riser pins are removed. The cope section is removed from the drag section and set aside

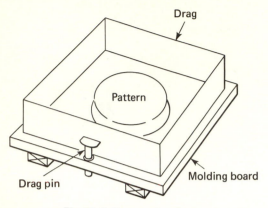

Fig. 10-1. Drag and pattern.

in a safe place. A draw pin is inserted into the pattern and rapped lightly (struck in different directions) to loosen the pattern. After the pattern has been removed from the drag section, two channels, or gates, are cut in the molding material, one to the sprue pin hole and one to the hole created by the riser pin. Both of these hand-cut gates open into the cavity impression caused by the pattern (Fig. 10-7).

All loose sand on the parting faces is removed and the mold is closed in preparation for the pouring operation. Placing weights on top of the mold will help prevent the possibility of the cope lifting up from the drag when the molten metal exerts pressure on the parting line.

DRAFT

Draft is the angular difference between the sides of the pattern and an imaginary vertical

Fig. 10-3. Hand rammer. (*Genevro Machine Company.*)

line drawn at an angle of 90° from the parting line. Draft allows the pattern to be removed from a molding medium without the rupture of the molding material or the loss of definition within the mold cavity. Draft usually begins at the parting line of a mold and increases in both directions (Fig. 10-8).

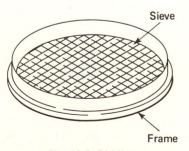

Fig. 10-2. Riddle.

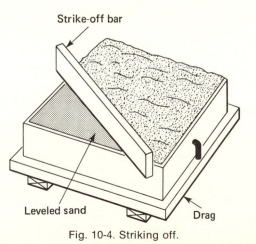

Fig. 10-4. Striking off.

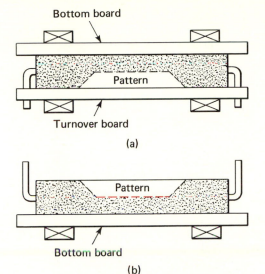

Fig. 10-5. Turning the drag. (a) Pins down; (b) pins up.

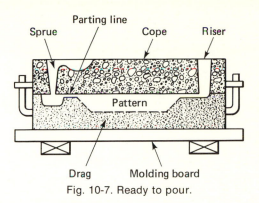

Fig. 10-7. Ready to pour.

The amount of draft, also called taper, is expressed in degrees, such as 1, 2, or 3°. The main pattern features that determine the amount of draft to be used include the depth of the draw face, the texture of the pattern material, the complexity of the design, and the type of molding medium (for example, the type of foundry sand used).

The length of the external draw face establishes the number of degrees of draft on a pattern because the pattern must be removed in order to form the cavity that accepts the molten metal. When the draw face is short, as little as ½° of draft may be adequate to withdraw the pattern. However, if the draw face extends deeply into the molding material, the amount of draft will increase to 2 or 3°.

External draft may be used on both sides of a pattern (Fig. 10-9a) or on only one side, with zero draft used on the other external face (Fig. 10-9b). Both of these methods are used in commercial foundries. However, the design of pattern b in Fig. 10-9 makes it possible to generate a right-angle corner that will require less cleanup of the casting after it is removed from the mold. Because extra cleanup is required when a pattern has a draft on both sides, constructing a pattern that uses draft on only one draw face is a time-saving consideration.

Internal draft is used when draw faces are in the interior of a pattern and when the interior area of the hole is large enough for the molding medium to support itself and the molten metal (Fig. 10-10). In this case, a casting with a hole in it could be produced but the hole must be large. Because the draw faces of a hole in a casting usually encircle the molding material, withdrawing the pattern is extremely difficult and necessitates the addition of 1 or 2° in the usual pattern draft (Fig. 10-10).

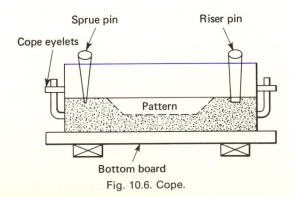

Fig. 10.6. Cope.

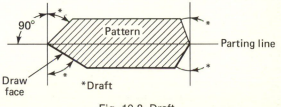

Fig. 10-8. Draft.

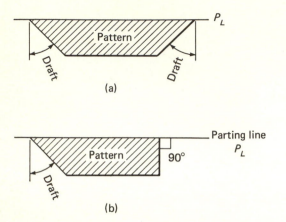

Fig. 10-9. Draft. (a) Two-sided (both sides); (b) one-sided.

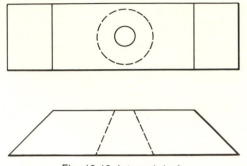

Fig. 10-10. Internal draft.

The texture of the surface of the molding pattern should be as smooth as possible. Surface roughness of a pattern increases the total contact area of a pattern and creates negative draft causing the mold cavity to deform after it is removed from the pattern. The most accepted method of achieving a smooth surface on a pattern is to coat the surface with a sealer. The common sealing agents include plastics, shellacs, lacquers, and practically all of the commercially available paints.

The type of molding material is also considered in determining the amount of draft that is built into the pattern. For example, foundry sand that is mixed with water requires more draft than oil-bonded foundry sand.

SHRINKAGE

When a molten metal is poured into a cavity and begins to solidify, the metal pulls away from the cavity walls. Each metal, pure or alloyed, has its own characteristic amount of shrinkage and rate of contraction. Consequently, when a pattern is designed, several factors determine the amount of extra size to build into the pattern to allow for shrinkage. These factors are: the metal or alloy being used; the optimum pouring temperature of the particular metal; the chilling effect of the

molding material; and the size of the mold and the core mass, if any, inside the mold cavity.

Although no absolute rules exist for determining the exact amount of excess material to allow for metal shrinkage, there are estimates that have been established. These estimates are based on the amount of loss of total volume during the solidification process in a solid, 12-in.^{3} block of metal. Many of these estimates have been transferred onto a 1-ft scale (Table 10-1). The patternmaker can use these estimates to build in a shrink allowance in the pattern. For example, if a pattern is being designed for use with aluminum, the fact that aluminum has an approximate shrinkage factor of $5/32$ in./ft is applied. The $5/32$ in. is added to a standard 12-in. scale stretching the standard to make a new scale that is $12 5/32$ in. long. All the index marks

TABLE 10-1. METAL SHRINKAGE PER INCH PER FOOT

Aluminum	$5/32$
Aluminum bronze	$1/4$
Gun-metal bronze	$1/8$–$3/16$
Manganese bronze	$1/4$
Phosphorus bronze	$1/8$–$3/16$
Yellow brass	$5/32$–$3/16$
Malleable cast iron	$1/8$–$3/32$
Grey cast iron	$1/10$–$5/32$
White cast iron	$1/4$
Magnesium	$5/32$
Steel	$3/16$–$5/16$

along this new rule have been moved proportionally to maintain 12 equal spaces. This new rule, called a *shrink rule,* is used for measuring when the pattern is built, automatically allowing for the proper amount of shrinkage to be built into the pattern.

SOLIDIFICATION

Metal solidifies in two directions. The force of gravity causes the heavier solid metal plane to rest at the bottom of the mold. Because there is a larger volume of heat entrapped in the larger mass, this section of a casting will solidify last, with the light sections of a casting solidifying first. Metal turns into a solid with directional impetus, and this motion of inward and upward freezing of a metal is called *directional solidification.* A pattern design is affected by the crystalline growth and directional solidification of a metal. A pattern that does not allow for directional solidification may produce castings with undesirable internal voids.

Another characteristic that must be considered is longitudinal and transverse contractions. These contractions take place in the solidus stage and are capable of causing the metal to tear itself apart (Fig. 10-11). These contractions can be controlled. For example, in Fig. 10-11, the heavy vertical mass of the pattern and the sprue system on the other end of the pattern act as immobilizers, allowing the contraction in the thin middle section. This pattern design does not allow the thin section to be fed adequately, causing the metal to exert extra force during solidification. In the maximum hindrance zone the structure will undoubtedly reveal macro- and microseparation.

PATTERN DESIGN

If a pattern is designed without allowing for directional solidification, then internal microshrinkage, entrapped gas, and large voids will occur in the casting because the molten

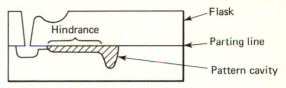

Fig. 10-11. Hindrance of shrinkage.

metal will freeze before the gating system and the mold cavity are completely filled. A bad pattern can be redesigned to produce uniform wall thickness and allow for directional solidification (Fig. 10-12).

Reinforcing the backside of a plate with ribs increases the strength of a casting with a flat surface, but using ribs to increase casting strength also increases the cross-sectional areas at certain locations. Enlarging an area can cause interior shrinkage at the junction of the rib with the main section of the casting. Interior shrinkage that is a result of concentrated mass is called a *hot spot* because of the nonfeeding characteristics of the entrapped molten metal. A hot spot is an area that is not fed metal from another area and does not allow for directional solidification. A means of predetermining hot spots is possible with a blueprint of the pattern and a draftsman's

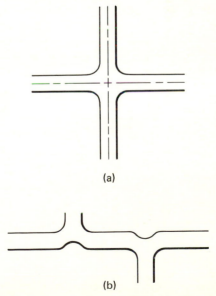

(a)

(b)

Fig. 10-12. Pattern design. (a) Original; (b) improved.

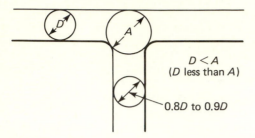

$D < A$
(D less than A)

0.8D to 0.9D

Fig. 10-13. Hot spot location—inscribed circle method.

compass. Inscribing circles at junctions in the design form identifies different sized mass areas (Fig. 10-13). This circle method usually indicates the exact location of a possible critical area of shrinkage.

Not only does a rib increase the area of a casting, but it also requires more precision when the pattern is removed and the use of a filleting material. Extra precaution must also be taken in designing the gating system in order to ensure a sound casting because criti-

cal areas of shrinkage occur at the junction of the rib and the casting.

The basic forms of ribs and junctions include the L, Y, H, T, X, and V shapes. These shapes are the easiest to produce when an original pattern is constructed. During the construction of the rib to the junction, the main concern is the filleting of the junction. Failure to fillet will cause a hot spot at the sharp corner, resulting in an unacceptable casting because the metal at this junction will be unsound. Figure 10-14 presents the two basic forms, L and Y in three stages of design. The relationship between the thickness of the piece X and the radius of the curve R determines the flow characteristics of the metal. A main point to remember is that a pattern should be designed with as many smooth flowing characteristics as possible; flow characteristics are also called isotherms.

All of the junctions in Fig. 10-14 represent enlargements in cross-sectional areas

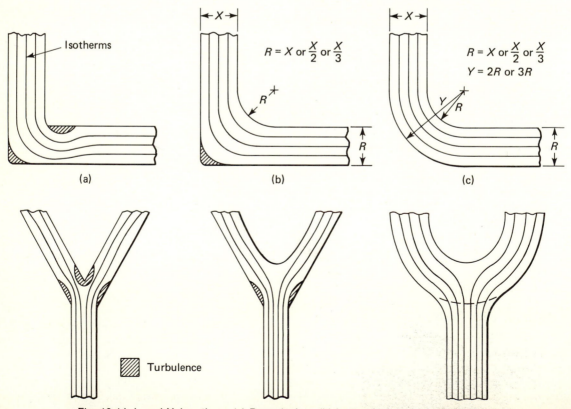

Isotherms

$R = X$ or $\frac{X}{2}$ or $\frac{X}{3}$

$R = X$ or $\frac{X}{2}$ or $\frac{X}{3}$

$Y = 2R$ or $3R$

(a)   (b)   (c)

Turbulence

Fig. 10-14. L and Y Junctions. (a) Poor design; (b) better design; (c) best design.

where hot spots may result when the cavity is filled with molten metal. The smaller feeding entrances freeze before the heavier center portions, therefore, the center section does not have any liquid metal to fill the voids caused by the solidification process. This void is called a *shrinkage defect*. The inscribed circle method that determines possible shrinkage locations is actually identifying the location of shrinkage defects.

The design of a pattern should be limited to as few junctions and ribs as possible. If junctions and ribs are included, some method of alleviating hot spots caused by these junctions will be required. If the design cannot be changed, T sections can eliminate hot spots. T sections can be adapted for use with external and internal chills, external insulators, cores, risers, or by reduction of area (Fig. 10-15). External and internal chills help to eliminate isolated, trapped areas of non-solid metal by creating a new interface, the chill. This new metal interface promotes the formation of small internal, equiaxed crystals and faster nucleation. Insulators can only be used externally because they are composed of material other than the metal being cast.

Insulating materials include asbestos, steel, plaster of paris, or any material that will absorb heat. Using a core or reducing area are two methods of achieving uniform thickness and allowing for directional solidification. The function of a riser is to create a new path for directional solidification.

If the top of the T is the main section of the casting and the stem is a minor section or support rib, the thickness of the main section controls the section width of the rib. The ratio of the main section to the rib varies between 1:8 and 1:9.

Another ratio that is important is the length of the change in sectional width. If the change is too abrupt, then turbulence, aspiration, and hot spots will result in the area. The change in thickness should be designed as a gradual slope, a wedge shape, to control the solidification process. The proportions of the wedge shape, length to width, should not exceed a ratio of 1:4. This proportion can be calculated by the formula

$$l = 4(W_a - W_b)$$

as illustrated in Fig. 10-16.

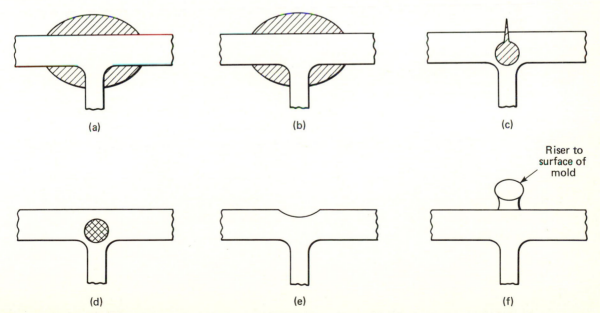

(a)

(b)

(c)

Riser to surface of mold

(d)

(e)

(f)

Fig. 10-15. Elimination of hot spots. (a) External chills; (b) external insulators; (c) internal chill; (d) core; area reduction; (f) riser.

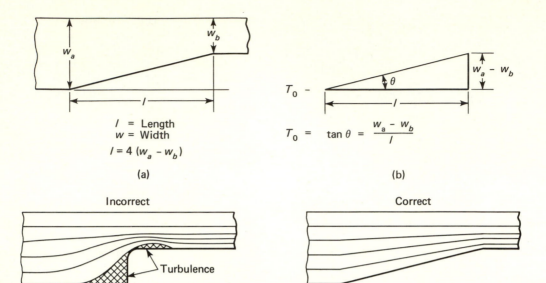

l = Length
w = Width
$l = 4 (w_a - w_b)$

(a)

$T_0 =$ $\tan \theta = \dfrac{w_a - w_b}{l}$

(b)

Incorrect

Correct

Turbulence

(c)

Fig. 10-16. Tapering. (a) Formula; (b) taper in degrees; (c) isothermic considerations.

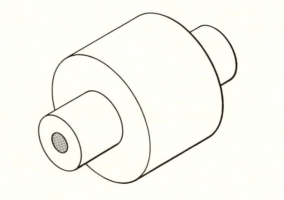

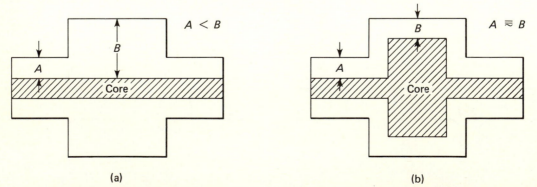

$A < B$

B

A

Core

(a)

$A \approx B$

B

A

Core

(b)

Fig. 10-17. Cored internal thickness. (a) Incorrect—nonuniform; (b) correct—uniform.

A design element that is easy to overlook is uniform thickness within a hollow symmetrical casting. The inexperienced pattern designer may forget to visualize how the internal and external portions of the pattern differ. Sometimes a casting will have uniform dimensions on the outside and not have uniform dimensions on the inside (Fig. 10-17). In Fig. 10-17, the problems of nonuniform thickness and resulting hot spots in a round casting with mixed heavy and light sections are solved by using a core for controlling internal thickness. A *core* is a shape that is preformed into the internal void of the pattern. Core material consists of foundry sand mixed with a binder, enabling the sand to maintain the desired shape and still, with rough usage, crumble. The core is supported in the mold cavity and the metal is poured around it.

Of major importance in pattern design is allowing for directional solidification. Solidification contraction is not controlled by the pattern shrinkage rule, but by the system of feeding the metal to the mold cavity. The pattern can only control the liquid and solid contraction stages of the solidification process. This lack of solidification control places an increased importance on the design of the gating, or feeding, system. Allowing for directional solidification should control hot spots, premature metal freezing, secondary growth of dendrites, and also internal shrinkage.

Testing for defects in a cast structure often incorporates a cross-sectional microscopic study of a suspected area of fault. The appearance of the microstructure of an area with a hot spot is illustrated by a nonfilleted L section in Fig. 10-18. The hot spots (which are illustrated by the dark areas in Fig. 10-18) could be responsible for the rejection of the complete casting because weakness may occur in the immediate area of the hot spot.

Types of Patterns

The basic pattern types include the loose pattern, the gated loose pattern, and the match-

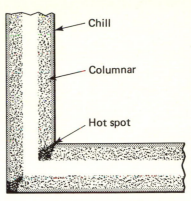

Fig. 10-18. Microstructure of a section.

plate pattern. There are, as well, special devices for making unique patterns.

LOOSE PATTERNS. Loose patterns can be solid, split, or loose-piece (multiple-piece) patterns. The material from which the pattern is formed does not in any way determine the basic type of pattern. The type is determined by the physical appearance of the pattern. The *solid pattern* can be either a regular or an irregular parting solid pattern, depending on the construction of the parting line during the molding process. The parting line is the cleavage point between the two sections of the molding flask or the plane on which the cope and the drag sections of the flask rest. The *regular parting solid pattern* is designed so that the portion resting on the parting line during the molding process is parallel to a single plane (Fig. 10-19).

The second type of solid pattern is an *irregular parting solid pattern*. This type may have been a forerunner to the split pattern because the more complex molding procedures used with the solid pattern have

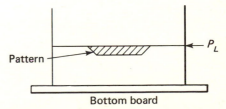

Fig. 10-19. Regular parting solid pattern.

been simplified in the molding procedures of the split pattern. The main difference between the regular and the irregular parting solid pattern is that the parting lines shift from a standard position in the regular pattern to a hand-formed parting line in the irregular pattern. The parting line must be moved when using an irregular pattern in order to remove the pattern from the molding medium. The removing of the excess molding material forms the new parting line. This hand forming of a new parting line to conform to the contour of a pattern is known as *coping* (Fig. 10-20a).

The irregular parting solid pattern can mold complex shapes that are otherwise impossible with a solid pattern. Another advantage is that it is more economical to construct a solid pattern that will perform the same function as a split pattern. A disadvantage of irregular parting line molding is that more skill is required in constructing the parting line manually. Also, a greater amount of time is involved in coping the parting line manually than when an automatically formed parting line is used.

The *split pattern* is adaptable to a wide range of applications because it can be designed about a centerline. The centerline of the split pattern is identical to the standard parting line employed between the cope and the drag sections of the standard flask, enabling the patternmaker to separate the pattern at the maximum draft area, the parting line. This characteristic makes it possible for more complex shapes to be molded in the same manner as with the regular parting solid pattern (Fig. 10-20b).

A third type of loose pattern is the *loose-piece pattern*. These patterns are separate; i.e., they are not joined together permanently. The loose-piece pattern is a pattern that has more than one section. One of these sections has to be removed from the molding medium separately. It cannot be removed from the mold in its assembled state. The pattern must be removed one part at a time. In Fig. 10-21, a loose-piece pattern with one

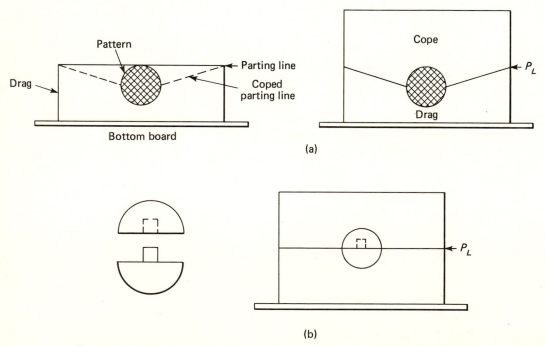

(a)

(b)

Fig. 10-20. Solid and split patterns. (a) Solid pattern (coped); (b) split pattern.

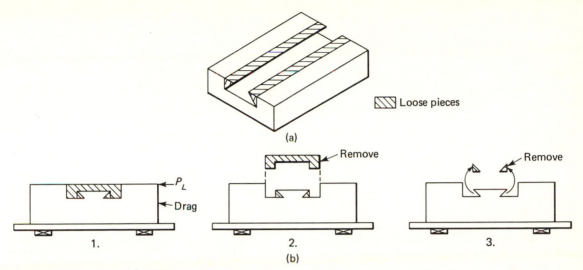

Fig. 10-21. Loose-piece pattern. (a) Pattern; (b) pattern removal.

main piece and two loose pieces is illustrated. Before the two loose pieces can be removed from the mold cavity, the main piece must be removed.

GATED LOOSE PATTERNS. The gated loose patterns can be any of the previously mentioned patterns with the addition of a feeding system which is permanently attached to the pattern. The advantages of permanently attached gates include rapid molding, elimination of possible errors in cutting gates by hand, and a reduction of skill needed by the person doing the molding. Often when the parts to be cast are small and must be reproduced many times, more than one part is attached to the gating system (Fig. 10-22). Factors that limit the number of patterns possible in one gating system include the size of the flask and the design of the casting. Some casting designs may not lend themselves to multiple-pattern gating systems because of the metal feeding requirements of the patterns and the systems.

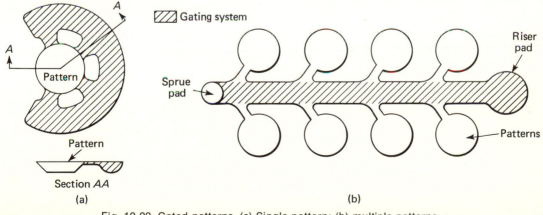

Fig. 10-22. Gated patterns. (a) Single pattern; (b) multiple patterns.

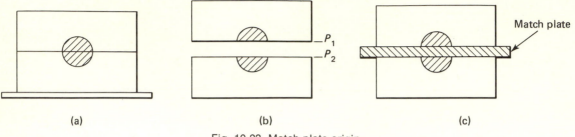

(a)   (b)   (c)

Fig. 10-23. Match plate origin.

MATCH-PLATE PATTERNS. A match plate is a flat plate placed between the cope and the drag to which patterns are securely mounted. Match plates have three applications in foundries. The patterns can be attached to the plates on both sides, on the drag side, or on the cope side. Both sides of the plate are not used all the time because production rates can be increased by using two people to do the molding with each ramming a cope plate or a drag plate at the same time (Fig. 10-23).

Drag and cope plates are also used in the production of castings with stack molding. Stack molding places a number of drag sections on top of each other with a pattern formed at every parting line and a sprue system common to all patterns (Fig. 10-24).

A *follow board* is a device that helps to establish a parting line with ease in a pattern that has an irregular shape. The follow board is a plate, like the match plate, that has a hole cut into it instead of patterns mounted on it. The hole will be just large enough to allow the pattern to be exposed from the ideal parting line up. The use of a follow board in the molding of a solid sphere is illustrated in Fig. 10-25.

Cones

Many castings have internal voids that are part of their design. These voids are formed by a sand core that is supported or immobilized within the mold cavity, as in the casting

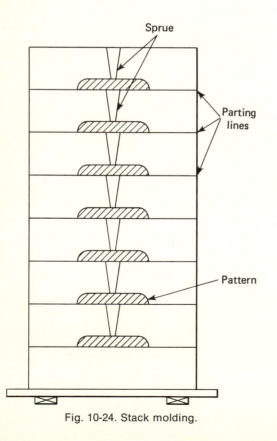

Fig. 10-24. Stack molding.

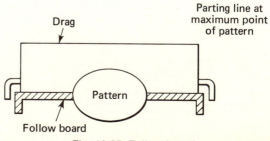

Fig. 10-25. Follow board.

of a cylinder or pipe. For a cylinder to be manufactured in a sand-casting system, the core must be fastened to the mold so that the core will not change position when the molten metal strikes it. The change in position of a core is called *core shift*. Core prints have been designed to eliminate core shift. A *core print* is an appendage on the pattern that forms an extra impression in the molding

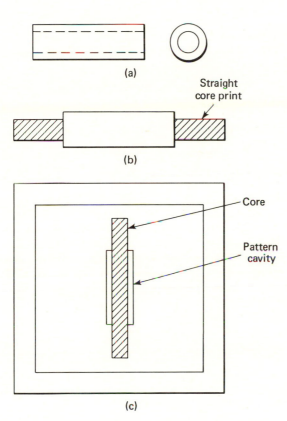

(a)

Straight
core print

(b)

Core

Pattern
cavity

(c)

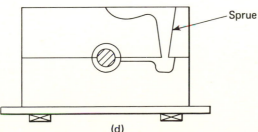

Sprue

(d)

Fig. 10-26. Core application. (a) Cast cylinder; (b) pattern with core print; (c) core placed in drag (top view); (d) complete flask.

material that will support a sand core (Fig. 10-26).

The shape of the core determines the design of the core print; therefore, core prints are many shapes and sizes. However, some of the more frequently used shapes include the straight print, the cone print, the stop print, and the tail print. The *straight print* (Fig. 10-26) does not refer to the shape of the core inside the mold cavity but to the area that supports the core body.

The *cone print* expedites the centering of the core of the mold cavity and, also, eases the procedure of closing the mold with the cope section. This last function has given the cone print a second name, the cope print. The cope (cone) print may be used with the straight print to ensure correct alignment of the core both vertically and horizontally. This combination is a logical one because the tapered sides of the cone print lock securely to the preformed impression (Fig. 10-27). The cone print can be any dimension, but a ratio has been established that works well, a ratio based on the diameter of the area of the print closest to the pattern shape portion of the core. It is recommended that the diameter of the base of the cone and the height of the cone be two-thirds of the base diameter, as shown in Fig. 10-28.

The *stop print* is a print that supports a core that forms a "blind" hole (Fig. 10-29). The requirements for the design of the stop print are that the volume of the core supported by the print should be larger than the volume of the core protruding into the mold

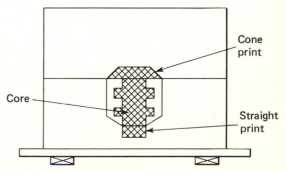

Cone
print

Core

Straight
print

Fig. 10-27. Vertical application of the combination of straight and cone prints.

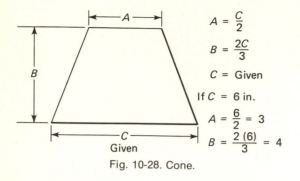

$A = \dfrac{C}{2}$

$B = \dfrac{2C}{3}$

$C = $ Given

If $C = 6$ in.

$A = \dfrac{6}{2} = 3$

$B = \dfrac{2\,(6)}{3} = 4$

Fig. 10-28. Cone.

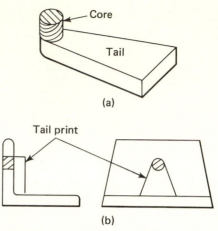

(a)

(b)

Fig. 10-30. Tail print. (a) Construction; (b) application.

cavity and that the core-print impression should be designed to forestall core shift. This type of core print would be used in the casting of a candleholder that has a cavity for a candle. The design of section X in Fig. 10-29 prevents core shift which would cause the casting to fail.

The *tail print* is another method of forming a cavity similar to the cavity resulting from use of the stop print. The stop print differs from the tail print in that the tail print is capable of locating a core support in areas where the pattern could not be withdrawn from the mold. The appendage (tail) of the print has the primary function of supplying positive draft to the cored area to help in the removal of the pattern. A tail print is an adaptation of the loose-piece pattern but without the individual pieces (Fig. 10-30).

Color Coding

Loose patterns with their core prints and core boxes are colored for easy identification in many foundries. This color coding establishes a basis for communication between the various individuals involved in the construction and use of patterns. The only drawback of the coding system is that the colors are not fully accepted by the whole foundry industry, but color coding is an attempt to standardize communications. The color code describes five components of the casting pattern (Table 10-2).

Stop-Offs

Stop-offs are pattern-reinforcing sections which are filled with molding material after the pattern is withdrawn from the mold. Their only function is to hold the pattern rigid during the ramming process. This rigid-

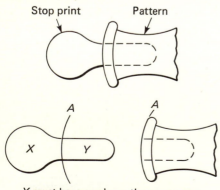

X must have a volume the same as or larger than that of Y.

Fig. 10-29. Stop print and core.

TABLE 10-2. PATTERN COLOR CODE

Black	Surface as-cast
Red	Machined finish
Yellow	Core prints and seats
Yellow/red diagonal stripes	Loose pieces
Yellow/black diagonal stripes	Stop-offs

TABLE 10-3. PATTERN MATERIAL CHARACTERISTICS

CHARACTERISTIC	ALUMINUM	PLASTIC	WOOD
Water corrosion resistance	Excellent	Excellent	Excellent
Machinability	Good	Good	Excellent
Repairability	Poor	Fair	Excellent
Strength	Good	Good	Fair
Wear resistance	Good	Fair	Poor

ity is important because if the pattern distorts during the compacting of the founding material, the pattern cavity will also be distorted, ruining the entire mold.

PATTERN MATERIALS

Choosing material for a pattern depends on the number of castings to be made from the pattern. Other factors that determine the selection of pattern materials include the method of mold ramming and the physical characteristics of the pattern design. Some of the more common materials used in the construction of patterns are wood, metal, plastic, and gypsum. Sometimes a pattern or a corebox will be made from a combination of these materials. For example, if there were an area of critical wear on a wood pattern, this one spot could be reinforced with a metal strip to decrease wear. This metal strip would extend the life of the pattern and reduce pattern replacement costs. This kind of reinforcement is often done because although wood patterns are more economical than metal ones, they deteriorate much faster.

Wood patterns are made out of either softwood or hardwood. Softwood patterns are designed for limited production, usually less than 10 castings, because softwood deforms easily and requires that more attention be given to the ramming of the mold. Hardwood patterns and coreboxes are made mainly from mahogany although other hardwoods can also be used.

Metal patterns are more difficult to make and more expensive than wood patterns, but they last longer. Because there is little wear, metal patterns are more accurate for a longer time than wood patterns. Metal patterns usually are used with match plates. Most of the plastics used for patterns are the cast plastics. These plastics can be cast into complex shapes and can be machined, like a metal pattern. They can have the accuracy of a metal pattern, yet be lightweight. An advantage of plastic patterns is that plastic does not absorb any of the moisture from the mold. Other advantages of plastic are its lack of oxidation and its ease of shaping. The major disadvantage of cast plastics is that pattern detail can be lost because of the abrasive action of the casting process.

Gypsum patterns are capable of producing castings with intricate detail and to very close tolerances. The two main types of gypsum are soft plaster of paris and hard metal casting plaster; either can be used to construct a pattern but the soft plaster does not have the strength of the hard plaster. Gypsum can be formed easily, has plasticity, and can be repaired easily.

Table 10-3 summarizes the characteristics of aluminum, plastic, and wood.

QUESTIONS

1. What is draft?
2. What is the difference between a bottom board and a turnover board?

3. Explain the steps in the ramming process.
4. How do certain patterns allow for shrinkage?
5. What is directional solidification?
6. How does directional solidification control pattern design?
7. Describe the circle method of hot spot location.
8. What are the basic rib forms in pattern designs?
9. How are hot spots eliminated?
10. Why is uniform thickness an important concept in pattern design?
11. What are the basic pattern types?
12. What is a match plate?
13. Explain stack molding.
14. What are the functions of a core print, a stop print, and a tail print?
15. Explain the procedure for developing a mold with a sweep pattern.

11

Gating

The process of metal casting requires that molten metal be transferred from some type of container to the mold cavity. The *gating system* is the plumbing that determines the direction of the flow and the amount of metal to reach the mold cavity. If the mold cavity is open on one side, uneven cooling of the metal will take place. Consequently, the mold cavity should not be open and only a few gates, or entrances, should be exposed to the atmosphere.

In order to design an effective and economical gating system for a particular pattern, one must first know the molding medium, the type of metal to be poured, and the design of the pattern.

SPRUE

The basic component of a gating system is the sprue. The function of the sprue is to provide an entrance to the mold cavity for the molten metal. Sprues may be designed with either a positive taper, a reverse taper, or no taper at all (Fig. 11-1).

In Fig. 11-1a and c, the designs of the sprues are weak because they promote rather than control turbulence in the molten metal. The main cause of the turbulence is the fall of

the metal into the bottom of the pattern cavity. Aspiration, or the gathering in of air, in the metal is the result of the turbulence because more metal is exposed to the atmosphere as the fluid tumbles down the sprue. Also, the design of the sprues in Fig. 11-1a and c does not confine the molten stream effectively and thus allows the metal to receive impurities from the air.

Of the three possibilities in Fig. 11-1, the positive-tapered sprue provides the best control of turbulence and aspiration in the metal. Metal contracts as it cools and loses a small amount of its volume. The temperature loss rate increases when the metal comes into contact with the mold face of the sprue and this further decreases the volume of metal within the sprue. The tapering of the sprue automatically decreases the cross-sectional area that the metal comes into contact with as it flows from the large end to the small end. The tapering of the sprue also slows the velocity of the flow stream, establishing a slower pouring rate that is easier to maintain and control. Figure 11-2 shows how aspiration is controlled.

Pouring Basin

A pouring basin added to the top of the sprue facilitates the pouring procedure. Pouring

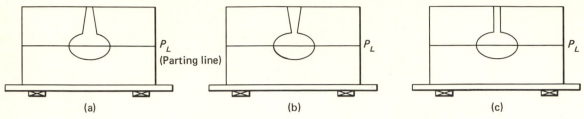

Fig. 11-1. Sprues. (a) Reverse taper; (b) positive taper; (c) straight—no taper.

basins have three distinct advantages over pouring metal directly into the sprue: They eliminate aspiration, make pouring easier, and give more control over the amount of metal poured. Pouring basins can be formed as an integral part of the sprue, or they can be separate molds placed over the sprue at the completion of the molding process.

The four types of pouring basins that enjoy widespread popularity in the foundry industry are: the concentric basin, the dam basin, the skimmer/dam basin, and the strainer core basin (Fig. 11-3). The pouring basin designs with dams must allow a minimum dam radius of 1¼ in. or the flow path of the metal will become too angular and create turbulence. All of these pouring basins are effective in controlling aspiration, although the concentric basin is not as effective as the others because it does not allow the metal to flow smoothly into the sprue hole. This design causes the metal to tumble, creating a vortex that encourages aspiration. The other three types are comparable, and selection of

the pouring basin type depends on the type of metal to be poured.

The combined height of the pouring basin and the sprue produces a taper for the sprue that will prevent the induction of impurities in the *downgate system* (the pouring basin and sprue). The appropriate amount of taper can be found by using the sprue taper formula (Fig. 11-4). For example, in Fig. 11-4, the pouring basin height is 4 in., the sprue height is 12 in., and the bottom of the sprue is to be ½-in. diameter. The problem is to determine the amount of taper or the diameter of the sprue entrance. First, the combined height, 16 in., of the pouring basin and the sprue is derived by adding 4 and 12 in. Then the problem is solved by rewriting the equation to solve for A. The solution is that the diameter of the top of the sprue should be 1 in. when the sprue exit, or bottom, is ½-in. diameter and the length of the sprue is 12 in. The size of the sprue entrance is determined by the sprue exit. The size of the sprue exit is determined by the flow rate of the metal

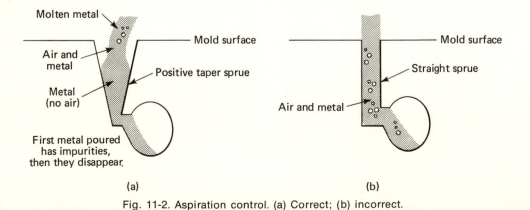

Fig. 11-2. Aspiration control. (a) Correct; (b) incorrect.

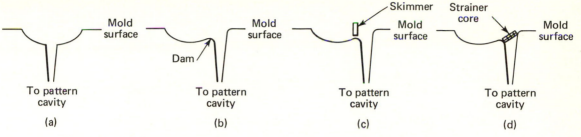

Fig. 11-3. Pouring basins. (a) Concentric; (b) dam; (c) skimmer/dam; (d) strainer core.

that the foundry worker uses to fill the mold cavity.

The metal poured into the downgate system is accelerated by gravity. The tapered sprue with the big end up limits acceleration. As the metal descends into the system, it is forced into a smaller and smaller cross-sectional area. This reduction in area produces a backing-up effect on the metal stream, slowing the metal and producing a standard velocity. The velocity can be measured by the amount of metal exiting from the sprue bottom. The taller the sprue, the greater the acceleration; and with greater acceleration, the velocity of the metal is more difficult to control. The velocity of the metal stream is usually expressed as the number of pounds of metal that passes a certain point in 1 s.

Sprue Base

Excessive velocity of fluid metal can be the cause of many casting problems. Some typical problems directly traceable to excessive velocity are: metal/mold interaction, washing of the cavity face, macroshrinkage, microshrinkage, and all types of porosity.

A satisfactory method for decelerating the flow rate of the metal is to add a basin, or sump, directly beneath the sprue exit. This sump acts as a shock absorber for the descending metal and changes the direction of the flow into channels, or runners, that feed the mold cavity.

Calculating the appropriate size of the sprue base depends on the size of the sprue exit. The diameter of the sump should be four to five times the diameter of the sprue bottom and can be expressed as a ratio of 1:4 or 1:5. The depth of the sump is also determined in relation to the exit diameter; this ratio should be 1:3 or 1:4. In the example in Fig. 11-4, the exit diameter of the sprue taper is ½ in. A sprue would have to be 2 to 2½ in. in diameter and 1½ to 2 in. deep to be of sufficient size so that the sump would function properly.

Bernoulli's Theorem

The sprue system should now be an adequate system, but additional information can be determined concerning its effectiveness. Bernoulli's theorem for calculating velocities in an idealized gating system helps a foundry worker predict the success of the gating system design. The theorem can be modified to take into account the energy loss that is not considered in the standard theorem; however, sufficient data have not been established

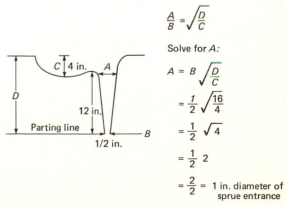

$$\frac{A}{B} = \sqrt{\frac{D}{C}}$$

Solve for A:

$$A = B \sqrt{\frac{D}{C}}$$
$$= \frac{1}{2} \sqrt{\frac{16}{4}}$$
$$= \frac{1}{2} \sqrt{4}$$
$$= \frac{1}{2} \, 2$$
$$= \frac{2}{2} = 1 \text{ in. diameter of sprue entrance}$$

Fig. 11-4. Sprue taper formula.

to make the modified theorem applicable to all gating systems. At any rate, Bernoulli's theorem can still be used as the best estimate as long as it is recognized that there may be differences between the idealized and the actual system. Bernoulli's theorem states

$$\frac{V_1^2}{2g} + \frac{P_1}{\mathbf{P}} + h_1 = \frac{V_2^2}{2g} + \frac{P_2}{\mathbf{P}} + h_2$$

where V = metal velocity, ft/s
g = acceleration due to gravity, ft/s
P = static pressure, lb/ft²
$\mathbf{P}$ = density of metal, lb/ft³
h = height of liquid, ft

Figure 11-5 demonstrates the application of this theorem with the no energy loss theorem modification. As a consequence of using this formula, it is possible to predict the sump exit velocity and flow rate for the sprue system illustrated in Fig. 11-4 with the addition of an estimate of the height of metal in the pouring basin. Point A is the estimated height of the metal during the pouring process. The distance from point A to point B is measured in feet. The velocity at A, determined by another formula called *Torricelli's theorem*, $2gh$, is equal to zero because point A does not move. The static pressure is equal to 1 atmosphere (atm) because there is no external pressure applied other than the force of gravity. The velocity of point B is the unknown. The static pressure is still equal to 1 atm, and the height of point B is the point from which vertical measurement is begun. The calculations for determining the velocity at point B are presented in Fig. 11-5b, establishing that the metal is flowing past point B at 8 ft/s.

Metal Flow Rates

The estimate of velocity resulting from the application of Bernoulli's theorem can be applied to a fluid flow equation that determines the flow rate of the metal. The equation for obtaining metal flow rates, called the *law*

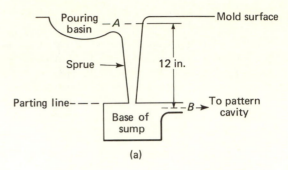

(a)

Point A	Point B
P_A = 1 atmosphere	P_B = 1 atmosphere
V_A = 0	V_B = unknown
h_A = 1 ft, or 12 in.	h_B = 0

Bernoulli's Theorem

$$\frac{V_A^2}{2g} + \frac{P_A}{\mathbf{P}} + h_A = \frac{V_B^2}{2g} + \frac{P_B}{\mathbf{P}} + h_B$$

$$\frac{V_B^2}{2g} = \frac{V_A^2}{2g} + \frac{P_A}{\mathbf{P}} + h_A - \frac{P_B}{\mathbf{P}} - h_B$$

$$= \frac{0^2}{2g} + \frac{1}{\mathbf{P}} + 1 - \frac{1}{\mathbf{P}} - 0$$

$$= 1$$

$$V_B = \sqrt{2g}$$

$$= \sqrt{2\,(32)}$$

$$= \sqrt{64}$$

$$= 8$$

Therefore the flow past point B is 8 ft/s

(b)

Fig. 11-5. Velocity determination. (a) Diagram; (b) flow calculations.

of continuity, is quantity equals area × velocity, or

$$Q = AV$$

where Q = flow rate, ft³/s
A = cross-sectional area, ft²
V = velocity, ft/s

In the preceding problem (Fig. 11-5) it was found that the velocity of the molten metal past point B was 8 ft/s. If the cross-sectional area of point B is known or can be determined, a flow rate estimate can be calculated for this gating system. Suppose the cross-sectional area of point B is 0.02 ft². It would now be possible to obtain an estimate of the flow rate in cubic feet, as follows:

$$Q = AV$$
$$= (0.02)(8) = 0.16 \text{ ft}^3/\text{s}$$

Another application of the law of continuity is in the estimation of velocities within a gating system, especially in estimating the effect on the flow rates and velocities of molten metal when the size of channels is changed. The changes in the cross-sectional areas in a channel affect the movement of the fluid metal within the channel, and these changes can be predicted (Fig. 11-6).

As illustrated in Fig. 11-6, when the flow rate is held constant, the velocity of the metal increases as the cross-sectional area of the runner decreases; and the velocity decreases when the cross-sectional area of the runner increases. This law can be used for any gating system, but it can only be applied to systems that are completely full of fluid.

The law of continuity, Bernoulli's theorem, and Torricelli's theorem are not absolute in their resolved conclusions. They are only best estimates concerning the foundry gating system, but they can be relied on for valuable predictions on the theoretical success of a gating system design. Perhaps in the near future a modification of Bernoulli's theorem that will include accurate data in the manipulation of energy loss in a gating system will be derived. For now, identifying loss in a gating system has too many variables for a general equation to be constructed. Some of the coefficients of energy loss that need to be identified and systematically evaluated include the effect of viscosity, texture of the gate walls, and angular changes in a gating system.

RUNNERS AND IN-GATES

The runners and in-gates pipe the metal from the sprue base to the mold cavity. The combination of the sprue, sprue base, runners, and in-gates completes the total pouring system of any casting.

Two main types of pouring systems that can be designed without adding external pressure to the metal stream are the pressurized system and the nonpressurized system. These systems differ in the ratios that they establish in certain cross-sectional areas within the gating structure.

Pressure Gating

The ratio used to determine the pressure classification of a gating system is based on a

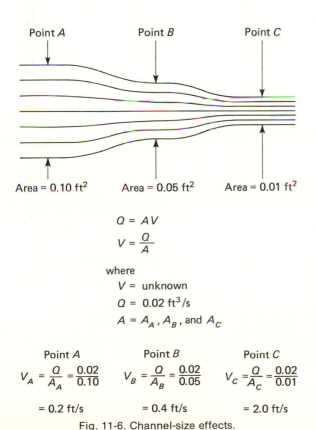

$$Q = AV$$
$$V = \frac{Q}{A}$$

where

V = unknown
Q = 0.02 ft³/s
A = A_A, A_B, and A_C

Point A
$$V_A = \frac{Q}{A_A} = \frac{0.02}{0.10}$$
$$= 0.2 \text{ ft/s}$$

Point B
$$V_B = \frac{Q}{A_B} = \frac{0.02}{0.05}$$
$$= 0.4 \text{ ft/s}$$

Point C
$$V_C = \frac{Q}{A_C} = \frac{0.02}{0.01}$$
$$= 2.0 \text{ ft/s}$$

Fig. 11-6. Channel-size effects.

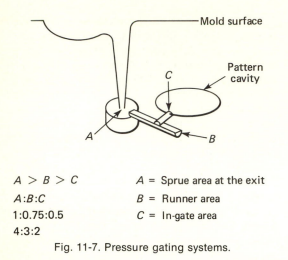

$A > B > C$ A = Sprue area at the exit

$A:B:C$ B = Runner area

1:0.75:0.5 C = In-gate area

4:3:2

Fig. 11-7. Pressure gating systems.

comparison of the cross-sectional areas of the sprue exit to the runner and to the total in-gates of a mold. In Fig. 11-7, this ratio is represented as 1:0.75:0.5. A gating system that conforms to a decreasing proportion can be identified as a pressuring gating system.

The numbers in the ratio are only unit proportions of the three cross-sectional areas under consideration; they do not represent linear quantities. For instance, the representative numbers for applying a ratio of 1:½:¼, may be 1:½:¼, 2:1:½, or even 12:6:3. In all cases the proportional distance between the various ratios are still identical, even though the numbers differ.

Pressurized gating is applied in the casting of ferrous metals, especially in the casting of grey cast iron. A disadvantage of pressure gating is the high velocity at which the metal enters the mold cavity, caused by the free flow of metal through the sprue and the runners before it is restricted finally at the in-gates of the mold cavity. This high velocity creates the high probability of mold face erosion.

No-Pressure Gating

The no-pressure gating system has the advantage of very low metal velocities. The metal just rolls lazily through the system and into the mold cavity (Fig. 11-8). The low velocity

reduces the chance of metal spurting into the mold. Because of the low turbulence and the greater use of atmospheric pressure with the no-pressure gating system, it is used with light-density metals.

No-pressure gating systems have disadvantages. It is extremely difficult to keep the sprue and runner full of metal during the pouring operation because there is no back pressure at the in-gates that allows the metal to be stored for later use. One method of gating that helps to alleviate this disadvantage is to form the runners in the drag and the in-gates in the cope section of the flask. This method dictates what part of the system will be filled with metal before the metal reaches the in-gates, thus requiring that all elements of the gating system be full before the metal enters the in-gates and the pattern cavity.

Gating System Ratios

Sprue runner in-gate ratios have been devised as a result of complex mathematical formulas and experimentation by the foundry industry. The ratios are based on a comparison of the cross-sectional area of the bottom of the sprue, the cross-sectional area of the runner, and the cross-sectional area of the total number of in-gates (Table 11-1). A typical gating system ratio for aluminum is 1:2:3. In this case, the cross-sectional area at the base of the sprue could be 1 in.^{2} and the total cross-sectional area of the in-gates could be

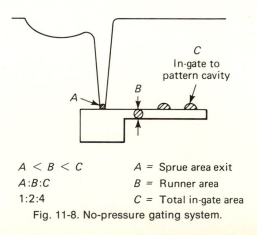

$A < B < C$ A = Sprue area exit

$A:B:C$ B = Runner area

1:2:4 C = Total in-gate area

Fig. 11-8. No-pressure gating system.

TABLE 11-1. SUGGESTED GATING SYSTEM RATIOS

METAL	RATIO
Aluminum	1:2:1, 1:2:3, 1:2:4, 2:2:1
Brass	1:1:1, 1:1:3
Ductile iron	10:9:8, 4:8:3
Grey cast iron	1:4:4
Steel	1:3:3, 1:2:2, 1:1:1

Note: A:B:C where A = sprue, B = runner, and C = in-gate.

3 in.² Again these numbers are only unit proportions. If the numbers were ⅝, 1¼, and 1⅞ in.², the ratio would still be 1:2:3.

This gating ratio controls the flow of metal at the base of the sprue, producing a no-pressure gating system. No-pressure gating is used on all light metals, and pressure gating is used on heavy metals. Pressure gating would be used on ductile iron, which has a ratio of 10:9:8 as shown in Table 11-1.

Figure 11-9 illustrates how the basic gating ratios are used in a no-pressure gating system for light metals. The base of the sprue is cross-sectional area size A. The runner is cross-sectional area size 2A, and the total area of the in-gates is 2A. Particular attention should be paid to the reduction of the runner size after the in-gate is branched off the main runner. This reduction in size controls the

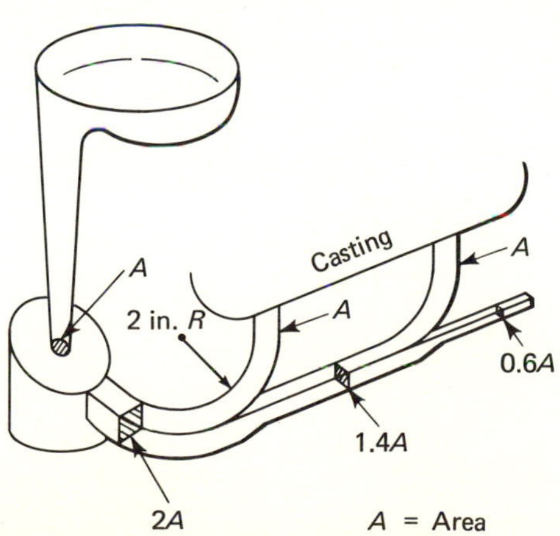

amount of metal to enter each in-gate, balancing the amount of molten metal entering the mold cavity. The runner is extended beyond the last in-gate so that some of the molten metal flowing down the runner will bypass the in-gates carrying all the impurities to the end of the runner.

Many gating types can be used that vary in design but still maintain the best gating ratios. All gates can be classified as either top gates, parting line gates, or bottom gates, depending on their location in relation to the casting (Fig. 11-10). Top gates are the easiest to mold, but they also create the most turbulence. Top gates often are used for the production of thin, flat plate. Gates located at the parting line are used the most because they, too, are easy to form. Although they do not control turbulence as well as bottom gates, they offer the advantages of speed and simplicity. The bottom gate is the least used because it is difficult to form, requiring extra skill to mold. Bottom gates many times use a core gating system, and they are capable of producing the cleanest castings.

The primary consideration in designing the pouring basin, the sprue base, the runner system, and the in-gates is the delivery of metal that is as free as possible of any impurity. If this end is to be achieved, the gating system must have the following characteristics.

1. It must be free of sharp corners or abrupt changes in cross-sectional size.
2. It must be free of all loose molding material.
3. The system must be placed at the proper location to maintain the low velocity of the metal.
4. The gating system must ensure that an appropriate amount of metal is received in the mold cavity.
5. It must control the distribution of metal through the in-gates, as well as control aspiration tendencies of the metal.
6. It must ensure adequate feeding of the metal during solidification.

Ceramic gating components are a means of presenting a smooth, friction-free gating

Fig. 11-9. 1:2:2 gating system.

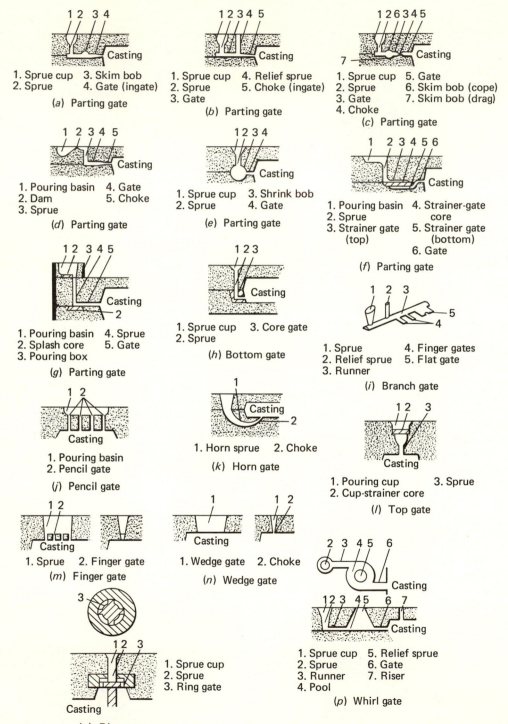

Fig. 11-10. Gating types. (*From D. C. Ekey and W. P. Winters, "Introduction to Foundry Technology," McGraw-Hill, New York, 1958.*)

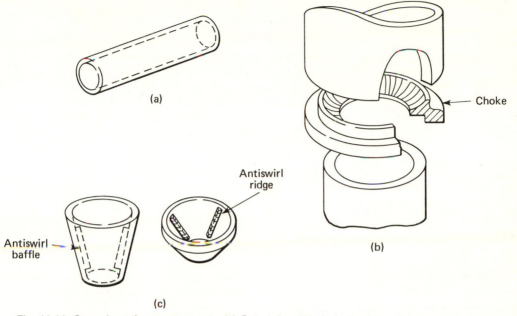

Fig. 11-11. Ceramic gating components. (a) Gate tubes (b) choke bushing; (c) pouring basin.

system to a mold cavity. These components are commercially available and have proved to be of great value to the foundry industry in the construction of gating systems (Fig. 11-11).

RISERS

A riser is used to feed metal to the casting as it solidifies. It ensures that there is the necessary amount of metal to complete a good casting. Risers should be the last portion of the casting that solidifies, enabling them to control, to some extent, the directional solidification of the metal. Risers are often incorporated directly into both the pressure and no-pressure gating systems.

The major shapes used in making risers include the cylindrical shape with a positive taper, the cylindrical shape with a reverse taper, and the straight and bulbous shapes (Fig. 11-12). Rectangular risers are also used, but this shape has some major drawbacks because it has less volume than cylindrical or conic shapes. The four important variables in the selection of a riser are shape, location, size, and type of connection to the casting. The shape of a riser determines its surface area relative to its volume. This relationship in turn determines the rate of heat transfer from the metal in the riser to the molding media.

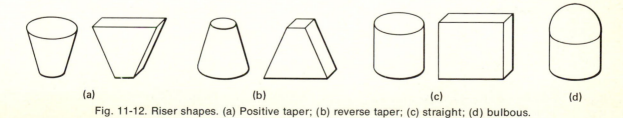

Fig. 11-12. Riser shapes. (a) Positive taper; (b) reverse taper; (c) straight; (d) bulbous.

N. Chvorinov has derived a mathematical model that approximates the time it takes for the solidification of the metal in a riser as compared to the volume and the area of the riser. The formula (an oversimplified formula) is that the solidification time T is approximately equal to the volume squared, V^2, divided by the square area of the riser, A^2

$$T = \frac{V^2}{A^2}$$

This theorem determines the ideal shape of the riser because geometrically a sphere has the best ratio of volume to area. The next most advantageous geometric shape is the cylinder; therefore, most risers are a combination of cylindrical and spherical shapes. Most blind risers are excellent examples of this combination (Fig. 11-13e and g).

The major types of risers are: top risers, side risers, lip risers, cored-gate risers, blind risers, insulated risers, blind risers with permeable cores, and risers with exothermic compounds. Exothermic compounds are those compounds that release heat or are used to generate extra heat at the top of the riser. This heat helps to control directional solidification. Most exothermic compounds are a mixture of aluminum, iron, and oxygen.

A rule of thumb for deciding on the proportion for a riser is that a riser should be 15 to 20 percent larger in diameter than the section it is going to feed, and its height should be approximately 1 to 1½ times the diameter.

Risers should be located so that they feed the heaviest section of the casting. More than one casting cavity in the mold can be fed by one riser. When this is the case, the castings should be located very close to the riser and in a circular pattern. Using multiple castings has advantages. The heat produced with multiple castings transfers to the molding media and helps to control directional solidification and helps to reduce heat loss in the riser, promoting good castings.

Surface-to-volume ratios of the riser relate directly to the surface-to-area-to-volume ratios of a casting. However, each ratio completely depends on the molding media, the type of metal being used, and the pouring temperature of the metal. Because figuring out the numerous surface-to-area-to-volume ratios is so complicated, these calculations have been done for only specific cases by particular companies. The cost prohibits figuring out these curves for all materials. Generally, the channel that connects the riser to the casting should always be large enough to ensure that it will not freeze before either the metal in the casting or the metal in the riser. If the connection of the riser freezes up, the riser then becomes useless; therefore, this connection should be large enough to maintain fluidity until the riser freezes.

Whenever possible a blind riser should be used. It is adaptable to automatic molding processes and can be used on gating systems

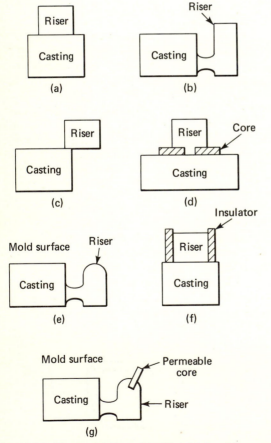

Fig. 11-13. Risers. (a) Top; (b) side; (c) lip; (d) cored gate; (e) blind; (f) insulator; (g) permeable core/blind.

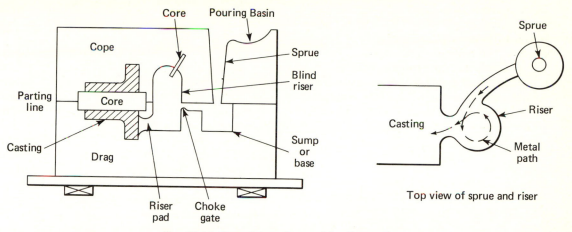

Fig. 11-14. Complete gating and feeding system.

and match plates. Blind risers can be smaller than a riser that opens to the mold surface because the molding material acts as an insulator. Blind risers also control directional solidification more than risers that go to the surface of the mold.

An adequate, efficient gating and feeding system (Fig. 11-14) begins in the formation of the pouring basin, which allows the metal to slide over the dam portion and down the tapered sprue with a control on the aspiration of the metal. As the metal falls down the sprue, it collects debris from the walls of the sprue. This debris is dumped into the sump or the sprue base. Often at the connection of the sprue base, a strainer is placed at the break line, further removing impurities and controlling the velocity of the molten metal. As the molten metal fills the sump base, clean, nonaspirated metal flows through the runner, through the choke gate (which is another control plane as is the bottom of the sprue), and into the cavity formed by the blind riser. The metal then flows to the pattern cavity. As the whole gating system fills, the pressure of the sprue helps to fill completely the blind riser, which is vented by a pencil or a Williams core. The riser, in turn, ensures the proper directional solidification of the casting.

Another means of controlling directional solidification when risers cannot be used is to place in the mold cavity pieces of metal which will act as nucleation centers in the solidification process. These artificial nucleation centers are called *chills*. Chills should only be used as a last resort for several reasons. Chills may not fuse with the casting, and they are more difficult to clean up. Chills may alter mechanical properties of metal in the casting; and often they have a tendency to shed, which can ruin a casting (Fig. 11-15).

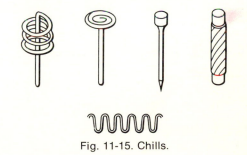

Fig. 11-15. Chills.

QUESTIONS

1. What are the basic components of a gating system?
2. Why should the sprue be tapered?

3. What is aspiration?
4. Explain the function of the sprue base.
5. Explain the law of continuity.
6. Why is velocity control important?
7. Explain the gating system 1:¾:½.
8. Where is the no-pressure gating system controlled? Why?
9. What is a riser and what is its function?
10. What is the best shape for a riser? Why?
11. What are the characteristics that ensure adequate gating systems?

12

Melting and Fluxing

The soundness of a casting depends on many variables related to the phenomena of metal melting. Of major importance is knowing the melting point, in Celsius or Fahrenheit, and the boiling point of metals. The melting point, or fusing point, of a metal is the temperature at which the solid metal becomes a liquid metal. Standard crucible furnaces are usually capable of producing approximately 3000°F. Obviously, metals must be put into furnaces that are capable of generating the heat necessary to bring the metal to its melting point. Care must always be taken that metals with a low boiling point, like aluminum, are not allowed to boil, because boiling increases the impurities within the melt. The melting point of pure aluminum is 1220°F. Usually, aluminum is poured at approximately 1250°F. In permanent molds, in sections of permanent molds, and in some types of plaster molding, the pouring temperature of aluminum will range from 1250 to 1550°F.

Another important consideration, the *latent*, or *hidden*, *heat of fusion* is the difference in the potential energy between the solid metal and the liquid metal. For example, the energy content in a metal in its solid state is lower than the energy content in its liquid state. Even though a constant temperature is maintained, when a metal reaches the melting point, additional heat must be added before the melting will continue. This additional heat is called the latent heat of fusion. The additional heat overcomes the basic bonding forces that hold the atoms in their space lattice system. The latent heat of fusion of ice is about 80 calories (cal) but the latent heat of fusion of iron is only 47.9 cal. It is easier to melt iron than it is to melt ice after the melting point of the two elements have been reached.

The latent heat of fusion is generally indicated by the gram calorie. One gram calorie is equal to a heat increase of 1°C in 1 g of water. This specific heat of water has a numerical value of 1; the specific heat of aluminum is 0.2096 (Table 12-1).

TEMPERATURE MEASUREMENT

Since the melting point of metals has such significance, a means of determining the temperature of the melt is extremely important. The instrument used for checking high temperatures is the pyrometer. Three types of pyrometers are used to test the temperature of metals: the immersion thermocouple pyrometer, the optical pyrometer, and the radiation pyrometer.

TABLE 12-1. MELTING POINT AND OTHER PROPERTIES OF METALS

ELEMENT	SYMBOL	ATOMIC WEIGHT	MELTING POINT, °C	MELTING POINT, °F	BOILING POINT, °C	LATENT HEAT OF FUSION, cal/(g)	SPECIFIC HEAT, cal/(g)(°C)
Aluminum	Al	26.97	660	1220	2450	94.5	0.215
Antimony	Sb	121.76	630	1166	1380	38.3	0.0495
Arsenic	As	74.93	Volatilizes	n.a.	Sublimes 450	88.5	0.076
Barium	Ba	137.37	704	1300	1000 appr.	n.a.	0.068
Beryllium	Be	9.02	1277	2331	2770	260	0.45
Bismuth	Bi	209.0	271	520	1560	12.5	0.029
Cadmium	Cd	112.41	321	610	765	13.2	0.0547
Calcium	Ca	40.08	838	1540	1440	52	0.145
Carbon	C	12.005	3727	6741	4830	n.a.	0.168
Cerium	Ce	140.13	804	1480	3470	n.a.	0.0447
Chromium	Cr	52.01	1875	3407	2665	96	0.104
Cobalt	Co	58.94	1495	2723	2900	58.4	0.099
Copper	Cu	63.57	1083	1982	2595	50.6	0.092
Galium	Ga	69.74	29.8	86	2237	19.16	0.079
Gold	Au	197.2	1063	1946	1946	16.1	0.0316
Indium	In	114.8	156	313	2000	6.8	0.057
Iridium	Ir	193.1	2454	4449	5300	n.a.	0.0323
Iron	Fe	55.84	1536	2797	3000	59.1	0.11
Lead	Pb	207.22	327	621	1725	6.26	0.0302
Lithium	Li	6.94	180.5	357	1330	104.2	0.79
Magnesium	Mg	24.32	650	1202	1107	88	0.246
Manganese	Mn	54.93	1245	2273	2150	63.7	0.115
Mercury	Hg	200.61	n.a.	n.a.	n.a.	2.8	0.0333
Molybdenum	Mo	96.0	2610	4730	5560	69.8	0.0659
Nickel	Ni	58.69	1453	2647	2730	73.8	0.103
Niobium	Nb	92.91	2468	4927	4927	69	0.065
Osmium	Os	190.9	2700	4892	5500	n.a.	0.0311
Palladium	Pd	106.7	1552	2826	3980	34.2	0.0592
Phosphorus	P	31.04	44.1	112	279	5.0	0.177
Platinum	Pt	195.23	1774	3225	4530	27.0	0.032
Potassium	K	39.10	63.6	147	758	16.0	0.177
Rhodium	Rh	102.91	1966	3571	4500	n.a.	0.058
Silicon	Si	28.3	1410	2570	2680	432	0.162
Silver	Ag	107.88	960.8	1761	2210	25	0.0556
Sodium	Na	22.997	97.6	208	877	27.5	0.295
Strontium	Sr	87.63	768	1414	1380	25	0.176
Sulphur	S	32.0	119	237	444.6	9.3	0.175
Tantalum	Ta	180.89	2996	5425	5425	38	0.034
Tellurium	Te	127.6	450	842	990	32	0.047
Thalium	Tl	204	302	576	1457	5.0	0.031
Tin	Sn	118.7	232	450	2270	14.6	0.0536
Titanium	Ti	47.9	1668	3034	3260	104	0.122
Tungsten	W	184.0	3410	6170	5930	44	0.034
Uranium	U	238.2	1132	2070	3818	n.a.	0.028
Vanadium	V	50.95	1900	3452	3400	80.0	0.119
Zinc	Zn	65.38	419.4	787	906	24.1	0.0918
Zirconium	Zr	90.6	1852	3366	3580	60	0.067

SOURCE: Foseco, Inc.
n.a. = not available

Immersion Thermocouple Pyrometer

In 1820, T. J. Seebeck found that if two different metals, such as copper and iron, are joined together to form a closed loop and if one junction is kept at a different temperature from the other, electric current will flow in the loop. This effect is known as the *thermoelectric effect*, or the *Seebeck effect*. The differences between the cold junction and the hot junction are registered on a millivoltmeter. A new scale which correlates directly with temperature is then placed on the millivoltmeter so that instead of a millivolt reading being taken by the meter, a temperature (either in Celsius or Fahrenheit) can be taken. Immersion-type thermocouple pyrometers generally are limited for use under 2500°F. At any temperature above this temperature the thermocouple ends start to disintegrate (Figs. 12-1 and 12-2).

Optical Pyrometer

The optical pyrometer is based on blackbody principles of emission. Blackbodies, for practical purposes, are nonreflecting materials (such as oxide coatings) that emit almost 100 percent of their radiant energy. Reflecting surfaces (such as molten metals) emit only a portion of their radiant energy; therefore, emissivity of a blackbody ranges from 1.0 down, where 1.0 is maximum radiation, or

Fig. 12-2. Immersion pyrometer. (*Pyrometer Instrument Company*.)

maximum release of radiant energy. Any material that is not a blackbody material must have an emissivity of less than 1. This relationship between blackbody and emissivity is generally stated as the ratio of radiant energy released by a heated mass to radiant energy emitted by a true blackbody. Temperature tests with optical pyrometers are based on the relationship between the emissivity of a perfect blackbody and the emissivity of the radiated heat.

There are three types of optical pyrometers: constant filament and disappearing filament (Figs. 12-3*a* and *b*), and also radiation. Temperature measurement with either the constant filament or the disappearing filament type is done the same way. The first step is to adjust the objective lens to the sharpest focus possible. Step two is to adjust either the movable optical wedge by the use of an external adjustment on the instrument or to adjust the variable filament by adjusting the rheostat knob on the disappearing filament. With either type, a test spot should be noted prior to adjustment. After the objective lens is focused, the contact which lights the

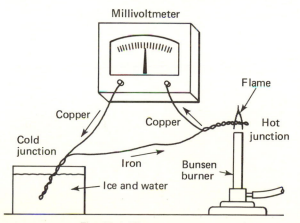

Fig. 12-1. Thermocouple.

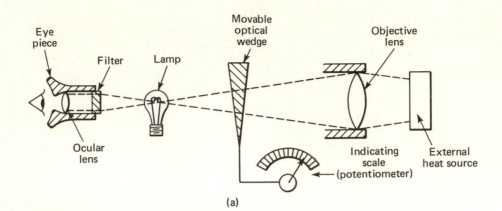

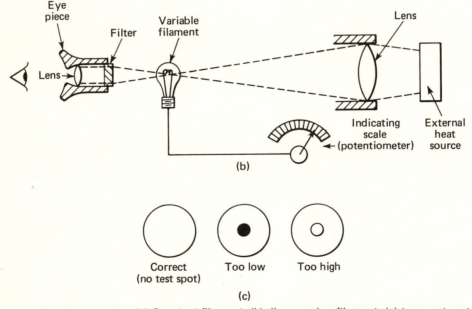

Fig. 12-3. Optical pyrometer. (*a*) Constant filament; (*b*) disappearing filament; (*c*) temperature test spot.

lamp is depressed and a temperature test spot will appear (Fig. 12-3*c*). Then, it is a matter of turning either the rheostat control or the variable optical wedge until the test spot disappears from view. A test spot that appears black will indicate too low a temperature setting of the rheostat or wedge. A test spot that resembles a hollow circle will indicate too high a setting. A correct setting is indicated when there is no visible spot opening.

Figure 12-4 shows an optical pyrometer with special scale for iron and steel.

Optical pyrometers are designed for use with temperatures above 1000°F. All optical pyrometers, whether constant filament, disappearing filament, or radiation, operate on the principle that the light source is a monochromatic light and that it is only of the red wavelength. The color red is used in optical pyrometers because red is the first color normally associated with increase in temperatures. Red is also the color that a color blind person can see, thus, anyone is capable of taking optical pyrometer temperature mea-

Fig. 12-4. Optical pyrometer for testing the temperature of iron and steel. (*Pyrometer Instrument Company*.)

surements. Another important factor is that red radiation is extremely sensitive to changes in temperature. In fact, the red radiation at 2500°F changes 12 times as rapidly as the increase or decrease in the emitted temperature. This ratio of 12:1 ensures the accuracy of optical pyrometers.

Radiation Pyrometers

The radiation pyrometer does not differ from the optical pyrometer in its principle of operation. Its operation is based on the theory that the heated object emits both heat

Fig. 12-5. Radiation pyrometer. (*Pyrometer Instrument Company*.)

and light waves and that this energy can be measured against a known blackbody standard (Fig. 12-5).

The radiation pyrometer is operated by merely pointing it toward the source to be measured and depressing the button that activates the power source. The distance from the heat source to the objective lens of the radiation pyrometer is important because radiation pyrometers usually have fixed focal lengths. The optimum distance from the objective lens to the heat source is 15 times the opening of the heat source. The radiated energy is collected by the objective lens. It passes through a red filter and strikes on a vacuum-enclosed thermocouple. The thermocouple is attached to a millivoltmeter (potentiometer) with a direct temperature indicated scale. The read-out is completely automatic (Fig. 12-6).

Radiation pyrometers are used to measure temperatures in muffle furnaces, annealing kilns, and other types of blackbody furnaces. They are used to determine the temperature of such materials as carbon, iron, and steel. When measuring with radiation and optical pyrometers, care must be taken to ensure that the view through the pyrometer is not obscured by smoke or fumes because any such interference will change the temperature readings. Again, as with the other two types of optical pyrometers, if metals other than iron or steel are measured, a conversion table must be consulted before an accurate temperature can be measured, because radiation pyrometers are set at 0.4 emissivity ratio.

FOUNDRY FURNACES

A furnace is a device capable of producing a controlled heat varying from hundreds to thousands of degrees Fahrenheit. This controlled heat is applied directly to the melting of metals. There are over 600 different designs, types, and sizes of furnaces. A furnace can be as simple as a hole in the ground or as complex as a tower over 40 ft tall. It may

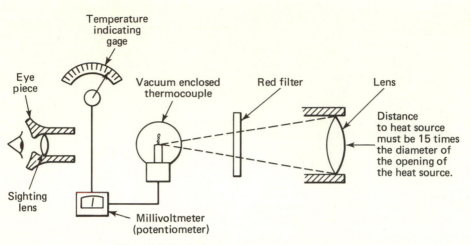

Fig. 12-6. Radiation pyrometer—fixed focus.

have a melting capability that ranges from a few ounces to hundreds of tons of melt at one time.

Furnaces, although they may differ in shape and size, have certain common features. Any foundry furnace must have a source of power to provide the necessary heat, a container to hold the metal to be melted, and a means of removing the molten metal after the melting is completed.

Fundamental to furnace construction is the use of materials that complement the functions of the furnace and thereby contribute to the quality of the finished cast product. The interior of the furnace is subjected to the severe eroding action of the high-temperature air movement and to corrosive reaction with the metals and fluxes that are added to the charge. The interior of the furnace must be constructed with a refractory material that is heat resistant and relatively nonfusible. The exterior of the furnace may be constructed of materials commonly used in industry such as iron plate or steel plate. The refractory materials have three chemical makeups: acid-based, basic, or neutral-based refractory materials. Acid refractories combine readily with oxides and consist of silica. The basic refractories possess no silica and consist mainly of metallic salts. The neutral refractories are composed of materials that are resistant to the combination of either acid or basic elements.

The type of refractory material used to line the furnace determines to a great extent the type of material produced, especially with ferrous materials. In ferrous-metal-producing furnaces portions of the lining are absorbed into the melt and change the chemical composition to produce either a basic ferrous metal (as in the basic oxygen process) or an acid ferrous metal.

The most common fuels used as power sources for foundry furnaces are oil, gas, coal, and electricity. As these fuel sources provide the heat source, the heat is transferred to the metal by means of conduction, convection, and radiation by either indirect or direct application of a flame to the metal.

The source of heat is a major factor to be considered when selecting a foundry furnace. In most industrial areas of the country, gas rates are relatively low compared to electric rates. But if the induction-type furnace is compared to the electric furnace which has advantages such as cooler working conditions, no fuel exhaust products, uniform alloy composition, uniform alloy temperature in the holding bath, electromagnetic fluxing, the lack of sludge problems, and longer refractory life, then the electric furnace becomes more competitive with the furnace that uses carbon fuels. Also, the electric furnaces do not have the same pollution problems as the furnaces using oil, gas, or coal.

Crucible Furnace

Crucible furnaces are capable of casting a maximum of approximately 2 tons of metal. When larger castings are required, the contents of more than one crucible must be poured into a common ladle or more than one crucible must be used to pour the casting.

While crucible furnaces have been made obsolete for large-scale industrial purposes by furnaces of different, more modern design, they still are used in many small foundries in industry and in schools. The construction of all crucible furnaces, regardless of their size, exhibits similar characteristics. A gas-fired crucible furnace, for example, is constructed with a steel outer shell and lined with a refractory material. The refractory material is usually silicon carbide preburned firebrick. Silicon carbide is used as a refractory material because it resists heat shock, abrasion, and erosion. It also has a heat transferability that makes it the best material available for the lining of the crucible furnace.

The fuel and air mixture generally is introduced into the furnace at an angle tangent to the inside diameter of the furnace. This angle causes the flame to rise from the bottom of the furnace, swirl around the base blocks, and create a cone of hot gases as the flames travel up around the crucible and out the top of the furnace. Crucibles should have refractory lids with an exhaust opening to expedite the escape of the hot gases. This opening usually ranges from 6 to 8 in. in diameter. The lids generally are hinged so that they can be swung out of the way for easy removal of the crucible. The vent in the lid of the crucible furnace is designed only for the escape of hot gases and is not really designed as a hole through which to charge the crucible. Metal is placed in the crucible by swinging the lid out and putting the metal directly in the crucible. In order to put metal into the crucible by means of the vent, the solid metal must be dropped into the crucible. Dropping metal into the crucible greatly shortens the life of the crucible and can be hazardous.

The round base, or pedestal block, is a key element in the proper functioning of the furnace. The diameter of the block must be the same as that of the crucible base in order to provide proper support. The block should raise the crucible so that a distance of 2 or 3 in. separates the bottom of the crucible from the bottom of the furnace and so that the crucible top is within 2 or 3 in. of the lid. In fact, from 2 to 3 in. is the ideal distance between the crucible and the walls, base, and top of the furnace. This distance ensures correct draft and proper combustion.

Fuel is generally natural gas, and it flows directly from the line source into the furnace. For proper combustion, air is forced into the furnace with the fuel. The air is supplied by small blowers with an operating pressure of only 16 oz but with a large cubic feet per minute airflow.

The furnace atmosphere, by commonly accepted descriptions, is classified as neutral, oxidizing, or reducing. The neutral atmosphere results from complete combustion of the fuel. It has an oxygen residue of approxi-

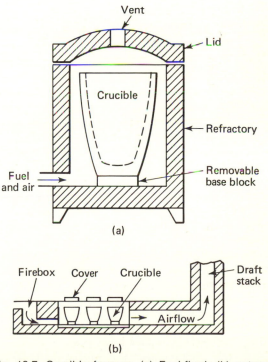

Fig. 12-7. Crucible furnace. (a) Fuel-fired; (b) natural draft.

mately ½ to 1 percent. This condition rarely exists in a fuel-fired, forced-air melting furnace. The reducing atmosphere occurs quite often. It indicates the presence of an excess of carbon monoxide. This condition results from a blower that is too small or an incorrect flow of air in comparison to the amount of fuel. The overabundance of carbon monoxide causes gas porosity in copper and aluminum if the molten metal is exposed to the reducing atmosphere for any length of time. The neutral atmosphere is the ideal atmosphere for foundry furnaces. A simple test to determine the atmospheric conditions of the furnace is the zinc test. A piece of zinc can be held over the molten metal for about 10 s. If the zinc turns black, a reducing atmosphere is present. If it turns grey, a slightly oxidizing atmosphere is indicated; if there is no change in the color, a neutral atmosphere is present.

A crucible furnace has provided small shops with a quick and economical method of melting nonferrous metal. A furnace will last years if properly handled and protected from strong alkali fluxes, the biggest enemy of crucible furnaces (Fig. 12-7).

Open-Hearth Furnace

The open-hearth furnace is a regenerative and reverberatory direct-flame furnace that ranges in capacity up to 350 tons of metal (Fig. 12-8). Depending on the lining of the furnace, the ferrous material produced may be either acid or basic. The type of ferrous material melted depends on the chemical composition of the insulating material of the furnace. The flame in the open-hearth furnace is directed onto the metal which is held in a hearth-shaped device encased in an inverted arch. The fuel and preheated air are introduced at one end of the oblong furnace, directed at the metal, and exhausted through the other end of the furnace. Open-hearth furnaces are used to heat large batches of metal and are designed primarily for large tonnages of metal to be melted at one time.

The open-hearth furnace operates on the principle of a baffle which reverses the direction of the airflow and the fuel nozzle flow approximately every 15 min. A simplified

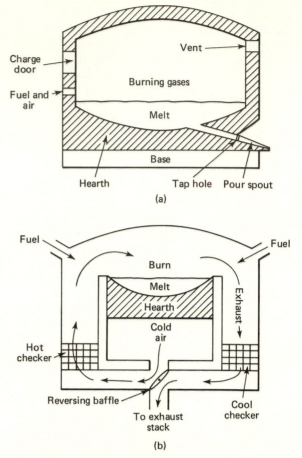

Fig. 12-8. Open-hearth furnace. (a) Components; (b) operating principle.

version of the operating principle is viewed in Fig. 12-8b.

The cold air is introduced into the ductwork. It goes through a device called a *checker*, which is a heat-retaining device. The checker has been preheated so that when the cold air goes through the hot checker, the air is preheated and prepared for ignition. The fuel is injected into the hot air, and when the fuel and hot air mixture strikes the slag that is covering the molten metal, the fuel ignites and burns. As more fuel and hot air are pumped in, the hot burnt gases resulting from the ignition of the fuel and hot air are forced over the cool checker, preheating the cool checker. The burning process is fully reversed when the hot checker starts to cool and the cool checker has reached a hot enough temperature. The airflow is then reversed by the reversing baffle, forcing the cool air up over the new hot checker. The fuel flow will be shut off on the original side and resumed on the opposite side.

As the insulation of the arch above the hearth and the hearth itself heat because of the combustion of the fuel and because of the melting of the metal, the lining also heats. As the lining becomes hotter, the heat reverberates and helps to melt the metal so that the metal is melted both by the ignition of the fuel and by the reverberatory process. The common vat melt length time for the open-hearth furnace ranges from approximately 5 to 8 h.

The rotary furnace is an adaptation of both the crucible furnace and the open-hearth furnace, because it combines principles from both of these furnaces (Fig. 12-9).

Cupola Furnace

The cupola uses a direct flame to melt metal through conduction, convection, and radiation. The basic component of a cupola is a steel pipe that may range from 20 to 40 ft high and from 10 to 50 in. in diameter. This pipe is lined with a refractory material and has hinged insulated doors at the bottom. Forced air is introduced by some means at the bottom of the pipe. A cupola furnace is very easy to operate, melts metal faster than many other types of foundry furnaces, is economical to maintain, and has a low operating cost.

Once the melting process is begun, the furnace supplies a continuous melt; that is, as the fuel, coke, limestone, and cast iron are melted and sink toward the slag spout and the tap spout, more layers of coke, limestone, and cast iron are placed in the charging door, creating a continuous supply of molten cast iron (Fig. 12-10). Inside diameters of the furnace vary, ranging from 6 in. for experimental furnaces up to 85 in. for production cupolas. For example, a small cupola with a 12-in. inside diameter is capable of producing approximately 1 ton/h of molten metal while large cupolas can produce up to 35 tons/h of molten cast iron.

The approximate melting rate for the cupola can be determined by estimating the inside diameter of the firebrick in square inches. Cupolas can melt approximately 10 lb of cast iron per square inch per hour.

The amount of material fed through the charging door determines the purity of the cast iron, the time needed to melt it, and its chemical composition. Typically, the flux layer will consist of limestone, fluorspar, or soda ash, and the total weight of the flux will be approximately one-fifth the weight of the coke charge. The most commonly used iron/coke ratio is 8:1.

The furnace is originally charged by ramming a bed of coarse silica sand on the bottom doors. Then, a thick layer of coke is

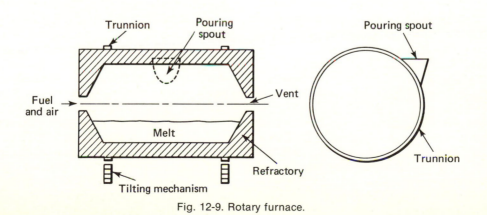

Fig. 12-9. Rotary furnace.

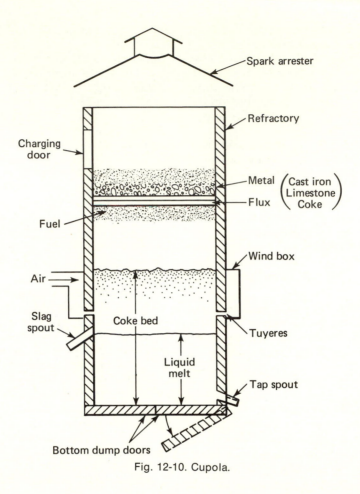

Fig. 12-10. Cupola.

placed in the furnace to above the tuyeres, or the air openings, in the furnace. Next, a layer of fuel is placed, then a layer of flux, and then a layer of metal. These three components are continuously built into the furnace following the order of fuel, flux, and metal. The furnace is then ignited and placed in operation.

The Converter Furnace

The converter furnace is a direct adaptation of the Bessemer furnace. Sir Henry Bessemer conducted his experiments in a crucible that was heated externally by a coke fire. The fire maintained the heat in the iron during a blowing operation, but this heat was found to be unnecessary. It was discovered that the heat increases as it is evolved within the iron through the oxidation of the impurities. In fact, so much heat is evolved that the temperature of the metal actually rises from approximately 1300 to 1600°C during the melting process. The Bessemer process has now been replaced by the open-hearth, the electric-arc, and the basic oxygen processes. The basic oxygen process (BOP) is a further refinement of the Bessemer process, introducing a blast of oxygen through the vent into the melt.

Converters based on the Bessemer furnace operation are not true melting devices, but are used to convert iron to steel by the action of a blast of air either over the surface or through the charge. The converter furnace

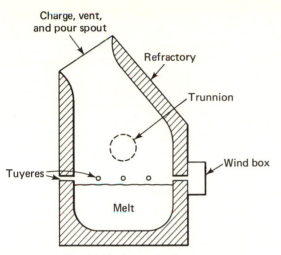

Fig. 12-11. Converter furnace

produces an oxidation reaction that exothermically promotes a superheated steel. This steel is often further refined in the electric-arc, the electric, or the open-hearth furnaces (Fig. 12-11).

Resistance Furnaces

Resistance furnaces consist of a power supply, resistors, insulators to support the resistors, an outer shell, and a refractory lining. The direct resistance furnace is used for a few special melting processes. It uses the material to be melted as a resistor. Current flow is established through the material from electrodes at each end of the material.

A more popular resistance furnace is the indirect resistance furnace that is designed with the resistor, or the heating elements, on the inside of the refractory lining. The resistors produce heat when the current flow passes through them. The furnace generates heat in the same manner as the common toaster that toasts bread for breakfast, except that a higher heat is generated. The material or metal to be melted is heated primarily through radiation and convection since the charge rarely contacts the heating elements. The two furnaces that are used most are the indirect resistance furnace (Fig. 12-12a) and the rod-resistor furnace (Fig. 12-12b).

Arc Furnaces

Electric-arc furnaces offer the advantages of high thermal efficiency, rapid heating, close temperature control, and strict atmospheric control. All of these features are desirable in the production of commercial-quality metals. Direct-arc furnaces derive their heat from the electric arc between electrodes and the material to be melted (Fig. 12-13a). The electrodes may be made out of carbon or graphite, making them nonconsumable electrodes; or they can be consumable electrodes comprised of steel rods with carbon cores.

Indirect-arc furnaces are normally horizontally mounted cylinders which can be ro-

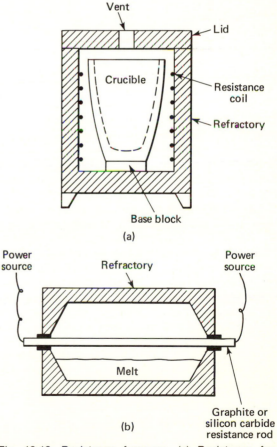

Fig. 12-12. Resistance furnaces. (a) Resistance furnance; (b) rod-resistor furnace.

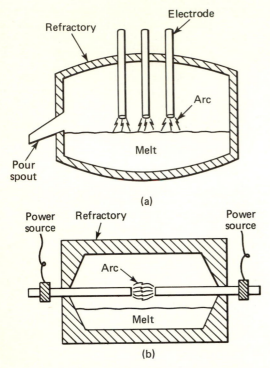

Fig. 12-13. Arc furnace. (a) Direct-arc furnace; (b) indirect-arc furnace.

tated through an arc of 180°. The carbon electrodes or the steel-tubed carbon electrodes are mounted along the horizontal axis of the furnace and automatically adjusted to maintain the correct distance for the proper arc column (Fig. 12-13b). In the indirect-arc furnace, the arc never touches the metal. Rather, the metal is melted by radiation from the heat produced by the arc and by conduction from the heat absorbed by the refractory lining. As the furnace is rotated, the refractory lining is heated and rotated back and forth, exposing the melt to a larger area of the heated lining. As in all ferrous melting furnaces, the basic or acid composition of the liner determines the type of ferrous material produced.

Induction Furnaces

Induction furnaces, using alternating current, create heat through hysteresis and eddy-current activity in a magnetic material. The heat is generated by the friction of the molecules in the metal as they try to align themselves with the ever-changing induced magnetic field. The molecules try to go in the direction of the magnetic field. When the magnetic field is changed, one molecule will try to turn, bumping into another and creating heat within the metal itself. If the fields are changed often enough and fast enough, the metal simply collapses into a molten state.

Induction furnaces originally were refractory-lined containers, like crucibles, that contained an induction coil and an iron core. The coil, called a *core*, was separated from the sides and bottom of the furnace by a

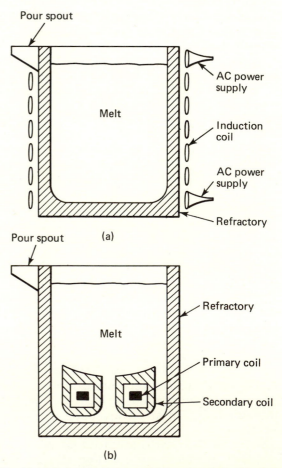

Fig. 12-14. Induction furnace. (a) Coreless induction furnace; (b) channel-induction furnace.

channel. When operating, the furnace could not function until that channel was filled with molten metal. The core or channel-induction furnaces, once placed in operation, had to be operated continuously for economic results. When the furnace was allowed to cool, the metal within the channel would solidify and destroy the furnace lining (Fig. 12-14*b*). Shutting the furnace down results in the relining of the furnace.

The channel-induction furnaces are used to melt only nonferrous metals. The advantages of induction furnaces led to the development of the coreless induction furnace (Fig. 12-14*a*). Currently, coreless induction furnaces are used to refine or melt many ferrous metals, and they are used in metallurgical research. Essentially, coreless furnaces are crucibles wrapped with a power coil which induces a magnetic field, melting the metal (Fig. 12-14*a*). Coreless furnaces can be completely emptied, shut down, cleaned, and restarted with a cold charge. Because of this, the furnace is suitable for small batch use as in the case of foundry research.

Many founders of nonferrous metals are starting to use devices that move the molten nonferrous metal from the furnace to the casting cavity by means of metal pumps.

These metal pumps generally operate on those metals that melt below 1200°F. Before pump part replacements are needed, 1 million lb of molten metal may be pushed through a pump (Fig. 12-15).

FLUXING

The goal of foundry workers is to produce ingots or cast products that are of rich quality and free from inclusions and gas porosity. The quality of the final cast product depends on the handling and melting of the metal in the production phase. The quality of the molten metal is judged by the following considerations:

1. Whether the metal meets the chemical requirements.
2. Whether the metal has the lowest possible level of dissolved or contained gases.
3. Whether the metal has a minimum number of nonmetallic inclusions.
4. Whether, metallurgically, the correct pouring temperature is used.

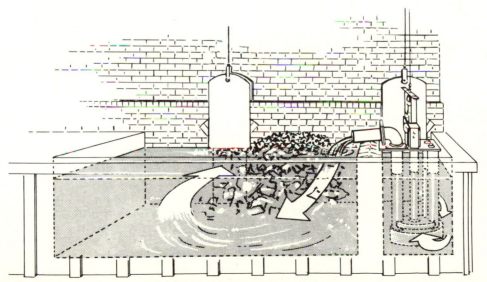

Fig. 12-15. Pumping molten metal.

All these considerations can be controlled by using the correct techniques and the proper equipment.

One of the most important controls is the flux added to the metal. Fluxes fall into five broad categories: covering, cleaning, degassing, drossing-off, and grain-refining fluxes.

Covering Fluxes

The purpose of the covering fluxes is to reduce the oxidation and to prevent contamination by atmospheric gases. The same function might be accomplished by melting a metal at the lowest temperature consistent with sufficient fluidity. However, prolonged holding of molten aluminum, for example, will cause the aluminum to pick up excessive amounts of hydrogen from the atmosphere and produce liquid hydrogen, causing porosity in the molten aluminum when it solidifies. Almost all commercial users of molten aluminum will hold a "bath" of aluminum for a considerable length of time. Commonly, mixtures of chlorides serve as sufficient covers or blankets at a reasonable cost and provide some cleansing properties as well.

Covering fluxes may be used to protect molten baths of aluminum from the atmosphere, but covering fluxes should not be used with the intention of cleaning. Most covering fluxes have no capacity for either wetting or coalescence with the nonmetallic properties that are suspended in the molten aluminum. Covering fluxes do absorb a certain amount of the metallic elements they are covering. The amount of metal lost to the covering flux depends on the melting point of the metal, the viscosity of the flux, and the temperature of the furnace or holding furnace.

Cleaning Flux

In order to rid the melt of the bath from nonmetallic impurities, cleaning flux can be added. It will produce excellent metal from contaminated, impure metal. For example, fluorides are added in order to clean aluminum. The fluoride produces a liquid flux within the molten aluminum. This flux has excellent cleaning powers because the fluoride wets the nonmetallic particles and floats them to the surface. However, all cleaning fluxes produce a dross which will float to the top of the melt and entrap not only the impurities in the dross but an amount of metal as well. Many times a cleaning flux and a drossing-off flux can be used at the same time. This dross also creates a type of covering flux that may appear the same as the product of the covering flux, but it will not give the molten metal the atmospheric protection that covering flux does.

Drossing-Off Fluxes

A drossing-off flux is used to avoid excessive metal loss. The flux must be applied before the furnace is tapped. These fluxes react with the caked, semisolid dross which forms on the melt surface and release the entrapped metal particles, reducing the semisticky, semisolid dross to a powder which is then skimmed off. Under the proper controls, drossing-off fluxes may reduce the precontent of aluminum dross from 5 to 65 percent of the metallic particles in the dross. Drossing-off fluxes work on the principle of exothermic reactions. Heat is given off when the metal-laden dross contacts the flux. Heat results because of the oxidation, or fast burning, of the metallic particles that rapidly heat, melt, and run back into the melt, producing a waste dross that is relatively low in metallic particles.

Degassing Fluxes

Degassing fluxes are added to the molten metal just prior to pouring the metal into the casting. Degassing is done by a chemical either in its solid state or in a gas state. For example, the method for degassing light metals in a crucible furnace is to turn the furnace off, wait until the temperature of the metal is decreasing, and then, with the aid of a plunger, shove the degassing pellet to the bottom of the crucible and hold it there. The degassing pellet releases a chlorine and ni-

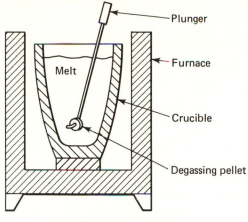

Fig. 12-16. Degassing light alloys.

TABLE 12-2. METAL/GAS COOLING REACTIONS

METAL	REACTION
Aluminum	$2H \rightarrow H_2 \uparrow$ (liquid hydrogen to hydrogen gas)
Copper	$2H \rightarrow H_2 \uparrow$
	$CO \rightarrow CO \uparrow$ (liquid carbon monoxide to carbon monoxide gas)
	$2H + O \rightarrow H_2O$ (liquid hydrogen and oxygen to water vapor)
	$C + O \rightarrow CO$ (carbon solution + oxygen to carbon monoxide)
	$CU_2 + 2O \rightarrow SO_2$ (copper sulfide + oxygen to sulfur dioxide)
Iron	$2H \rightarrow H_2 \uparrow$ (liquid hydrogen to hydrogen gas)
	$Fe + H_2O \rightarrow FeO + H_2$ (iron + water vapor to iron oxide and hydrogen gas)
	$FeO + C \rightarrow CO + Fe$ (iron and oxygen + carbon to carbon monoxide and iron)
	$2FeO + S \rightarrow 2Fe + SO_2$ (iron and oxygen + sulfur to iron + sulfur dioxide)
Nickel	$2H \rightarrow H2 \uparrow$ (liquid hydrogen to hydrogen gas)
	$2N \rightarrow N_2 \uparrow$ (liquid nitrogen to nitrogen gas)
	$C + O \rightarrow CO$ (carbon + oxygen to carbon monoxide)

Note: Arrow ($\rightarrow$) indicates a gas.

trogen mixture that bubbles up through the liquid metal, removing the absorbed hydrogen. This bubbling action also helps to clean the molten light metal by bringing nonmetallic inclusions to the surface (Fig. 12-16).

Test specimens of aluminum have proved that degassing improves the soundness of a casting and produces aluminum with greater density. Controlling gas porosity is one of the major problems in the melting of metals. Studies have revealed that the gases most commonly associated with gas porosity include hydrogen, oxygen, and nitrogen, and compound gases of carbon monoxide, carbon dioxide, and sulfur dioxide. Gas porosity is responsible for the voids and pinholes that occur in a casting. The major gas that must be controlled in order to control gas porosity in aluminum or magnesium is hydrogen. The heavy metals (copper, iron, and nickel) seem to have more gas reactions during metal cooling with more complex gases released by the molten metal (Table 12-2).

Grain-Refining Fluxes

Many commercial fluxes are available for refining molten metals. The exact way in which the fluxes refine the metal is not completely understood, but most metallurgists agree that the **addition of grain-refining fluxes** serve as nuclei for crystal formation at many points rather than just a few as in the normal nucleation process. The result is a much smaller and more nearly uniform grain size with the advantages of improved mechanical properties and better appearance. For example, the addition of inoculants to grey cast iron greatly improves its mechanical and physical properties. Essentially what happens is that the inoculants redistribute the graphite in the cast iron by controlling the distribution, shape, and size of the graphite during the solidification process. This control of the graphite refines the grain and greatly affects the tensile strength and hardness of the grey cast

TABLE 12-3. COPPER-BASED FLUXING PRACTICE

METAL	TREATMENT	FLUX	EFFECT	POURING TEMPERATURE, °F BY SECTION SIZE, in.		
				0–½	½–1½	OVER 1½
Copper—high conductivity. Copper of over 99% purity can be produced with electrical conductivity in excess of 85% IACS (International Annealed Copper Standard).	Melt down under a reducing cover of Cuprit 8. Deoxidize by plunging deoxidizing CB tubes (containing calcium boride) immediately before casting.	2 lb Cuprit 8 1 Deoxidizing CB 5 tube (to be plunged)	Reducing atmosphere combined with a cleansing slag, effective deoxidation without reducing conductivity properties.	2280	2190	2100
Copper—commercial. Copper containing small quantities of zinc, tin, and other impurities. To a total of about 50% IACS.	Melt down under a cover of Cuprex 100. Deoxidize by plunging twice, if necessary, deoxidizing PC tubes (containing phosphorus) immediately before casting.	1 lb Cuprex 100 3 Deoxidizing PC 4 tubes	Prevention of hydrogen pickup. Stronger deoxidation treatment than possible with HC copper.	2280	2190	2100
Tin bronze 88-10-0-2 or "G" bronze. 88-8-0-4 or modified "G" bronze. Leaded tin bronze. Steam or valve bronze (navy "M"). 80-10-10. 87-8-1-4 (navy P-c).	Melt charge on top of Cuprex blocks 14 in bottom of crucible or melt down under a cover of Cuprex 100. Deoxidize by plunging Deoxidizing PC tubes immediately before casting.	1 lb Cuprex blocks 14 or 1 lb Cuprex 100 1 Deoxidizing PC 3 tube	The modern oxidation-deoxidation technique, i.e., oxidizing and scavenging action, prevents hydrogen pickup and cleans melt, while deoxidation removes excess oxygen, oxides and improves fluidity. (Residual phosphorus 0.02–0.03%.)	2190	2120	2050
High-leaded tin bronze. Alloys containing more than 10% lead: 78-7-15, 70-5-25.	Melt down under cover of Plumbral 2. Superheat and wait 5 min before pouring, plunge further amount of Plumbral 2.	½ lb Plumbral 2 (as cover) ½ lb Plumbral 2 (to be plunged)	Pickup by hydrogen, hydro-carbons, and sulfur is curtailed. Lead and tin oxides are dissolved, which also increases metal fluidity. The final plunging operation helps to prevent lead segregation.	15% lead 1975 to 2010	20% lead 1920 to 1960	30% lead 1885 to 1925
Leaded red brass 85-5-5-5 or No. 1 composition. Commercial red brass 83-4-6-7. Valve composition 81-3-7-9.	Melt charge on top of Cuprex blocks 14 in bottom of crucible or melt down under a cover of Cuprex 100. Deoxidize by plunging Deoxidizing PC tubes immediately before casting.	1 lb Cuprex blocks 14 or 1 lb Cuprex 100 1 Deoxidizing PC tube	The modern oxidation-deoxidation technique, i.e., oxidizing and scavenging action, prevents hydrogen pickup and cleans melt, while deoxidation removes excess oxygen and oxides and improves fluidity. (Residual phosphorus 0.02–C.03%.)	2190	2120	2050
Copper-nickel alloys 12% leaded nickel silver 20% leaded nickel silver 25% leaded nickel silver	Melt down under an oxidizing cover of Cuprex 100. For pressure-tight castings, plunge regenerator 17 about 10 min before pouring. Deoxidize by plunging Deoxidizing NS tubes.	2 lb Cuprex 100 ¼ lb Regenerator 17 1 Deoxidizing NS 6 tube	Oxidizing and scavenging action prevents hydrogen pickup and cleans melt, while deoxidation removes oxygen and oxides.	Monel, 2840 12% Ni, 2350 25% Ni, 2460	Monel, 2785 12% Ni, 2325 25% Ni, 2400	Monel, 2730 12% Ni, 2325 25% Ni, 2350
Phosphor bronze. Tin up to 10%. Phosphorus 0.03–0.50%.	Melt charge down on top of Cuprex blocks 14.	1 lb Cuprex blocks 14	Oxidizing action prevents hydrogen pickup and tin "sweat" is curtailed. Deoxidizing PC tubes increase phosphorus content when necessary.	2010	1960	1900

TABLE 12-3. COPPER-BASED FLUXING PRACTICE (cont.)

METAL	TREATMENT	FLUX	EFFECT	POURING TEMPERATURE, °F BY SECTION SIZE, in.		
				0–½	½–1½	OVER 1½
Leaded yellow brass High copper yellow brass. Commercial No. 1 yellow brass. Alloys not containing aluminum.	Melt down under cover of Cuprit 49 or use Cuprit blocks 1. Finally plunge Deoxidizing PC tubes immediately before casting.	1 lb Cuprit 49 (as surface cover) or 1 lb Cuprit blocks 1 (at bottom of charge) 1 Deoxidizing PC 1 tube	Fluic cover prevents zinc loss and has a general cleansing action. Increased fluidity obtained by "deoxidation" treatment.	2010	1920	1870
Yellow brass Alloys containing small percentages of aluminum as an impurity.	Melt down under fluid cover of Albral 2 and plunge a further quantity a few minutes before pouring. If aluminum is to be removed, use Eliminal 2. In either case, finally plunge Deoxidizing PC tubes.	1 lb Albral 2 (¾ as cover, ¼ to be plunged) or 1 lb Eliminal 2 (used as above) 1 Deoxidizing PC 1 tube	Albral readily dissolves aluminum oxide and reduces its formation during melting. Eliminal removes aluminum and gives a general cleansing action. Increased fluidity obtained by "deoxidation" treatment.	2100	2010	1960
High-strength yellow brass manganese bronze Leaded manganese bronze No. 1 manganese bronze	Melt down under a fluid cover of Albral 2 and when pouring temperature is reached, plunge in further small quantity. Finally plunge Deoxidizing MB tubes.	1 lb Albral 2 (¾ as cover, ¼ to be plunged) 1 Deoxidizing MB 2 tube	Aluminum oxide dissolved and its formation reduced. Good cleansing and degassing action. "Deoxidation" treatment coalesces suspended non-metallics and improves fluidity.	1975	1905	1830
Aluminum bronze 5–15% aluminum up to 10% iron, with or without manganese or nickel	Melt down under a fluid cover of Albral 2 and when pouring temperature is reached, plunge in further small quantity. Finally plunge Deoxidizing AB tubes.	1 lb Albral 2 (¾ as cover, ¼ to be plunged) 1 Deoxidizing AB 5 tube	Aluminum oxide dissolved and its formation reduced. Good cleansing and degassing action. "Deoxidation" treatment coalesces suspended non-metallics and improves fluidity.	2280	2190	2100
Silicon bronze Silicon 1–5% Everdur	Melt down under a fluid cover of albral 2 and when pouring temperature is reached, plunge in further small quantity. Finally plunge Deoxidizing PC tubes immediately before casting.	1 lb Albral 2 (¾ as cover, ¼ to be plunged) 1 Deoxidizing PC 2 tubes	Curtails oxidation and reduces metallic oxides combined with general cleansing action. "Deoxidation" treatment coalesces suspended non-metallics and improves fluidity.	2190	2120	2050

SOURCE: Foseco Inc.

iron. Silicon is used for grain refinement in aluminum by controlling the nucleation process. Titanium, used in combination with boron, is also used for the grain refinement of aluminum. The exact amounts used of both metals vary with the chemical conditions expected of the aluminum.

Many commercially available fluxes serve more than one function. For example, a commercially available flux for aluminum may have a certain amount of covering properties, cleansing properties, and grain-refining properties, all included in the same flux so that the application is simplified. Table 12-3 identifies one manufacturer's recommended fluxing practices for copper-based metals.

QUESTIONS

1. What is the melting point of aluminum and what is its pouring temperature?
2. Explain latent heat of fusion.
3. Explain the working principle of the immersion pyrometer and the optical pyrometer.
4. Why are furnace linings important to the chemical makeup of metals?
5. What are the most common fuels used for foundry furnaces?
6. What is the function of the opening in the lid of the crucible furnace?
7. List and explain the basic fluxing categories.
8. How do the checkers work in an open-hearth furnace?
9. Explain the continuous cupola melting cycle.
10. What is the key element in crucible furnace construction? Why?

13

Sands and Binders

Sand lies in abundance all over the earth, near water, deserts, deltas, and eroded mountains. Rivers carry loads of minerals in them as they flow. Swift current can carry both coarse and fine materials; but if the current is slow, the water can transport only fine materials. When rivers enter a lake or an ocean, the velocity of the water decreases. The coarser sand is deposited first, then the medium-grain sand is deposited, and finally the finer grains are carried into quiet waters.

Silica sands were formed by sand that was deposited along coasts of ancient oceans. Where these deposits were buried under large thicknesses of later deposited sediment, the sand was transformed into sandstone. The heaving and shifting of the surface of the earth have exposed layers of sandstone in some areas, making it an easy operation to mine the sandstone and convert it into foundry sand.

Bank sands are the sands along the banks of a river, or they can be a product of disintegrated sandstone. These sands were blown by the wind and deposited in small banks. Bank sand varies in its degree of impurity, depending on the minerals with which it is mixed.

Lake sands are produced by the erosion of rocks in and along the shore that are deposited on the beach. Some of the surface sand has been shifted by the wind and is sometimes referred to as dune sand.

The American Foundry Society has classified foundry material into sizes (Table 13-1). The sand sieves used to classify sand size are called *U.S. standard sieves*. The numbers of U.S. standard sieves represent the number of openings per square inch in the sieves. For example, a no. 6 sieve would have 6 openings per square inch and a no. 200 sieve would have 200 openings per square inch. The greater the number of the standard sieve, the finer the material that can flow through it. To further identify sieves, foundry workers have arbitrarily assigned terms to sieve sizes, so that sieve sizes from 6 to 12 are called large grains, and sieve sizes from 270 to 400 are called *flour sizes*.

SAND STRUCTURES

Foundry sands are classified according to their structure. They are round, angular, subangular, and compounded (Fig. 13-1). Research with foundry sand has shown that angular sand provides a greater interlocking strength if it is properly rammed. Round-grain sands flow better, have higher grain compression strength and better venting

TABLE 13-1. FOUNDRY MATERIAL CLASSIFICATION

NAME	SIZE
Boulders	10-in. diameter or larger
Cobbles	2½- to 10-in. diameter
Gravel	5-mesh sieve to 2½ in.
Granules	10- to 5-mesh sieve
Sand	250- to 10-mesh sieve
Silt	70 microns to 250-mesh sieve

properties. The properties of subangular sand lie somewhere between round-grain and angular-grain sand. Compounded sands are not used often because of their unpredictable final properties. This unpredictability is caused by two things: the lack of control of the grain size or the combining of round, angular, and subangular grain shape.

Angular-shaped sand has superior bonding strength because of the larger surface area of the grains. If round, angular, and subangular grains of sand are passed through a 70 to 100 U.S. standard sieve to assure the same sand size for the three types of sand, and if the surface area of these three types is estimated, it can be shown that round-grain sands have a surface area of approximately 159 cm²; subangular grain, 191 cm²; and angular grain, 211 cm².

Although no standard specification for foundry sand exists, specifications for foundry sand are agreed upon between the seller of the sand and the user of the sand, the foundry worker. Each foundry sets its individual requirements, which are usually expressed by the desired sieve size, shape of the sand, and clay content.

The major sand used in foundries is silica sand (Table 13-2). Silica sand is white and has a fusion temperature of 3200°F. Its chemical activity ranges from slightly acid to acid in the major minerals. Silica sand is available in angular, subangular, or round-grain sizes.

SPECIALTY SANDS

Silica sand is used extensively by the foundry industry because it is easy to get and inexpensive. However, specialty sands are being used more in the foundry industry for several reasons. They are comprised of more complex materials; they contain mixtures of inorganic compounds; and even though they cost more, they offer better high-temperature stability than ordinary silica sand. This better stability at high temperatures produces better cast surfaces. Some of the major specialty sands used in foundries in the United States include olivine, chromite, zircon, staurolite, and aluminum silicate sands (Table 13-2). The three specialty sands used most often are olivine, chromite, and zircon. They have the widest applications for both mold making and core making. These three sands can be used as facing sands or for the total mold.

Silica sand is much less expensive than the specialty sands; in fact, the cost of olivine is usually 10 times the cost of silica sands, and chromite and zircon are twice as expensive as olivine. Specialty sands cost more because complex processing is required to change the sands from their raw mined states into a controlled molding medium. Specialty sands are sometimes imported from overseas and that adds extra costs.

MULLING

The quality of molds and castings produced in foundries greatly depends on the preparation of the sand. So, thorough mixing and mulling become one of the critical steps in the production of quality castings. Once

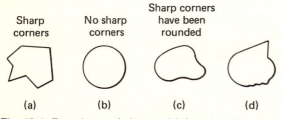

Fig. 13-1. Foundry sand shapes. (a) Angular; (b) round; (c) subangular; (d) compound.

TABLE 13-2. SANDS

SAND	COLOR	FUSION TEMPERATURE, °F	GRAIN SHAPE	CHEMICAL ACTIVITY	MAJOR MINERALS
FOUNDRY SAND					
Silica	White	3200	Round, angular, subangular	Acid	Quartz
SPECIALTY SANDS					
Aluminum silicate	Beige	3335	Round	Neutral	Kyanite, sillimanite, quartz
Chromite	Black	3450	Angular	Basic	Various spinels
Olivine	Green	3400	Angular	Basic	Olivine
Staurolite	Brown	2895	Round	Neutral	Staurolite
Zircon	Light beige	3900	Round; angular in flour grades	Acid	Zirconium silicate

foundry sand has been mixed and mulled, it is known as *green sand*. There are two varieties of green sand: (1) *facing sand*, the sand used next to the pattern cavity, and (2) *heap sand*, the sand used as backing for the facing sand. Facing sand requires more preparation and more control than heap sand. Once the casting is done, the facing sand is lost in the ingredients of the heap sand. Many foundries do not use facing sands. Instead, they mull the heap sand to a consistency sufficient for use alone.

There are many different ways to mull sand. What mulling method will be used is determined by such variables as the foundry facilities available, the type and the amount of sand required, and the amount of tempered water or oil desired. The manufacturers of mulling equipment establish a timed cycle for each piece of equipment so that the best performances can be achieved with given materials. If the timed cycle for a muller is reduced, the quality and the green strength of the sand coming through the muller are also reduced.

The process of mulling the sand differs from the mixing of the sand both in theory and in process. Mixed sand has various additives dispersed throughout it. The sand can be mixed either manually or mechanically, and this mixing can be accomplished simply with a shovel or hoe, as in the mixing of concrete. However, the mulling process gives

foundry sand the correct green strength and plasticity. These two physical properties are developed by working the sand under pressure, a process impossible to do by hand. The amount of pressure it takes to indent a rammed green sand surface is known as *green strength*. Working the sand is much like kneading bread, under pressure, and gives the sand more strength; in fact, mulled sand will have approximately 25 to 100 percent more strength than unworked sand.

Rollers are usually used to mull the sand. Often devices that prepare foundry sand are both mixers and mullers: mixing the ingredients into the foundry sand, forcing the additives to coat the separate grains of sand by rolling wheels over the sand, and applying pressure to the sand at the same time. The rotational speed of mullers usually ranges from 40 to 50 revolutions per minute (r/min). If the r/min of the pressure wheel is faster than this, the temperature of the sand being mulled will increase, possibly destroying some of the desired properties achieved by the mixing-mulling process.

Types of Mullers

Some of the major types of mullers in the foundry industry are the mix muller, the pan mix muller, the horizontal wheel mullers, the paddle mixers, and the belt mixers.

The *mix muller* is used most with clay-bonded foundry sands and also for mulling clays for the ceramic industry. The typical mix muller has two or more wheels that rotate in the bottom of the tank. The sand is mulled between the bottom of the wheels and the bottom of the tank, and then the sand is forced out from under the muller wheels under extremely high pressure. The *pan mix muller* is similar to the standard mixer muller, except that it has been adapted for use with bentonite-bonded sands (Fig. 13-2).

A new type of muller is the *horizontal wheel muller.* It differs from the other types in that the sand is mulled on the sides of the tank instead of on the bottom. Centrifugal force throws the sand against the wall and the wheels then run over the sand, applying pressure to the sand in the mulling process. Plow sweeps help to sweep the sand into the path of the wheels on the sides of the tank. Horizontal wheel mullers run at much higher speeds than do vertical mix mullers. They also cool sand much more effectively because the sand is lifted into the air. Sometimes horizontal wheel mullers have air inlets that force air up through the sand as it is being mulled.

Paddle mixers do mixing mostly and very little mulling so that the green sand developed with paddle mixers has only a portion of the green strength of bentonite sand mixtures coming from standard mullers. Paddle mixers are used to aerate and mix sand and are usually used in conjunction with a mulling system. *Belt mixers* are efficient, compact units that mix, mull, and aerate in alternate processes, and they have large sand preparation capacity. Because of their speed and their varied functions, the number of installations of belt mixers has increased in existing systems.

All of these mulling systems have one main purpose: to develop the correct green properties in the molding sand. The mulling cycle must allow sufficient time to accomplish this purpose without over- or undermulling. Many overmulled sand mixtures lose both their permeability and their green strength.

In the total sand cycling system, the returning sand must undergo proper rebonding and retempering. Controlling the preparation of completely new molding sand is easier than the rebonding of the circulated sand because the recirculated, or used, sand will contain unknown ingredients. Also, many properties of the green sand are lost from burnout when a pour is made and a certain amount of guesswork must be used to restore these burned out ingredients.

A basic problem encountered when sand is recycled is how to determine the order in which additives are placed in the sand to be reconditioned. A general rule is that temper water should always be the last ingredient placed in the muller. Thus, the order of operations should be as follows: First, the solid ingredients are placed in the muller with the sand to be reconditioned. The muller is then run for specified lengths of time to coat each sand grain thoroughly with the solid ingredients. The temper water or temper oil is placed in the muller last.

BINDERS

Some of the major binding media used in the foundry include clays (such as bentonite), no-bake binders (such as carbon dioxide, fenal, and furan), and oil or water. There are two types of tempered sand: oil-tempered and water-tempered. Each has its advantages. Water-tempered sand has the advantage of lower cost, while oil-tempered sand has the advantage of less steam because it lacks water.

Many of the characteristics that temper water gives to the foundry sand result in a specialized vocabulary. For example, the water that is added to foundry sand mixture is called *temper water* because it tempers the foundry sand. The sand is then known as *green sand* and is ready for molding. The amount of pressure it takes to indent a rammed green sand surface is known as *green strength.*

Both synthetically bonded and naturally bonded sands use water which acts as a binder. In lake sands, the grain strength is greatest at about 1 percent moisture content. More water will not increase the strength of

(a)

(b)

Fig. 13-2. Mullers. (a) Batch mix muller; (b) continuous mix muller. (*National Engineering Company.*)

the sand. In fact, adding too much water will lower grain strength in water-tempered, or water-bonded, sand. The naturally bonded sands are water-deposited sands with natural clay minerals in them. Naturally bonded sands contain approximately 70 percent sand grain and 30 percent clay or other mineral bonding material mixed intimately with the sand grains. These sands can be used without refinement by simply adding temper water.

There are optimum percentages of water to be added to foundry sand in order to achieve maximum green strength. If too little water is added, the sand will lack green strength because the moisture content will be too low to hold the coated sand particles together. On the other hand, if the percentage of water in the green sand is too high, the coating of the sand particles will become sticky instead of slippery, like mud when it rains, and the green sand will lose some of its green strength (Fig. 13-3a).

Permeability, another physical characteristic that is affected by the amount of temper water added to the foundry sand, is the ability of the sand to breathe. Examples of nonpermeable material would be metal or plastic, materials that air or liquid cannot pass through. A material with extremely high permeability is dry sand. A permeability range in foundry sand can be controlled by the percentage of temper water added to the sand (Fig. 13-3b).

A relatively new development in the foundry industry is the use of certain types of oil to replace the temper water in bonding.

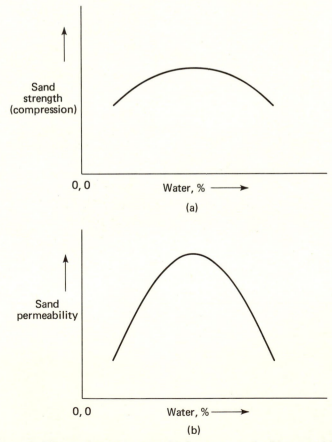

Fig. 13-3. Effects of temper water. (a) Green strength; (b) permeability.

Oil-tempered molding sands are reusable and can be rebonded in much the same manner as water-tempered sands. One of the advantages of the oil-tempered foundry sands is less gas evolution. Also, because of the extremely low water content, the possibility of steam is greatly reduced. Cast finishes are improved, too, because finer grain sizes can be used. Oil-bonded sand can be rammed much harder and can be kept without being used for long periods of time, possibly indefinitely. Other advantages are: (1) oil-tempered sand does not have to be remulled after each casting use, (2) the remulling is done only if it is determined that there has been a loss of green strength, and (3) oil bonding does not have the chilling effects of water-bonded sand, making it possible to cast finer detail.

A typical mixture for an oil-bonded sand is 100 lb dried silica sand, 5 lb commercially available oil-bonding agent, 2 lb bonding oil, and 1 oz catalyst.

Clays

Clays originate in three ways. Some are formed by the decomposition of rock and are called *residual clays*. Other clays are formed by the alteration of rock of igneous origin by underground waters. Still others are deposited as sediments and are known as *sedimentary clays*. The first class forms irregular deposits; both the second and the third classes are found in deposits that vary in extent and thickness.

Clays used as bonds in synthetic sands include fire clays, bentonite, Fuller's earth, and illite. The two most common types of mineral clays used in the foundry industry are bentonite and fire clay.

Bentonite clay is the primary clay used in the foundry industry as a bonding agent. It derives its name from Fort Benton of Rock Creek, Wyoming, where it was first mined. It is a clay derived usually from the decomposition of volcanic ash that is composed of hydrous silicate of aluminum or the mineral montmorillonite. It has the ability to absorb up to 13 times its original volume of water,

quickly soaking up water to form a light yellow paste or gel. In its gel form it will repel water completely, and repeated drying and wetting do not change this characteristic. Bentonite will also absorb up to five times its own weight in oil. Because of its absorptive qualities, it is dropped from airplanes to fight forest fires. Because it repels water in its gel form, it also is used to line the bottom of artificial lakes. The two types of bentonite that are used in foundry work are referred to as western or southern bentonite according to where in the United States they are mined. Bentonite is used as the main bonding material in both oil- and water-tempered foundry sand.

Fire clays are composed of the mineral kaolinite that is mined in Illinois and Ohio. It is available in grinds ranging from flour to very coarse. Fire clay does not form a gel when water is added so that it generally is used with some other bonding agent, such as bentonite.

Fuller's earth has been used primarily because it has great bleaching qualities. It is closely related to bentonite and is used as a clay bond.

Illite is found in most clays and sometimes forms a large percentage of clay deposits. Illite, when watered too heavily, becomes sticky.

Cereal

Cereal binders have been used in foundries for thousands of years to give green strength to cores in the green state. After the cores have been baked at temperatures of 450°F or above, corn cereal binders deteriorate and lose their effectiveness. Cereal binders are also used in molding sands in iron foundries and in facing sands in steel foundries to give a rubbery state to the foundry sand enabling the molten metal to move over the sand and not burn in or penetrate the mold itself. All cereal binders will burn out at approximately 700°F, but by then they will have fulfilled their functions.

Higher permeability is attained by the use of cereal core binders because an open core with a sharp angular sand can be produced, yielding a high green strength. Because the cereal used in cores burns out rapidly, the core collapses completely, giving the cereal core the advantage of an easy shake out. Common amounts of cereal used range from ½ to 1 percent of the volume of the mixed foundry sand.

Oils

Oils are used primarily to prevent deterioration of cores when they are baked over 450°F. Oils contribute to dry tensile strength and allow a longer shelf life for molds and cores because their moisture content will not change as with water. Oils used for bonding sand for cores generally are derived from the vegetable oils, with linseed oil being used as a primary oil binder, while oils used to bond oil-bonded sands for molding are petroleum oils. Oil binders are often used in conjunction with cereal binders in cores because oil does not impart green strength as cereal binders do. As an oil-cereal core bakes, the oil undergoes a complex process of polymerization as well as oxidation. Polymerization changes one compound into another compound. Although the new compound has the same elements as the original, it has different physical properties. A common example of polymerization is paint. Once paint has been dried, it cannot be restored to its original liquid form.

Resins

Resins, sometimes called gums, are binders that cure by heat, not oxygen, the way molasses cures. A resin is usually used as a supplement to other binders rather than as a primary binder. Naturally occurring resins are not used as primary binders, but synthetic resins are used as primary binders.

THERMOSET BINDERS. When phenolic resins come in contact with heat for the first time, they go through three stages. First, the resins melt into a liquid; second, the liquid changes to a rubbery solid; and last, the rubbery solid changes into a hard, strong,

almost insoluble material. These stages mark the polymerization process in phenolic resin.

This thermosetting process is often referred to as the shell process, and it is now being used more frequently in the foundry industry. Phenolic resins are used primarily for this process. In the shell core process, the cores are cured before they are removed from the corebox, thus no green strength is involved in the shell core process. The shell may be a complete mold or a core, but it can be used only once.

The simplest type of shell process occurs when a heated match plate or pattern plate is clamped to a dump box containing a sand that

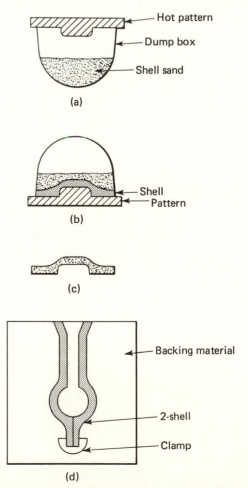

Fig. 13-4. Shell molding. (a) Heated metal pattern plate; (b) contact; (c) shell; (d) ready to pour.

has been mixed with thermosetting phenolic resin (Fig. 13-4). After the hot match plate has been securely fastened to the dump box, the box is inverted and the coated sand is dumped on the hot plate. The phenolic resin goes through its three stages until it reaches its solidification stage, a timed process. Then the dump box is returned to its original upright position and is further treated by being baked in an oven, a step that produces a shell of the pattern. Usually this shell will include a complete gating system if it is to be a mold. The two molds are clamped together and an appropriate backing material that supports the mold during pouring is placed around the two clamped shells. While the shells are still warm, the metal is poured into them.

FURAN BINDERS. Furan no-bake binders are also thermosetting binders that consist of either the furfuryl alcohol formaldehyde resins or the furfuryl alcohol urea formaldehyde resins. Basically they are air-setting, with the thermosetting action controlled by a phosphoric acid. All furan resins are thermosetting and exothermic when they come into contact with an acid catalyst.

The air-setting process was originally developed to shorten the baking cycle of large cores. A binder, oxidizing agents, and a catalyst were mixed with the sand and quickly rammed up into the corebox. After an initial hardening time, the core was taken from the box and then baked in an oven. From this beginning, the process has advanced to a complete air-setting process that is being used more frequently by the foundry industry.

The air-setting process has many advantages. It allows faster ramming of very large cores. The mixed sands allow the metal to flow, a characteristic called good flowability. Also, the core collapses easily after pouring, called good collapsibility, allowing easy shakeout. The process reduces labor costs. The metal does not need as much rod reinforcement as in the baked core processes.

Small foundries usually mix a liquid resin with the foundry sand and hold this mixture until it is needed. Just prior to using

the sand, the third component, the catalyst, is added to the liquid resin and foundry sand mixture, and then the molding sand is rammed into either a corebox or the complete mold. Once the catalyst has been added, the liquid resin turns into a solid resin with a residue of heat and a small amount of water vapor. The speed of this reaction is influenced by the temperature of the sand, the type of sand, the mixing speed, and the amount of catalyst. For the best results when using a furan no-bake system, the water content of the sand should be under 0.25 percent, the temperature of the sand should be between 25 to 80°F, and the sand should be clean. When the liquid resin binder makes up about 2 percent of the volume, the phosphoric acid is added to make up between 20 and 30 percent of the binder. With 20 percent phosphoric acid in the mixture a working life of 30 to 40 min will be ensured, with complete hardening taking from 60 to 80 min. A 30 percent application of the catalyst to the binder will result in a working life of 10 to 20 min, with the complete reaction taking place in a total of 30 to 40 min, a very fast reaction time especially when used with large castings. The furan air-setting binding system compares favorably in most respects to the cereal binder system (Table 13-3).

Carbon Dioxide

The carbon dioxide, or CO_2, process is a relatively new one, but it has proved to be a pro-

TABLE 13-3. BAKED CORES AND NO-BAKE CORES

	BAKED (OIL/CEREAL)	NO-BAKE (FURAN)
Collapsibility	Fast	Moderate
Curing	Dehydration	Polymerization
Reproduction accuracy	Fair	Excellent
Shakeout	Good	Good
Smoking (pouring)	Slight	Moderate (sometimes irritating)
Storage	Indefinite	6 months–1 year

ductive and valuable process for the foundry industry.

The CO_2 process, developed in Germany in 1952, is based on the fact that when CO_2 is introduced into a silicate solution, it precipitates a gelatinous silicic acid. When sand grains that are covered with sodium silicate are exposed to CO_2, they are cemented together at their connection points by the silicic acid gel. During casting, the water vapor present in the gel is given off slowly so that gas evolution is kept at a minimum. The CO_2 binder is mixed with the core sand, and the corebox is filled and rammed, and then an amount of CO_2 is injected into the rammed sand, hardening the core. The core is then removed from the corebox and is ready for use. Complete molds have also been made with the CO_2 process using this same system.

Actually very little extra equipment is needed in order to install the CO_2 process. The major pieces of equipment include a cylinder of CO_2, a regulator for the cylinder (usually an oxygen regulator), a hose, and a valve nozzle at the end of the hose. The CO_2 can be injected into the rammed sand by using either the muffle board technique or the lance, or probe, technique (Fig. 13-5). The muffle board is designed so that an air space is created above the core to be solidified. This air space is generally between 1/8 and 1/4 in. thick. CO_2 gas is injected into this air space, permeating the core which then solidifies. The lance, or probe, works on the same principle as a hypodermic needle except that the end of the probe is plugged and there are holes drilled along its sides. The probe is inserted directly into the core and CO_2 gas is injected into the core at various depths. It is common practice when using the probe to use a 4-in. penetration pattern, a technique that ensures complete gassing of the core. The recommended amount of carbon dioxide gas in either technique is a maximum of 20 psi working line pressure for approximately 20 to 25 s.

ADDITIVES

A foundry sand additive is a material that does not produce any binding qualities but rather imparts some other physical property to the foundry sand. Many times an additive is used in order to produce a facing sand that has a smoother texture than the sand backing it. Sea coal, wood flour, and silica flour are the three main additives used in most foundries. Many other things are added by individual foundry workers. The use of sea coal improves the surface of a casting and prevents sand burnout. A common practice is to add sea coal in amounts from 1 to 4 percent of the total weight of the facing sand.

Wood flour is pulverized, soft wood that in its major uses controls the sand expansion created by temper water. It also improves collapsibility. A secondary advantage of wood flour, as of all flour grades, is that it improves cast finishes.

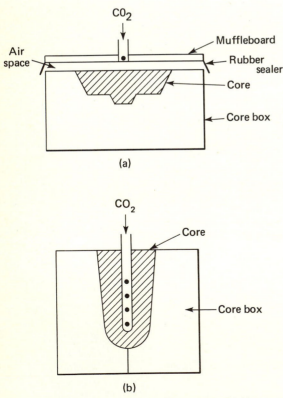

Fig. 13-5. CO_2 gassing. (a) Muffle board; (b) lance or probe.

Silica flour is used by many foundries in the molding material to reduce metal mold penetration or interaction. A certain amount of flour-grade material always burns out of the foundry sand in the area of the casting so that it is common practice to add 5 to 10 percent silica flour with the facing sand. Some of the flour will be burned out, and the remaining silica flour will be lost to the heap sand.

QUESTIONS

1. Identify the three shapes of foundry sand.
2. Explain the term *U.S. standard sieve.*
3. Why have specialty sands?
4. What are some advantages of olivine, zircon, and chromite?
5. Explain the difference between mixing and mulling.
6. What are the major types of mullers?
7. What are the functions of sand binders?
8. How are clays formed?
9. What is foundry flour?
10. What are additives? Why are they used?
11. Explain the furan binder process.

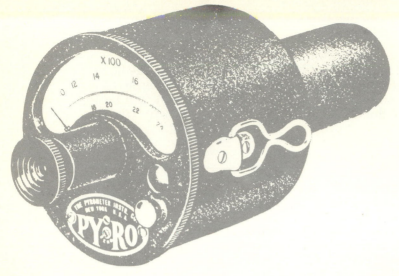

14

Sand Casting

Sand or mineral molds have been used since prehistoric times. Metal molds, or permanent molds as they are known today, are relatively recent developments in making castings. The basic operations involved in ramming a mold have not changed. Equipment to do difficult tasks has simply been added; and even when the equipment became automated, none of the basic concepts were changed. Besides being the oldest casting method, sand casting is still the most widely used casting method.

SAFETY PRECAUTIONS

As in any work involving tools, machines, and materials, certain hazards exist. Most of these hazards can be greatly reduced if common sense is applied. The greatest reduction in accident rates through the use of modern safety methods and procedures has been made in the foundry industry. Industries using steel and nonferrous metals rank low in both the frequency and the severity of accidents when compared to other industries. Besides common hazards inherent in any industry, several special problems exist in metal casting. The proper handling of molten

metal demands special attention. Other hazards result from the dust and fumes that are generated in the foundry process.

Personnel who handle molten metals must wear protective clothing, such as face shields or safety goggles, asbestos or leather gloves which do not have gauntlets but are tight at the wrist, protective aprons that will protect both from heat and from molten particles, leggings which extend over the shoe tops, and work shoes or safety shoes.

General housekeeping of the casting area should keep the area neat and free from clutter, especially in the pouring area, as is true in all areas where hot metals are handled. A fire blanket or fire extinguisher should always be readily accessible. Another hazard in the foundry pouring area includes the presence of water that may fall into the molten metal, causing the metal to explode. And, of course, adequate ventilation should be provided to remove smoke and gas fumes that result from the pouring process.

Although every furnace manufacturer will stipulate lighting instructions for the particular furnace that is being used, the cover of the crucible furnace should be opened before attempting to light any gas-fired furnace. Also, a good practice is to allow a blast of air to cleanse the interior of the furnace before any fire is applied. The gas should always be turned off first in any gas-fired furnace when it is shut down. A common mistake of the beginning foundry worker is to add, or to charge, damp metal into a hot crucible. In such a situation there is always a chance that the metal will contract rapidly and literally explode out of the crucible. Consequently, the metal should always be checked to assure that it is absolutely dry.

When molten metal is poured from a crucible into a mold, it is good practice not to look down a sprue or a riser hole because of the fumes that may be emitted. Also, it is good practice to inspect the crucible thoroughly prior to picking it up. Should the bottom fall off a crucible, the molten metal will go over the feet of the individual who is preparing to pour. After the pouring process has been completed, and the crucible replaced in the furnace, the casting will be hot for some time. Shaking out a casting too hastily can result in second and third degree burns on the hands and feet from the hot foundry sand. Assuming that all metals in the pouring area are hot and that they can burn is a good safety precaution to observe.

HAND TOOLS

The major hand tools used for the manual operation in casting are: spoons and slicks, trowels, sprue cutters, draw pins or draw screws, rammers (bench rammers or air driven, or pneumatic, rammers), lifters, bellows, and shovels (Fig. 14-1). Slicks, spoons, and trowels are used to smooth, patch, or refinish mold surfaces. Sprue cutters, used to cut sprues into the mold, may be either straight-sided or tapered. The draw pin, or draw screw, is a metal pin that aids in withdrawing the pattern from the mold cavity. Rammers are available in three types: bench rammers, floor rammers, which are longer rammers, and pneumatic rammers. The lifter is a tool designed for lifting small particles of sand from the mold cavity, and bellows are used to blow loose sand from deep recesses in the mold cavity.

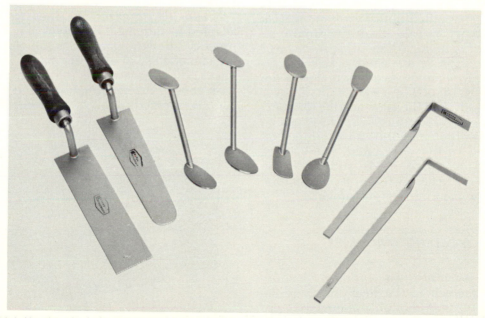

Fig. 14-1. Hand tools. *Left:* trowels; *middle:* slicks and spoons; *right:* lifters. (*Genevro Machine Company.*)

FLASKS

The four types of foundry flasks used most in industry are: the standard flask (Fig. 14-2); the snap, or spread, flask; the taper, or slip, flask; and the jacket. Flasks can be constructed of either wood or metal. Wood flasks have the disadvantage of burning if molten metal is poured on them, and they swell when they are exposed to water-tempered foundry sand. They also cannot maintain the rigidity that a metal flask can. Primarily, magnesium, aluminum, and steel are used in the construction of metal flasks.

Standard flasks have solid walls and are composed of a drag and a cope. Adaptations of the standard flask have led to the development of the snap, or spread, flask. Once the mold has been rammed in a snap flask, the flask sides can be spread apart and the flask removed, giving the advantage of using one flask to generate many molds. A standard flask, because of its construction, can ram only one mold at a time. The mold is poured and then shaken out. The taper, or slip, flask is also designed so that the rammed mold can be removed. However, instead of the flask spreading apart, the interior walls of the flask are on a taper and the flask can simply be lifted from the mold. When either the snap or slip types of flasks are used, a jacket is required to reinforce the sand mold during the pouring operation. The jacket will slip over the mold and bond the cope and the drag sections of the mold together. The jacket can be slipped over the mold or it can be slipped off and moved to the next mold. Many times there will be bare molds sitting on the pouring floor, each with a jacket so that pouring can continue uninterrupted.

MOLDING MACHINES

Molding machines can relieve foundry workers of much of the heavy work of the foundry process. Although molding machines do not eliminate all the work, they perform operations faster and easier than a person

could. The basic molding machine is referred to as a *jolt-squeeze machine*. The flask, with accompanying pattern plate, is assembled on the table of the jolt-squeeze machine. The operator fills the cope or the drag, whichever is on top, with sand. Then a hydraulic device is actuated which picks the lower table up and drops it, jolting the sand and settling it over the pattern. The top plate is then lowered and the sand is squeezed, the same process as ramming. In the next step, the flask rolls over, exposing its cope half. The operator then dusts the parting line lightly, riddles a small amount of facing sand in, and heaps in the backing sand. The flask is again jolted, which settles the sand over the mold face. Additional sand is placed in the flask and then the flask is squeezed. A mechanism lifts the cope from the drag, and the operator removes the mask plate, cleans out any excess sand in the cope or the drag section, and closes the flask. This operation is called the *jolt-roll over-squeeze-draw-and-close*. A quick time can be established with small flasks by an experienced operator of the molding machine, approximating a pace of 3 to 4 min per mold. This pace, however, is difficult to maintain (Fig. 14-3).

The jolt-squeeze machines have been adapted to automatic processes (Fig. 14-4). A process called the *conventional molding loop* accommodates 36 × 36 in. flasks and produces 240 poured molds per hour. First the flask goes to the cope molding, and then the cope is directed to the mold closure station.

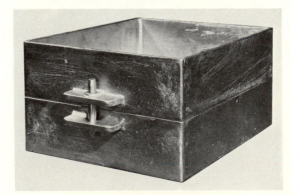

Fig. 14-2. The standard flask. (*Genevro Machine Company.*)

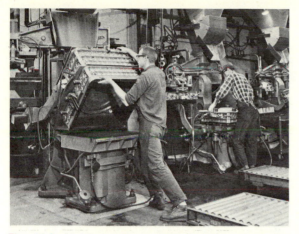

Fig. 14-3. Molding machine. (*Osborn Manufacturing Company*.)

In the next step the cope is cleaned. It goes through a drag molding, and the drag is then directed to a plate- or a core-setting area. The drag then meets the cope section, with a mold closing machine placing the cope on top of the drag, closing the mold. Weights are then placed automatically on the flask to prevent cope-drag separation. The final step is automatic pouring of the metal.

Automatic sand-casting systems have rel-

atively high maintenance, but they are high-production systems that are used throughout industry. The application of the automatic sand-casting flask system in the production of brake drums (Fig. 14-4) can produce 960 brake drums per hour.

Flaskless Molding Machines

There are now single pieces of equipment that will produce a flaskless mold, pour the mold, and strip the mold, accomplishing all the steps within one compact unit (Fig. 14-5). Flaskless molding generally entails specific steps. The first step is the filling of a premachined mold cavity. After the mold cavity is filled with sand, the pattern is automatically positioned and a hydraulic or pneumatic device squeezes the sand. The pattern is then stripped from the mold surface, and the mold is rotated and inserted into a pouring device. The mold is poured, allowed to cool, and stripped. Flaskless molding machines are capable of producing 240 molds per hour, and the castings may range up to 650 lb. The flaskless molding casting system is capable of replacing the very large flask molding system (Fig. 14-6).

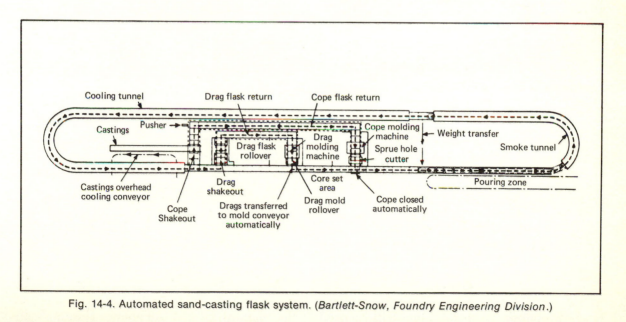

Fig. 14-4. Automated sand-casting flask system. (*Bartlett-Snow, Foundry Engineering Division*.)

Fig. 14-5. Automatic molding. (*Osborn Manufacturing Company.*)

MATCH PLATE

Many small foundries use loose patterns to produce castings. However, to produce consistent castings with loose patterns requires a high degree of skill. Using match plates ensures the accuracy of each casting and, at the same time, lessens the skill required of the foundry worker. Match plates are costly to create and this must be kept in mind in relation to the total number of castings. Often the match plate will be used on small jobs not warranting permanent molds or in jobs that will use sand as the casting medium. Match plates should not be used if just a few castings are to be made. The major factors to consider in choosing a match plate instead of a loose pattern are the number of castings to be produced, the time involved in creating the match plate, and the cost savings of the match plate compared to the loose-piece pattern.

Match plates include a sprue base and the complete gating and risering systems of the pattern. Fully automatic systems can

Fig. 14-6. Flaskless molding/casting system. (*Calhoun Foundry Company Installation*.)

even mold sprues. On semiautomatic or standard jolt squeeze produced moldings, the sprue is cut with a sprue cutter (Fig. 14-7).

Aluminum, wood, and steel are the primary materials used for match plates. Match plates completely cast of aluminum are best for permanent cast match plates for several reasons. Aluminum can withstand mechanical jarring and sudden heat shock. It is the easiest material to cast and can easily be worked with hand tools. Wood match plates can swell, warp, or dent with improper care, resulting in lower quality castings. Steel, while very durable, distorts when heated. Steel also makes it difficult to cast the many intricate shapes demanded by the match plate. The necessity of working the steel forms with machine tools makes a steel match plate cost more than an aluminum match plate.

Aluminum match plates are cast from plaster molds to very exact tolerances. Molten aluminum is forced into the plaster mold under pressure. The aluminum match plate allows very fine detail because the molten aluminum is forced into the plaster mold under pressure and the plaster mold is poured as soon as it is recovered from the heating furnace. Standard sizes and shapes of match plates have been adopted by the foundry industry as a result of a working arrangement with the various manufacturers of flasks and pattern plates (Fig. 14-7).

Guide pins are shaped and constructed to give assurance of a perfect fit between the match plate, the cope, and the drag. Guide pin holes are standard and will fit any flask no matter what manufacturer produced it. Holes for attaching vibrators are also standardized and positioned in such a way that

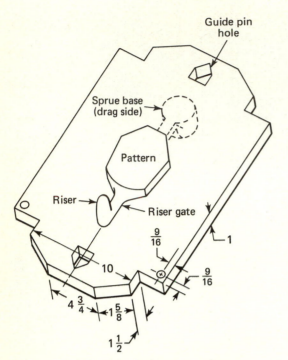

Fig. 14-7. Match plate, cope view.

the vibrator can be attached at any angle. Enough plate is extended beyond the sides of the flask to ensure a firm hold when the match plate is removed from the rammed mold.

Patterns mounted on plates are like any other removable pattern or loose-piece pattern. They must have positive draft and must not have any sharp edges so that they can be removed without their edges catching and tearing the sand away.

Follow boards are sometimes mistaken

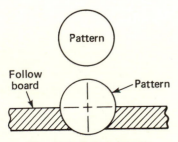

Fig. 14-8. Follow board.

for match plates. A follow board establishes a new centerline for a pattern. The pattern would be placed in the follow board and then the follow board would be used in the same manner as a match plate. A follow board is not attached to the pattern like a match plate, and it would have to be used with a pattern that does not have a flat side, as in a pattern for a round ball (Fig. 14-8). Follow boards are used on one-piece patterns of irregular shape or in patterns with shapes that require its use for ease in ramming the mold. The follow board is only an aid to the molder and takes the place of coping out the mold.

CENTRIFUGAL CASTING

Metal flows into a mold cavity in many ways. The most common and the oldest method for controlling flow is by gravity pouring. Other methods include vacuum casting, low-pressure casting, and centrifugal casting. Centrifugal casting involves pouring metal into a revolving mold. In centrifugal casting, centrifugal forces create pressures far in excess of gravity to force the metal into the mold. For instance, an aluminum alloy rotated at 2,600 r/min is subjected to pressures of 32 psi at about a 4-in. diameter and larger pressures are generated at larger diameters. In fact, in this situation, the pressure exerted with centrifugal casting would exceed that achieved by a gravity-feeding system with a sprue 26 ft tall.

Centrifugal casting is subdivided into three major categories: true centrifugal casting, semicentrifugal casting, and centrifuge casting (Fig. 14-9). Centrifugal casting is often more economical than other casting methods, especially when casting symmetrical objects such as pipe. The pressure which results from the centrifugal force allows thinner sections to be cast than can be cast with gravity casting or with static pouring methods. Castings that weigh from only a few ounces (such as automotive piston rings) to over 42 tons (such as paper mill rolls) can be centrifugally cast.

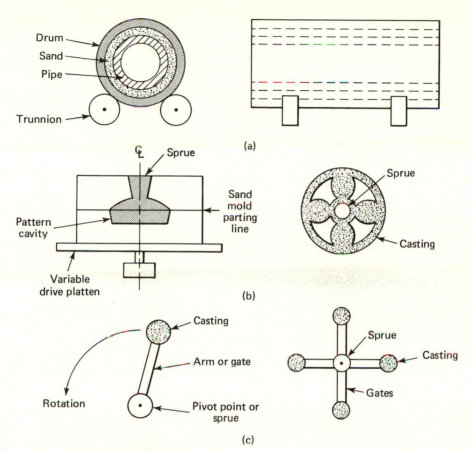

Fig. 14-9. Types of centrifugal casting. (a) True centrifugal; (b) semicentrifugal; (c) centrifuge.

True Centrifugal Casting

True centrifugal casting results in a casting that has a dense structure. The impurities are forced to the center by the pressure exerted on the metal and frequently the center is machined out.

True centrifugal casting is used for pipes, liners, and any symmetrical object which can be cast by rotating the mold about its horizontal or vertical axis. The metal is held against the wall of the mold by centrifugal force so that no core is required to form the interior wall of the casting. Because the impurities in the casting are forced toward the center of the casting, items such as brake drums, airplane cylinders, and motorcycle cylinders can be cast by the true centrifugal process. All that is

needed to clean up a cylinder casting, for example, is to bore the casting. This step removes all the impurities and produces a true centrifugally cast object with few or no metallic impurities (Fig. 14-9a).

Semicentrifugal Casting

Semicentrifugal casting uses centrifugal force to cause the metal to flow from a central sprue into one or more sand molds which are rotated around the same central axis. For example, all railroad wheels are cast in steel by the semicentrifugal method because they can be cast accurately and relatively free of impurities. As with true centrifugal casting, the semicentrifugal process also is used for items that have centers which will be removed by machining; but the rotational speed for this form of casting is considerably less than the rotational speed for true centrifugal castings. An advantage of semicentrifugal casting is that stack molding can be employed. This technique allows numbers of objects to be stacked on each other, poured at the same time, and fed by one central sprue system (Fig. 14-9b).

Centrifuge Casting

Centrifuge casting differs from other centrifugal casting methods in that the casting itself is on the end of a rotating arm or end gate. The casting is located at one end of this gate and the sprue is the pivot point. Castings may be rotated in either direction and numbers of castings may be located up and down the sprue at various angles to the sprue. The castings themselves need not be identical or uniform. As the casting is rotated around its pivot point, or sprue, metal is poured in and thrown through the armlike gates to the casting where the metal hits the casting cavity. Because the mold cavities are filled under the pressure of the metal being thrown out through the arms, very sound castings are produced. The rotational speed of the casting depends on a number of factors such as the molding medium (sand, metal, or ceramic), the size of the casting, the kind of metal being used, and the distance the casting is from the pivot point. Centrifuging the casting creates a slightly more dense grain structure than can be obtained in static types of castings (Fig. 14-9c).

Experimentation in all three types of casting has revealed that centrifugal forces of 50 to 100 gravities (g) are best, all things considered, with 75 g being the most common force used. A general formula for determining the revolutions per minute is to divide 1,675 by the square root of the radius of the casting in inches, or

$$r/min = 1,675/\sqrt{R}$$

The result will approximate the 75 g. After the gravitational force is derived by this for-

mula, the revolution speed can be adjusted when the formula is applied in making a casting.

FULL MOLD PROCESS

The full mold process uses a pattern made of a cellular material called *expanded polystyrene*, shaped into a mold and rammed in green sand, dry sand, sodium silicate-bonded sand, or any other molding material. A conventional gating system is used and molten metal is poured through the sprue so that the material is replaced as the metal comes in contact with it, resulting in a pattern. Upon burning, polystyrene material leaves a harmless small residue of carbon, 0.1 percent by weight. Expanded polystyrene foam is familiar to everyone in the form of white throwaway coffee cups. It is possible to take one of these foam coffee cups, attach polystyrene sprue runners and risers to it, and cast it with either a ferrous or nonferrous material. A full mold process is often used for product research in the foundry industry. Also, very large one-of-a-kind machine bases can be cast simply by shaping large blocks or sheets of expanded foam, placing them in a dry sand mold, and pouring them. The low vaporization point of polystyrene, approximately 175°F, ensures that molten metal will vaporize and replace it.

Proper gating and pouring are most important in the full mold process. The mold must be filled rapidly so that the hot metal enters the mold cavity from many gates, not just one or two. The hot metal must also displace the polystyrene foam evenly. Because of the amount of smoke and fumes released by the burning of the polystyrene foam, blind risers should always be used, coupled with a pop-off device (Fig. 14-10). Blind risers are also used so that an excess amount of oxygen will not enter the mold. Too much oxygen will allow the foam to ignite prematurely, causing the mold cavity to collapse. The pop-off is constructed by placing a welding rod or a wire from 1/8- to 1/4-in. diameter into the blind

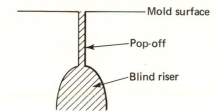

$\frac{1}{8}$ to $\frac{1}{4}$ D Hole

Mold surface

Pop-off

Blind riser

Fig. 14-10. Blind riser with pop-off.

riser, ramming the sand, striking the sand off, and then extracting the welding rod, leaving a small hole that leads to the blind riser. This pop-off will control smoke and fumes as well as provide adequate feeding and ventilation to the casting. As in all types of castings, the use of exothermics in sprue tops also aids the feeding of the casting. All nonferrous metals used in the full mold process should be poured 50°F hotter than when they are used in standard sand-casting processes. When the pouring is begun, a small puff of black smoke will come from the sprue and the risers but, as in regular sand casting, the sprue should be kept full from the moment the pouring starts until it stops.

SAND-CASTING DEFECTS

Knowing the probable causes of defects in sand castings can help eliminate them. *Blow air holes* in castings can be caused by low sand permeability or venting. Molding green sand that is too wet causes steam and can also result in blow air holes. Another defect, called a *complete runout,* is caused by failure to secure the cope to the drag. This causes the cope to lift and molten metal to run out of the parting line. A *cold short* occurs when the metal fails to fill the pattern cavity completely. In this case, the casting will have voids with rounded edges. A *core fault* is caused by some structural damage or deficiency in the core that causes its collapse or deformation.

A fifth defect, *core settling,* results when the core print either is not large enough to support the weight of the core and the molten metal or is not correctly aligned. *Crush* occurs when too much weight has been applied to the top of the cope, causing the sand to fill the mold cavity. A *dirty casting* is caused by leaving sand particles within the pattern cavity or by crush. *Drop* occurs when cope sand drops into the pattern cavity as a result of cope settling or as a result of crush. *Excess porosity* in a casting can be caused by the poor quality of the scrap being used in the melt, not properly fluxing the melt, or by adding cold metal to the hot melt.

Metal fault is a term used for a casting that is defective because of a number of things: gas porosity, misalignment, the wrong alloys of metal, or incorrect gassing of the metals. For these defects or a number of others, the casting is rejected. A *miss-run* occurs when the entire mold cavity is not filled with metal but not as a result of a cold short. For example, such a situation exists when the quantity of molten metal that is estimated to fill the casting is not large enough. *Pattern fault* is an error that can be traced to a faulty or incorrect pattern. *Poured short* is a term that identifies a faulty estimation by the foundry worker of the amount of metal needed to complete the pouring and to fill the mold.

Another defect, called *ram-off,* occurs when the sand next to the pattern cavity has been rammed correctly but the backing sand is too soft, causing the mold cavity to move. *Shift* results when the cope part of the cavity is not aligned properly with the drag portion of the pattern cavity. *Strained,* also called *flashing* or *finning,* is a defect that occurs when a small portion of metal flows out from the pattern cavity at the parting line. Usually this metal can be cleaned up by trimming. If the sand next to the mold cavity is too soft, then the molten metal pushes out the sides of the pattern cavity. This defect is called *swell.* And a final defect, called *warp,* occurs when castings are shaken out too quickly, causing them to lose their proper alignment or resulting in their nonuniform cooling.

QUESTIONS

1. What protective clothing should be worn when pouring molten metal?
2. How does water affect molten metal?
3. Why are metal flasks superior to wood flasks?
4. Name four of the flasks that are used most by the foundry industry.
5. Identify the operations of a jolt-squeeze machine.
6. How do flaskless molding machines produce castings without flasks?
7. What are follow boards?
8. Describe the uses of a match plate.
9. What are the advantages of centrifugal casting as compared with sand casting?
10. Identify and describe the major categories of centrifugal casting.
11. Why should pop-off risers be used in the full mold process?
12. Explain the following casting defect terms: crush, miss-run, and cold short.

15

Semipermanent Casting

Semipermanent castings are those molds that have long shelf life and can be used more than once but are capable of producing only a limited number of castings. Processes that come under the semipermanent category include plaster castings, investment casting, shell casting, and cement casting.

SHELL MOLDING

The shell molding process for producing castings is a modification of the sand-casting process. Instead of using a regular foundry sand mixture enlarged by clay binders, a fine dry sand is mixed with a resin that is applied to a pattern and heated to approximately 450°F. The resin coating on the sand melts and then hardens, acting as a bond for the grains of sand. The shell is then ejected from the pattern and cured. At this point, the shells are mated together and are ready for pouring.

In place of regular sand molding equipment, an open-faced box mounted on trunnions is used in the shell casting process (Fig. 15-1). The equipment used for making shell molds can be simple and small for experimental or job shop use, or it can be large and complex for mass production. Regardless of the equipment, the funda-

mental operations of investment, curing, and stripping remain the same. All apparatus, whether manual or automatic, is designed to perform these three basic operations.

Shells are molded for a single use. Once they are set and cured, the shells become hard and brittle, making it almost impossible to modify the mold cavity without changing the original pattern and repeating the investment process with a new resin mixture.

Most shells range from $3/16$ to $5/8$ in. thick depending on the density of the metal to be poured and whether or not the shell uses a backing system. The thickness of any shell can be controlled by the type of thermosetting resin, the type of grain shape of the sand, the temperature of the pattern, and the length of time that the unbonded sand is in contact with the hot pattern.

Carefully planned gating and riser systems are important in shell casting. The hardened, glazed sand with its resin surface offers little resistance to the flow of incoming metal. As a result, the gating system is more critical than in sand casting and should be designed so that pouring turbulence and splashing are kept to a minimum. The velocity of the metal entering the pattern cavity should be controlled to a moderate speed. These conditions can be obtained by using a tapered sprue along with a slag well and

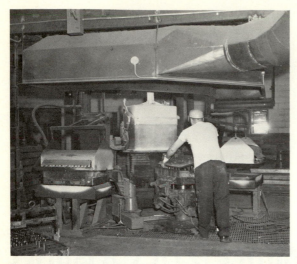

Fig. 15-1. Shell molding system—two station machine. (*Shalco Systems.*)

runners with a cross-sectional area greater than that of the lower portion of the sprue. Bottom gating and the use of the tapered sprue bring metal to the lowest part of the casting pattern cavity, aiding in the reduction of turbulence in the metal.

Whether or not risers are used with shell castings depends on the cross-sectional area of the casting and the thickness of the shell. Often, when the cross-sectional area is small, shrinkage can be eliminated by modifying the gating rather than by adding a riser. When the thickness of a shell is ½ to ⅝ in. thick, a riser becomes necessary to provide for the elimination of gases.

In the early days of shell molding, the majority of castings were poured with a vertical gating system which required less floor space for the pouring than conventional sand molding (Fig. 15-2a). Today, most shell molds are poured horizontally (Fig. 15-2b). Horizontal pouring allows the metal to drop from a lesser height; consequently, elaborate provisions are not required to reduce the turbulence. The horizontal position also allows more jobs to be poured without backup material. It establishes a more even pressure throughout the mold and requires less gating. The techniques of overlapping and stack molding have been incorporated to offset the increased floor space requirements.

Removing the pattern from the pattern plate is accomplished by extending recessed bolts through the pattern plate close to the pattern or incorporating the bolts in the pattern. These bolts extend through the pattern plate and are all the same length. The pattern plate is pushed down and the bolts extend upward, causing the shell to be pushed from the pattern. Without these ejection pins, it would be impossible to remove the shell from the pattern plate (Fig. 15-3). After the mold has been removed and cured in an oven, the molds are aligned. Molds that are poured horizontally are usually glued firmly together. There are a number of ways to fasten shells together; however, gluing or cementing the shell halves prevents distortion of the shells by providing a means by which the static pressure of the metal is overcome (Fig. 15-4). The basic resin used in the shell binding system is used as a glue.

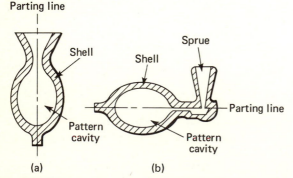

Fig. 15-2. Types of shell molds. (*a*) Vertical; (*b*) horizontal.

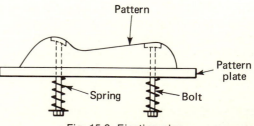

Fig. 15-3. Ejection pins.

Fig. 15-4. Shell bonding fixture. (*Shalco Systems*.)

Once the shells are glued, they are usually bedded in sand and poured. Gravel, steel shot, or copper shot is used as backing material if it is needed. Shot is the most acceptable backing material used in industry because of its density and the ease with which it is mechanized. It should be kept in mind that some light metals in small castings with thin cross-sectional areas can be poured without the use of any bedding or backing material to support the mold.

Troubleshooting

Table 15-1 identifies many of the basic problems encountered in shell molding and their possible solutions. For example, when there are *bubbles* in the shell, the bubble is usually noticed on the exterior wall of the shell. The two major reasons for these bubbles are insufficient mixing of the dry-mix-type shell coating or overmulling of the resin-coated sand. *Drop-off* occurs when por-

tions of the shell drop off into the dump box, leaving the pattern clean. *Fall-off* occurs when the shell splits, leaving a part of the fused shell sand clinging to the pattern and part of it dropping off. *Fill-out* occurs when the pattern has not been covered completely during the dump process. *Seizure* indicates that the mold is difficult to remove.

INVESTMENT CASTING

The lost-wax, or investment, casting process began with the early settlers along the Mediterranean. In the early process, the actual molding was done in wax over an earthen core, and then another layer of earth was firmly packed around the pattern. The wax was melted out and metal poured into the form. This early method was lost and then rediscovered during the Italian renaissance. Great sculptors and artists such as Cellini and Michelangelo used the lost-wax process in

TABLE 15-1. SHELL MOLDING TROUBLESHOOTING

PROBLEM	CAUSE
Bubbles in shell	Insufficient mixing (dry mix)
	Overmulling (resin-coated sand)
Drop-off	Excessive lubrication
	Excessive resin
	Wrong resin
	Pattern temperature too low
Fall-off	Pattern temperature too high
	Too much resin
	Dump time too long
Fill-out	Dump box rotated too fast
Seizure	Curing time too long
	Pattern temperature too high
	Need slower-setting resin
Sticking	Wrong lubricant
	Pattern fault
	Improper pattern temperature
Warpage	Oven temperature too high
	Pattern temperature too low

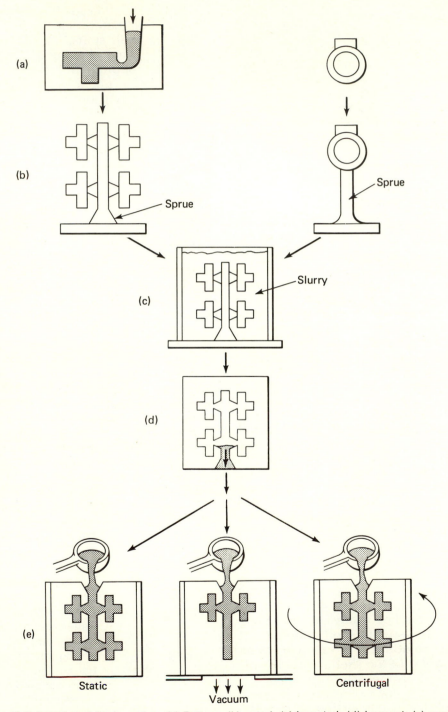

(a)

(b)

Sprue

Sprue

(c)

Slurry

(d)

(e)

Static

Vacuum

Centrifugal

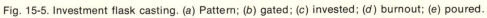

Fig. 15-5. Investment flask casting. (a) Pattern; (b) gated; (c) invested; (d) burnout; (e) poured.

their metal casting work. Later, other artisans, such as jewelers and dentists, started to use the lost-wax process. During World War II, many techniques allowed the investment casting process to be adapted as an effective production tool. The only difference between the modern process and the early process is that a silica slurry is now used over the pattern instead of the layer of packed earth. In the early 1950s, investment casting began to be categorized as either investment flask casting or investment shell casting.

Investment Flask Casting

The pattern for investment flask casting is derived by either carving objects out of wax or injecting a molten wax, plastic, or mercury into a die (Fig. 15-5). One or more patterns are attached to a wax sprue with wax gates, and then the completed pattern is placed upside down in a canister that is usually lined with an asbestos paper. The pattern is invested in a refractory ceramic material. The investment is allowed to dry for a length of time before the complete canister is placed in a burnout oven. The burnout of the pattern requires that an oven be set at a low temperature, reducing the amount of water within the slurry until the temperature is raised enough for the wax pattern to melt and flow out. This wax or plastic is then recovered. After the major amount of the wax has been melted out of the pattern cavity, the furnace temperature is raised to 1200 to 1800°F, a temperature which will vaporize any residue wax located in areas where it cannot run out. After the burnout is complete and the mold is still hot, the mold is inverted and may be poured either by using the gravity static method (as in standard sand casting) or by placing the mold on a vacuum table and drawing a vacuum down through the slurry which will help suck the metal right into the mold, or by placing the canister in a centrifugal casting machine and pouring the metal in this manner.

After pouring, the canister and the metal are allowed to cool. Then the investment is broken away by using either the hammer and chisel or water and air pressure. The castings are then cut from the gating systems and the end-gate areas are cleaned for shipping.

There are many modifications of investment flask casting. For example, changing the wax in the pattern to mercury, which is injected into a die pattern and then frozen, is called a *Mercast system*. The mercury in its frozen state is invested and then reclaimed by allowing the invested flask to come to room temperature so that the mercury will flow out of the pattern cavity. Then the flask is put through the heating and curing process. Other low-melting-point alloys can also be used as pattern materials.

A number of materials can be used as investment materials. The investment mold, as well as the materials from which it is made, can only be used once. Usually, fine grain silica sand with a suitable binder is used. The binder may be plaster of paris or other gypsum products, sodium silicate, alumina cement, calcium phosphate, ammonium phosphate, ethyl silicate, and many other materials (Table 15-2). As in sand casting, investment casting uses additives to control such qualities of the investments as contraction and thermal stability. Some of these additives include alumina, magnesia, zircon, talc, and silica flour.

A recently developed technique in investment casting is the glass cast process in which finely ground vycor glass serves as a mold refractory. Vycor glass is in the silica family, has an extremely low coefficient of thermal expansion, and does not undergo phase transformation in heating as does quartz.

TABLE 15-2. INVESTMENT FLASK SLURRY

BINDER	SILICA SAND REFRACTORY, %	WATER, %
Alumina cement 5%	95	27–30
Ethyl silicate 3–7%	97–93	Trace
Sodium silicate 3–7%	97–93	Trace
Calcium phosphate 6–7%, MgO 2.30%	91.7–90.7	51

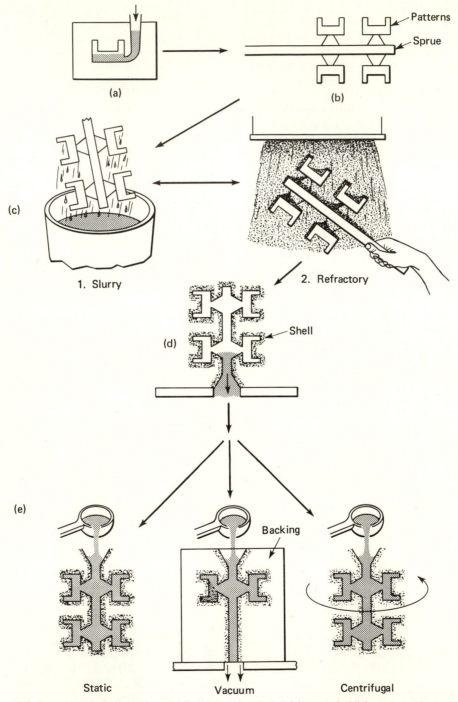

Fig. 15-6. Investment shell casting. (*a*) Pattern; (*b*) gated; (*c*) invested; (*d*) burnout; (*e*) poured.

Investment Shell Casting

Investment shell casting goes through some of the same operations as investment flask casting. A pattern is developed by either carving a pattern from wax or plastic or by injecting the pattern material into a die, and gates are attached in the same manner as in flask casting. The difference is in the investment of the slurry (Fig. 15-6).

Materials used for investing shells include rundom, arclay, silica flour, silica glass, sillimanite, and zirconium. These are the basic binders used in the creation of the investment slurry. The pattern, after being dipped in or exposed to a slurry mixture of these materials, is placed under falling particles of refractory. These sprinkle particles may be emory, fire clay, silica sand, or silica glass (Table 15-3).

The process of dipping the pattern into a very liquid slurry and then sprinkling refractories onto the wetted pattern is repeated until there is a gradual buildup of a ceramic shell from $3/16$ to $5/8$ in. thick. When the shell is the desired height, the wax is burned out in the same manner as in investment flask casting, and pouring is accomplished by either static pouring, vacuum pouring, or centrifugal pouring methods.

The advantages of using the investment casting process are that very intricate forms with undercuts can be cast easily; a smooth surface can be cast with no parting line; and unmachinable parts can be cast with high dimensional accuracy. Investment casting can be competitive with die casting when complicated parts with superior strength are need. Much less tooling is required with investment casting than with die casting. When

high production is not the most important consideration in choosing the casting process, substantial savings can be achieved with investment casting.

An Old Lost-Wax Casting Method

Complex mechanical devices are not necessary for a practical application of the lost wax or investment casting process. For example, in Thailand, foundry workers work with the barest minimum of materials. Their investment slurry is composed of a mixture of two parts earthen clay to one part charred rice husks to one part water buffalo dung. The high organic content of the dung increases the permeability, or porous quality, of the slurry and enables the slurry to dry rapidly. The organic content also controls the shrinkage and absorption of wax during the casting process.

The first step in making the pattern is molding a crude form in the shape of the item to be made. These forms generally are made around a spindle. The spindle is placed in a rack and the form is permitted to dry completely. When the form is dry, the spindle is placed in a simple, hand-operated lathe and turned to a crude form of its desired finished pattern shape. The beeswax is then prepared. It is first cooked to remove its impurities, then it is extruded through a length of hollow bamboo with a hole in the end of it that is the size desired for the wax wire. Fire-softened wax is inserted into the bamboo tube, and a plunger of solid wood is inserted into the open end of the bamboo tube. The plunger is pushed against the body and a wire of wax is formed at the other end of the tube (Fig. 15-7a).

Beeswax in wire form is then used to wrap the clay form. This wire serves several purposes. It enables the artisan to have a uniform thickness of wax, facilitates the handling of the waxed form, and serves in some cases as a decorative factor in the finished product. When the base form is completed, the spindle may be returned to the hand lathe and the wire flattened to form a smooth surface. In most cases, the project then has its sprues and risers attached to the wax form

TABLE 15-3. INVESTMENT SHELL MATERIAL

REFRACTORY	SPRINKLE PARTICLES
Corundum, artificial	Emery
Fire clay	Fire clay
Silica flour	Silica sand
Silica glass	Silica glass
Sillimanite	Emery
Zirconium	Emery

(a)

(d)

(b)

(e)

Fig. 15-7. Lost-wax castings from Pa-Ao, Thailand, (a) Wax preparation; (b) gating; (c) investing; (d) pouring; (e) shakeout.

(c)

(Fig. 15-7b). The investment is now formed around the inner form. Care must be taken in applying the investment so that a tolerance exists to allow for clay shrinkage and so that the investment wall is sufficiently thick to withstand the heat of the casting.

Generally the investment is applied by pushing small wads so that the clay is stretched slightly. At the sprue end of the casting, the outer form is shaped with a cup, with the sprue and risers exposed. Another form is shaped which is the crucible. Bronze pieces of metal are put inside the second form and the two halves are sealed together to complete the total investment, crucible, and pattern cavity (Fig. 15-7c). The two forms are now placed mouth to mouth and sealed together with more clay investment, making the interiors one dumbbell-shaped cavity that is pinched where the necks are joined.

A furnace is now constructed to complete the castings. A cavity is dug in the clay soil and a bellows is constructed next to the clay cavity. The simple furnace is composed of two large hollow trunks of bamboo with plungers that resemble feather dusters. At the base of the bellows, two bamboo pipes lead into the furnace to supply the air (Fig. 15-7d). The furnace is fired with charcoal. The entire invested form is placed end down near the fire crucible. It is heated slowly and the wax melts and runs into the bottom crucible. When the invested form has reached a temperature high enough not to explode upon contact with the furnace temperature, the mold is placed in the furnace with the crucible end still down. The mold/crucible unit is not heated until it is past the melting point of the bronze. Usually the clay mold will glow "white" at this point. The wax will melt and vaporize through the porous investment. The unit is then gripped with a double green bamboo thong and inverted. The metal then runs from the crucible into the mold cavity.

After the mold is permitted to cool briefly, the clay shell is broken and the finished casting is removed. The cores are removed and the castings are shaken out in the traditional manner (Fig. 15-7e). The product is then finished or **burnished** on the hand lathe.

PLASTER MOLDS

Plaster molds usually are not considered competitive with either sand or permanent molds. Instead, the plaster mold method allows the production of castings that would otherwise be impossible to produce because of the time, money, or surface texture involved. Many industrial uses have been found for plaster molds. The smooth surface of the plaster mold gives an excellent surface texture to the casting. This smooth surface achieves far greater accuracy than can be achieved with precision sand casting.

One of the main advantages of a plaster mold is that castings may be produced to very close tolerances requiring little or no machining besides cleanup. Another advantage of these castings is that they have uniform hardness and machinability because of their slow directional solidification. This slow directional solidification helps to relieve the internal stresses of the castings. It is a result of the lack of moisture in the plaster after the plaster has been baked out and the lack of foundry sand. This chilling action, or slow solidification, is controlled by some foundries by adding silica sand to the slurry mixture to improve the chill action of the mold.

The procedure for producing plaster molds includes the following steps. First, the pattern is coated with a thin film of oil and is placed on a bottom board within a flask. The pattern should be situated in such a way that there is at least a 1-in. clearance between the sides of the pattern and the flask. The flask should also extend at least 1 in. higher than the pattern. The slurry is then poured over the pattern filling the flask. After the flask has been filled completely, it should be vibrated to settle the plaster and to ensure that the plaster mold has completely surrounded the pattern.

After approximately 30 min, the mold should be hard enough to turn over to drill aligning hollows near the corners. These aligning hollows will aid in aligning the mold halves. After the drag section of the mold is thoroughly dry, the cope is placed on the drag and the entire surface of the plaster and the pattern is covered with a light petroleum-based oil. Then more slurry is mixed, poured, and vibrated. The plaster of paris is allowed to set again for approximately 30 min, and then the flasks are separated both by tapping the flask and by applying air pressure.

Many foundries implant an air pipe that extends to the parting line prior to pouring the second slurry application. This air pipe will allow an external air hose to be fastened to the pipe and the air will then apply pressure to the parting line, enabling the cope to be separated from the drag section of the flask (Fig. 15-8). The pattern is removed and appropriate end gates, sprues, and risers are cut into the plaster of paris. The cope and drag sections are kept separate and placed in an oven at about 400°F and baked for 20 h. This baking dehydrates the plaster of paris.

The easiest way to check the dehydration of the mold is to insert a thermocouple in the slurry prior to the initial setup of the mold. After the initial setup, the mold is placed in an oven at approximately 1000°F and left there until the reading of the thermocouple exceeds 212°F. The mold will not exceed 212°F as long as there is water or water vapor present in the investment. When the mold reaches approximately 220°F, the absence of all water vapor is ensured. The oven is turned off, and the oven temperature is allowed to reach about 400°F before the complete cured plaster mold is removed to prevent too great a thermal shock to the mold. The mold should never be allowed to heat above 600°F. The molds are allowed to cool

to room temperature and are stored, or they may be readied for assembly and poured.

The last step before pouring molten metal into the mold is to coat the mold. Several methods may be used to create mold facings. Plumbago, or graphite, makes one of the best facings. A plumbago paste is made by mixing graphite and denatured alcohol together. While the paste is still wet, it is painted onto the mold surface. As soon as the surface has been covered, the facing is ignited with a match and the alcohol is allowed to burn off, leaving a slick covering which helps in removing the castings and aids in reducing the thermal shock of the molten metal.

After the castings have been allowed to cool, the plaster mold is broken away by hot water and air pressure. Sometimes live steam or a hammer and chisel are used. The castings are cleaned up in the usual manner by grinding or machining.

Slurries

There are three slurries that can be used in the creation of plaster molds: the plaster of paris, or standard gypsum, molds; the in situ mold; and the separately generated foam mold. The standard slurry does not have a great deal of permeability, so the in situ and the separately generated foam molds were created with greater permeability. After the slurries have been generated by any of the three processes, they are all applied to the pattern in the flask in the same manner. The only difference among them is in the way that they are generated.

GRAPHITE MOLDS

Graphite is used for molding in much the same manner as plaster. Graphite is available in an investment type of mixture which can be molded to shape. Graphite molds have an advantage over plaster molds because they may be reused. Currently, graphite molds are limited to a maximum size of 20 × 18 × 10

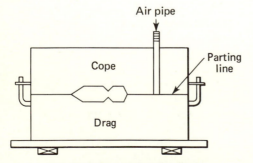

Fig. 15-8. Separating the flask.

in. and the heaviest casting produced to date has been approximately 50 lb. Graphite molds are capable of withstanding the heat of grey, ductile, or malleable iron; steel; copper alloys; aluminum; and most other ferrous and nonferrous metals.

QUESTIONS

1. What foundry processes are included in semipermanent casting?
2. Explain the shell casting terms *seizure* and *warpage.*
3. Why are shell-cast gating systems different from sand-cast gating systems?
4. How are shells fastened together?
5. Why are backing materials sometimes necessary in shell casting?
6. Explain the investment casting process.
7. Explain the shell casting process.
8. What is Mercast?
9. How is plaster mold separated from the pattern?
10. What is plumbago?

Permanent Molds

16

Molds that are not destroyed after each casting are called *permanent molds*. They are made of metal and have a high degree of permanence. These molds are capable of producing from 3,000 to 10,000 iron castings and from 10,000 to 25,000 or more aluminum castings.

The simplest type of permanent mold is the book mold, so named because of its resemblance to a book, with two mold halves that are hinged or clamped together to close the mold (Fig. 16-1). Permanent molds, however, are made in a variety of ways and can have two or more parts. The way the mold opens can vary. A simple book mold can be opened manually. Molding machines can open and close molds by the use of a mechanical link system or by an air cylinder or a hydraulic cylinder system (Fig. 16-2). All permanent molds are made so that they can be opened and closed easily and so that the complete casting and gating system can be removed. Molds can be made for items as small as 1 oz with a wall thickness of 0.10 in. or as heavy as 50 to 75 lb. The design of the mold must be kept simple because the casting must be ejected after the pouring.

The standard procedure for pouring a permanent mold involves the following steps. First the permanent mold is coated with a casting release agent, such as burnt carbon from a fuel source. Second, the mold is clamped shut and pressure is applied to the mold halves. This pressure keeps the mold from opening during the pouring process. The mold is poured and the exterior surfaces of the casting are allowed to solidify. The casting is ejected by opening the mold. The cavity surface is again coated with a casting release agent and the process is repeated. This pouring process is identical whether the book-type mold (Fig. 16-1) or the straight-line retraction-type mold is used (Fig. 16-2).

The straight-line retraction-type mold is used more by industry because it can be adapted to automatic or semiautomatic production lines. The typical turntable permanent molding production line is a device that is mounted on a turntable which revolves constantly from 2 to 7 r/min with approximately 4 or 5 work stations (Fig. 16-3). The tasks at the stations include mold coating, coring, pouring, solidification, and shake out or ejection. Each station may have a person performing each task, or the whole operation may be accomplished by one person, depending on the rotational speed of the turntable. Usually, the center of the turntable has a cooling station that blows cool air over the molds. There are also heating units which keep the permanent molds themselves as close to the correct pouring temperature as possible. A 12-station turntable permanent

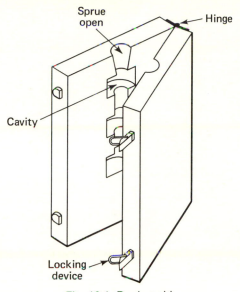

Fig. 16-1. Book mold.

mold, for example, may be set to rotate one complete revolution every 3 min. In this case, a mold is poured every 15 s. The casting production rate is set by the revolution time of the machine.

CORES

Metal cores are used for nonferrous metals. The two major types of metal cores are pin cores (Fig. 16-4a) and collapsible cores (Fig. 16-4b). Pin cores are usually polished steel cores that are simply retracted from the casting. The collapsible core is composed of two or more parts: the side core itself and a tapered center core that is removed to allow the side core to fall to the center of the cored area for retraction. Whenever possible, collapsible multipart cores are avoided because they are expensive and they slow down the casting cycle. When grey-iron permanent molds are cast, metal cores cannot be used; sand cores are used instead. Using a combination of metal molds and sand cores is often referred to as *semipermanent mold casting* because the sand cores are destroyed in each casting.

The core, as well as the mold face, must be protected with a refractory coating so that the casting is released from the permanent mold surface and so that the mold will have a long life. Also, this procedure provides a smooth surface for the mold and helps to control the cooling rate of the cast metal. Two types of refractory agents and mold release agents are (1) a refractory slurry of graphite, clay, or whiting for nonferrous metals and (2) carbon black, the residue of hydrocarbon burning, for ferrous metals. Often when cast iron is poured into a cast-iron mold, the refractory slurry is painted on and then carbon soot is added to ensure mold release.

GATING

Because permanent molds are made from materials that are not permeable, such as cast iron, the gating systems have to vent the casting to the atmosphere. The primary gating system used in most permanent molds is a parting line gating system, placed where the two mold halves come together. It is important to vent the molds by slightly misaligning the mold halves. Another method of venting permanent molds is to drill small vent holes from the casting through the exterior wall of the permanent mold. The holes should be large enough to allow the flow of air out of the mold cavity but small enough to prohibit metal from flowing through them.

The standard parting line gate used in most gating systems is a bottom entry gating system, composed of a down sprue, an end gate, a runner, and a bottom gate (Fig. 16-5). The advantage of a bottom gating system is that there is more control of the metal as it enters the mold cavity. The velocity of the metal is controlled to a greater extent than in any other end-gate system, and what turbulence exists is minimized by bottom gating systems. Permanent molds can contain either single or multiple patterns. Regardless of the number of castings, the recommended method for gating the castings is through the use of down sprues and bottom gates. Risers

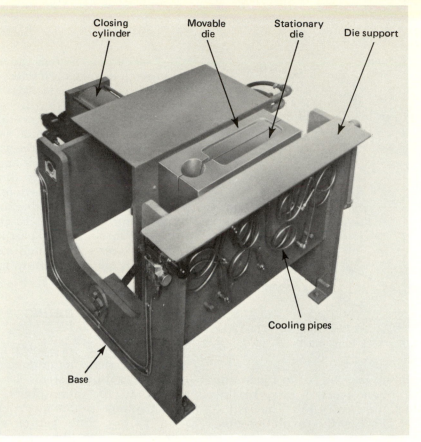

Fig. 16-2. Permanent mold casting machine. (*The Centrifugal Casting Machine Company*.)

Fig. 16-3. Turntable permanent molding. (*The Centrifugal Casting Machine Company*.)

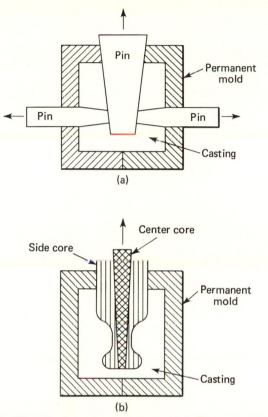

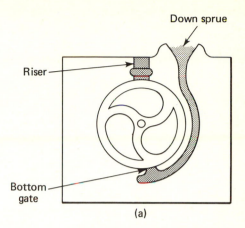

Fig. 16-4. Permanent mold cores. (a) Pin core; (b) center, or collapsible, core.

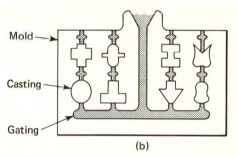

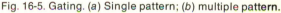

Fig. 16-5. Gating. (a) Single pattern; (b) multiple **pattern.**

generally are required on all permanent molds to counteract the lack of permeability of the metal molds, and they are larger than comparable risers used in sand castings. The risers should be designed, as in all castings, to be the last molten metal to solidify.

A method to control turbulence further in permanent mold castings is the use of tilt pouring devices. A tilt pouring machine allows the operator to pour the molten metal into a measured holding cup that will hold only the amount of metal needed to fill the casting cavity. The total mold is then tilted, allowing the molten metal to enter the casting. Upon solidification, the casting is ejected from the mold, and the mold is resurfaced with refractory. It is then closed and placed in the original position so that more metal can be ladled into the holding device (Fig. 16-6).

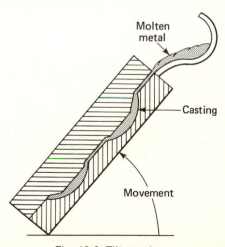

Fig. 16-6. Tilt pouring.

SQUEEZE MOLDING

Squeeze molding is a relatively new process that was developed in the Soviet Union. The metal is poured into a mold and then, instead of the mold simply closing, the mold is closed and a pressure of 50 tons is applied to the mold surface, compressing more metal into the mold cavity than can possibly be there under 1 atm of gravity pressure (Fig. 16-7). Little is known about this process, but it is said to increase greatly the mechanical characteristics of the poured metal. The squeeze molding process has not yet been adapted to production in the United States as it is still in the research stage.

LOW-PRESSURE CASTING

Approximately 1 atm of air pressure is used in low-pressure permanent mold casting to inject the molten metal up a riser tube through a control plate into the permanent mold. The pressure is released, the control plate solidifies, the metal is allowed to drop back into the sealed crucible, and the casting is ejected from the permanent mold. The mold is then recoated with the refractory and the process is repeated. The low-pressure permanent mold casting process is easy to automate. One

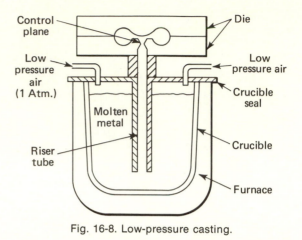

Fig. 16-8. Low-pressure casting.

major advantage of the low-pressure casting system is that the riser tube extends close to the bottom of the sealed crucible allowing only clean metal to be forced up the riser tube to the permanent mold (Fig. 16-8). Because the molten metal has fewer impurities in it, the as-cast finish of the casting produced by this process is superior to the finish on the casting produced by gravity permanent molding. The low-pressure permanent mold casting process produces castings that are much sounder than castings produced with the gravity permanent mold process, and it also produces castings that are more homogeneous in structure.

SLUSH CASTING

Slush casting is a permanent mold casting process that produces hollow castings without the use of cores. It is used mainly for ornamental objects such as toys, statuettes, and other novelties. Slush casting is accomplished by pouring a molten metal into a permanent mold, allowing the metal to solidify slightly, and then inverting the mold and draining the still molten metal out of the mold. The metal in contact with the permanent mold surface will form an inner shell that is composed of chill and columnar crystals of solidified metal (Fig. 16-9).

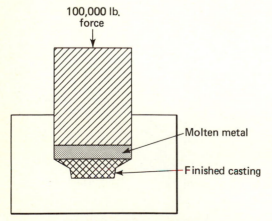

Fig. 16-7. Squeeze molding.

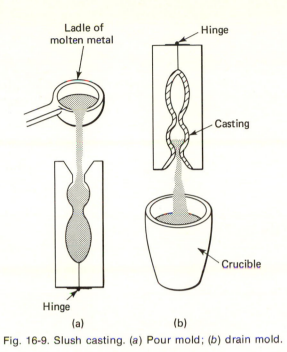

Fig. 16-9. Slush casting. (a) Pour mold; (b) drain mold.

DIP CASTING

In the dip casting process, a male permanent mold is dipped into a molten metal and then removed from the metal, allowing a certain portion of metal to solidify on the male mold before the shell is removed (Fig. 16-10). The electronics industry uses dip casting for casting electronic component

forms. Electronic parts are placed in these castings and an insulating material is poured into them. The material solidifies; and once this insulation material and the imbedded components are satisfactorily combined, the dip-cast mold, which is composed of a low-melting-temperature metal, is melted away, leaving the completed, smooth-finished electronic component exposed. Only the extremely low-melting metals (such as lead, tin, and zinc) are being used in industry for dip casting.

CORTHIAS CASTING

Corthias casting, or pressed casting, is a little-used technique that allows hollow castings to be made in permanent molds. Corthias casting uses a permanent mold with a permanent core. The permanent mold is filled to a prescribed fullness, and then the permanent core is pressed into the molten metal, allowing the metal to fill the molding cavity to create the hollow casting (Fig. 16-11). Pressed castings are used mainly in the production of toys. This method also is limited to use with only low-temperature alloys.

DIE CASTING

The die-casting process, another form of permanent mold casting, involves forcing a

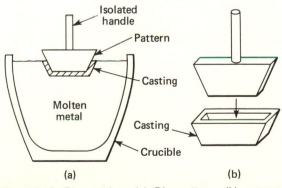

Fig. 16-10. Dip casting. (a) Dip pattern; (b) remove casting.

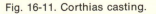

Fig. 16-11. Corthias casting.

molten metal into a permanent mold cavity under pressure. Metals used for die casting include tin, lead, zinc, aluminum, and to a small extent, copper and iron alloys. The actual process of die casting is referred to as a one-step process because the metal is changed from a liquid to a solid state in one step.

Pressure and Gravity Die Casting

Much consideration has been given to the advantages of the gravity die-casting system over the pressure die-casting system (Fig. 16-12). Pressure die casting forces molten metal into a die with air, hydraulic, or mechanical pressure. Gravity die casting pours molten metal into a die and uses gravity to force the molten metal into the die cavity. Gravity-poured castings are superior in metallurgical structure to the castings poured under pressure because gravity-set castings solidify as the molten metal flows into the die, progressively freezing the metal. Each

freezing layer is fed by the liquid layer above it, allowing the gases in the metal to escape through the molten metal and giving the casting a sound grain structure. Besides a stronger metallurgical structure, gravity-fed castings have less total shrinkage and can be pressure tight.

In the pressure-fed die-casting system, molten metal that comes in contact with the die surface solidifies immediately, as in other types of casting processes, but gases are entrapped in the molten metal. The gases cannot escape through the gating system because the gating system has pressure forcing the metal in instead of allowing the air to come out. Since the entrapped air is not allowed to escape, it is forced into the metallurgical structure of the metal, causing porous and weak castings.

Die-Casting Machines

Die-casting machines consist of three main parts. First, there is the frame, which must be

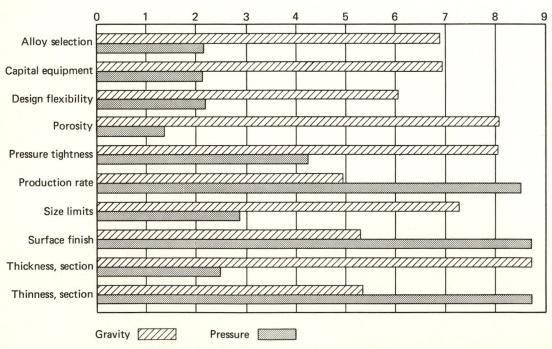

Fig. 16-12. Die casting, pressure versus gravity.

rigid and strong enough to support the weight of the dies. Then there is the mechanism for opening and closing the dies, driven by air, an electrical motor, or fluid (either water or oil). Last, there must be an apparatus for injecting the molten metal into the die, an operation that may be done either mechanically or manually.

While there are a number of die-casting machines, all have basically the same operating procedures. First, molten metal is forced into the closed die. The dies usually are water-cooled when used in high-production runs. Next, the metal is forced into a system of runners and gates and then into the mold cavity itself. After the metal solidifies, the split die opens and the casting is removed with ejector pins which have been built directly into the dies. After the casting has been ejected, the parting lines and gates are removed by trimming the excess metal from them. The item is then ready for the finishing operation. In order to increase production of small items, dies with numbers of cavities are used and these are called *multiple-cavity dies*.

The two basic methods of die casting include the hot-chamber method and the cold-chamber method. The hot-chamber method is accomplished with either the gooseneck machine or the plunger machine.

PLUNGER DIE-CASTING MACHINE. The hot-chamber plunger die-casting machine is used primarily with lead- and zinc-based alloys containing aluminum. The charging chamber rests in a reservoir of molten metal. The chamber has an opening in its wall just below the surface of the molten metal and the mechanically powered piston or plunger. The neck of the chamber is positioned in the sprue in the stationary half of the die. With the piston in the *up* position, metal enters the opening in the chamber wall. As the piston begins to travel downward in the cylinder, or the charging chamber, it closes the opening in the side and the compression cycle begins. The pressure buildup ranges from a few hundred to 5,000 psi. This pressure forces the metal through the gooseneck, into the sprue, and into the die where solidification occurs.

The pressure of the plunger is released. The casting is allowed to solidify and then is ejected, completing the cycle which can be repeated. This pressure system must be used only on those metals that do not dissolve iron and steel. If metals are used that dissolve the piston in the chamber, the close-fit tolerances could not be maintained, resulting in the metal being squeezed out between the pistons with an accompanying loss of pressure. Such conditions would greatly affect the quality of the castings (Fig. 16-13).

AIR-INJECTION DIE-CASTING MACHINE. The gooseneck, or air-injection, hot-chamber die-casting machine is designed primarily for use with aluminum-based alloys, although it also is used with zinc alloys and combinations of aluminum and zinc. It is limited to an air pressure under 700 psi, with the usual operating air pressure from 300 to 600 psi. At an operating pressure above 700 psi the gooseneck will burst. The gooseneck machine can handle larger castings than the plunger-type die-casting machine because the gooseneck cavity is larger and can handle larger amounts of molten metal.

The first step in the operating procedure

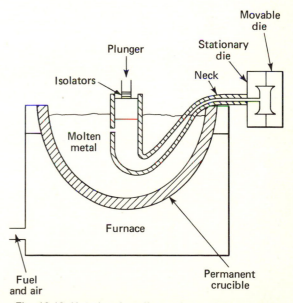

Fig. 16-13. Hot-chamber die casting—plunger type.

is the lowering of the gooseneck into the molten metal, allowing the molten metal to enter at the nozzle end. After the gooseneck is filled, the neck and nozzle assembly is raised and the nozzle is inserted into a receptacle in the stationary half of the die. The metal enters the die in a spray of finely divided particles. Because of this spraying action, air is entrapped in the cavity, resulting in porosity of the casting. Since there is an absence of moving parts, fits and allowances are critical. Again, metals which have a dissolving effect on iron and steel should not be used (Fig. 16-14).

The restriction of this machine to a low number of alloys is a disadvantage to its use. For example, magnesium solidifies in the nozzle, which has the effect of restricting the flow and causing the metal to spurt out between the nozzle and the die. Also, the molten metal becomes contaminated by contact with the ferrous metal that the gooseneck is made from. These disadvantages, coupled with the low-pressure design of the machine, cause castings to be of poor metallurgical quality and to have a low density. Consequently, the machine gradually has been replaced by the cold-chamber die-casting machine.

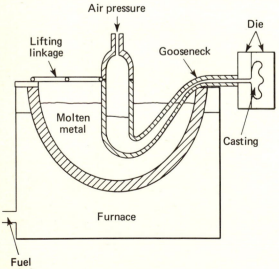

Fig. 16-14. Hot-chamber die casting—air-injection type.

COLD-CHAMBER DIE-CASTING MACHINE. There are two types of cold-chamber die-casting machines. One is operated in the vertical position, and the other is operated in the horizontal position. These cold-chamber die-casting machines can be used for any metal that can be cast and can be contained in a permanent die. The primary metals used for cold-chamber die casting include aluminum, magnesium, and copper-based alloys.

The horizontal casting machine cycle begins when molten metal is ladled from a holding pot into the shot hole (Fig. 16-15a). The plunger is then activated and, as the plunger progresses toward the stationary die, the charging hole is covered. Pressures are built up that range from 2,500 to 50,000 psi, forcing the metal into the die. The piston travel, according to the machine size, may vary from 5 to 250 in./s. After solidification, the die is opened and the plunger continues its forward motion, pushing the slug or the metal remaining in the sprue out of the cylinder. Ejector pins are activated in the movable die half, forcing the casting from the die cavity (Fig. 16-15b).

The vertical cold-chamber die-casting machine operates on the same basic principle, varying mainly in the sequence of the steps. The chamber is oriented vertically with the top open. At the lower end of the chamber a piston-like valve is positioned, covering the sprue hole. When the charge of molten metal is introduced into the chamber, the metal rests on the top of the lower piston. The upper ram is then positioned at the top of the opened cylinder and activated. As the compression begins, the lower piston is forced down, exposing the sprue hole and allowing the metal to be forced into the die under pressure. After solidification, the upper ram is withdrawn and the lower piston is activated. As upward travel begins, the pistons shear the remaining metal in the chamber from the sprue and force it out of the top of the charging chamber. The movable die opens, the casting is removed, and the lower piston then returns to its original starting position so that the machine is ready for the next complete cycle. The vertical cold-chamber die-casting machine can pro-

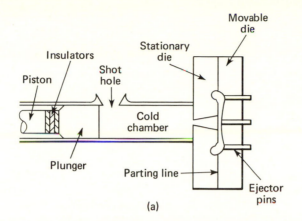

(a)

(b)

Fig. 16-15. Cold-chamber die casting. (a) Principle; (b) application. (*American Die Casting Machinery Company*.)

duce die-cast products that have greater densities than the products of any of the other die-casting processes.

Gating

Runner and gating design is important in the making of dies. The object of gating is to fill the cavity in an orderly manner without undue eddies or entrapment of air in the casting. General rules are that the sectional area of runners should be considerably greater than that of the gates they feed and they should be slightly tapered, decreasing gradually in the direction of flow. Passages should be smooth and gradual rather than sharp so that eddies and flow currents in the molten metal will not be created.

The pressure and speed of the shot are the primary factors that affect the structural soundness as well as the surface of a die casting. The quality of aluminum and zinc castings is adversely affected when the injection pressure drops at the end of the stroke of the plunger. Machine designers have developed pressure intensifiers, which are not part of most die-casting machines. These devices are usually entirely self-contained and automatic, functioning as a part of the injection cylinder unit without presetting or adjustment. They function by increasing the pressure from two to six times that of the starting pressure. This great increase in pressure packs metal into the die with tremendous force, increasing the density of the casting and, consequently, improving the quality and mechanical strength of the casting. The control of the injection speed and the elimination of plunger bounce are other important factors that need to be considered when die-casting machines are designed.

QUESTIONS

1. What is a book mold?
2. Why preheat a permanent mold before use?
3. What are the major types of cores used in permanent molding?
4. Explain permanent mold venting.
5. Explain permanent mold gating systems.
6. How is turbulence controlled in permanent mold casting?
7. What metals are cast by the permanent mold process?
8. Why are risers usually required?
9. Explain squeeze molding, dip molding, and slush molding.
10. What are the differences between pressure and gravity die casting?
11. What are the general rules regarding the design of gating and runner systems for successful die casting?

17

Powder Metals

The powder metal technique of forming metal parts is a simple process, consisting of pressing finely powdered metals into a die to form the desired shape and then heating, or sintering, the granular compact to cause the individual metallic particles to weld together. It is one of the cheapest mass production processes for manufacturing high-quality, high-strength, complex parts with a high degree of accuracy.

POWDER METAL PROCESS

Metal parts manufactured by the powder metallurgy process are produced in three basic steps: blending, compacting, and sintering, or heating (Fig. 17-1).

In the blending stage the metal powder is mixed with lubricants, other metals, and any additives that might be used. These materials are weighed to ensure the correct proportions before they are mixed into a homogeneous blend.

The next stage, compacting, consists of filling a die with its required amount of blending mixture and then compressing it between two or more punches. The pressure exerted ranges from 20 to 50 tons/in.² The pressure and production rate vary according to the size and shape of the part and the density of the powdered metals being compressed. After the powdered metals are compressed, the solid mass, called a *briquette* or a *green compact,* is ejected from the die. This green compact can be handled, but it is relatively fragile. If the green compact were dropped, it would probably crack or fall apart. The green compact is said to have green strength, the same as foundry sand.

The sintering, or heating, of the green briquette is usually done in a continuously operated furnace with a highly controlled reducing atmosphere. The final step of the process is carried out at a temperature well below the melting point of the base metal but high enough to bond the particles together to produce parts with good physical and mechanical characteristics. After the part is sintered, it may be ready for use. If desired, however, further processing may be performed to obtain additional characteristics. These additional processes include coining, or sizing, resintering, and infiltration (Fig. 17-1).

Compacting

Compacting, or briquetting, is more important than any other individual operation in producing powder metal parts. The methods

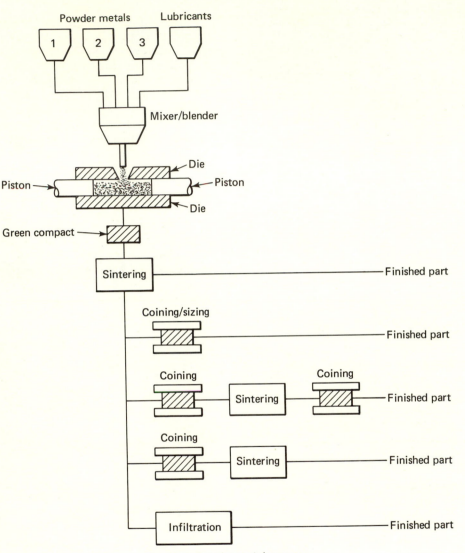

Fig. 17-1. Powder metal process.

used and the shape and the size of the article depend on the metal or alloy being used. The purpose behind compacting, or briquetting, is to increase the contact surface between the metal particles and to cold weld the particles together into a green compact (Fig. 17-2). Usually during pressing the height of the powder is decreased three or four times.

DIES. The basic tool in powder metallurgy is the die. The die is the piece of equipment that is responsible for forming the powder metal into a usable mass. The die consists of the matrix, the punch, and the support (Fig. 17-3). The matrix forms the sides of the compact and the punch forms the top of the compact and applies the pressure for the compacting process. The support forms the bottom in a single-end die. In a double-end die, two punches are used from opposite ends with one punch supplying the support and the other supplying the punch. However, both punches will be movable (Fig. 17-4).

Even with the use of double punches,

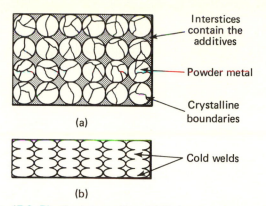

Fig. 17-2. Plastic deformation. (a) Before compression; (b) green compact.

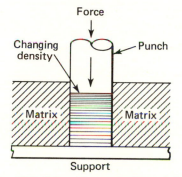

Fig. 17-3. Briquetting—single-end die.

powder metal compacting creates a serious problem of pressure gradients on objects that are of irregular shape. These pressure gradients have led to the use of multiple punches that control the powder metal better by applying varying pressures on it (Fig. 17-5).

Dies are classified as collapsible dies or noncollapsible dies. The noncollapsible die is used whenever the green compact can be forced out of the die cavity without harming the compact. If the design of the product is such that the green compact cannot be forced out of the die cavity, then a collapsible die, or a die that can have panels removed, must be used. Collapsible dies are more expensive and have longer production cycles than non-collapsible dies. More complicated designs can be produced by collapsible dies than by noncollapsible dies. The major design requirement when constructing a noncollapsible die is that the finished article must have positive draft or the article cannot be extracted from the die cavity (Fig. 17-6). This draft is the same type of draft used when constructing foundry patterns. Draft in powder metallurgy dies is usually under 1°.

The design of the green compact is usually limited to those parts that have less than 10-in.² cross-sectional area figured by using

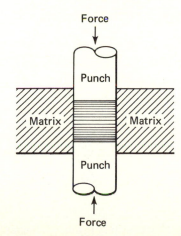

Fig. 17-4. Briquetting—double-end die.

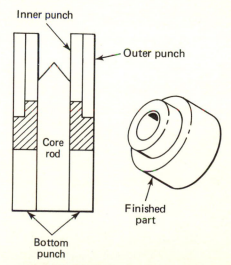

Fig. 17-5. Multiple-punch compact.

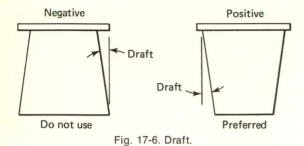

Fig. 17-6. Draft.

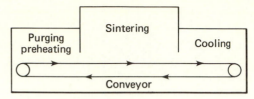

Fig. 17-8. Sintering furnace.

the formula

$$H = \sqrt{L \times H}$$

or the height (H) is equal to the square root of the cross-sectional area ($L \times H$). For example, if an item is 3 in. wide and 3 in. long, the length times the width equals 9 in.^{2}. The square root of 9 is equal to 3; therefore the height of the green compact has a maximum limitation of 3 in.

PRESSES. The green compact may be produced by either a mechanical or a hydraulic press. Mechanical presses are used for producing green compacts that require less than 150 tons pressure, and hydraulic presses are used for those compacts that require from 150 to 2,000 tons pressure. The production speed and the pressure are the two main differences between mechanical and hydraulic presses. Mechanical presses are adaptable to high production; some are capable of producing up to 1,000 green compacts per hour. Hydraulic presses are slow by comparison; usually their top production limit is 100 green compacts per hour when a large press is used.

Sintering

When the green compact is removed from the die, it is not very strong and is very brittle. If dropped on the floor, it would probably disintegrate. Therefore, it must undergo further processing in order to be a usable powder metal product. This further processing is sintering, i.e., a heating process. The article is placed in a furnace and allowed to soak in the heat until the individual particles are no longer discernible.

The sintering process accomplishes several things. First, residual stresses are relaxed and minute changes occur in the shape of the individual particles. Second, the process forces the particles to go through solid-state diffusion-bond welding that originates at the cold weld zones and continues until all of the metallic particles are welded into a coherent mass. The impurities that are a part of the metal particles are forced out of each individual interstice into small impurity voids within the sintered compact (Fig. 17-7). Also, individual crystals may be recrystallized within the compact if the sintering tem-

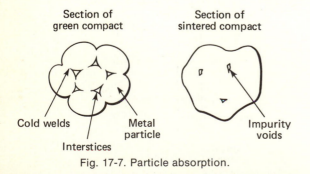

Fig. 17-7. Particle absorption.

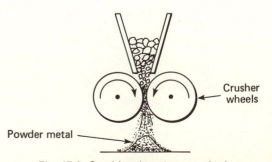

Fig. 17-9. Crushing (gyratory crusher).

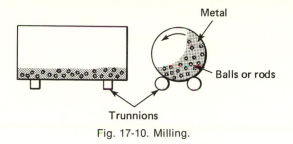

Fig. 17-10. Milling.

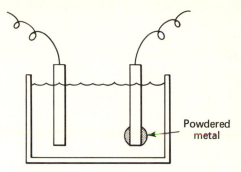

Fig. 17-12. Electrolysis (or electrodeposition).

perature is high enough to have an effect on the crystalline structure.

FURNACES. Furnaces for sintering vary greatly depending on the temperatures desired, the sintering time needed, and the nature of the protective atmosphere within the furnace.

The major type of furnace used is the electric resistance furnace. The temperature, the hydrocarbons, and the nitrides can easily be controlled in the electric reverse resistance furnace, whereas in a gas-fired furnace, controlling the atmosphere within the furnace is more difficult.

The typical sintering furnace has three main parts: the loading, purging, and preheating portion; the sintering portion; and the cooling portion (Fig. 17-8).

MANUFACTURE OF POWDERS

The range of metal powders available has been extended by recent technological developments to nearly an infinite range of metal alloys. Many nonmetallic powders can be used with metallic powders to produce new and different alloys. Powdered metals are obtained from ores, salts, or other compounds, and from bulk metals or alloys. Powdered metals can be produced in a number of ways, by crushing ore, by milling, machining, graining, atomizing, or by evaporation, condensation, reduction, precipitation, displacement, electrodeposition, and disintegration (Figs. 17-9 to 17-12).

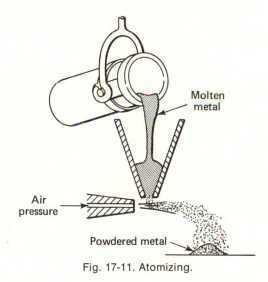

Fig. 17-11. Atomizing.

QUESTIONS

1. What is sintering?
2. Explain the major ways metals are converted into powder form.
3. What is a green compact?
4. Identify and describe the different types of dies used in powder metallurgy.
5. What is the major type of furnace used in powder metallurgy? Why?

18

Forging

Forging causes plastic deformation of a metal by imposing external stresses on it through hammering or squeezing operations. One of the basic metalworking manufacturing processes, forging consists of working a piece of metal, usually hot, to a predetermined shape by using one of the major types of forging processes: hammering, upsetting, pressing, extruding, or rolling. Of all machine shop work performed, casting and forging operations make up 90 percent. More steel is manufactured by forging than any other metal.

The major advantage that the forging process has over all other processes (such as casting, machine tool, and powdered metals) is that it produces a tougher fibrous structure. The fibrous structure is known as *grain flow*. In a machine gear blank that has not been forged, the grain flow would go straight across the metal. In other words, the flow would be in the direction of the flow in the plate from which the gear blank was cut. In a forged gear blank, however, the grain flow, appearing from the center of the forged gear blank, radiates to the sides of the gear blank, thus strengthening the metal (Fig. 18-1). Because of this characteristic of grain flow in forged metal, metal parts produced by forging are stronger than parts produced by any other metalworking process.

CRYSTALLINE STRUCTURE

When a metal is forged, the crystalline structure of the forged part undergoes a change and internal stresses are built up. If left in their as-forged state, most metals would eventually tear themselves apart because of the internal stresses. Forged parts must go through a second operation of heat treating, an operation called *recrystallization* (Fig. 18-2).

The recrystallization, or annealing, process is accomplished by placing the forging in a furnace and allowing it to heat up beyond the lower transformation temperature until grain refinement starts. The forging is soaked in the heat long enough to ensure total recrystallization throughout the forging. Then the forging is removed from the furnace and either quenched in a quenching agent or allowed to cool to room temperature. The choice depends on what machine operations need to be performed on the forging. This recrystallization also removes all worked-in stresses, yielding a stress-free forging with a fine-to-medium crystalline structure.

If the temperature of the forged metal is allowed to increase above the upper transformation temperature, grain growth will again

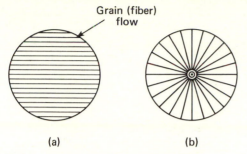

Fig. 18-1. Metallic grain flow. (a) Machined gear blank; (b) forged gear blank.

TABLE 18-1. HOT-WORKING TEMPERATURES OF SELECTED METALS

METAL	HOT-WORKING TEMPERA- TURE, F°	LOWEST RECRYSTAL- LIZATION TEMPERATURE, F°
Aluminum	600–900	300
Brass	1,100–1,650	400
Copper	800–900	212
Nickel	1,600–2,300	1,100
Steel, low carbon	1,500–2,200	900
Steel, high carbon	1,400–2,000	1,000

start, increasing until the forging is either removed from the furnace or melts. Table 18-1 identifies some of the hot-working, or forging, temperatures of selected metals as well as the lowest recrystallization temperature for the metals. The single most important aspect of forging is the hot-working temperature of the metal. If the metal is allowed to overheat, the resultant metal properties will not be the ones desired; and if the forging is allowed to cool too much while being hammered or pressed, excessive stresses will be set up within the forging and will ruin it.

METHODS OF SHAPING

Three major types of forging actions may be taken to shape metal. The metal may be drawn out, which increases the length of the workpiece. The metal may be upset, which

decreases the length of the workpiece. Or the metal may be squeezed, which increases the length of the workpiece in two or more directions (Fig. 18-3). The major ways that hot metals are deformed are: hammering, upset forging, pressing, extruding, and rolling. These five basic types of forging processes are controlled by the equipment used.

Hammering

The simplest way of shaping a piece of metal is to strike it with a hammer while holding the workpiece against an anvil. Hammering may be accomplished by hand or by machine. The basic process of hand hammering, begun in antiquity, has not changed. Hand hammering depends primarily on the skill of the hand forger, not on the equipment used. The

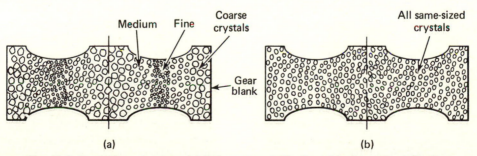

Fig. 18-2. Crystalline structure. (a) Before recrystallization; (b) after recrystallization.

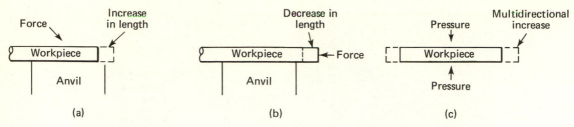

Fig. 18-3. Major types of forging actions. (a) Drawing; (b) upsetting; (c) squeezing.

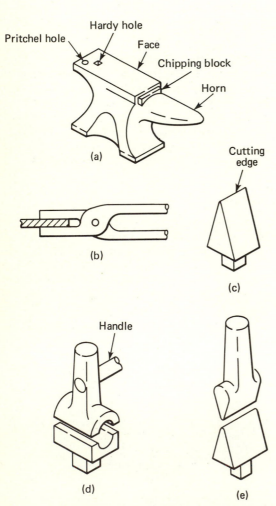

Fig. 18-4. Hand forging tools. (a) Anvil; (b) tongs; (c) hardies; (d) swages; (e) fullers.

basic equipment used for hand hammering, or hand forging, is the anvil, tongs, and hammers. Hammers usually range in weight from 1 to 16 lb. Other tools of the hand forger, or smith, are hardies, swages, and fullers. Hardies are cutting devices; swages shape hot metal into a preformed shape; and fullers are necking down devices (Fig. 18-4).

The demand of modern industry for many repetitions of a part has resulted in mechanical hammering (Fig. 18-5), relegating hand hammering to very special work. The die apparatus attached both to the hammer of a mechanical hammer and to the anvil has replaced the necessary expertise of the operator in hammer forging.

Hammer forging equipment can be divided into three fairly broad classifications. The board, the airlift gravity drop, and the steam piston are all used as hammer forging mechanisms. Hammer forging is more commonly known now as *drop forging*. The main function of the drop forge is to form metal, which has been heated to a plastic state, into a desired shape by the blows of the falling weight of the hammer.

DROP FORGING. Drop forging consists of hammering heated bars of metal inside closed impression dies. This process is accomplished by kneading and forming the hot plastic metal into dies that have been machine ground to close tolerances. These dies control the shapes and sizes of the worked pieces. The impact pressure of the hammer blows refines the steel billets and improves the physical properties of the metal. The drop forging process is capable of producing forgings that range in weight from less than one ounce to several hundred pounds.

Guides

Lifting device

Hammer

Anvil (platen)

(a)

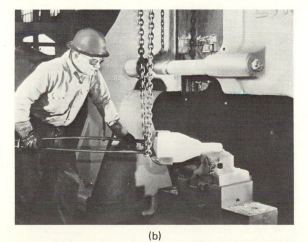

(b)

Fig. 18-5. Hammer. (a) Parts of a hammer; (b) application (*American Iron and Steel Institute*).

At the heart of the drop forging system are the forging dies. Forging dies are made from high-carbon, nickel-chromium-molybdenum alloy steel blocks which have been forged to achieve the maximum grain refinement and resistance to shock. Special heat treatment of these forging dies ensures a maximum resistance to wear.

Before any die shapes or impressions are cut into the rough die blocks, shanks are shaped into the blocks for locking the dies in the forging equipment. These shanks, or locking devices, are designed specifically for one piece of equipment. After the locks have been shaped, the blocks are then squared for perfect alignment. The striking surfaces are planed to make sure that the two die surfaces (the interface) are parallel.

The next step in creating a die is the cutting of the impression into the die material, or die block. Six types of impressions may be cut into the die: The *swager* reduces and draws out the stock when the differences in cross-sectional area make it necessary. The *edger* or roller distributes the stock so that it will fill the next impression or cavity without excessive waste. The *bender* impression forms initial curves or angles in the forging before it is subjected to a finishing impression. Often this finishing impression can be omitted. The *blocker* impression gives the forging its general shape and allows the proper gradual flow of the metal that is necessary to prevent overlapping and cold shut outs. It has the same contour as the finished part except that extremely large fillets and contours are used permitting the easy flow of metal. The *finisher* impression presses the forging to its final size. The *gutter* removes the excess metal (the flash) which is forced out of the finishing cavity at the last hammer stroke. After any of these impressions have been cut into the die block, the next step is to heat treat the die and then grind it with special diamond-dust graining tools. The die is then heat treated again.

When a forging die is designed, several things must be taken into consideration. Of major importance is the draft of the die. *Forging draft* is the angle or taper that must be added to the surfaces of the forged part so that the forging will be released easily from the die. Forging draft ranges from 3 to 5° on external surfaces and from 5 to 10° on internal surfaces.

Another item to be considered is the shrinkage of metal. The hot metal used in forging shrinks as it cools. Steel is the metal used most in forging. It is forged at temperatures that range from 2100 to 2400°F (Table 18-1). At these temperatures steel is greatly expanded and during the forging process, which is also a cooling process, the metal shrinks. The die impressions, then, must allow for volumetric shrinkage in order to produce the proper sized finished part. The dies used for steel forgings are cut with a 3/16-in. shrink rule, the same shrink rule as is used in the foundry process.

IMPACT FORGING. Impact forging is an adaptation of the drop, or closed-die, forging machines. Impact forging machines, however, are designed so that the impact force is delivered to the stock horizontally (Fig. 18-6). Impact forging is anvilless forging; consequently, the shock that is imparted from the hammer to the anvil is not present. The full force of the impact is delivered to the stock. Impact forging machines are usually automated so that the delivery of the stock as well as the forging stroke is automatic. These machines can deliver 40 forgings per minute, but the forgings are limited in size to items that weigh less than 20 lb.

Upset Forging

Upset forgings are produced by a squeezing pressure rather than by an impact force. The forging machines used for upsetting the metal are designed to furnish the necessary pressure. The closed impression dies that are

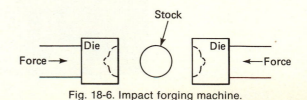

Fig. 18-6. Impact forging machine.

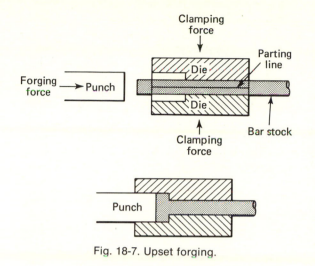

Fig. 18-7. Upset forging.

pressure exerted on the hot metal ranges from 1 to over 25 tons/in.². Most of the presses employed in this method of forging are either hydraulic or pneumatic.

Large forgings that require heavy hammers to shape them can be formed with a hydraulic press, which is smaller than the pneumatic press. The press forging process is faster than hammer forging too. Usually the forging dies have only one impression, and the forging is completed with one pressing. Because the impression dies are not subjected to the hammering of the drop hammer, they can be made with less draft, and they will yield a more accurate forging—an important advantage of press forging.

used with the machine are designed to grip the metal, acting as the anvils. Hot plastic metal is pushed into the dies by a punch that is held in the header ram (Fig. 18-7).

The first step in performing upset forging is to place a heated bar of stock between the two halves of the die and against a gage which permits the correct amount of metal to stick out beyond the gripping parts of the die. The bar is then upset into the impression chamber by the header ram. Upset forging is similar to drop forging in that it takes one or more steps in order to derive the finished shape. After the preliminary shaping has been completed, the heated bar is moved through a series of dies until all shaping has been completed. Some upset forgings can be completed in a die with one single impression, while other more complex forgings require as many as six or seven impressions before the product is completely forged. There is no flash to trim in upset forging as there is in drop forging.

Press Forging

Press forging employs a slow squeezing action in order to deform a hot plastic metal to the desired shape. The pressure is applied slowly, allowing time for the flow of the metal. The slow pressure results in changes that penetrate deeply into the forging. The

Roll Forging

Rolling may be regarded as a continuous form of open-die forging in which the hammer and the die rotate instead of work in a line. A metal bar is passed between a pair of metal rollers which rotate in opposite directions. When the workpiece is passed between the rollers, it retains its volume but its length is increased and its width is decreased. The cross-sectional size of the rolled forging can be shaped to almost any size. Rolling is by far the most used forging process in the United States particularly for structural shapes such as I beams, angles, and wide flange beams. Rolling equipment is expensive and designed primarily for large production runs. While rolling is not limited to ferrous metals, over 90 percent of all metals rolled are ferrous.

Two important items to be considered to ensure a quality product from rolled forgings are the angle of the bite and the temperature of the metal being rolled. The *angle of the bite* is the amount of deformation or the amount of reduction in area that results as a forging moves through the roll forge (Fig. 18-8a). If the angle of the bite is too severe, the metal will be torn and ripped because too much stress is placed on it. If the angle of the bite is too small, repeated passes through the roll will be necessary in order to form the metal into the finished product.

The rolls in a rolling mill are supported

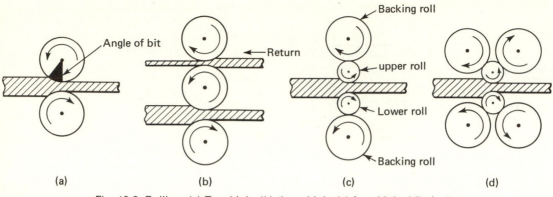

Fig. 18-8. Rolling. (*a*) Two high; (*b*) three high; (*c*) four high; (*d*) cluster.

at either end and tend to deflect under load, a characteristic which produces material that is thicker in the middle than at either end. One way to compensate for this difference is to make the rollers larger in the middle. This means of compensation is not widely practiced because it is not completely accurate. A better solution provides support for the working rollers by using massive backup rolls (Fig. 18-8*c*). These backup rolls keep the smaller working rolls from bending and thus keep the workpiece forging at a constant thickness.

ROLL RECRYSTALLIZATION. One advantage of hot rolling is that as the metals enter the angle of bite, the hot crystals are deformed into long crystals. This rapid deformation of crystals generates enough heat so that the stretch crystals begin a recrystallization

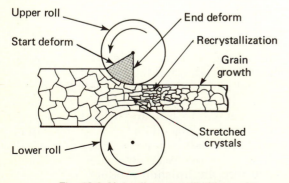

Fig. 18-9. Hot-roll recrystallization.

process. The grains grow and, as they grow, they are placed farther and farther from the forging rolls. As the temperature of the forging decreases, the crystalline growth is arrested. The crystalline growth is controlled by the spacing between each stand (Fig. 18-9).

Extrusion

Extrusion is an uncomplicated hot metalworking manufacturing process that can produce some of the most complex shapes of all the hot metalworking manufacturing processes. For example, extrusions are used to manufacture all standard structural shapes. They also are used to make such products as the mast of a sailboat that must be lightweight and have high strength with the added complication of having sail guides designed into the mast. In Fig. 18-10 examples of extrusions are illustrated.

The two basic types of extrusions are the direct and the indirect (Fig. 18-11*a* and *b*). The direct type of extrusion places a hot billet within a chamber that has a die at one end. A punch forces the hot billet through the die opening, producing the extrusion. The indirect method places the hot billet in the hot chamber; the die, which produces the extrusion, is attached to a hollow punch. As the punch travels forward, the hot metal is extruded through the die. Indirect extrusion does not require as much force as direct ex-

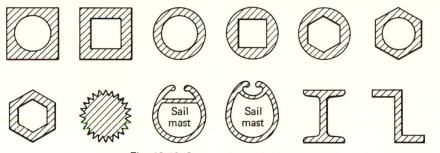

Fig. 18-10. Some extruded shapes.

trusion because no force is required to move the hot billet inside the chamber walls. The hot metal rubs against the chamber walls, an action which raises the pressure requirements for extrusion. The dummy block is used in both direct and indirect extrusion. The dummy block used in direct extrusion separates the punch from the hot metal; in indirect extrusion the die plays the part of the dummy block.

Direct extrusion has two major process variations, direct sleeve extrusion and hydrostatic extrusion. In direct sleeve extrusion the dummy block does not touch the walls of the chamber containing the billet. The dummy block is approximately one-eighth smaller than the diameter of the billet chamber. As the punch moves forward, the exterior surface of the billet remains stationary, producing a shell approximately ⅛ in. thick. Direct sleeve extrusion is used to counteract extrusion defect, a condition that exists when contaminants (such as the oxides that exist on

the exterior walls of the billet) are mixed into the final extrusion as the billet is pushed through the extrusion die. The direct sleeve extrusion method is one technique used to combat the inclusion of impurities in the final product.

In hydrostatic extrusion, a punch does not push on the hot billet. Instead, the billet is surrounded by a hydraulic fluid in a closed chamber, and the punch acts on the hydraulic fluid, which then acts on the hot metal, producing the extrusion. An advantage of hydrostatic extrusion is that all sidewall friction between the metal billet and the interior of the cylinder chamber is absorbed by the hydraulic fluid.

Indirect extrusion has been adapted to the manufacture of such soft metal thin-walled cylinder items as toothpaste and medicine tubes by the impact extrusion method. The impact extrusion method is not a hot metalworking technique. Because it extrudes metal without the use of heat, it is usually lim-

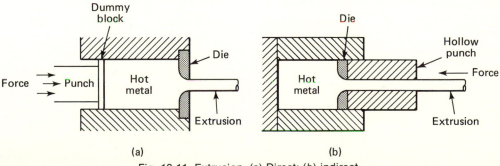

(a)   (b)

Fig. 18-11. Extrusion. (a) Direct; (b) indirect.

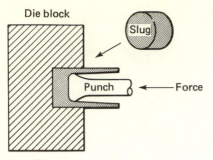

Fig. 18-12. Impact extrusion.

ited to use with soft nonferrous metals. In this process, a slug of soft metal is first placed in a die block. A punch is then forced against the slug, and the metal extrudes around the slug, producing a soft metal cylinder. The cylinder usually has an excellent finish and is accurate in size. Also, cold-working of the metal slug increases the mechanical properties of the soft metal, producing a fine grain structure that has a grain flow running the length of the cylinder (Fig. 18-12).

QUESTIONS

1. What is grain flow?
2. Why is the crystalline structure of a forging superior to that of a casting?
3. What is recrystallization?
4. Describe the three major types of forging actions.
5. What is swaging?
6. Why is there more than one impression in a drop-forged die block? What are the six types of impressions that may be cut into the die?
7. What is the angle of bite?

Part Four

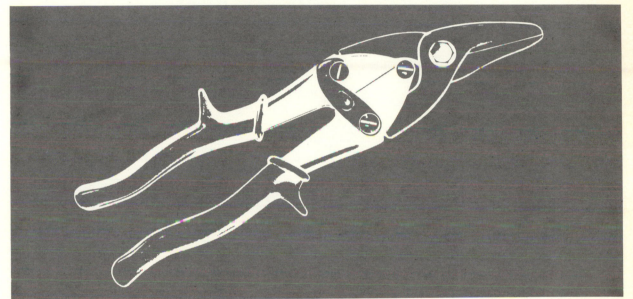

Cold Metalworking

19

Squeezing

Cold-working of metal occurs when metals are deformed below their recrystallization temperature. Cold forming can be accomplished by either squeezing, bending, or shearing. Squeezing includes the areas of cold-rolling, cold forging, drawing, swaging, and cold extrusion. Cold-working is used primarily as a finishing process and usually follows hot-working, which has been used to accomplish the major portion of deformation of the metal. Cold forming includes a series of processes that produce metal parts that have already been hot formed into rough shapes.

Certain advantages result from working metals below their recrystallization temperatures. First, a smoother surface finish is possible when metals are worked at lower temperatures. Surface oxidation, or *scaling* of the work, is virtually nonexistent, but any existing scale on the surface of the metal to be cold formed must be removed. Another advantage of cold forming is that closer dimensional tolerances can be achieved than in the hot forming of metals because there is no thermal expansion in the cold-working processes. A third advantage of cold forming metals is that higher tensile strengths and more uniform grain structures result.

Cold forming has some disadvantages. Most significant is that more energy is needed, so more expensive equipment is required.

EFFECTS OF COLD-WORKING

Metals are composed of irregularly shaped crystals of various sizes. Each crystal, or grain, is composed of a series of atoms arranged in an orderly pattern. This orderly arrangement is known as a *space lattice*. When a material is cold-worked, the space lattice becomes internally stressed, causing structural changes in the space lattice (Fig. 19-1). Each crystal is composed of a series of shearing, or slip, planes. If a metal is worked until all the slip planes have been fractured, the metal ruptures. The ideal condition in cold-working is to use as many of these slip planes as possible within a crystal without allowing the metal to fail completely. The amount of cold-working a metal will withstand depends on its ductility. Because pure metals are more ductile than alloyed metals, pure metals can withstand a greater amount of deformation. Pure metals also will not strain harden as quickly as an alloyed metal.

Tensile Properties

The relationship of tensile properties to cold-working identifies the suitability of a metal to cold-working. This relationship is usually studied by means of stress-strain diagrams (Fig. 19-2). For example, metal will not

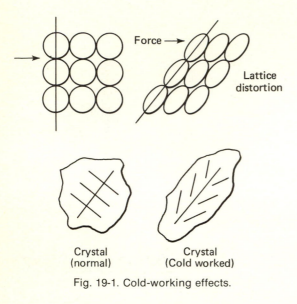

Fig. 19-1. Cold-working effects.

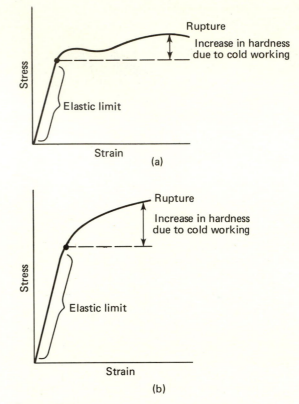

Fig. 19-2. Tensile properties. (a) Low-carbon steel; (b) high-carbon steel.

be deformed permanently unless the strain or deformation is done above the elastic limit of the metal. If the metal is not deformed above its elastic limit, it will resume its original shape when the strain is removed from it. The metal must be worked into its plastic range.

Crystal Deformation

When a metal is cold-worked, major changes in the shape and strength of each individual crystal occur. Before cold-working, crystals are usually equiaxed and may appear in many shapes. After the metal has been subjected to cold-working, the shapes of the crystals are elongated at an angle of 90° in the direction that the force is applied (Fig. 19-3). These cold-worked crystals will have locked-in residual stresses, the reason for their greater tensile properties in one direction. However, the crystals are weak if force is applied in a direction that is perpendicular to their elongation.

Preparation of Metals

Metals must be given special preparation before they are cold-worked. First, the scale must be removed from the metal to avoid abrasions and pitting of the dies that are used in cold-working. Scale is usually removed by some form of pickling, that is, dipping the metal in an acid bath and then washing the acid off the metal. Many metals used for cold forming are then given a light cold forming before the major cold forming. Finally, a

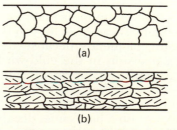

Fig. 19-3. Crystalline structure. (a) Before cold-working; (b) after cold-working.

third treatment given to metals to be cold-worked is annealing prior to the cold forming. If a metal that is to be cold formed is not going to be worked immediately, its shelf life can be extended by applying a light coat of oil to its surfaces. This light oil coating also acts as a die lubricant.

COLD-ROLLING

Cold-rolling, like hot-rolling, is accomplished by rolling metal through a series of roll stands. These roll stands are spaced far enough apart so that the metal going through them will not sag. As the metal enters the first stand, it is reduced in size slightly. This small reduction in size increases the length of the metal so that the second in the series of stands will be turning faster than the first stand, and the third stand will be turning faster than the second stand. Between the stands there is a spray device which sprays an oil-based coolant on the metal. This cools both the working rolls and the metal being reduced in size and also puts an oil coating on the finished product. The coolant also keeps the metal from expanding too much because of heat. The last stand of rolls that the metal passes through is called the *sizing stand*. The sizing stand is the finish tolerance stand for the metal and ensures that all metal passing through it will be of uniform thickness (Fig. 19-4).

SWAGING

Swaging, very similar to closed-die forging, reduces the area of a metal. The swaging process is used for reducing, tapering, and pointing bars and tubing. It is accomplished between two or more dies that strike the metal to be formed, reducing the metal in size. Cold swaging usually is done on a rotary swaging machine, which has a series of rollers that act as hammers, driving the anvil in the die toward the center of the rotary

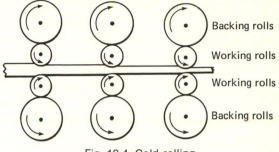

Fig. 19-4. Cold-rolling.

head. The article to be formed is simply hand-held in the dies.

The swaging machine consists of heavy stationary rings, in which rollers are mounted at close intervals, and a moving ring, carrying two mounted dies and a stationary ring. The dies are mounted facing the axis and are free to slide back and forth. The dies are blocks of hardened steel with impressions or shapes cut into them that indicate the shape the die will produce. One end of the die is flared to allow unshaped stock to be placed in the die (Fig. 19-5).

The swaging action of the machine takes place when the dies that are mounted to the inner race rotate. Attached to one end of the die is the anvil. As the anvil strikes the stationary rollers, it is forced toward the center of the swaging machine, squeezing or compressing the stock or material between the rollers. As the inner race of the swaging edge rotates, further centrifugal force throws the die blocks toward the outer race, opening the die. When the die is opened, the anvil strikes the next set of stationary rollers and is compressed again and thrown open. This cycle is repeated, resulting in the work being rapidly hammered from all sides while being contained in a die.

Swaging is the best method for tapering welds, seamless tubes, or drawn tubes. Also, swaging is economical when applied to the reduction of rods, bars, and wires. An excellent example of the swaged tube is the oxygen cylinder used in oxyacetylene welding. The threaded portion of this high strength tube has been swaged. Other examples of products produced by swaging include golf

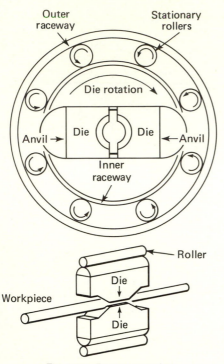

Fig. 19-5. Rotary swaging.

club shanks and fishing poles. Swaging is sometimes used to attach end pieces to cables, tubes, and wires, as well as to seal ends of tubular pieces.

COLD FORGING

Cold forging is the same basic operation as hot forging but without the heat. Most cold forging is simply done with closed-die forging equipment. Cold forging is used for the production of such items as bolts, nails, and rivets. It also is used as a secondary step in assembly, as in joining two pieces of material together by forming the head on a rivet. An example is the riveting used to join sheet metal.

The basic operation of closed-die cold forging, or cold-heading, includes the following steps. First, stock is cut to length and placed in a clamping device. The head is then partially formed. The die head rotates and finishes forming the head. The die is then withdrawn, and the ejector pin ejects the item. The production of such items as nails, bolts, and rivets readily lends itself to automation. Many times the cold forging of such items will be done with a cutoff device, a rough shaping die, a finishing die, a final sizing die (as in the case of bolt heads that are part of a coining die), and an ejection point. All are incorporated in a multiple die head that simply rotates in positions to the stock being formed (Fig. 19-6). *Coining*, the positive displacement of a metal between two closed dies, derives its name from the production of coins by the U.S. Mint. Coining is the process by which blank slugs of metal, such as copper, are turned into coins. The faces of the two opposing dies have designs cut into them and the design is impressed on the metal (Fig. 19-7).

Riveting

Riveting is a cold forging process that is used to join two or more pieces of material together. Riveting can be done either by hand or by machine. Generally, cold riveting is confined to use with light or sheet metal; hot riveting is used for plates and structural shapes, such as those used in the erection of high-rise buildings. The basic cold riveting device is a die punch, called a rivet set, and a bucking bar. The rivet set is the die punch and has a cavity formed in the head. The rivet head is placed in the bucking bar, the material is put onto the rivet through the hole, and then the head is formed (Fig. 19-8).

Consistent results are highly desirable. All heads must be formed alike in regard to height, expansion, and general appearance. A single installation may employ several hundred rivets that must all appear the same, as in, for example, an airplane. If they are slightly under- or oversized or have different widths, the riveting job will not only appear messy and nonuniform but the job may also be rejected, creating more hours of work to replace the rejected rivets.

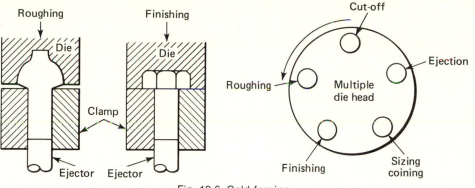

Fig. 19-6. Cold forging.

COLD-DRAWING

The cold-drawing process changes the cross-sectional area of a rolled bar by pulling or drawing the bar through a die opening (Fig. 19-9a). Machines which accomplish this process are known as *drawbenches*. The length of these benches varies according to the space available and the length of the finished drawn bar, with the usual length between 30 and 60 ft. The drawbenches consist primarily of a pointing head for the bar, a die holder, the drawhead carriage, and a drive machine. The pointing head grips the bar and forces it through the die about 7 or 8 in. The bar is then gripped by the drawhead. A chain connects the drawhead to the system of pulleys that pulls the drawhead carriage backward until the bar stock is drawn com-

pletely through the die, producing a bar with small diameter. Wire is produced in the same manner (Fig. 19-9b).

There are various lubricants applied to the bar being drawn through the bench. These lubricants reduce the force needed to draw the bar through the die and increase the life of the die. Some lubricants currently used are heavy greases, soluble oils, petroleum oils, detergents, and cotton seed oils.

The commercial drawing speeds vary from 40 to 100 ft/min depending on the equipment, the size of the area being reduced, the finished design, and the metallic composition of the bar being drawn. One of the major factors in controlling the drawing speed is the amount of heat liberated at the die. The die must remain cool or it will gall the bar, deforming the surface of the drawn

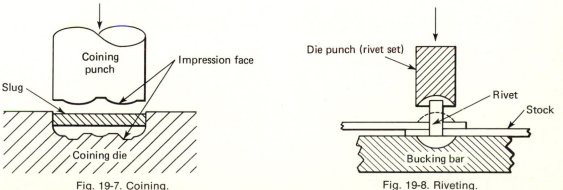

Fig. 19-7. Coining.

Fig. 19-8. Riveting.

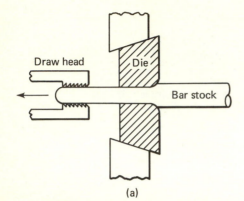

(a)

(b)

Fig. 19-9. Cold-drawing. (a) Principle; (b) application. (*American Iron and Steel Institute.*)

bar as well as the die, greatly reducing die life.

Practically any ductile metal can be cold-drawn. Steels with up to 0.50 percent carbon content are the most economical steels to draw. Alloy steels are slightly more difficult to draw, and stainless steels present a problem for the cold-drawing process. Low-carbon, open-hearth produced, resulfurized steel is the most used cold-drawn metal. Higher carbon, open-hearth steels have to be annealed prior to cold-drawing because they work harden so readily. Stainless steels are

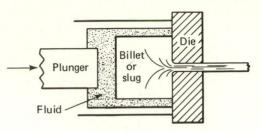

Fig. 19-10. Hydrostatic extrusion.

the most difficult to draw, and if drawn they generally are restricted to use with very simple shapes. Cold-drawn shapes of stainless steel are used when corrosion resistance and appearance are important factors.

COLD EXTRUSION

In cold extrusion, unheated slugs of metal are forced to flow around punches and into shape-forming dies. The tool design is probably the most critical factor affecting successful cold extrusion. Cold extrusions are done by a hydrostatic process, by forward extrusion, reverse extrusion, and a combination

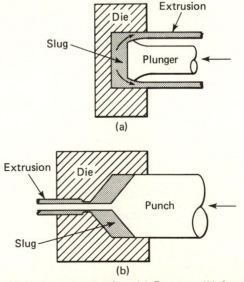

Fig. 19-11. Impact extrusion. (a) Reverse; (b) forward.

of forward and reverse extrusion processes.

Hydrostatic extrusion uses a fluid to transmit the force from the plunger to the slug, reducing the amount of friction the slug exerts on the die walls (Fig. 19-10). Standard reverse impact extrusion places a slug between the plunger and the die, and the extrusion moves in a direction opposite to the plunger movement. Forward impact extrusion occurs when the extrusion flow is in the same direction as the plunger, or punch, movement (Fig. 19-11).

Cold extrusions are usually done at room temperature. It is a quick process, and the metal only heats up to several hundred degrees for a fraction of a second. Cold extrusion may range, however, up to 500°F slug temperature. Such metals as magnesium and zirconium usually are heated up to 500°F before cold extrusion is used. Other metals, such as lead and tin, are already in the recrystallization range at room temperature so that these two metals lend themselves very readily to cold extrusion.

Cold extrusion is used to produce specific shapes and to improve physical properties of metal. The improvements of physical properties are much the same as in all coldworked metals. Common examples of cold extruded parts are gear blanks, hydraulic and shock absorber cylinders, risk pins, rocket motors, automotive pistons and heads, ammunition cases, fire extinguisher cases, toothpaste tubes, and all kinds of shaving cream tubes.

QUESTIONS

1. What are the effects of cold-working on the metal being worked?
2. What are the advantages of cold-working?
3. How do slip planes control the amount of cold-working a metal can withstand?
4. Why are metals cleaned before cold-working?
5. Explain the swaging process.
6. What is cold-rolling?
7. What is a bucking bar?
8. What are the differences between the hot and cold extrusion processes?
9. Compare and contrast forward and reverse extrusion.

20

Forming

Cold forming of metals applies a force to a metal blank causing permanent contour changes in the metal. All forming forces that create stresses in metals must do so below the nominal tensile strength of the metal. If higher forces occur in the forming process, failure will result and the metal blank will be rejected as scrap. All forming must take place below the ultimate strength of the metal. In forming, the stresses applied may range from zero stress at certain areas to stresses approaching the yield point in a corner bend.

The main characteristic of all forming is that stresses in the metal occur only in specific areas. For example, bending metals in a brake will result in stretching and compression stresses being applied at only the area of the bend (Fig. 20-1). Any time metal is formed, or changed in shape by bending, tensile and compression stresses always occur in the bend area. The outside of the bend will undergo stretching, or tensile stresses, and the inside of the bend will always be placed under compression. The forming or bending stresses of the metal must be applied below the ultimate tensile strength of the metal. If the metal is stretched too far, it will crack and the piece will be ruined. In bending, however, the portion of the metal not being bent is not stressed during any of the forming operation.

NEUTRAL AXIS

There is a point in time between the compression and tensile strength stresses during which a *neutral axis* exists in the metal. The neutral axis is normally near the center of a sheet of metal at rest. As stress is placed on the metal, the neutral axis moves in the direction in which the metal is bent. In the radius of a bend, the neutral axis shifts toward the compression stress side.

Before bending, the metal blank has a specified length. The length of the neutral axis is always exactly equal to the original blank length. The outside length of the sheet metal increases and the inside length decreases when the metal undergoes forming, but the length of the neutral axis does not change. The neutral axis then is the only true representation of the original metal blank length, so that the neutral axis is the measurement used for pattern development. When bending bar stock, for example, the neutral axis is located at a distance that is one-third of the bar thickness inside the bend. On sheet metal, the distance the neutral axis moves is usually four-tenths of the thickness of the sheet metal (Fig. 20-2). The same theory of the neutral axis applies to all forming operations.

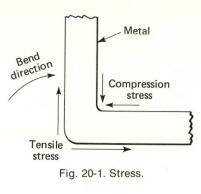

Fig. 20-1. Stress.

METAL FLOW

Metal flow usually occurs when metals are subjected to a forming process. The tensile stresses cause the metal to flow, reducing the thickness of the metal in the immediate bend area. The metal flow results in a change in cross-sectional shape so that as the metal reduces in thickness, the metal flow causes an increase in the width at the bend area. For example, in bending bar stock, the increase in the width of the bar stock may range up to as much as one-eighth.

Metal flow is more evident in round stock than in flat stock because the round stock is uniform in size. However, the same metal flow action results when bending or forming flat stock. This flow may not be noticed because the flat stock is often wider than it is thick, but thinning at the bend joint occurs nevertheless. The metal flow accounts also for the wrinkling effect found on the inside of rods or hollow tubes when they are bent. The major way to combat wrinkling is to increase the radius of the bend.

SPRINGBACK

Springback is the effort of metal that is not stressed beyond its elastic limit to reshape itself into its original position. If the metal nearest the neutral axis has been stressed below the elastic limit, the metal will try to return to its preformed shape when the forming forces are removed. The metal that has been stressed beyond the elastic limit will resist returning to its original shape, but a certain amount of springback will occur in a formed part. The forces causing springback are just the reverse of the stresses placed on the metal during forming. In fact, the metal is trying to come to a rest state again.

The three methods currently used for controlling springback are overbending, bottoming, and stretch forming. *Overbending* is putting a higher degree of bend than is needed onto the part and allowing the piece to spring back to the desired shape. *Bottoming* is accomplished by striking the metal at the radius of the bend area while the metal is under the bending stress. *Stretch forming* consists of stretching the blank so that all of the metal is past the elastic limit, completely eliminating springback.

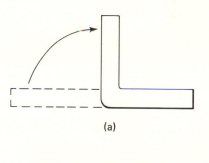

(a)

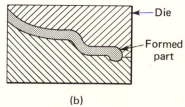

(b)

Fig. 20-3. Bending and forming. (a) Bending; (b) forming.

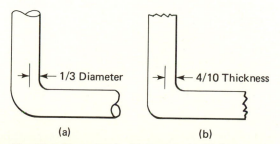

Fig. 20-2. Neutral axis. (a) Bar stock; (b) flat stock.

BENDING

Bending and forming are sometimes thought to be synonymous terms. However, forming occurs when complete items or parts are shaped, and bending occurs when forces are applied to localized areas, such as in bending a piece of metal into a right angle. *Bending* is the term applied to the phenomenon that occurs at the points where stresses change. It incorporates angle bending, roll bending, roll forming, and seaming. *Forming*, on the other hand, usually refers to the process in which dies encompass the metal blank and bend it to a predetermined shape (Fig. 20-3).

Angle Bending

Angle bending usually is accomplished with a cornice brake, a box and pan brake, a bar folder, or a press brake (Fig. 20-4). For example, with a cornice brake a piece of sheet metal is placed between the stationary jaw and the upper movable jaw and clamped into place. A bending leaf is then rotated and the metal blank is bent to the desired angle (Fig. 20-5). A box and pan brake, also known as a finger brake, is used for angle bending, too. It is used primarily in the construction of metal boxes. The box and pan brake has movable fingers, or jaws, that can be set to specified widths so that they fit inside previously bent metal parts. The movable jaws usually are set

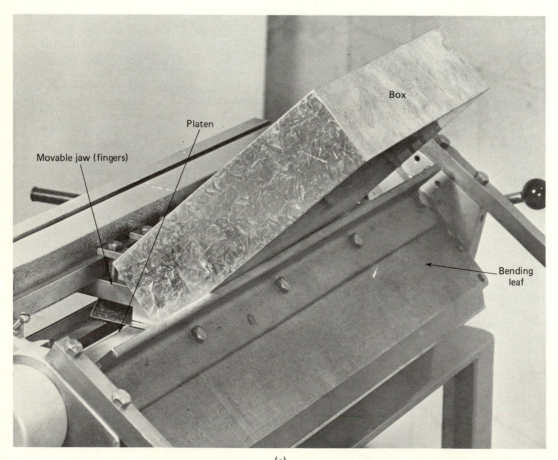

(a)

Fig. 20-4. Brakes. (a) Box and pan; (b) press. (DiAcro.)

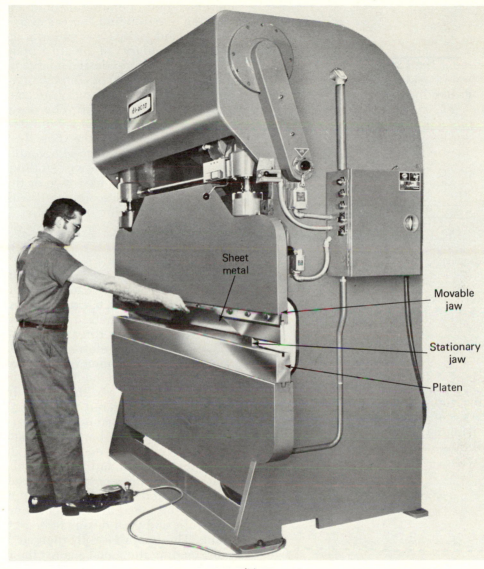

Sheet
metal

Movable
jaw

Stationary
jaw

Platen

(b)

in combinations that range from ¹/₂ to 4 in. long, and they may be assembled in combinations that generate many different jaw, or finger, widths.

Another machine used in angle bending is the bar folder. The bar folder is also used for producing hems. The bar folder is operated by setting the gage that determines the width of the hem. The metal is inserted against the gage and the bending leaf is rotated. Most bar folders have both a 45° and a 90° stop incorporated within the gaging system so that these two bends can repeatedly be made accurately (Fig. 20-6).

The press brake is rapidly replacing the other types of metal brakes because of its

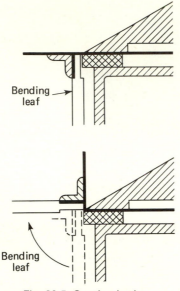

Fig. 20-5. Cornice brake.

wide application. The press brake does not require highly skilled operators as do the other types of equipment. The press brake has a set of dies and a stationary jaw in a movable jaw that forms the metal. The dies make simple tasks of such hand operations as bending, flanging, hemming, seaming, wire edging, ribbing, and crimping. Some of the

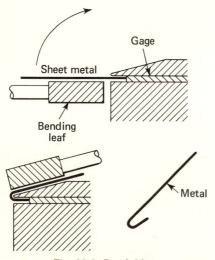

Fig. 20-6. Bar folder.

more detailed operating techniques of press working are bulging, corrugating, beating, bossing, and many types of forming.

The popularity of the press brake has led many companies to design a large number of die forms that can be interchanged in the press. The die forms usually are composed of a male and a female die. The design of the die determines the shape of the finished formed part. Many of the dies also incorporate more than one stage of operation within them. For example, in wire rolling, or tube rolling, the die may have two or three separate work stations incorporated within it for the complete forming of the tube.

Rolling

Rolling is used in the production of cylindrical metal objects made of either sheet metal, flat plate, rod, bar stock, or angle stock (Fig. 20-7). Sheet metal rolls are capable of rolling metal under 16 gage. Rolls for metal above 16 gage are referred to as plate rolls. Some plate rolls commercially available are capable of rolling metal 3 in. thick.

Regardless of its thickness, the metal being rolled is entered into the rolling machine in the same manner. The first step is to raise the metal or prebend it right at the tip. If the metal is not prebent at the tip, it will not strike the rear roll and will be deflected upwards. Many times on thicker metal the rear roll is operated hydraulically, dropping down to allow the metal to enter between the two front rolls and then raising to bend the metal blank. The two front rolls then act as feeder rolls, feeding the metal against the rear rolls. The height of the rear roll determines the diameter of the rolled part (Fig. 20-8).

Roll Forming

The two types of roll forming that are used most are continuous strip rolling and sheet, or plate, piece rolling. Continuous strip rolling is used most in high production because of its speed in forming metal. Continuous roll forming is the most versatile when compared to sheet or plate rolling because

Fig. 20-7. Slip roll former (*Peck, Stow, and Wilcox Company*).

machines have been designed with interchangeable rolls that are capable of creating a wide variety of designed roll forms.

The way a piece of metal is formed is determined by the design of the finished product. A simple design may take only two sets of rolls, while intricate designs may require twelve or more pairs of rolls. The basic roll-forming operation remains the same, however. For example, when constructing continuous gutter for a house, a roll of metal is placed on the roll-forming machine and started into the first set of rolls. This first set of rolls makes primary bends in the metal which enable it to feed into second and third rolls. A second set of rolls completely forms the strip metal into a gutter shape (Fig. 20-9). Continuous gutters that have no joints can be fabricated very quickly with this operation. Roll-forming machines are also compact so that they may be mounted on trucks. These trucks can be moved onto the job site, the

specified metal fed into the machine, and the continuous gutter formed. This example is just one of the many uses of roll forming.

Seaming

Sheet metalworking incorporates a wide variety of seams and joints. Popular seams that are either riveted or soldered are: the lap, the butt strap, the outside corner, the dovetail, the cash box, and the slip seams or joints (Fig. 20-10). Often sheet metal is joined by using popular locking seams such as the grooved lock, the bottom lock, the Pittsburgh lock, the clip lock, the corner clip lock, and the double bottom lock.

Most of the locking seams can be formed

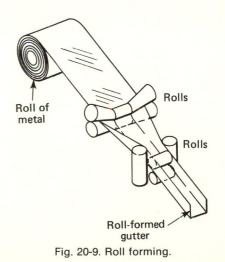

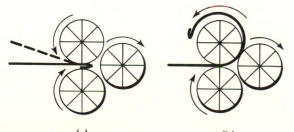

(a) (b)

Fig. 20-8. Using the forming roll. (*a*) Enter; (*b*) roll.

Fig. 20-9. Roll forming.

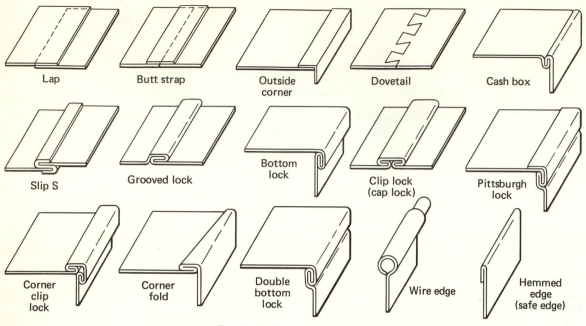

Fig. 20-10. Seams and joints.

either by hand with the use of the cornice brake, the press brake, or the bar folder, or they can be formed with roll-forming machines. Many forming machines can produce more than one lock seam. For example a popular seam, the Pittsburgh lock, is available with roll-forming machines. By simply changing the roll dies, a grooved lock or a clip lock seam may also be produced with the same piece of roll-forming equipment.

DIE FORMING

When metal is formed with dies the terms *bending* or *forming* are used interchangeably because the dies produce a bending action to the part as well as forming the total part. Forming dies are designed to bend metal parts into various shapes, which are usually irregular. The shapes are produced by pushing the metal blank into cavities or depressions that are cut into the die block.

A simple form of bending die would be

one having an upper part that has a punch shape which would correspond with the depressions in the die face. The metal is placed between the punch and the die, and then the pressure is applied. This pressure shapes or forms the metal blank between the punch and the die. The forming or bending stresses exerted on the metal should always be below the ultimate tensile strength of the metal but above its elastic limit. As in bending, if the metal is stretched or shaped too much, it will crack and the piece will have to be discarded. Knowledge of the elasticity of the metal being used is an important factor in any forming operation. If a metal is brittle or has a low tensile strength, the amount of forming it can withstand is limited. If the metal has high elasticity, its forming capabilities are much greater.

DRAWING

The drawing processes can be divided into two categories, deep drawing and shallow

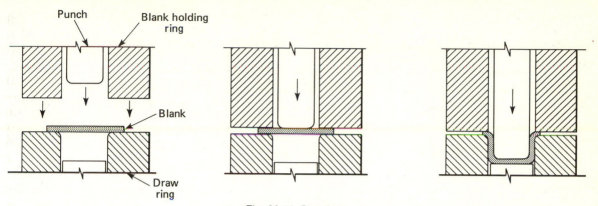

Fig. 20-11. Drawing.

drawing. If the length of the object to be drawn is deeper than its width, the process is called *deep drawing*. If the length of the object to be formed is less than the width, it is called *shallow, or box, drawing*. An example of box drawing would be the production of common household pots and pans.

The drawing operation is performed by placing a metal blank over a stationary die and exerting a calculated pressure from a punch against the blank. The blank is forced into the shape of the die. The pressure and resulting stress cause the metal to change permanently into the shape of the die. There is no movement of metal through space, but the metal flows through the opening between the die and the punch as the punch exerts a force on the blank (Fig. 20-11). The construction of the dies is of prime importance for ensuring quality control over drawn products. All the die surfaces have to be free of nicks and must be polished. Nicks in the die surface will result in ridges and bumps in the finished product, causing it to be rejected. Consequently, precision machining and close tolerances are required in the construction of both dies and punches.

Lubricants are extremely important in the drawing processes. The lubricant provides a film between the workpiece and the die, facilitating forming and reducing friction and wear on blank, punch, and die. The lubricants also protect the dies and the punches against corrosion and reduce some of the stress placed against the blank holder and the draw ring. Some of the major types of lubricants used for drawing include waxes, soap fats, dry film lubricants, mineral oils, soluble oils, and synthetic oils.

Solid-Die Forming

A solid forming die presses or stamps the part into shape between the male and the female dies (Fig. 20-12). These parts have to be machined to the desired contour to produce the finished product. The solid forming die is probably the simplest and least expensive to construct. The number of parts to be manufactured determines to a large degree the cost of designing the die assembly. Because of the

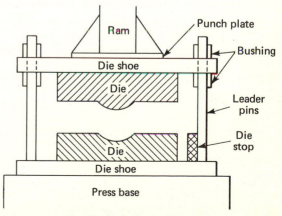

Fig. 20-12. Solid-die forming.

simplicity of solid forming dies, many different die techniques can be used in their construction. An example of solid forming dies are those that are used in the production of the sheet metal in automobiles (such as in the doors, the roof, the hood, and the trunk lid).

PRESSES

The presses that are used to perform all of the cold forming operations are the C frame press, the straight-sided frame press, and the horning press. Of these three types, the C frame is used most. A typical C frame press is a 25-ton mechanical OBI C frame press. *OBI* means *open back inclinable*. It is open back so that the parts can fall from the die plate into a carton for transportation. The press is inclined so that gravity will move the part from the die and provide the transportation to storage. C frame presses range from a 1-ton bench model to about a 200-ton floor press (Fig. 20-13a).

The straight-sided press is capable of generating higher pressures over larger areas. It can be as large as 50,000 tons. The straight-sided presses are usually hydraulic; whereas C frame presses are usually mechanical-drive presses. Hydraulic presses are slower than the mechanical presses, but they are capable of generating much more force.

Horning presses are used mostly for secondary operations such as punching holes, riveting parts together, or deforming small areas in a piece. Horning presses are smaller and are not capable of generating the amount of force of either the C frame or the straight-sided frame press (Fig. 20-13b).

GUERIN FORMING PROCESS

Rubber forming is a widely accepted method of forming sheet metal. Rubber under pressure can serve as an effective female die to form a metal blank around the solid punch or forming block. Under high pressure, rubber responds in much the same way as a hydraulic fluid, exerting equal pressure in all directions. Rubber has a high resistance to permanent deformation so that it returns to its original shape after being deformed by the forming process. Rubber die forming has many advantages: low cost for tools, elimination of costly die matching, and rapid tool fabrication and setup. This process usually is used when there are small production runs like those which occur within the aircraft industry.

The Guerin forming process uses a large hydraulic press, ranging from 1,000 to 7,000 tons. A rubber pad is secured to the bottom of a recessed platen that is placed on the upper ram of the press. The rubber pad then presses the blank over the profile of the male die. Two to four plates can be mounted on conveyor rails to speed production, enabling unskilled operators to unload formed parts from one platen and to reload it with new blanks while the press is forming the blanks on another platen (Fig. 20-14).

When simple shapes are formed, the pressure exerted by the rubber is usually adequate. However, complicated shapes sometimes may require additional pressure at specific points. The additional pressure is provided by small auxiliary or secondary rubber pads placed at strategic locations. The working face of the pad is capable of producing thousands of parts before replacement, if care is taken in the operation of the process. Proper rubber pad treatment involves such things as changing the position of the dies so that they do not strike the rubber pad at only one point, eliminating burrs on the blanks, avoiding the flow of the rubber into narrow channels, and providing a lubricant, such as graphite, for the rubber.

For long runs male dies are made of die tool steel. Some male dies are made of regular steel plate or cast iron. For shorter runs plastics, hard woods, and some of the nonferrous alloys are suitable for die materials. However, nonferrous die forming blocks are short-lived.

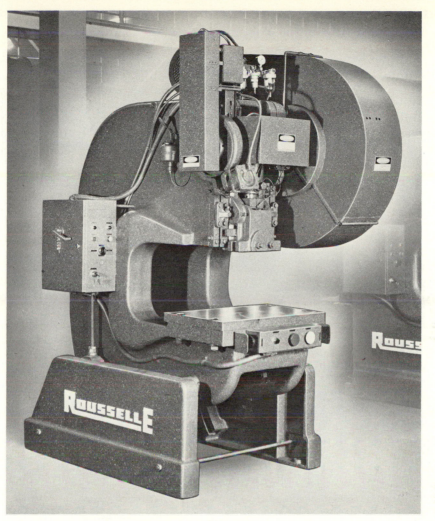

(a)

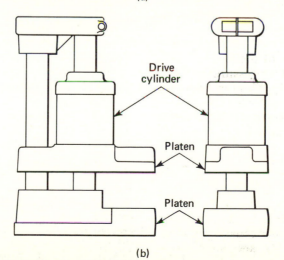

Drive
cylinder

Platen

Platen

(b)

Fig. 20-13. Presses. (a) C frame (*Rousselle Corporation*); (b) horning.

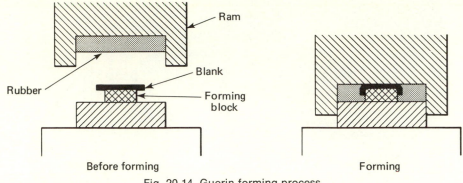

Fig. 20-14. Guerin forming process.

VERSON-WHEENLON FORMING PROCESS

The Verson-Wheenlon process is used mainly to develop higher side forming pressure than is possible with the Guerin process. The rubber used for the pad is softer and can be elongated much more than the rubber pad in the Guerin process. As a result, the press can form larger pieces with higher flanges or sides. The height varies according to the material used, but a rule of thumb is that approximately 6 or 7 in. more side height can be achieved. Shallow parts can also be produced with the female die or with the draw ring. Very deep draws are not recommended because of the limitations of the fluid cell being used.

The main feature of the Verson-Wheenlon process is a fluid cell, a rubber bag, mounted on the top of the press. When inflated, the cell exerts pressure on the rubber female die. There are no mechanical moving parts on the press except the trays that hold the blanks to be formed. The cycle time of the press is slow compared to that of mechanical presses, but production can be accelerated by employing two or more loading trays (Fig. 20-15).

The soft rubber under high pressure can be pressed easily into deep holes and around semisharp protrusions. However, very deep cavities in high projections cause excessive **wear** of the rubber pads and should be

avoided. Rubber pads can be protected from excessive wear, especially from sharp edges, by inserting either expendable rubber pieces or leather sheets between the rubber and the blank. Often the soft rubber pad has a leather binding glued directly to it. As the leather wears, it is pulled off and a new piece reglued.

Tool and die steel usually is used to make the male die. Masonite, plastic, or hard wood can be substituted for the die form when simple shapes are used and short production runs are made.

MARFORM PROCESS

The Marform process differs from the Guerin process in that it uses a special blank-holder mechanism that automatically controls the applied pressure, making it possible for deep shells to be fabricated with an accuracy that usually is associated with all-metal or solid-die forming but at a much lower tooling cost. Usually the parts that are formed are free of wrinkles as well as external tooling marks.

The equipment used for the Marform process includes an inverted container of steel. The container, which must be deeper than the shell to be drawn, is filled with laminated rubber pads and is mounted on the ram or the punch of the hydraulic press (Fig. 20-16). For long runs and deep draws, well-polished steel punches are used. The

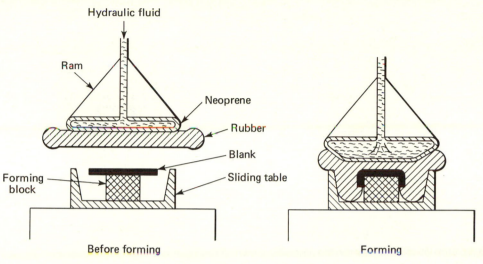

Fig. 20-15. Verson-Wheenlon forming process.

punches should be lubricated lightly to prevent scoring of the punch and the formed piece. An approximate depth of 33 times the diameter of the part can sometimes be obtained. The diameter and the depth sizes of the formed pieces depend on the size and the capacity of the press used. A cast zinc alloy is often used as a punch material when forming light gage metal.

In the operation of the Marforming process, the punch comes down and the rubber contacts the metal blank. The blank holder then applies pressure against the rubber that is securing the blank. As pressure continues to be applied, the piston descends into the hydraulic chamber. The oil in the hydraulic chamber offers resistance to the ram that is lowering the rubber pad and pushes the punch into the rubber pad. When the punch has achieved the necessary depth of penetration into the pad, the pressure is released. The blank holder then acts as a stripper, stripping the part from the punch (Fig. 20-16).

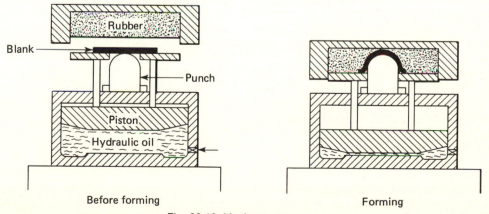

Fig. 20-16. Marform process.

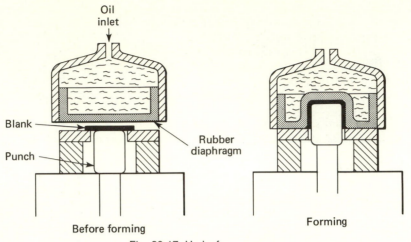

Fig. 20-17. Hydroform process.

HYDROFORM PROCESS

The hydroform process employs a hydraulic press that is designed and constructed especially for the deep drawing of metals. This process eliminates the die and the upper blank holder of conventional cold forming processes. They are replaced by a pressurized forming chamber sealed by a rubber diaphragm. The largest commercially available hydroform machines can form blanks up to approximately 30-in. diameter or draw a shell to about 10 in. long. Parts that require three or four operations when being made by other processes can often be produced in one stroke by the hydroform press with one set of tools.

The hydroform press operation provides continuous control of the plastic deformation of metal blanks. A forming cycle starts when a metal blank is placed on the blank-holder ring. The forming chamber is lowered over the blank and a small pressure is applied to hold the blank down. The punch rises and forces the sheet metal blank upward into the pressurized, flexible chamber to form the part. The punch is then lowered and the blank is formed into a finished shape. The hydraulic pressure then ejects the part from the rubber diaphragm (Fig. 20-17).

Tooling consists of punching the shape of the part to be drawn and a draw ring around the punch. Cast iron or tool steel is used in punches for long production runs. Oil hardening alloy steel can also be used for punches. The rubber dies help protect the punch because it is not forced against another block of steel. Instead, it is pressed against a rubber diaphragm, helping to reduce punch wear as well as to cushion the vibrations created by the machine.

Usually a light lubricant oil is sufficient to sustain a good finish on the product. Often graphite is used to protect the rubber diaphragm. The punches and draw rings are highly polished so as to prevent any snagging of the diaphragm or any imperfections being imparted to the metal blank.

QUESTIONS

1. Why must metals be formed below their ultimate strength?
2. What is a neutral axis?
3. Why is metal flow more evident in round stock?

4. Explain springback.
5. Explain how the box and pan brake can form a box.
6. Identify the steps in operating a forming roll.
7. Compare and contrast rolling and roll forming.
8. What are the differences between deep and shallow drawing?
9. Explain the drawing process.
10. How does solid-die forming differ from the rubber forming processes?
11. What is an OBI press?
12. Identify and explain the functions of the three major types of presses.
13. Compare and contrast the Guerin and the Verson-Wheenlon forming processes.
14. Explain the hydroform process.

21

Pattern Developing

The accurate layout of the sheet metal used in the production of any cold-formed product is of major importance. This original layout can determine the accuracy of the finished product. Most sheet metal and plate objects are formed into three-dimensional shapes by squeezing, bending, or forming a predetermined pattern stretchout (Fig. 21-1). The purpose of the pattern stretchout is to determine the exact amount of sheet metal or plate that is necessary to fabricate the product. Many times a drafter will originate a three-dimensional sketch and a stretchout of the item to be manufactured. The drafter will create a pattern that can be used to transfer specific dimensions onto the stock metal. Often, however, the metalworker is required to produce this information or to develop the pattern directly on the metal.

A stretchout can be drawn for only one-half of the object, but these half-patterns can only be used when the object is symmetrical. *Tabs* are the extra material left on the stock that is used to produce a metal seam. Many companies draw stretchouts without tabs; but many companies do incorporate tabs on stretchouts. Both stretchouts and patterns drawn directly on the metal are originated by one of four methods of pattern development: straight-line method, parallel-line method, radial-line method, or the triangulation method.

STRAIGHT-LINE METHOD

The straight-line method is used for such items as boxes, cylinders, or flat pieces. The basic tools needed for the straight-line method of pattern development include a straight edge or ruler and a set of dividers. The easiest way to prepare a straight-line pattern is to draw the pattern directly on the metal. First, the metal must be squared so that its sides are parallel. The divider is set to the correct measurements and one point of the divider is dragged against the edge of the metal while the inside point of the divider scribes the line (Fig. 21-2).

For example, a box is constructed by squaring the metal to the length or the width of the box. The dividers are set at the appropriate distance and the total pattern sides are drawn. The various side lengths, heights, tabs, and end pieces can be incorporated directly into the pattern simply by varying the width of the divider points and scribing the line. All lines should start at the outside edge of the sheet of metal. When dividers with points are used in this method, it is poor practice to go over the scribed lines more than one time. Repeatedly scribing the same lines can result in errors or more than one scratched line on the surface of the metal.

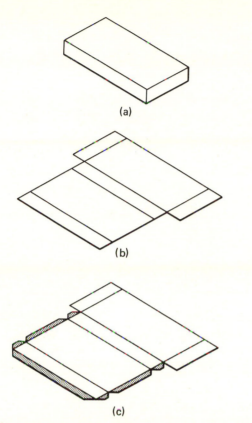

Fig. 21-1. Stretchout. (*a*) Object; (*b*) stretchout; (*c*) stretchout with tabs.

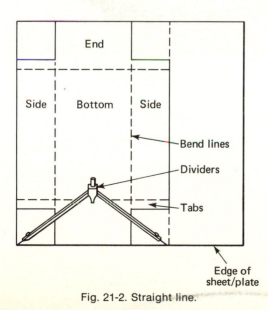

Fig. 21-2. Straight line.

PARALLEL-LINE DEVELOPMENT

Parallel-line development is used for stretchouts of Y shapes, T shapes, and elbows. It is also used for areas where pipes intersect flat surfaces at an angle (Fig. 21-3). Parallel-line development derives its name from the parallel lines used in the construction of the stretchouts.

The basic procedure for constructing stretchouts consists of the following steps. First, a plan view that has true length outside lines is drawn. Drawing true length lines is basic to the total parallel process. For example, when one cylinder connects to another, as in a T shape, there is no way to visualize the correct line length of all the various points along the line that connects one cylinder to another. One way to generate an accurate stretchout is by the parallel-line procedure in which a plan view, or elevation, is constructed. The next step involves drawing a stretchout line at an angle of 90° to the plan view. Measuring lines are placed perpendicular to the stretchout lines, and parallel lines for the cut are transferred from the elevation, or plan, view to the stretchout line. This transferred line is drawn parallel to the stretchout line (Fig. 21-4).

Accuracy in performing each step is imperative if an accurate stretchout is to result. This accuracy can be achieved more easily if the front view of the intersection is used; and in the case of a T shape, if a circle of the adjoining connecting pipe is drawn. This circle is divided into 12 or 16 parts. The higher the number of equal parts, the greater the accuracy of the stretchout, as long as mistakes are not made in the dividing. These parts should be of equal arc length. Once the length of the arc is determined, the divider is set to the arc length and then the distance is transferred to the stretchout line, generating the circumference of the circle. Notice that line number 1 on Fig. 21-4 starts as well as stops the stretchout so that when the metal is rolled, the two number 1 points become the same.

When these 12 equal distances have been generated, perpendicular lines are drawn

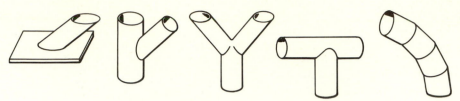

Fig. 21-3. Basic forms of parallel-line development.

from the stretchout line. The lines are transferred from the front view across to the arc length lines intersecting them with each intersection yielding one point. The points then are joined together by an irregular curve. Often the points are joined together by sketching freehand from point to point. When extreme accuracy is demanded, only three points on the irregular curve should be connected before moving ahead one point, so that two points always generate the third point.

If the stretchout has been made on metal, the next step is to cut the metal. If it has been made on drawing paper, the next step is usually to transfer it to a metal template. One thing to remember in the use of parallel-line development is that this method does not establish any means for attaching one end of the metal to the other so that tabs must always be incorporated either on the stretchout itself or on the metal after the stretchout has been transferred to the metal. Although it is not mandatory, the stretchout is usually located to the right-hand side of the front view.

The elbow, one shape used extensively in sheet metal, is constructed by following the procedure for parallel-line development. The first step is to draw a front view and a diameter view of the elbow, either top or bottom. The diameter view is segregated into 12 or 16 equal arc length parts, and then parallel lines are drawn from the arc lengths across to the line bisecting the elbow. The arc lengths are again transferred to a stretch-

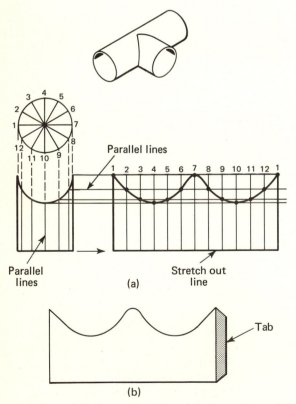

Fig. 21-4. Cylinder connector. (a) Procedure; (b) stretchout.

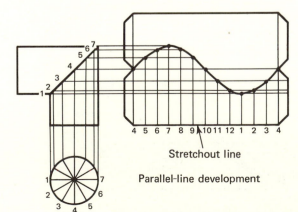

Stretchout line

Parallel-line development

Fig. 21-5. Elbow.

out line and vertical parallel lines are extended. The point at which the arc length lines of the bottom view meet the bend line is established and transferred onto the arc length lines that previously were established on the stretchout lines (Fig. 21-5). Following this procedure for all elbows, no matter what their degree of bend, will always establish the true line lengths at each of the parallel lines on the stretchout.

RADIAL-LINE DEVELOPMENT

Radial-line development is used to develop items that are either pyramid or cone shaped. The bases may be round, square, hexagonal, octagonal, or any of the other regular polygons. An example of a section of a pyramid is a pan with tapered sides with a round bottom and a round top opening. If imaginary lines were extended out, the pan would become an inverted cone. Figure 21-6 identifies the typical forms of products used in radial-line development.

Pyramid

The stretchout development of a pyramid requires a straight edge, a scribe or pencil, and a set of dividers. The stretchout may be drawn on paper and transferred to sheet or plate metal, or it may be drawn directly on the metal. The basic steps for developing a pyramid include drawing a plan view and an elevation view that will generate one or more true line lengths. The pyramid is drawn, as shown in Fig. 21-7, because this procedure is the only method of generating the true line length from the base to the point of the pyramid. The only true line lengths generated are the outside lines of the pyramid. The centerline of the pyramid appears shorter in the drawing, but it is the same length as the outside lines. This illusion is another reason for using a radial-line development procedure for producing the stretchout. The plans used can be either a top view or a bottom view of the elevation view. The elevation view is usually a front view.

After the plan and elevation views have

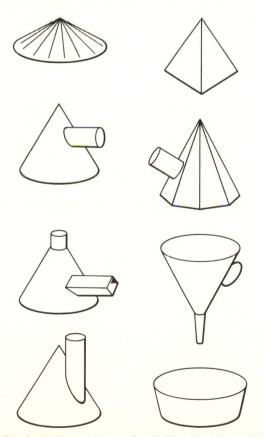

Fig. 21-6. Typical forms of radial-line development.

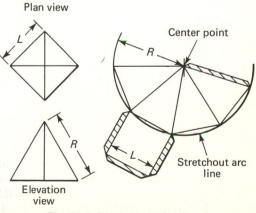

Fig. 21-7. Pyramid (radial line).

been drawn, the dividers are set for the distance of the radius on the elevation view. This distance is transferred to the drawing paper or to the metal, and then a center point is determined for the stretchout. The center point is indented on the metal when dividers are used. Next, the dividers are set to the true length of the base as shown in the plan view, and an arbitrary edge line is constructed from the stretchout arc to the center point. The dividers are set at the point at which the arbitrary edge line and the stretchout arc meet. The dividers are used to scribe a point on the stretchout arc. The plan view true length line is that point. This step is repeated as many times as there are sides in the plan view. In the example given in Fig. 21-7, there are four sides so that four lengths L will be scribed on the stretchout arc line. Then these points are connected to the center point, yielding both bend lines and the basic shape of the stretchout. If the finished product is to have a base, a base is drawn at this time to one of the segments of the stretchout arc. Also, if pads are to be used for connecting the sides of the finished part, they must be drawn at this time.

Cone

The procedure followed for radial-line development of a cone is basically the same as the procedure for a pyramid. The cone also requires that a plan view and an elevation view be drawn. The stretchout arc is constructed in the same manner from a specified center point. It is general practice to draw the plan view and the elevation view on scrap material that can be either paper or metal, with only the stretchout drawn on the metal. This practice saves drawing many unwanted lines on the finished part. Only a divider is required to transfer true line lengths from paper to the stretchout arc.

Cones usually have a round base, making it necessary that a circle be divided into equal parts. Again 12 or 16 divisions normally are used for dividing circles into their individual elements or parts, which will be transferred directly onto the elevation view, establishing specific points where the part is to be

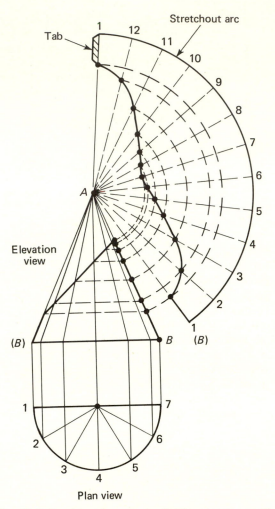

Fig. 21-8. Frustum of a cone (radial-line development).

cut. These intersections are transferred to the edge of the elevation view (from point A to point B in Fig. 21-8), because this is the only true length line represented in the elevation view. Then at the points where the plan view divisions intersect, Fig. 21-8, the divider is set. These lengths are then transferred to the stretchout arc yielding two points for each arc length on line AB. The points can be connected either by freehand drawing or by the use of the irregular curve. The choice of whether to draw freehand or to use the curve depends on the degree of accuracy required.

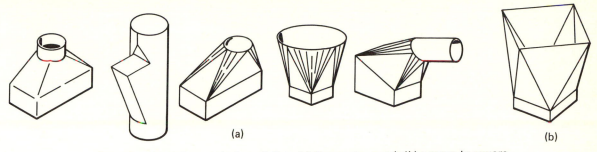

Fig. 21-9. Basic forms of triangulation. (a) Square to round; (b) square to square.

TRIANGULATION

The construction of straight and parallel lines depends on parallel lines for pattern development. Radial-line development uses a center point and an arc with lines radiating from the center point to the arc. Triangulation uses a series of small triangles to generate various patterns and stretchouts. The basic shapes of triangulation include a square-to-square transition, or square-to-round transition (Fig. 21-9a and b). Triangulation uses a number of small triangles to generate various changes in the shape of a product. Of major concern in pattern development are the true line lengths of the series of triangles. The instruments used are a straight edge, scribe, and dividers, the same as with the other methods of development. Two or more dividers can be used to speed up the drawing of the stretchout with the triangulation method.

Square-to-Square Transition

The simplest form of triangulation is in a square-to-square transition (Fig. 21-10). First,

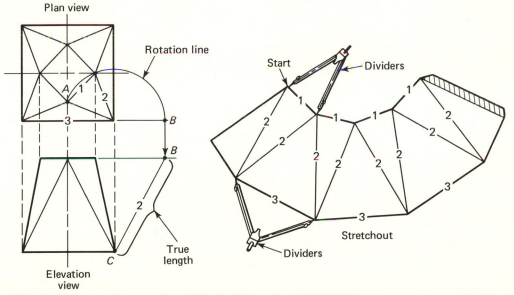

Fig. 21-10. Square-to-square transition.

an elevation view and a plan view of the part to be produced are drawn. Although the plan view will determine two of the true length lines needed for the transition piece, it will not yield a true length line for the bend lines of the transition piece. One further step is needed in order to determine the true length line, the number 2 line in Fig. 21-10, in the square-to-square transition.

A number 2 line, an important true length, is available only by rotating the plan view and transporting this arc to the elevation view with a compass or a divider. An outside corner that is close to the elevation of the plan view is chosen and a line is started at point A. With dividers or a compass, an arc is swung to point B. The same reference point is established on the elevation view. A true length line extends from point C on the elevation view to the constructed point B on the elevation view, which establishes the true length of the number 2 line (Fig. 21-10).

The stretchout can now be constructed. First one pair of dividers is set to length number 1. Another pair is set to length number 2, and a third divider is set to length number 3. One divider can accomplish the same operation but it is more troublesome to use just one pair of dividers. Arbitrarily a starting point is established and a line is extended from it. An arc of length number 1, as

pictured in Fig. 21-10, is swung. Arc number 2 is also swung, yielding two points. Next, the second set of points is connected by a straight line, and then the action of swinging arc lengths 1 and 2 is continued until the piece is completed. The complete stretchout will be nothing more than a series of intersecting arcs whose lines can be joined to create the finished stretchout. Always remember that tabs have to be added to any stretchout.

Square-to-Round Transition

The square-to-round transition, probably the most used transition piece, is constructed in basically the same way as a round-to-round transition. The equipment used to generate square-to-round transitions is the same as that used to generate square-to-square transitions. The major difference is in the number of rays that are radiated from a given point. These rays, or bend lines, are all true line lengths. As in the case of square-to-square transition, the square-to-round transition elevation and plan views do not yield the true line length of the rays that radiate from each corner of the piece to the top of the piece (Fig. 21-11).

As usual when working with anything that is circular, the circle is divided into an

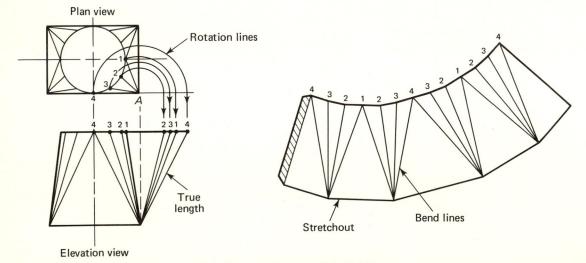

Fig. 21-11. Square-to-round transition.

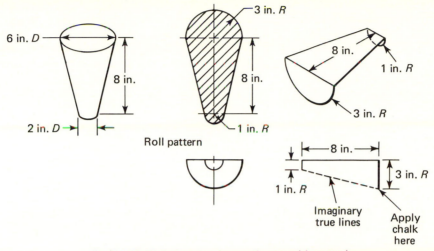

Fig. 21-12. Rollation development—round to round.

equal number of portions, a step that usually is accomplished in the plan view. Common practice is to make 12 or 16 equal portions with 12 being the number that is used most. The plan view (Fig. 21-11, numbered 1, 2, 3, 4) indicates equal divisions. These lines are drawn onto the elevation view. Usually the true length lines are generated by using the plan view for the rotation lines and then transferring these lines to the elevation view. This transfer is accomplished by placing a compass or divider at point A and swinging intersect lines, as shown in Fig. 21-11. The lines are transferred to the elevation view

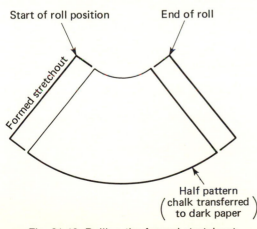

Fig. 21-13. Rolling the formed stretchout.

points, and then the true length lines are plotted. These true length lines correspond directly to the bend lines in the stretchout. Again, it is much simplier to use two sets of dividers. One divider is set to the segment which is one-twelfth of the circle, and the other divider is used to transfer the true length lines for the construction of the stretchout.

ROLLATION DEVELOPMENT

Rollation is a short-cut method to generate a series of true line lengths. Basically, it establishes a centerline pattern that will yield an imaginary true line (Fig. 21-12). For example, in a round-to-round development, all that is needed are the dimensions of the part to be made. The dimensions are transferred onto a roll pattern and cut out of sheet metal. If the diameter of the top piece were 6 in., a 3-in. arc would be swung; in the case given in Fig. 21-12, a 1-in. arc is swung. Connecting the lines produces the pattern. Then the pattern is bent at the appropriate bend line, creating a true centerline length for all the lines. The pattern is placed on the edge of the sheet metal with chalk or some other coloring device, and the sheet metal is rolled against a dark paper. The chalk transfers to the dark

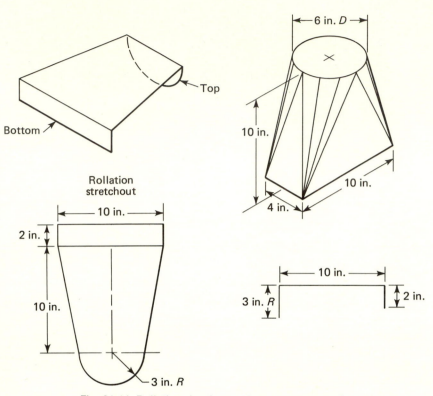

Fig. 21-14. Rollation development—square to round.

paper, generating a half-pattern stretchout (Fig. 21-13).

The short-cut method of rolling a stretchout can generate all shapes accomplished with parallel-line development, radial-line development, and triangulation. The critical point in rollation is the accuracy of the centerline section as well as the accuracy of the transfer of the chalk or bluing to the stretchout. This method also can generate pieces that are nonsymmetrical around the centerline by making two or more rollation patterns. Figure 21-14 is an example of a square-to-round transition.

QUESTIONS

1. What is a stretchout?
2. What types of patterns can be developed by the straight-line method?
3. Identify an advantage of the straight-line method.
4. Explain the parallel-line method of pattern development.
5. How is the irregular curve correctly joined?
6. What are the pattern shapes that can be developed by the radial-line method?
7. Explain the triangulation method of pattern development.
8. Compare the parallel-line, radial-line, and triangulation methods of pattern development.
9. What is a true line length? Are there false line lengths?
10. What is the concept behind the rollation method?

22

Shearing

Shearing is a cutting operation that is performed without creating chips or waste products. This procedure leaves a clean edge on the piece of metal that is sheared or cut. The basic shearing operations are: cutting apart to final size; trimming; notching; piercing, which is the creation of holes; and blanking (Fig. 22-1).

SHEARING ACTION

Shearing action has three basic stages: plastic deformation, shear, and fracture (Fig. 22-2). The metal is placed between the upper and lower blades of the shear, and the blades are forced together; one blade may be stationary and the other blade forced toward it. The blades close and the elastic limit of the material is reached as the blade penetrates the metal. At this point, plastic deformation takes place in the metal. As the blade continues to descend through the material, the shearing portion of the cutting cycle is accomplished. The shearing action is noted by small deformations on the surface of the metal which extend into the interior of the metal from 5 to 40 percent of its thickness. The penetration of the shear zone depends on the type of metal being sheared. As continued pressure is ap-

plied to the cutting blade, the fractures start at the cutting edge of each blade, the points of the greatest stress concentration. As the blade descends further, the small fractures meet and the metal is then sheared.

The same shearing action takes place when a punch and die are used (Fig. 22-3). The only difference in punch and die work is that the shear part is pushed completely through the die. The part is called either a slug or a blank. The term *slug* refers to waste material; and the term *blank* refers to an item that requires further forming or cutting in order to make washers, pots, pans, and other formed materials. A careful study of the slug or blank can explain a great deal about

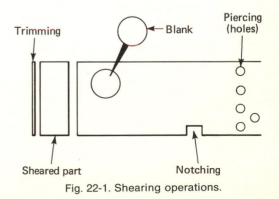

Fig. 22-1. Shearing operations.

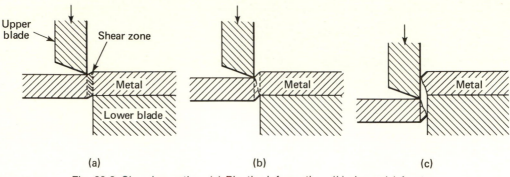

Fig. 22-2. Shearing action. (a) Plastic deformation; (b) shear; (c) fracture.

the quality of the shearing process. A well-sheared slug has a smooth burnished surface for about two-thirds of its thickness and a rough fractured surface for approximately the remaining third of the metal thickness (Fig. 22-3b).

SHEARING EQUIPMENT

Shearing equipment can be classified into two categories: hand shears and machine shears.

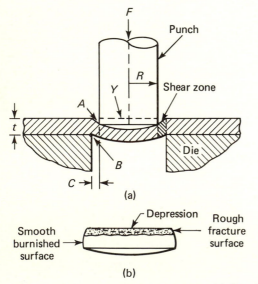

Fig. 22-3. Punch and die shearing action. (a) Plastic deformation; (b) slug.

Hand shears, commonly known as snips and punches, are available in a wide variety of shapes and types. Common snips are combination snips, circular snips, hawkbilled snips,

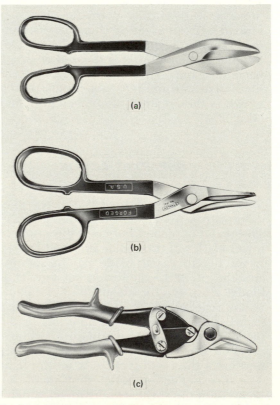

Fig. 22-4. Hand shears. (a) Combination snips; (b) hawk-billed snips; (c) aviation snips (left-handed). (*Stanley Tools.*)

and aviation snips (Fig. 22-4). Hand punches are also available in a wide variety of sizes and are capable of shearing a variety of metal thicknesses. However, the use of most hand shears and punches is usually limited to metals that range in thickness to a maximum of 16 gage. The use of the hand punch also is limited to metals 16 gage or lighter and to sizes that range from a $1/16$-in. punch die to approximately ¾ in. Punch sets that consist of a die and a punch are available in sizes that start at $1/16$ in. with sizes increasing in steps of $1/64$ in.

Shearing machines are divided into two main groups according to the thickness of metal they cut. Shearing machines that are capable of cutting metal 10 gage or thinner are called *sheet metal machine shearers*. Those machines that shear metal 10 gage and thicker are called *plate shearers*. Common sheet metal shearers are the foot-squaring shears, the punch, and the notcher (Fig. 22-5). Both the foot-squaring shears and the notcher operate by the use of a straight shearing blade. Their primary function is the production of sheet metal parts. The machines come either as power-operated shears or as mechanically activated shears.

The shearing sequence for both the foot-squaring shears and the notcher includes the following steps. First, a piece of metal is placed under the moving blade, and the machine is activated. A clamping bar that is fastened to the upper blade descends, clamping the metal firmly. Then the metal is sheared. Ring and circle shears use a rotary cutting blade, much as an electric can opener does. The center of the metal is determined and placed under a stationary radius point, which is a fixed distance from the cutter blades. The material is rotated through the cutter blades, generating a circle or a ring. Plate and angle shears are used in the same manner as sheet metal shears except that the machines are larger and the amount of energy exerted by the machine onto the cutting blade is much greater because the metal to be cut is thicker. Plate shears can shear steel up to 3 in. thick.

PIERCING AND BLANKING

The ability to pierce or blank coupled with the forming processes has given designers wider ranges of possibilities for solving design problems. Press pierced, blanked, and die-formed parts make it possible for lightweight, high-strength products or parts to be produced, parts that are used in such things as radios, business machines, automobiles, all types of household items, and in thousands of other useful items. Approximately 40 percent of all the sheet and strip steel annually produced in the United States is used in the piercing and blanking metal forming industry.

DIE CONSTRUCTION

Dies can be designed and constructed as either drop-through dies or as standard dies (Fig. 22-6). The most popular die design is the drop-through design because the part that has been punched, whether it is a slug or a blank, simply falls through the die block and press bed into a waiting container. Standard die construction occurs when the die block is solid and die cutters are mounted onto the die block. The punch travel is restricted so that it never strikes the die block, traveling only far enough to shear the metal sufficiently. So that the punched part can be removed easily, a pad is placed on top of the die block between the die cutters. This pad can be made of rubber or even of three-ply cardboard, like that used in the container industry.

Both drop-through and standard dies are composed of four basic parts: the die block, the punch, the die shoe, and the stripper. The *die block*, the female part of the blanking die, has an opening that is the size of the blank desired. The punch is the male part of the die which forces the blank through the opening of the die block. The *stripper*, a device to keep the metal from riding up on the punch as the punch is withdrawn from the metal

(a)

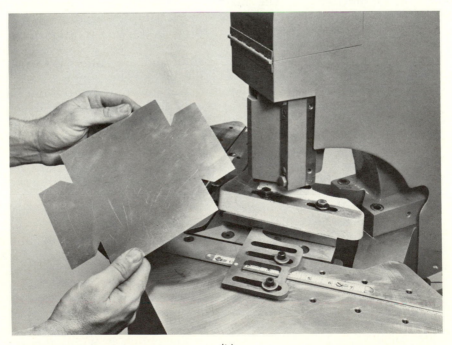

(b)

Fig. 22-5. Machine shears. (a) Foot-squaring shears (*Di-Acro Houdaille*); (b) notcher (*Di-Acro Houdaille*); (c) punch (*E. G. Heller's Son*).

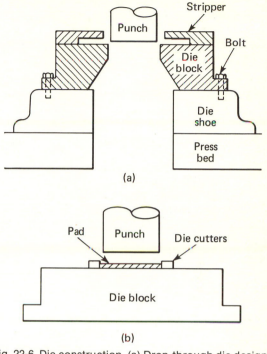

Fig. 22-6. Die construction. (a) Drop-through die design; (b) standard die design.

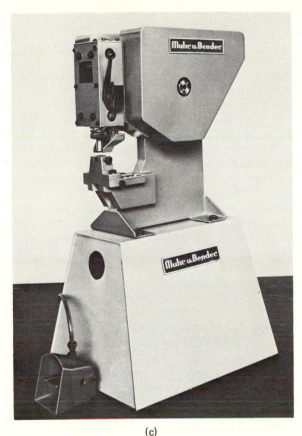

(c)

Fig. 22-5. (cont.)

stock, ensures that the punched metal is held to the surface of the die block. All of these devices rest on the base, or the *die shoe*. The shoe is mounted to the press platen or press bed and remains stationary. The punch is mounted to the ram of the press and is movable (Fig. 22-7).

The many secondary parts used in die sets include punch holders, back gages, feed mechanisms, return springs, blocking devices, and lubricating devices. Punch holders are used sometimes to secure a punch to the press rim, and they can also serve as a spacer to shorten the distance that the ram must travel in order to mate the punch into the die block. The back gage is used as a stop gage to help align the metal to be sheared. Many times the back gage is incorporated directly into the stripper mechanism so that the one part performs the actions of both.

Feed mechanisms are usually not part of the die set itself but are incorporated into the total shearing system. In certain circumstances dies are made with a device that advances the material after each punch cycle

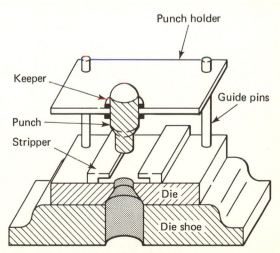

Fig. 22-7. Die set.

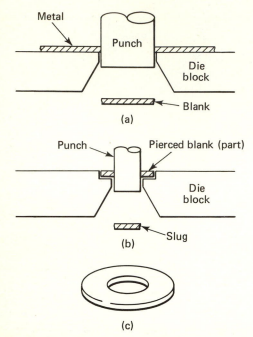

Fig. 22-8. Single operation, two-station piercing and blanking (cut washer). (a) Blanking; (b) piercing; (c) finished part—cut washer.

cation usually is done by the operator of the equipment.

The thickness and type of material control the cutting clearances of the die set. The *cutting clearance,* or *angular clearance,* is the amount of space between the side of the punch and the side of the die block. Proper cutting clearance determines the life of the die as well as the quality of the sheared part. Cutting clearances, expressed as a percentage of the thickness of the metal to be cut, are available to die makers in very complex tables. These tables, however, only state a starting point for the clearances, and each die set must be machined and tested a number of times before the correct cutting clearance is established for one particular die set. A common practice for the die maker is to start with a slightly smaller clearance angle than the table states and to proceed by a system of trial and error, enlarging the clearance until a satisfactorily finished blank is produced.

PROCESS TYPES

and uses the action of the ram itself to trigger the feed mechanism. Locking devices can be incorporated directly within the stripper or are attached to the punch. Lubricating systems are used only on those punching systems that have been automated. When the punching system is operated manually, lubri-

Piercing and blanking can be accomplished by three different dies: separate, progressive, or compound dies. With separate dies, one die produces one part (Fig. 22-8). Progressive dies have a series of punches and die openings and are capable of producing a number of blanks or pierced holes during one

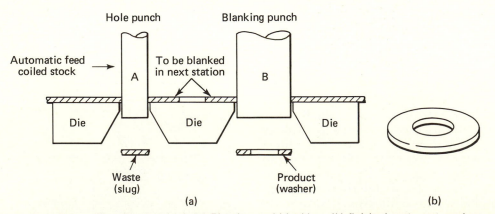

Fig. 22-9. Progressive dies (washer). (a) Piercing and blanking; (b) finished part—cut washer.

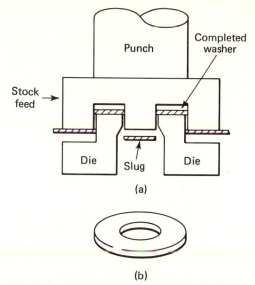

(a)

(b)

Fig. 22-10. Compound die (washer). (a) Piercing and blanking; (b) finished part—cut washer.

shearing action, or one release of the ram (Fig. 22-9). Compound dies pierce and blank at the same time (Fig. 22-10). Separate dies are the least expensive of the three types, although the labor costs for separate dies are more than doubled when compared to the other two methods. The accuracy in separate dies or single operation dies is not as high and the speed of production is not as fast as with progressive or compound dies.

Progressive dies initially cost more than separate or single-operation dies. However, progressive dies significantly cut labor costs. The accuracy when progressive dies are used is much higher than when separate dies are used, and the production rate is significantly greater with progressive dies. The only disadvantage to compound dies is their relatively high cost. Compound dies offer the advantage of perfect accuracy in the alignment of blank parts. Locating the position of the pierced holes from one pierced hole to another as well as from the pierced hole in relationship to its position on the blank is performed with great accuracy. The inherent accuracy of the compound dies is created by the precision with which the compound die sets are made. The production rate of compound dies is slightly higher than the rate of progressive dies. An advantage of the compound die is that the burrs on the blanks and holes are always on the same side; whereas many times with progressive dies the burrs are on opposite sides.

QUESTIONS

1. Explain shearing action.
2. What is a slug?
3. How does the slug indicate proper shearing action?
4. How does the shearing action differ for hand shears and machine shears?
5. Explain piercing and blanking.
6. What is the function of the die block?
7. How do the functions of a progressive die set differ from the functions of the compound die set?

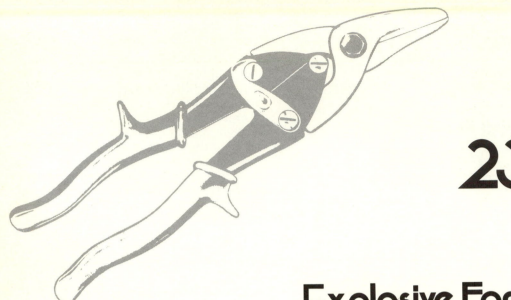

23

Explosive Forming

The conventional methods of forming can be contrasted accurately to the explosive method of forming by demonstrating the differences between the use of energy by the two methods. The use of kinetic energy is equal to one-half the mass times the velocity squared, or

$$K = \tfrac{1}{2}MV^2$$

The principle behind conventional forming methods is concerned with the M in the equation, the mass. The mass involved is the size and weight of the hammer or the ram used to perform the work. If the ram velocity is at a very low level, perhaps only a few feet per second, an increase in the power for the conventional forming machine can be achieved by increasing the ram mass. Although this principle is workable, it has led to extremely large, heavy, and costly machines.

The method of using explosives to perform the deforming work on the workpiece deals with another factor in the kinetic equation. The principle involved with explosive forming is the velocity, the V in the kinetic energy equation. Instead of using a heavy, slow-moving ram to do the work, an explosion is used, creating a pressure pulse, a wave front, or a gas bubble, which causes the

deformation of the workpiece. The power is achieved by increasing the velocity of the wave front and not by increasing the mass of the prime mover, or the ram. Expensive presses are not required, making this method ideal for large items that have short-run capabilities.

Devices that form metal at a rate of over 10 ft/s are called *high-velocity forming devices*. The major types of high-velocity forming to date include pneumatic-mechanical forming, explosive forming, electrohydraulic forming, and electromagnetic forming (Fig. 23-1).

ENERGY REQUIREMENTS

Energy requirements play an important part in choosing whether to use high-velocity forming or conventional forming. A rule of thumb can be that when the energy requirements for forming exceed 2 million joules (J), high-velocity forming should be used. A pound of explosives delivers between 1.6 and 2 million J of energy. A *joule* is equal to the work done when a current of one ampere is passed through the resistance of one ohm for one second. Or, a joule is the force needed to displace one newton, one meter in the

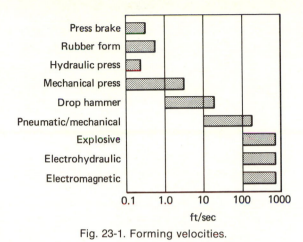

Fig. 23-1. Forming velocities.

direction of the force. A *newton* is the force that 1 kilogram of mass has when accelerated one meter per second. The joule (also expressed as foot pounds) describes the energy, the work, or the quantity of heat.

The explosion used to form the metal can be divided into two general categories: high explosion values and low explosion values. This classification does not have anything to do with the power source, which may be electrical, gaseous, or explosive; but it defines the energy conversion time, the burn rate, and the pressure generated. Explosive forming when using, for example, a combustible gas mixture of propane, methane, hydrogen, and an oxidizer, creates a shock front which moves at a rate of 1,000 to 8,000 ft/s. This rate would be considered a low explosion rate. A high explosive burning rate is more rapid. It may range from 6,000 to over 28,000 ft/s. However, many power sources, such as an electrical power source, do not have burn rates, so that the energy conversion time is used for a comparison. For example, a measurement that could be used for the rate of expansion of an electromagnetic field is 6 microseconds (μs). The 6 μs would be the energy conversion time. With high explosives, the energy conversion time is extremely short, usually ranging from 4 to 10 μs.

The energy conversion time is important because it is directly proportional to the amount of pressure exerted by the explosion on the surface to be formed. The example above of the electromagnetic energy that is released in 6 μs develops up to 560,000 psi. With high explosives, the pressures can range from 2 to 4 million psi. The range with the low explosives is from 30,000 to 60,000 psi. However, the low explosive pressure is contingent on the explosive charge being used with proper confinement.

TRANSFER MEDIA

Explosive forming can use water, sand, gas, and almost any other fluid as an energy transfer medium. Water, because of its abundance, low cost, and low compression factor, is used the most. When an explosion is detonated, a spherically shaped pressure pulse travels away from the center of the explosion. A gas bubble of the same basic pattern is generated immediately after a pressure pulse. After the gas bubble expands to the maximum diameter, it collapses, and then builds up again, repeating this action like waves in the ocean. Each oscillation produces a weaker pressure pulse, until the gas bubble rises to the surface of the water and dissipates into the atmosphere.

The energy, or the pressure pulse, created by the explosion is what deforms the workpiece to the desired shape. The impulses are either uniform or nonuniform. Uniform pulses result when sheet explosives are used in the area of explosive contact. The explosive sheet being detonated from one edge will produce a pulse of very short duration when there is direct contact between the metal and the explosive. The explosion products are free to expand and do so very rapidly, allowing also for a rapid reduction in pressure. The pressure pulse usually is a wedge shape (Fig. 23-2).

A nonuniform pulse results when a cylinder with an internal explosive contact charge is used. At the moment of detonation two fronts are generated: the *original detonation wave front* and the *energy released front*. The energy released front must always follow

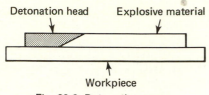

Fig. 23-2. Detonation wave.

the detonation wave. The released front is completely dependent on the detonation front, and it only achieves two-thirds of the velocity of the detonation head so that the two wave fronts constantly increase the distance between themselves. Eventually, the detonation front reaches the end of the explosive material, causing another energy release front to start moving back in the opposite direction. These two release fronts meet each other at a distance of about six times the length of the explosive material. When the two waves meet at this point, the release of the largest amount of energy occurs.

FORMING PROCESSES

High-velocity forming processes may be divided into four categories depending on the power supply, or energy, used for forming. The four types are: explosive forming, electrohydraulic forming, pneumatic-mechanical forming, and electromagnetic forming.

Explosive Forming

Most explosives are used with a die. The metal is pressed into the die by the explosive force of the charge. Because wrinkling is hard

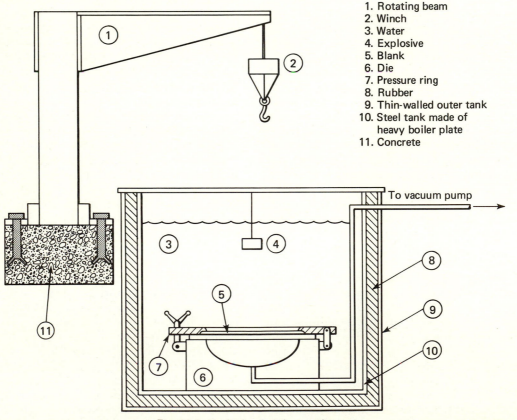

1. Rotating beam
2. Winch
3. Water
4. Explosive
5. Blank
6. Die
7. Pressure ring
8. Rubber
9. Thin-walled outer tank
10. Steel tank made of heavy boiler plate
11. Concrete

Fig. 23-3. Explosive forming equipment.

to control when a metal is formed over a punch, most of the dies used are female, or internal, dies. The basic explosive forming equipment is a die, a rubber seal, a vacuum pump, a chamber that will hold the water in the die, and the explosive charge (Fig. 23-3). The metal blank to be formed is bolted securely to the die. A vacuum, usually about 29.9 inches of mercury, is set up inside between the blank and the die. The die is lowered into the water tank, and an explosive charge is suspended at a strategic point above the workpiece. The charge is set off and the force bubble drives the metal blank against the die. The vacuum between the workpiece and the die ensures that the metal forms easily against the die face.

The hardest high tensile metals can be contoured with explosive forming with less fracture and with less springback than with other metal forming processes. The explosive shock wave acts as a free, frictionless rim, causing the metal to flow freely into the die cavity without any excessive stretching as occurs in press forming. Thus, explosive forming does not have the detrimental effects of the press forming process. The only limiting factor for explosive forming is the construction of the die.

Explosive forming is also accomplished in other ways. For example, it is used with closed dies (Fig. 23-4). The closed die uses a parabolic reflector and a shaped charge. The workpiece is placed between the closed dies and the shaped charge in the die cavity. Both the reflector and the charge must be shaped

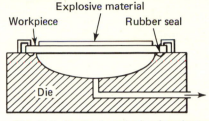

Fig. 23-5. Contact explosive forming.

to direct the explosive force toward the work. Another process, contact explosive forming, places a flat high explosive in direct contact with the workpiece. The workpiece is then placed on top of the female die. A vacuum is drawn and the charge is ignited, driving the metal blank into the die form. Many times contact explosive forming is done without the aid of a fluid transfer medium; instead air is used as a transfer medium (Fig. 23-5).

Explosive forming also is used for bulge forming. A bulge forming device is a split die in which a cylindrical metal blank has been inserted. A charge is lowered into the cylinder blank and then ignited. The force drives the cylinder into the die face. Bulge forming can be done either in a fluid transfer medium or in the air (Fig. 23-6).

Another method of explosive forming uses a rubber container full of oil which is placed on the metal blank. The explosive force is directed into the rubber and transmitted through the oil to the work blank. The

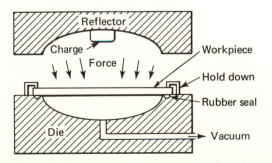

Fig. 23-4. Explosive forming with a parabolic reflector (closed die).

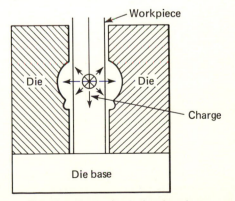

Fig. 23-6. Explosive bulge forming.

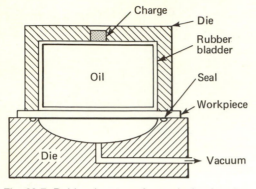

Fig. 23-7. Rubber bag transfer explosive forming.

blank then forms on the die. Gun powder cartridges usually are used for this type of explosive forming. The oil and rubber bag is used to distribute the force more evenly over the entire surface of the workpiece. Vacuum again is used under the workpiece preventing any air pockets and ensuring that the flow of metal into the die is not retarded (Fig. 23-7).

Electrohydraulic Forming

Electrohydraulic high-velocity forming (HVF) is similar to explosive forming, except it uses electric energy rather than chemical energy to generate the shock wave. The wave is generated by the storing of electricity in a capacitor bank. The current is discharged, creating a spark between the two electrodes. Sometimes these two electrodes are connected by a small wire in order to create the initial path, a wire which is destroyed when the capacitor bank is fired. The shock wave is needed to produce the high-velocity wave which transfers through the fluid (usually water) and strikes the workpiece, forcing it into the die form that has previously been evacuated by a vacuum pump (Fig. 23-8).

The major difference between electrohydraulic forming and high-explosive forming is the magnitude of the pressure wave. Because the capacitor banks do not usually store sufficient quantities of power, the process of electrohydraulic forming is restricted to use with small parts. Although large parts and

large capacitor banks can be constructed, the cost of such construction when compared to the cost of explosive forming is high. The average amount of energy released by electrohydraulic forming is a shock wave of about 20,000 ft/s. Normally, the electrical discharge occurs in less than 40 μs, and the complete forming process takes place in less than 400 μs.

Pneumatic-Mechanical Forming

The pneumatic-mechanical high-velocity forming and forging machines superficially resemble those that operate in a conventional manner, because workpieces are formed in a die system driven by a ram. The essential differences involve the mass and the speed of the ram. The mass of the explosive forming ram does not have to be as large as in conventional machines, and the ram travels a great deal faster than rams in conventional machines.

The initial cost of high-velocity forming compares favorably with that of conventional machines. Although high-velocity forming machines are not capable of performing many of the operations which are routine to a conventional forming press, they do offer many advantages. The high-velocity forming machine does not require a special foundation and it can be located in any area zoned for medium or heavy industry, areas in which

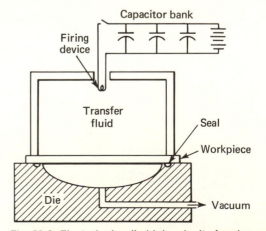

Fig. 23-8. Electrohydraulic high-velocity forming.

conventional forming or forging hammers, for example, are restricted. The forgings produced by high-velocity forming machines can be designed with no draft, produced with excellent surface finishes, and formed with careful control of grain flow. Added important advantages of these machines are that they can work superalloys and refractory alloys and can repeat the production of parts accurately and at a high rate of speed.

The pneumatic-mechanical machines obtain their necessary deformation energy through the transfer of kinetic energy. These machines are operated with completely enclosed gas systems. Adiabatic expansion, allowing no energy loss, accelerates one or more power pistons which are attached to the press platen in such a manner that the platens move together, transferring the energy to the die. The inward piece of the die is attached to the platen and when the dies contact each other, a high amount of energy is expended to deform the workpiece. The gas in the system is compressed by hydraulic or special gas compressors. The ultimate speed of the ram depends on the amount of gas pressure released, and the closing energy of the dies depends on the length of the stroke of the ram piston and the mass of the platens (Fig. 23-9).

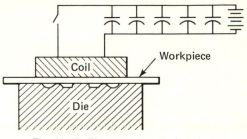

Fig. 23-10. Electromagnetic forming.

Electromagnetic Forming

Electromagnetic forming, sometimes called magnetic-pulse forming, uses an ultra rapid capacitor discharge into a specially prepared electrical coil to produce the necessary forming forces. The result of this rapid electrical discharge is a high momentary current that passes through a coil, setting up an intense magnetic field for a short duration. The result of this magnetic field is the generation of eddy currents and an electrically conductive workpiece within a close proximity. The magnetic forces created accelerate the workpiece toward or away from the coil and the coil windings. The direction of the movement of the workpiece depends on the discharge of the coil (Fig. 23-10).

Magnetic forming can be classified into

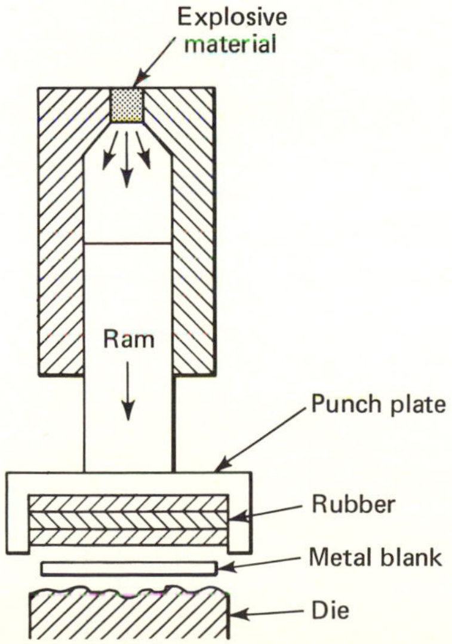

Fig. 23-9. Pneumatic-mechanical high-velocity forming.

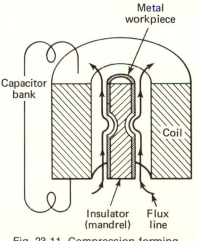

Fig. 23-11. Compression forming.

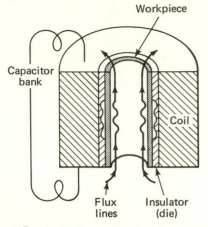

Fig. 23-12. Expansion forming.

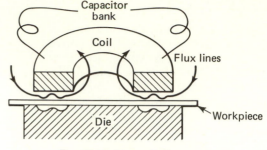

Fig. 23-13. Magnetic hammer.

three categories: compression forming, expansion forming, and hammer forming. In compression forming, the object to be formed, such as an aluminum tube, is formed around a mandrel. The magnetic field is pulsed under a few microseconds so that the field is kept within the aluminum tube. When the magnetic field collapses, the metal tubing is squeezed around the mandrel or die (Fig. 23-11). Allowing the magnetic field to build causes the magnetic field to be created outside the tubing, resulting in the further compression of the tube.

Expansion electromagnetic forming is the opposite of compression forming. The insulator die is joined directly to the coil, and the metal to be formed is placed inside the die instead of on the outside. The magnetic field is created and collapses, drawing the workpiece onto the die and forming the finished product (Fig. 23-12).

Magnetic hammer forming uses a flat die and strikes the metal plate into the die in the same manner that a hammer would, except that the striking force is very smooth and occurs over a large area. The magnetic hammer forming principle is used both for original production as well as for repair work. The workpiece is formed by placing it between the insulated die and the coil. The hammer is the magnetic field that is created (Fig. 23-13).

Commercial magnetic forming machines are capable of forming pressures of 5×10^4 psi in pulse duration, with a pulse duration of 10 to 20 μs. The electric energy to produce the force required demands a capacitor storage capability as high as 30,000 dc volts (V) and 10,000 amperes (A), a capability which will produce 300,000 gauss (G) or 3×10^5 G.

QUESTIONS

1. What is high-velocity forming?
2. Explain $K = \frac{1}{2}MV^2$ as it pertains to forming.
3. What are the major types of high-velocity forming?
4. Compare and contrast high and low explosives.
5. What is energy conversion time?
6. Why is water the most used transfer medium?
7. How does electrohydraulic forming differ from explosive forming?
8. Explain pneumatic-mechanical forging.
9. How does the magnetic hammer work?
10. What is the function of the insulating mandrel in electromagnetic forming?

Part Five

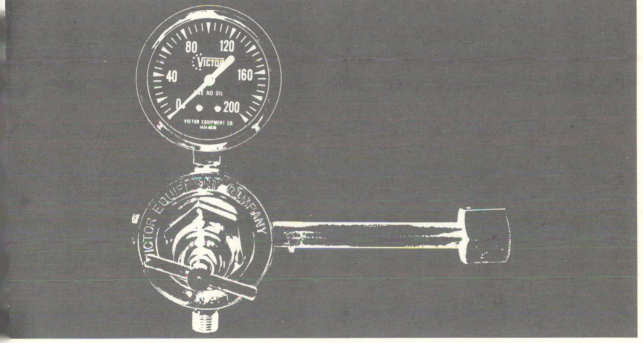

Welding Processes

24

Shielded-Arc Welding

Present-day shielded-arc welding is accomplished by producing an electric arc between the work to be welded and the tip of the electrode. This type of welding has the advantages of less heat loss and less oxidation than that of the oxyacetylene flame.

ARC COLUMN THEORY

The arc column is generated between an anode, which is the positive pole of a dc power supply, and the cathode, the negative pole. Metal ions pass from the positive to the negative pole because they are positively charged and thus attracted to the negative pole.

The arc is one of the most efficient means for producing heat that is available to modern technology. Approximately 50 percent of the electric energy put into the arc system comes out in the form of heat energy. Approximately two-thirds of the energy released in the arc column system is always at the anode (the positive pole). This is true in all dc systems. Another type of arc power source used in shielded-arc welding is alternating current (ac). When an ac power supply is used, the heat in the arc column generally is equalized between the anode and the

cathode areas, so that the area of medium heat is then in the plasma area (Fig. 24-1).

THE ARC COLUMN AND POWER SOURCES

The welding circuit consists of a power source, the electrode cable, the ground cable, and the electrode (Fig. 24-2). The two basic types of power sources for arc welding are direct current and alternating current. Each of these two power supplies has distinct advantages. In dc welding, the electron flow is in one direction; in ac welding, the electron flow is in both directions. In dc welding, the direction can be changed by simply reversing the cables at the terminals located on the generator. The different settings on the terminals indicate that the electron flow will be either from the electrode to the work, which is the positive ground, or from the work to the electrode, which is the negative ground.

Two-thirds of the heat is developed near the positive pole while the remaining one-third is developed near the negative pole. As a result, an electrode that is connected to the positive pole will burn away approximately 50 percent faster than one that is connected

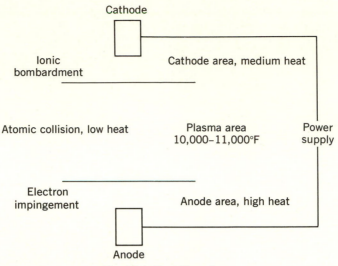

Fig. 24-1. Heat liberation.

to the negative pole. Knowing this information helps a welder to obtain the desired penetration of the base metal (Fig. 24-3). If the positive ground is used, the penetration will be greater because of the amount of heat energy supplied to the work by the electrode force. At the same time, the electrode will burn away slowly. If the poles are reversed and there is a negative ground, two-thirds of the heat will remain in the tip of the electrode. For this reason, the penetration of the heat zone in the base metal will be shallow when compared to the penetration depth of the positive ground arc column. Alternating current yields a penetration depth that is approximately half that achieved by the dc

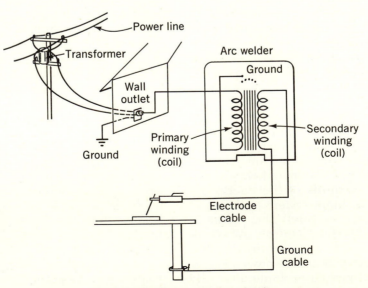

Fig. 24-2. Typical ac welding circuit.

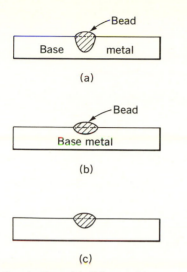

Fig. 24-3. Penetration. (a) DC—positive ground; (b) DC—negative ground; (c) ac.

positive ground. Since electron flow switches ground every time the ac cycle changes, the penetration of the heat zone in the base metal is approximately between the two dc types.

In *straight polarity,* the electrode is negative and the work is positive. The electron flow goes from the electrode into the work. When the electrode is positive and the work is negative, the electron flow is from the work to the anode, a characteristic called *reverse polarity* (Fig. 24-4). When reverse polarity is used, the work remains cooler than when straight polarity is used.

In both the ac and dc power sources, the arc serves the same purpose: producing heat to melt metal. If two pieces of metal that are to be joined are placed so that they touch or almost touch one another and the arc from the electrode is directed at this junction, the heat generated by the arc causes a small section of the edges of both pieces of metal to melt. These molten portions along with the molten portions of the electrode flow together. As the arc column is moved, the molten puddle solidifies, joining the two pieces of metal with a combination of electrode metal and base metal.

The coatings on the electrodes burn as the electrode wire is melted by the intense heat of the arc. As the electrode wire melts, the

electrode covering, or the flux, provides a gaseous shield around the arc, preventing contamination (Fig. 24-5). The force of the arc column striking the workpiece digs a crater in the base metal. This crater fills with molten metal. As the flux melts, part of it mixes with the impurities in the molten pool causing them to float to the top of the weld. This slag protects the bead from the atmosphere and causes the bead to cool more uniformly. The slag also helps to design the contour of the weld bead by acting as an insulator. By insulating the heat-affected zone (HAZ), located in the parent metal or the base metal and completely surrounding the weld bead, the slag allows an even rather than an erratic heat loss from this heat-affected zone, thus helping to control the crystal, or grain, size of the metal.

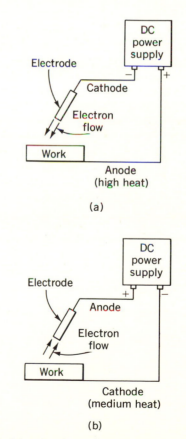

Fig. 24-4. DC polarity. (a) Straight polarity; (b) reverse polarity.

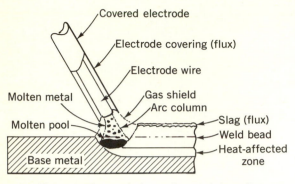

Fig. 24-5. Covered electrode metal deposit.

The arc column reaches temperatures from 5000 to 7000°F. These temperatures have a harsh effect on the parent metal. The molten pool, which must maintain a temperature of approximately 2800°F, radiates heat outward and changes the crystals surrounding the weld bead. Many times after welding, a part must be heat treated to change the size of the grains in the weld bead and the surrounding area (Fig. 24-6). The heating of the base metal by the arc stream and the resultant molten weld puddle or crater generally extend deep into the base metal. The extent of the heat-affected zone can be observed by studying the crystalline structure of the base metal in this zone. It generally is represented by a large grain. The grains in the unaffected areas of the metal are smaller. Because of the protection of the flux, the weld bead itself has medium-sized grains that extend to large grains at deeper penetration. It is not necessary to heat treat mild steel; but, with many metals, the heat from

welding will result in locked-in stresses that must be relieved either through peening or further heat treatment of the entire piece of metal.

Magnetic Arc Blow

Magnetic arc blow is experienced when direct current is employed for welding; however, this peculiarity is sometimes experienced when using alternating current for the power supply. When using alternating current, there is only about a 1 percent chance that magnetic arc blow will be encountered.

When current flows through a conductor, it produces a magnetic flux that circles around the conductor in perpendicular planes. The centers of the flux circles are located at the center of the conductor (Fig. 24-7). The magnetic flux is produced in the steel and across the arc gap. The arc column is mainly influenced by the lines of force crossing the gap. As the weld joins the pieces together, there is less and less chance that the magnetic field will concentrate in the arc gap. As the weld is filling the gap of the joint, it pushes the magnetic flux ahead of the arc. As long as the flux can travel, no serious arc blow will interrupt the weld. When the flux ceases to move, however, it piles up, and a magnetic field of considerable strength develops. The buildup of the flux causes a deflection of the arc column as it pulls away from this heavy concentration of magnetic force. Ionized gases that carry the arc from the end of the electrode wire to the workpiece are acting as a flexible conductor. This concentration of flux that pulls the arc from its intended path is called *arc blow*.

When the slag runs under the arc, conti-

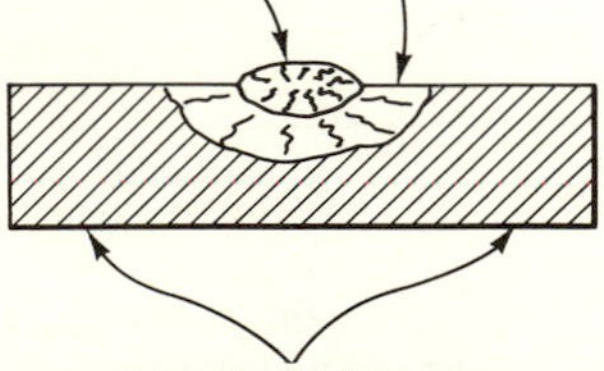

Fig. 24-6. Heat-affected zone.

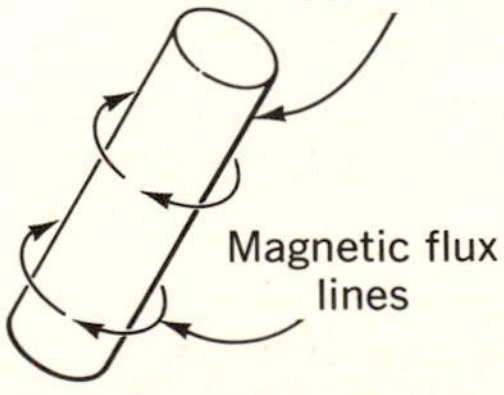

Fig. 24-7. Magnetic flux motion.

nuity of the weld bead is broken. The arc column is not self-starting, so if it is extinguished it must be reestablished. Two essential factors are involved in proper continuity: (1) The arc column must be maintained, and (2) the electrode must be fed into the weld puddle at a continuous rate in order to maintain the proper spacing between the electrode and the work. As the arc column becomes longer, more arc voltage is required to maintain the arc. The type of coating on the electrode also changes the amount of arc voltage that is required to maintain an arc column within a range of optimum fusion. If arc voltage is insufficient or overabundant, fusion of the weld bead will be inadequate. Oxidation and porosity can also be kept to a minimum by keeping the arc column within an optimum fusion range, which helps to control the problem of arc blow.

The base metal, which is also a conductor, has a flux field around it as current passes through it. These lines of force are perpendicular to the current passing through the work. Magnetic lines of force circle around the electrode, around the arc column, and around the workpiece. The *right-hand rule* used for finding the direction of the flux is as follows: When the thumb of the right hand points in the direction of the current flow, the forefinger points in the direction of the flux lines.

There are three areas of magnetic field travel. The first field is created by the current passing through the electrode. The second is created in the base metal by the ground. The third is created by the electrode arc column that comes in contact with the base metal. The current passes through the arc column into the metal. Of these three types of flux fields, or magnetic fields, the type created in the base metal by the ground is desirable because it causes a slight forward pull in the arc column. The other two types should be controlled.

Magnetic fields created by the flux can never be removed, but they can be controlled by various methods. One method is to set up a magnetic field of sufficient strength to neutralize the force caused by the flux. Other methods of controlling arc blow include

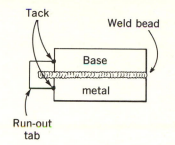

Fig. 24-8. Runout tabs. (*Note:* Extend the weld bead well into the runout tab.)

welding away from the earth ground connection; changing the position of the earth connection on the work; wrapping the welding electrode cable a few turns around the work; using runout tabs (Fig. 24-8); reducing the welding current or the electrode size; welding toward a heavy tack or portion of the weld already completed; reducing the rate of travel of the electrode; shortening the arc column length; or changing the power supply to alternating current.

Mechanism of Transfer

The transfer of metal from the tip of the electrode to the base metal is actually a method of short-circuiting. The electrode makes contact with the base metal every $1/400$ s. This short-circuiting creates a problem in the welding machine where the short circuit plays havoc with the amperage control within the machine. This short-circuiting effect, or *mechanism of metal transfer*, results from various distinct forces. One is the electromagnetic force, which is responsible for the pinch-off effect; another is the electromotive force (emf). Another force, resulting from the ion-electron travel, directs the metal from the electrode to the base metal. The force of gravity, especially in the flat welding position, the force resulting from the rapid expansion of gases, and the force of capillary attraction, resulting from the lessening of the surface tension of the base metal, also aid in the transfer of metal.

The short-circuiting of the electrode has four basic stages: *the heat stage, the deform stage, the contact stage,* and *the pinch-off*

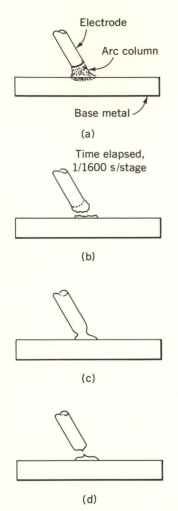

Fig. 24-9. Transfer of electrode metal. (a) Heat stage; (b) deform stage; (c) contact stage; (d) pinch-off stage.

stage (Fig. 24-9). After the arc column has been created between the electrode and the base metal, the electrode tip and the target area heat up, causing the metal to become plastic. The forces listed above aid in the deformation of the heated tip of the electrode and the heated spot in the base metal until the electrode metal comes into contact with the base metal. The arc column is extinguished at this time; however, current flow is maintained. The current flow creates a pile-up of electromagnetic lines of force which pinch off the electrode. The arc column is

restarted in order to begin another short-circuit cycle. This four-stage cycle occurs in as little time as $1/400$ s.

The short-circuit transfer mechanism, coupled with the magnetic arc pull, causes the weld metal to flow in the direction of the ground (Fig. 24-10). An arc crater is formed by the force of the arc column striking the base metal. The digging action that produces the crater results from the expanding gases of the fluxing shield and from the electron stream striking the metal. This crater fills with molten metal. The electrons continually bombard the center of the molten pool, making temperatures higher in the center of the crater or molten pool than they are at the edges. The edges solidify first so that the edges of the crater control the width of the weld.

Metal transfer is also accomplished through the spray arc. The short-circuiting method is based on low arc voltage, which ranges from 14 to 26 volts (V). The spray-arc method of metal transfer is also based on arc voltage, but of a higher range, usually from 20 to 40 arc V. The increase of potential voltage means an increase in the emf. This increase explodes particles of metal off the electrode tip. The higher the emf, the finer the particle size; in fact, the particles leaving the electrode tip in the form of a spray have much the same appearance as the paint ejected from a paint spray gun. The electrons leaving the surface of the electrode have a higher velocity than those leaving the electrode in the short-arc method of metal transfer. This high velocity is thought to create small air pockets under the surface of the tip of the electrode,

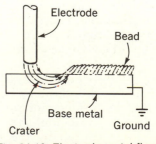

Fig. 24-10. Electrode metal flow.

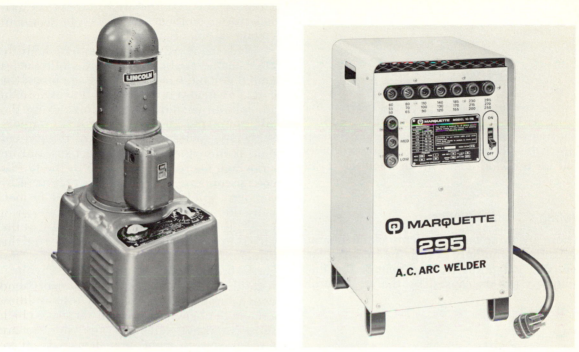

(a) (b)

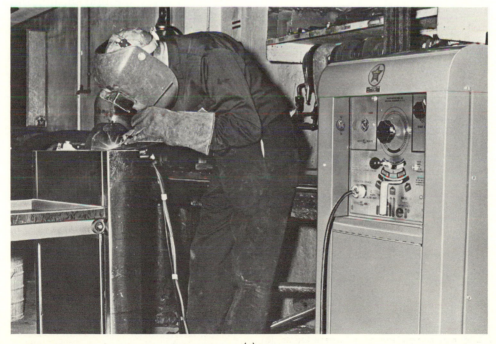

(c)

Fig. 24-11. Power supplies. (*a*) DC power supply (*Lincoln Electric Co.*); (*b*) ac power supply (*Marquette Corp.*); (*c*) ac-dc power supply (*Miller Electric Manufacturing Co.*).

making it easier for the particles to fly off from the surface of the electrode.

POWER SUPPLIES

Power is needed to supply the current that supports the arc column for fusion welding. There are three types of welding power supplies: dc motor generators, ac transformers, and ac transformers with dc rectifiers (Fig. 24-11).

Voltage Characteristics

There are three major current-voltage characteristics commonly used in today's arc welding machines to help control the fluctuating currents caused by the arc column.

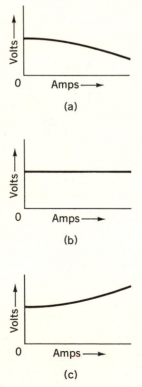

Fig. 24-12. DC voltage-amperage characteristics. (a) Drooping-arc voltage (DAV); (b) constant-arc voltage (CAV); (c) rising-arc voltage (RAV).

They are the drooping-arc voltage (DAV), the constant-arc voltage (CAV), and the rising-arc voltage (RAV) (Fig. 24-12).

The machine that is designed with the DAV characteristics provides the highest potential voltage when the welding current circuit is open and no current is flowing. As the arc column is started, the voltage drops to a minimum and the amperage rises rapidly. With DAV, when the length of the arc column is increased, the voltage rises and the amperage decreases. The DAV is the type of voltage-amperage relationship preferred for standard shielded-arc welding that is manually done.

The CAV and a modification of it called the RAV are characteristics preferred for semiautomatic or automatic welding processes because they maintain a preset voltage regardless of the amount of current being drawn from the machine. These voltage-amperage characteristics are sensitive to the short-circuiting effect of the shielded-arc mechanism of metal transfer. With these types, the spray arc method rather than the short-circuit arc method of metal transfer is used. The spray arc, much like a spray gun spraying paint, works on a principle different from that of the short-circuit pinch-off effect of welding with a stick electrode. An advantage of the RAV over the CAV characteristic is that as the amperage requirement is increased, the voltage is increased automatically, thus helping to maintain a constant-arc gap even if short-circuiting occurs. This RAV is adaptable to the fully automatic processes.

Voltage Controls

Controls for dc welding machines may be of several types, ranging from a simple rheostat in the exciter circuit to a combination of exciter regulators and a series of field taps. A third means for controlling current is a mechanical provision for shifting the generator brushes on a self-excited machine to vary the current output. On certain types of generators, leakage of the magnetic field may be imposed artificially to give the desired current output. The rheostat, however, has a maximum number of fine adjustments and is be-

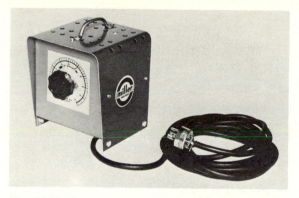

Fig. 24-13. Remote current controls. (*Miller Electric Manufacturing Co.*)

coming the preferred method of amperage control.

Some available arc welders are equipped with remote-control current units that permit the machine to be located in another part of the job site or plant. The machine operator may adjust the voltage-amperage to the desired level without leaving the work station. These units are useful when the operator must climb up, down, in, or out of a work station for the adjustment or readjustment of the current (Fig. 24-13).

Voltage and amperage meters are sometimes available on welding machines. On some machines they indicate the polarity in addition to the efficiency of the current values and the potential values. Some machines have individual meters for the voltage and the amperage. Voltmeters on dc welders range from 0 to +100 to −100. The amperage meters register both positive and negative current values with the scale going above the rated capacity of the machine.

EQUIPMENT

Machine Accessories

The equipment accessories for the arc welding machine are the cables or leads; the electrode holder, or stinger; appropriate lead connectors; and the ground attachments.

The leads that carry the welding current

to the work are very flexible and generally are made of copper or aluminum wire. The wires that carry the power are generally very fine, but consist of between 800 and 2,500 wires for maximum flexibility and strength. The wires are insulated by a rubber covering that is reinforced by a woven fiber covering that in turn is reinforced with a heavy, exterior rubber coating. The welding leads, then, are strong for their weight. Aluminum cables weigh approximately one-third as much as copper cables or leads, but the current-carrying capacity for aluminum cables is approximately 60 percent of that of copper cables. The proper aluminum cable size can be determined by simply going to the next higher step for similar copper welding lead, and the current capacity will be approximately the same (Table 24-1).

The shielding of the metal leads is sufficient because the potential voltage carried by the leads is not excessive. The voltage carried by the leads varies between 14 and 80 V. Connectors for the electrode lead should be designed so that the current-carrying capacity of the lead will be allowed for. Welding leads are connected either by mechanical connectors or by soldering, welding, or brazing. The mechanical connectors are the connection leads that are most used because they can be assembled and disassembled more easily (Fig. 24-14).

TABLE 24-1. COPPER WELDING LEAD CHARACTERISTICS

SIZE NO.	CAPACITY	
	0–50-ft LEAD,* A	100–250-ft LEAD,* A
4/0	600	400
3/0	500	300
2/0	400	300
1/0	300	200
1	250	175
2	200	150
3	150	100
4	125	75

* Combined length of both the stinger and the ground lead.

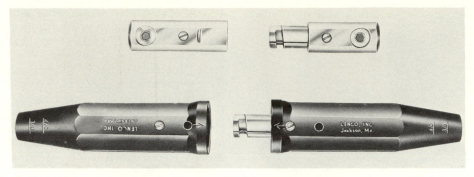

Fig. 24-14. Welding cable connectors. (*Lenco Inc.*)

Electrode holders, or stingers, come in a variety of sizes, ranging from 150 to 500 amperes (A). They generally are matched to the size of the lead, and the lead in turn is matched to the amperage output of the arc welder. Most electrode holders have grooves cut into the jaws which enable the electrode to be held at various angles for easy manipulation. Larger electrode holders, when high amperage is used, provide a heat shield in order to protect the operator's hand from the excessive amount of heat and the radiation that is liberated during the arc welding process (Fig. 24-15).

The ground clamp that completes the circuit between the electrode and the welding machine generally is fastened to the metal being welded with a clamp, a bolt, or some other means, depending on the size of the metal (Fig. 24-16). The connection must be clean and easy to install. Many times, if the arc welding is done at a welding table, the table is grounded by having the ground clamp bolted directly to the cable. Then the material to be welded is simply laid on the table to complete the circuit.

Operator Accessories

Operator accessories fall into two groups: weld bead cleaning accessories and safety accessories. The main implements for cleaning the weld bead are the chipping hammer and the wire brush (Fig. 24-17). The chipping hammer is chisel-shaped and is pointed on one end to aid in the removal of slag. The wire brush, which removes small particles of slag, generally is made of stiff steel wire embedded in wood. Of course, power wire wheels, when available, may be used in place of wire brushes, but many times these are not as available to the welder who is working in the field as to the welder working in a shop.

Provisions for the safety of the operator are most important, especially in arc welding, because the light that is given off by the arc column is harmful to the skin and eyes. Lenses for eye protection are extremely important because large quantities of infrared and ultraviolet radiation are given off by the arc. This radiation can burn the retina of the

Fig. 24-15. Electrode holder. (*Lenco Inc.*)

Fig. 24-16. Welding ground clamp. (*Lenco Inc.*)

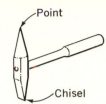

Point

Chisel

Chipping hammer

Wire brush

Fig. 24-17. Chipping hammer and wire brush.

(a)

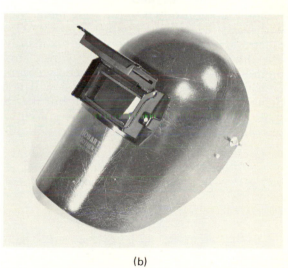

(b)

Fig. 24-18. Face shields. (a) Solid lens; (b) flip-front lens. (*Hobart Brothers Company.*)

eye and can even cause third-degree burns on the skin. The helmet face shield and the hand-held face shield are two commonly used protection devices. The face shield covers the entire face, down to the lower throat. All that is exposed is a small $2 \times 4\frac{1}{2}$ in. opening that has a shaded lens to stop the infrared and ultraviolet rays. The lens is capable of stopping 99.5 percent of these rays. The color density of the lens depends on the type of welding amperage being used. For standard stick electrode welding with the electrode diameter size ranging from $\frac{1}{16}$ to $\frac{3}{8}$ in., the shade number for the colored lens would be between a no. 10 and a no. 14 lens. However, no. 9, no. 10, and no. 11 shade lenses are the most popular with welders. Even with the eyes protected by shaded welding lenses, ultraviolet rays from arc welding may cause eye pain if welding is performed for periods of time that exceed tolerance. This time period may be from 8 to 18 h, depending on the sensitivity of the individual.

The face shield may be hand-held, or it may be a head helmet with either a solid lens or a flip front (Fig. 24-18). The solid lens is stationary. The flip-front lens shading revolves upwards so that the welder can see the weld bead in order to clean it. It also allows maximum eye protection from hot slag while chipping.

Long gauntlet gloves protect the hands

from minor burns during the chipping operation. The gloves should be worn at all times during the welding process. Even though these gloves are excellent protection from the heat of the arc column, they should never be used to pick up hot metal or be held in the arc column because they will not protect against burns in these cases.

The work clothes that should be worn by

the welder consist mainly of long-sleeved cotton shirts and long pants with cuffs that have been sewn shut or no cuffs. Shoes should be high topped. If street shoes are worn, small globules of molten metal may drop into them. Also, some mechanical means should be provided to remove the fumes produced by arc welding when welding indoors. Often some type of fan or air duct is used to draw out the semitoxic fumes.

OPERATION

Striking the Arc

Starting, or striking, the arc is accomplished by either tapping or scratching (Fig. 24-19). With the *tap method,* the electrode is brought straight down to the base metal and withdrawn as soon as contact is made. The electrode is withdrawn to only approximately the diameter of the electrode wire. This method is preferred by experienced welders because the beginning arc column will not deface or destroy the base metal, but it is a more difficult technique. There is a greater possibility that the electrode or rod will ad-

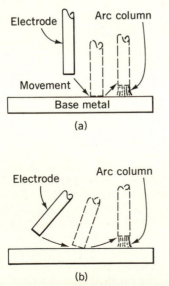

Fig. 24-19. Striking an arc. (a) Tap method; (b) scratch method.

here to the base metal because of the surge of current during the initial contact of the electrode. The *scratch method* is usually preferred by beginning students. It is comparable to striking a match. After the arc is started with the scratch method, it is held the same distance from the work as with the tap method, approximately the diameter of the electrode. The major hindrance in using the scratch method is that if the electrode is not immediately retracted upon contact with the base metal, it will deposit unwanted molten metal on the base metal or it may adhere to the metal because of the surge of high current.

The correct electrode distance and amperage and current settings are indicated when the sound emitted from the arc column sounds like bacon frying in a skillet. After the arc length has been established, it should be maintained at this distance. A too short arc length results in poor penetration and a drop in the current and voltage settings. An arc length that is greater than the diameter of the electrode will result in the molten metal splattering on the base metal.

The manipulation of the electrode falls into two categories according to the thickness of the flux coating on the electrode. Electrodes with a light flux coating require more physical manipulation of the electrode tip than do semicoated electrodes because of the manner in which the arc length is established. The lightly dusted electrodes are kept from touching the base metal, referred to as the *standoff technique.* The heavier coated electrode can be allowed to touch the base metal. This technique is often referred to as *contact welding* or a *drag technique* in welding.

The basic weld movements depend on the operator of the welding machine (Fig. 24-20). Popular weld movements include the J movement, the C movement, the circle, and the U movement. All these movements are designed to control the weld puddle so that the crater can create a penetration depth that the filler material will completely fill. The most common mistake made by beginning welders in running beads is that they do not allow the arc crater to fill sufficiently. Optimum movement allows for a hesitation

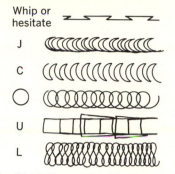

Fig. 24-20. Types of weld movements.

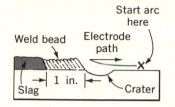

Fig. 24-21. Restarting a weld bead.

period when the arc is standing still. This hesitation allows part of the crater to fill with molten metal. Then the arc is moved rapidly away from this puddle to allow the molten puddle to cool slightly. Next the arc column is moved quickly back in order to start a new weld puddle. From puddle to new puddle should be approximately $\frac{1}{16}$ in. This distance creates the ripple effect of the weld bead. Arc welding then is simply depositing one small puddle on another which in turn creates a bead.

During the time that these independent weld puddles are being stacked on one another, the arc column is never moved far enough away to allow complete solidification of each independent puddle. If the arc is withdrawn from the puddle so that the metal begins to solidify, the gaseous slag portion of the puddle will rise to the surface of that puddle and take a solid form. Under this condition, when the arc is moved back over the previous puddle, the slag will be entrapped in the molten bead, resulting in a porous weld. It is important also to maintain a constant arc length during the puddling operation. A short arc, or an arc length of approximately the diameter of the electrode wire, must be maintained. If the arc length is too great, the gaseous shield that results from the flux coating will not be sufficient to protect the molten puddle from the atmosphere, resulting in a poor weld.

Restriking an Arc

Sometimes a weld bead must be interrupted for some reason and then restarted. A weld bead, after it has once been interrupted, is restarted by first chipping and brushing the solidified slag from the weld bead and approximately 1 in. from the crater, a step which ensures that no slag will be entrapped in the restarted arc puddle. The welder strikes the arc approximately ½ to 1 in. in front of the crater on the side opposite the weld bead (Fig. 24-21). After the arc is struck, a long arc is maintained until the arc is moved to slightly above the center of the crater on the bead side. The arc is then shortened to a standard arc length or to slightly shorter than a standard arc length and held for an instant until the cool crater fills with molten metal. Once this crater is full of molten metal, the electrode must be moved quickly in the direction of travel. The greatest problem facing a welder when restarting a bead is hesitating too long when filling the cooled crater with molten metal. A long hesitation allows the molten metal to overflow, resulting in a bead starting point larger than the previous bead width or height.

WELDING POSITIONS

The Flat Position

There are four basic positions in which arc welding can be done: flat, horizontal, vertical, and overhead (Fig. 24-22). Most shielded-arc welding is done in the flat position. In fact, arc welding not done in the flat position is referred to as out-of-position welding. Usually most welding done in shops is done in the flat position. Elaborate fixtures have been designed that will rotate the work so that this position can be used.

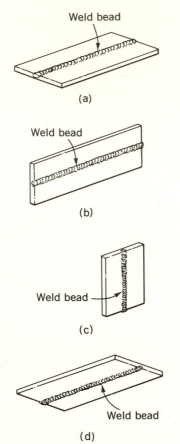

Fig. 24-22. Welding positions. (a) Flat (F); (b) horizontal (H); (c) vertical (V); (d) overhead (O).

ticular modes of operation. The typical rod movement for the flat position is either a simple movement of the electrode while maintaining the correct arc length or the hesitate-move type of movement. In the hesitate-move movement, the end of the electrode moves ahead approximately ¼ in., hesitates for an instant allowing the molten puddle to fill, sweeps ahead about ⅜ in. to allow the molten puddle to cool, then goes back to approximately ¹/₁₆ in. ahead of the previous molten puddle where it hesitates again.

Weld beads that are exceedingly smooth and free of slag spots can be accomplished easily in the flat position. The flat position is adaptable for the welding of all metals, whether nonferrous or ferrous. Many metals, such as cast iron, almost require that the flat position be used. The importance of the flat position is indicated by the emphasis placed on it by the electrode manufacturers. There is a whole class of electrodes that have been designed specifically for use in the flat position. These are high-production, high-deposit-rate

This favored position is the most popular because it requires the least amount of skill in order to produce a sound bead. A semicoated electrode, such as the iron-powder electrode, can simply be pulled across the metal to deposit the metal with little operator skill involved.

The electrode in the flat position is held usually at a 90° angle to the work, with the electrode slanted from 10 to 25° in the direction of travel (Fig. 24-23). There are no absolute rules for the angle at which the electrode should be held. This angle depends on the voltage and amperage settings of the machine and the thickness of the metal. With a little practice, novice welders can determine approximate rates of travel for their own par-

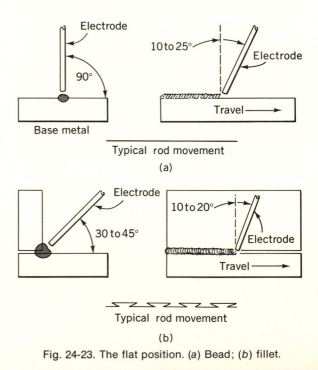

Fig. 24-23. The flat position. (a) Bead; (b) fillet.

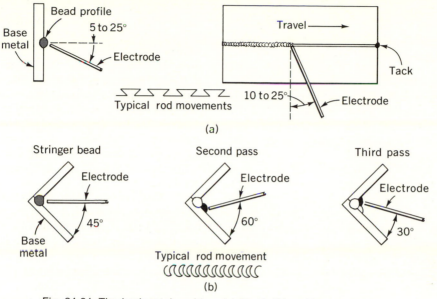

Fig. 24-24. The horizontal position. (*a*) Bead; (*b*) multiple-pass fillet.

electrodes, suitable for single-pass welding procedures.

The Horizontal Position

The horizontal arc welding position is the second most popular position because it enables the welder to deposit a large amount of weld metal although not as much as in the flat welding position. The manipulation of the electrode can be made with the same movements that are used in the flat position. Preferred movements are the C, the J, and O; the hesitate-move method can also be used (Fig. 24-24). The angle of the electrode should be from approximately 5 to 25°, tipped up in order to help alleviate the influence of gravity on the molten pool, and inclined from 10 to 25° in the direction of travel (Fig. 24-24). The major errors to watch for when welding in the horizontal position are under-cutting and overlapping of the weld zone (Fig. 24-25). These problems are caused by the force of gravity on the molten puddle which makes the puddle more difficult to control in any out-of-position welding.

The sagging of the molten puddle may be prevented by maintaining a shorter arc than in the flat position and by making quicker movements instead of the slow and easy movements of the flat position. Out-of-position welding requires that the movement of the electrode be accelerated in order to help the cooling of the weld puddle. Delay in moving the electrode will cause the metal to sag. The 5 to 25° inclination of the electrode also helps fight the force of gravity on the weld bead and allows the electrode force being emitted in the arc column to impinge upwardly on the base metal.

The Vertical Position

For welding in the vertical position, the welder can choose whether to deposit the

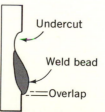

Fig. 24-25. Sagging of the horizontal weld bead.

bead in an uphill or downhill direction. The uphill weld is used most because the heat of the electrode goes deeper into the metal, thus allowing deeper penetration of the weld. It is also the stronger of the two welds and is used when strength is a major consideration. If the metal to be welded is ¼ in. or more thick, the welding should be done in the uphill direction. The downhill welding position is used for a sealing operation or for welding thin metal. It is much faster than uphill welding. To fight the force of gravity, the welder generally inclines the electrode to an angle between 10 and 25°. Welding in the vertical position is still simply the laying of one weld puddle directly on the next weld puddle (Fig. 24-26).

The typical rod movements are the oval, the C with hesitations at the end of the C, and

the whip movement, which is the most popular. The whip movement allows the electrode to establish a weld puddle; it is then whipped vertically ½ in. to allow the molten puddle to cool, and then the electrode is brought back to approximately 1/16 in. above the previous puddle where it is allowed to hesitate in order to start a new pool. This procedure is the basic movement for vertical welding.

Any movement can be used in all of the positions, depending on the choice of the operator, and there is really no best movement. The best movement for an individual is the one that can be manipulated satisfactorily for a length of time and one that does not allow the entrapment of slag within the weld puddle.

One of the major things to avoid with any

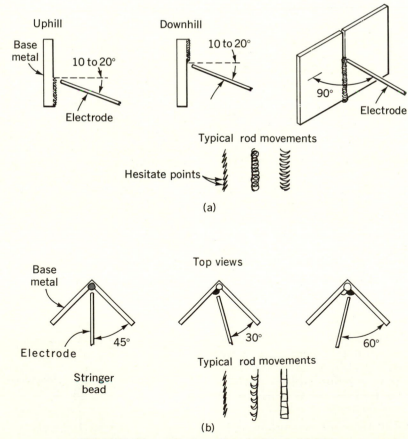

Fig. 24-26. The vertical position. (a) Bead; (b) fillet.

of the movements in any position is breaking the arc, losing the arc column, and restarting the column without cleaning the deposited weld metal. The breaking of the arc column can occur often in the vertical position because of the upward whipping motion of the electrodes. Many welders break contact and lose the arc column every time the electrode is whipped up. When this happens, too much solidification takes place in the weld pool, causing slag to change from a fluid to a solid material that is entrapped in the puddle. This problem must be avoided.

The same motions that are used in uphill vertical welding may also be used in downhill welding. The major drawback to downhill welding is that the slag often runs in front of the bead and is entrapped. Downhill welding should never be used for a strength weld.

The Overhead Position

The overhead position, while the most hazardous because of the flying sparks and the possibility of the molten puddle dripping onto the operator, is not the most difficult of the four positions. The manipulations and the weld angles are the same as those used in the flat and the horizontal positions. The only difference in overhead welding is that the weld bead is in a more awkward position (Fig. 24-27). Instead of the weld puddle beginning to sag, the puddle will tend to drop from the work. However, by main-

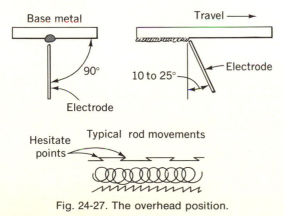

Fig. 24-27. The overhead position.

taining a short arc length and by using electrode manipulation, this tendency may be overcome. In all the welding positions, the welder may find it necessary to drape the electrode cable over a shoulder and allow an arm's length of cable to lie over the shoulder. This technique prevents the electrodes from being deflected because of contact with the cable. It also keeps the arm and hand from tiring, because they will not be supporting a large amount of welding cable.

ELECTRODE CLASSIFICATION

Electrodes are classified and given an identifying number by the American Welding Society (AWS). This number gives the strength of the weld, the weld positions in which the electrode will give the best results, and the current requirements of the electrode.

The AWS electrode classification system is the most efficient that has yet been devised (Table 24-2). An electrode numbered E6010 indicates by the letter E that it is an electrode. It has a tensile strength of 60,000 psi, indicated by the first two digits of the four-digit numbering system. In a five-digit numbering system, the first three digits times 1,000 psi give the tensile strength of the electrode. The third digit indicates that the electrode can be used in the flat, horizontal, vertical, and overhead welding positions. If the number 2 were used, the electrode could be used only in the flat and horizontal positions. If the digit 3 were used, the electrode could then be used only in the flat position.

The last digit in the AWS classification system identifies the type of flux used to coat the wire electrode. The type of flux action determines to a great extent the penetration characteristics as well as the arc digging action, which is the result of electrons impinging on the base metal. Usually the last digit also determines the power supply to be used with the electrode. In the example E6010, the last digit is 0; in this case because the next to last digit is 1, the power supply would be dc+, or DCRP (direct current, reverse polarity). The arc action would be

TABLE 24-2. AWS ELECTRODE CLASSIFICATION SYSTEM (EXXXXX OR EXXXX)*

LAST DIGIT	LAST-DIGIT CHARACTERISTICS			
	POWER SUPPLY	ARC ACTION	TYPE OF FLUX	PENETRATION CHARACTERISTICS
0	10, dc+; 20, ac; or dc	Digging	10, organic; 20, mineral	10, deep; 20, medium
1	ac or dc+	Digging	Organic	Deep
2	ac or dc	Medium	Ductile	Medium
3	ac or dc	Soft	Ductile	Light
4	ac or dc	Soft	Ductile	Light
5	dc+	Medium	Low hydrogen	Medium
6	ac or dc+	Medium	Low hydrogen	Medium
7	ac or dc	Soft	Mineral	Medium
8	ac or dc+	Medium	Low hydrogen	Medium

* E = electrode. First set of digits (XXX or XX) = tensile strength × 1,000 psi. Next-to-last digit: 1 = all positions; 2 = flat and horizontal positions; and 3 = flat position only.
SOURCE: T. B. Jefferson, "The Welding Encyclopedia," p. E-4, Monticello Books, Morton Grove, Ill., 1968.

strong and would create a deep crater, yielding in turn a deep penetration of the metal. The penetration is indicated by the type of flux which is represented by the last two digits also. Table 24-2 applies to electrodes for all low-alloy ferrous metals. The E6010 electrode is often referred to as a *universal* or *all-purpose electrode;* it is used often because of its adaptability and the strength of its weld bead.

The E6011 electrode duplicates many of the operating characteristics of the E6010 electrode, but it uses alternating current as a power supply. Because of the advantages of alternating current, the weld deposit of the E6011 electrode usually yields a weld bead with slightly higher ductility, higher tensile strength, and a higher weld-bead strength.

The E6012 electrodes are often referred to as the *poor fit-up electrodes* because they provide smooth welds over broad joint openings, also called root gaps. Their characteristics are: a smooth, even ripple on the weld face, a heavy slag with a medium penetration pattern, and a very quiet arc. The E6012 electrode is usually suitable for high-speed, single-pass horizontal fillet welds.

The E6013 electrode is similar to the E6012 electrode, except it has a quieter arc, a smoother ripple on the bead, and more easily removed slag. The E6013 electrodes are replacing the E6012 electrodes because they can weld lighter metal more easily.

Other commonly used low-alloy-steel electrodes are the E6014, the E6024, and the E6027. These electrodes have a large amount of iron powder in the flux coat covering. Much of the iron powder within the flux becomes part of the weld upon solidification of the weld zone. This feature provides a welding speed with these electrodes that is approximately twice that of conventional electrodes. Slag removal when using iron powder rods is exceptionally easy. The welder simply taps the bead and the slag falls off. Iron-powder rods are known as contact rods. For welding, the rod or electrode is simply drawn across the surface and the flux covering is allowed to touch the base metal. Drag or contact welding generally is accomplished with electrodes that have thick flux coatings, like the semicoated electrodes. If the electrode is dust coated, the standoff method is used to achieve correct arc length. Electrodes of the low-alloy series are available in E45XX, E60XX, E70XX, E80XX, E90XX, E110XX, and E120XX series. The E120XX series produces a bead that has a 120,000-psi tensile strength.

QUESTIONS

1. What is the proper arc length for any electrode?
2. What are the methods of striking an arc?
3. What are the advantages of the flat position?
4. What are the basic movements in manipulating the electrode and the weld puddle?
5. What is the proper sequence for restarting the arc for a continuous weld bead?
6. How does the angle of the electrode affect the weld bead?
7. Why is the vertical position the most difficult welding position?
8. What are the major power supplies used for arc welding?
9. What are DAV, CAV, and RAV?
10. Why must the welder be protected from the arc column?
11. What are the tools used to clean the slag from the weld bead?
12. Why are long gauntlet gloves mandatory for welder protection?

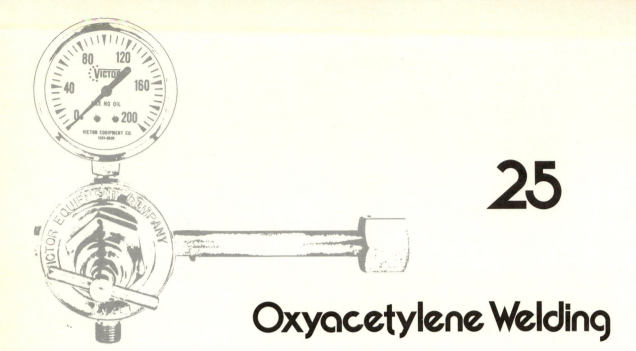

25

Oxyacetylene Welding

Oxyacetylene welding is a fusion-welding process with the coalescence of metals produced by an oxygen-acetylene flame. Extreme heat is concentrated on the edges or on the edge and surface of the pieces of metal being joined until the molten metal flows together. A filler metal may be used to complete the weldment depending on the type of joint design. If filler metal is added, it is inserted into the molten puddle of the base metals. The puddle then solidifies, making the weld bead (Fig. 25-1).

The extremely high heat is produced by a mixture of two gases: oxygen and acetylene. The oxygen supports higher combustion; the acetylene is the fuel for the combustion.

Acetylene gas under pressure becomes very unstable and in the free state will explode before reaching a pressure of 30 psi. The safe working pressure of acetylene gas is 15 psi. This instability necessitates special requirements for the storage of acetylene. A storage cylinder is filled with a mixture of calcium silicate, a material that is 92 percent porous. The cylinder is then filled with acetone, the solvent agent of acetylene gas which has an absorptive capacity of up to 35 volumes of acetylene per volume of acetone per atmosphere of pressure. This enables about 420 volumes of acetylene to be compressed at 250 psi. Under these conditions,

the gas is present in the form in which it is to be used. Acetylene comes out of the acetone solution at a slow constant rate as the pressure in the cylinder is released. The rate, however, depends on the temperature of the gas (Fig. 25-2).

The burning of oxygen and acetylene is accomplished in five steps. First, the cylinder pressure is released to a working-line pressure by means of special regulators. The gases are transported, usually by hoses, to the torch body where they are mixed in the mixing chamber. Then this mixture is ejected into the atmosphere (Fig. 25-3). All that is needed now to supply combustion is for the mixture to be ignited. The three requirements for oxygen-acetylene flame are those required for any combustion: an oxygen source, a fuel source, and a kindling (or ignition) temperature.

THE OXYACETYLENE FLAME

The approximate temperature range that can be attained by the oxyacetylene flame is from 5000 to 6300°F at the inner cone, around 3800°F in the middle of the envelope, and approximately 2300°F at the extreme end of the secondary combustion envelope (Fig.

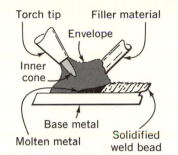

Fig. 25-1. Oxygen-acetylene welding.

25-4). The inner cone and the secondary envelope are the two stages of combustion. The temperatures in these two stages can be varied by changing the mixture of gases or by causing an improper balance in the volume of oxygen and acetylene ejected from the tip of the torch. This imbalance usually is accomplished by adjusting the needle valves on the blowpipe or torch body.

Flame Adjustment

The first step in igniting the flame is to open the acetylene valve on the torch and ignite the acetylene gas coming out of the tip. Enough oxygen will be drawn in from the atmosphere to burn the fuel gas partially. The needle valve should then be opened until the

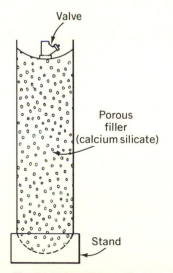

Fig. 25-2. Acetylene cylinder.

flame separates from the tip. Then the valve is closed just enough for the flame to join the tip, a method used to estimate proper acetylene flow. The main characteristic of this flame is the abundance of free carbon released into the air. In fact, this flame is sometimes used to apply carbon to mold faces in a foundry, for the carbon acts as an insulator between the molten metal and the mold face.

There are three types of flames: the carburizing, or reducing, flame; the balanced or neutral flame; and the oxidizing flame. The *carburizing*, or *reducing*, *flame* has an excess of acetylene (Fig. 25-5) and is characterized by three stages of combustion instead of two as in the other two types of flames. The extra combustion stage, called the *intermediate feather*, can be adjusted by the amount of acetylene imbalance induced by the torch body needle valve. The length of the intermediate feather usually is measured by eye in terms of the inner-cone length. A 2X carburizing flame, then, would be a feather approximately twice as long as the inner cone (Fig. 25-5). The carburizing flame does not completely consume the available carbon; therefore, its burning temperature is lower and the leftover carbon is forced into the metal. This action is characterized by the molten weld puddle appearing to boil. After this carbon-rich weld bead solidifies, the weld will have a pitted surface; these pits can extend through the entire weld bead. The bead will also be hardened and extremely brittle because of the excessive amount of carbon that was injected into the molten base metal. This excess of carbon, however, is an ideal condition when welding high-carbon steel.

Upon further adjustment of the torch needle valves, the intermediate feather can be drawn into the inner cone. The oxygen usually is increased in order to maintain the minimum amount of acetylene flow. Increase of the oxygen flow causes the intermediate feather to recede into the inner cone. The instant that the feather disappears into the cone, the oxygen-acetylene mixture produces a *balanced*, or *neutral*, *flame*. This two-stage neutral flame (which has a symmetrical inner cone and makes a hissing sound) (Fig. 25-4),

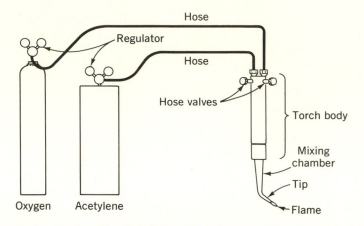

Fig. 25-3. Gas welding system.

is the most used flame in both the welding and the flame cutting of metals. It has little effect on the base metal or the weld bead and usually produces a clean-appearing, sound weld bead with properties equal to the base-metal properties. The inner cone of the neutral flame is not hot enough to melt most commercial metals, and the secondary combustion envelope is an excellent cleanser and protector of ferrous metals.

Further opening of the oxygen needle valve on the torch body shortens the inner cone approximately two-tenths of its original length. The inner cone then loses its symmetrical shape, and the flame gives off a loud roar. These three actions characterize the *oxidizing flame,* the hottest flame that can be produced by any oxygen-fuel source. The oxidizing flame injects oxygen into the molten metal of the weld puddle, causing the metal to oxidize or burn quickly, as demonstrated

by the bright sparks that are thrown off the weld puddle. Also, the excess of oxygen causes the weld bead and the surrounding area to have a scummy or dirty appearance. A slightly oxidizing flame is helpful when welding most copper-based metals, zinc-based metals, and a few types of ferrous metals, such as manganese steel and cast iron. The oxidizing atmosphere creates a base-metal oxide that protects the base metal. For example, in welding brass, the zinc alloyed in the copper has a tendency to separate and fume away. The formation of a covering copper oxide prevents the zinc from dissipating.

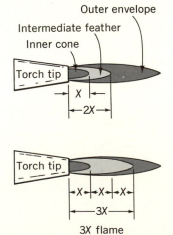

Fig. 25-5. Carburizing or reducing flame.

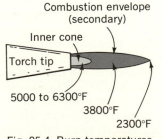

Fig. 25-4. Burn temperatures.

TYPES OF WELDS

The oxyacetylene torch can be applied to three basic types of welding: fusion welding, braze welding, and brazing. One of the major considerations in joint design is the type of welding that will be performed.

Fusion welding occurs when the base-metal molten puddle intermingles with a filler material or with other base metals. When the metals combine into a homogeneous structure, the strongest type of oxyacetylene weld is created. Oxyacetylene welding can be accomplished both with and without filler material, as shown in Fig. 25-6. If filler material is used, it can be part of the base metal or it can be supplied by a filler rod.

In *braze welding,* the filler material generally is composed of copper and zinc. Sometimes tin is added. A requirement of braze welding is that the filler material must have a melting point below that of the base metal but above 800°F. It generally is necessary to use a cleansing flux, and usually a slightly oxidizing oxyacetylene flame is used. The principal limitation of braze welding is that the weld loses its strength as temperature increases so that braze welding can be used only when the weld will be subjected to low-temperature environments.

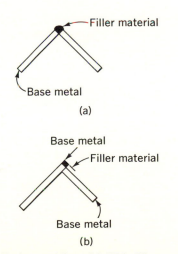

Fig. 25-6. Fusion welding. (*a*) With filler material; (*b*) without filler material.

Brazing, sometimes referred to as hard soldering, is also done above 800°F. The difference between brazing and braze welding is the placement of the filler material. In braze welding the filler is placed in the weld joint. In brazing, the filler material is dispersed over the closely fitted surfaces by capillary attraction. The filler material in brazing acts as a wetting agent that flows out over the base metal, breaking its surface tension. The base metal is not in a molten state as it is in fusion welding. The joint design and the distance between the pieces to be brazed are extremely important. The root openings for the distance between pieces range between 0.002 and 0.010 in. If these tolerances are exceeded, the brazed joint may be weak either because of an inadequate amount of filler material or because of an excessive amount of filler material.

EQUIPMENT

The basic equipment for oxyacetylene welding consists of a cylinder of oxygen, a cylinder of acetylene, an oxygen regulator, an acetylene regulator, a hose system to carry the gases, and the torch.

Oxygen

Oxygen is available commercially in two forms: gaseous and liquid. The gaseous oxygen is compressed into steel cylinders for delivery to the consumer. It can be stored in this manner almost indefinitely and is ready for use in an instant. These two qualities make the cylinder the most popular storage medium for gaseous oxygen among consumers of small and medium amounts of oxygen.

The three common sizes for cylinders or tanks are 80, 122, and 244 ft^3. Even though cylinders may vary in size, they are all filled to 2,200 psi at 70°F. Outside temperature changes will, of course, change the pressure within the tank. For example, if the outside temperature drops to a few degrees below freezing, the pressure within the tank would drop to approximately 2,000 psi. This drop in pressure within the tank would not indicate any loss of oxygen; it would merely indicate that the cooled oxygen had been reduced in volume. If the temperature of the cylinder increases above 70°F, the pressure inside the cylinder would increase accordingly.

Because of the possibility of the oxygen pressure becoming high enough to rupture the steel cylinder, a safety device has been designed into the oxygen valve (Fig. 25-7). The oxygen-cylinder safety device is a special two-seated valve that must be either completely off or completely on since a partially open valve results in the escape of oxygen into the atmosphere. The lower valve seat shuts or seals the cylinder during storage, and the upper valve seat prevents the leakage of oxygen around the valve mechanism when the valve is opened completely.

The time during which oxygen cylinders are being transported is most hazardous. A protector cap or safety cap should be screwed over the valve to ensure that no damage to the valve with a consequent instant release of high-pressure oxygen into the atmosphere is possible. If such an accident should occur, the tank could become an operational rocket and could travel a considerable distance, doing damage to all in its path. It would react

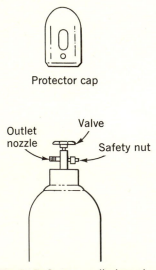

Fig. 25-7. Oxygen cylinder valve.

in the same way as a child's balloon when the compressed air inside it is released.

Acetylene

Acetylene gas can be manufactured either by the water-to-carbide method or the carbide-to-water method. The carbide-to-water method is the primary method of production in the United States. The water-to-carbide system may still exist but only in a few special instances, such as in miners' lamps. These lamps are seldom used now because they might ignite gas fumes in a mine.

There are two types of carbide-to-water generators: low-pressure and medium-pressure. The low-pressure generator produces less than 1 psi, and the medium-pressure acetylene generator produces from 1 to 15 psi. The 15-psi limit has a built-in safety margin to ensure against any free combustion.

Either type of generator can be portable or stationary. However, the low-pressure generator usually is considered portable, while the medium-pressure generator is considered stationary. Acetylene production by the low-pressure portable generator ranges upward from 30 ft³/h. The medium-pressure stationary generator can produce up to 6,000 ft³/h.

The acetylene cylinder is a steel container that meets or exceeds the standards established by the Interstate Commerce Commission (ICC) for gas-pressure vessels. Safety plugs are located in the top and the bottom of the acetylene cylinder to allow the acetone and the acetylene to escape in case of a fire. These plugs simply melt at 220°F, allowing the fluids in the cylinder to flow out. When the plugs melt, the steel casing of the cylinder will not build up any excessive pressure that would cause the tank to rupture.

The acetylene stored in these cylinders is considered dissolved rather than generated acetylene. The most common cylinder sizes for dissolved acetylene are 60-, 100-, and 300-ft³ containers. These sizes reflect the maximum amount that the containers will hold; however, it is practically impossible to fill a container to its maximum rated capacity. The consumer purchases dissolved acetylene only by the actual amount within the cylinder. The consumer determines the size of acetylene cylinder needed according to the number of cubic feet per hour that will be used. Dissolved acetylene is released from the acetone carrier at the rate of approximately one-seventh of the cubic-foot capacity per hour. For example, a 60-ft³ cylinder of dissolved acetylene will release approximately 60/7 or 8.5 ft³/h, and a 300-ft³ cylinder of dissolved acetylene will release approximately 300/7 or 42.8 ft³/h. If more than these amounts are drawn from the cylinders, acetone will be siphoned from the cylinder with the dissolved acetylene. This mixture of acetone and acetylene burns erratically and turns the oxyacetylene flame a purplish color. A cylinder of dissolved acetone should never be laid on its side because the acetone will mix with the acetylene.

Pressure Reduction Regulators

Gas pressure is reduced by equalizing pressure in a chamber. An equal-pressure chamber usually is regulated by a diaphragm-controlled valve (Fig. 25-8a). The high-pressure gas enters the equal-pressure chamber and exerts a force against the diaphragm. As the pressure (pounds per square inch) in the chamber increases, the diaphragm automatically flexes away from the high-pressure inlet. A closing valve is fastened to the flexibile diaphragm that closes the high-pressure opening when the pressure inside the chamber is slightly greater than the spring tension supporting the diaphragm. The gas trapped inside the chamber is allowed to flow out of the low-pressure outlet, which, in turn, relieves the chamber pressure. As the chamber pressure is relieved, the pressure on the diaphragm is relieved, reopening the high-pressure valve.

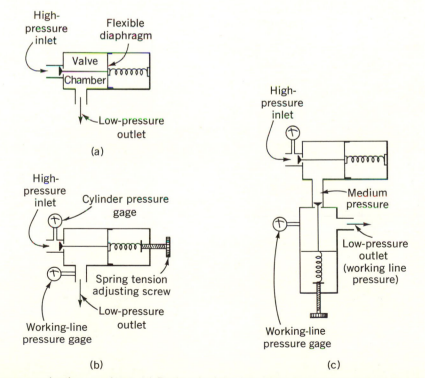

Fig. 25-8. Pressure reduction regulator. (a) Basic principle; (b) single-stage regulator; (c) two-stage regulator.

There are two types of regulators: the single-stage and the two-stage. The single-stage regulator uses the basic principle of pressure reduction with the addition of a spring-tension adjusting screw (Fig. 25-8b). This adjusting screw varies the pressure that the spring exerts on the diaphragm and thus controls the amount of pressure allowed within the valve chamber. A pressure-sensitive gage indicates the pressure within the valve chamber. A single-stage regulator is all that actually is needed for both oxygen regulation and acetylene regulation for oxyacetylene welding. For convenience, the cylinder-pressure gage is added to the basic regulator in order to indicate the amount of pressure remaining in the cylinder.

The two-stage regulator (Fig. 25-8c) combines the basic principle of automatic pressure reduction with the operation of the single-stage regulator. The connection to the high-pressure side of the regulator, called the cylinder-regulator connection, allows high-pressure gases to flow into an intermediate valve chamber that reduces the pressure to a preset amount. This amount of pressure is built into the regulator by a factory-set spring tension on the intermediate valve chamber. The chamber furnishes the adjustable valve chamber with an even amount of relatively low-pressure gas and minimizes pressure fluctuation to the adjustable second stage. This preset amount of gas enters the second stage of the regulator where the pressure is further reduced by the amount of tension on the spring diaphragm adjusting screw. The last stage of the two-stage regulator is identical in operation to that of the single-stage regulator.

Regulators for different gases are basically the same, except the pressures that they control differ vastly (Fig. 25-9). When manifolding acetylene gas cylinders or installing acetylene generators on a manifold system, a fire safety device usually is installed between the acetylene supply and the work site. This safety device, a flashback arrestor or hydraulic back-pressure valve, is a mechanism allowing gas to flow in only one direction. If a flash or a fire travels back up the acetylene line, the shock bubble in front of the fire would close the one-way valve. It is

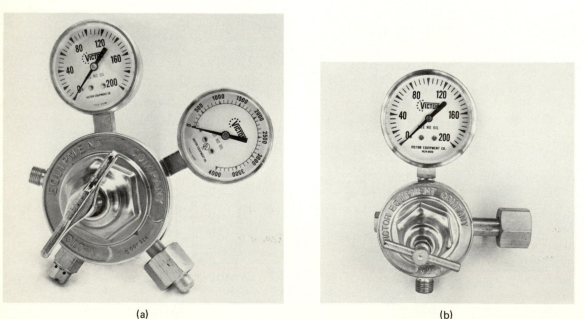

(a)   (b)

Fig. 25-9. Oxygen regulator. (a) Standard; (b) line or station. (*Victor Equipment Company.*)

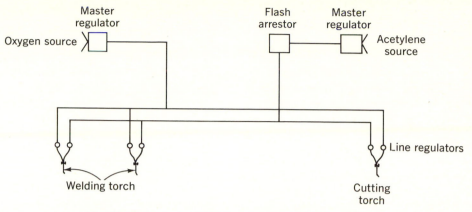

Fig. 25-10. Typical manifolding oxygen-acetylene system.

generally good practice to install small in-line flash arrestors either at the connection of the regulator to the manifold line or at the connection point of the standard acetylene regulator to the acetylene cylinder (Fig. 25-10).

Hoses

The currently available industrial gases may be piped through steel tubing, stainless steel tubing, brass tubing, bronze tubing, and cloth-reinforced rubber flexible hose. The only combination that should be avoided is copper and acetylene. When acetylene gas comes into contact with copper, copper acetylide forms in low portions of the piping system and turns into a gel. This compound will explode even when just slightly shocked or tapped.

The most common method of piping both oxygen and acetylene is by means of reinforced rubber hoses, which are black, green, or red. The green hose usually is used to transport oxygen; the red hose is usually the fuel-gas hose; and the black hose usually is used to transport other available industrial welding gases. These colors are not standardized, but many times they are used this way.

As a safety precaution, *all* oxygen and compressed-air hoses are right-hand threaded, and *all* fuel-carrying hoses are left-hand threaded. This standard arrangement is

unvaried and prevents oxidants from combining with fuel, a situation which could result in an explosion.

The hoses are manufactured in various diameters. The more popular diameters are $3/16$, $1/4$, $5/16$, $3/8$, and $1/2$ in. These industrial hoses always are measured by inside diameter and come in standard lengths of 25, 50, and 75 ft. Usually hoses for the oxyacetylene or oxygen-fuel systems have a webbing that holds the oxygen hose and the fuel hose together (Fig. 25-11). Hoses of standard lengths can be purchased with connection fittings attached by the factory or with connection that can be added by the consumer. These connections are similar to those used on a garden hose and are readily available and simple to install.

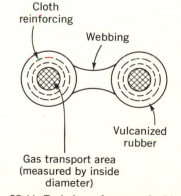

Fig. 25-11. End view of oxygen-fuel hose.

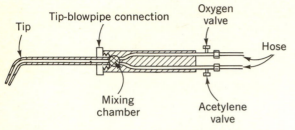

Fig. 25-12. Welding torch or blowpipe (with tip).

Certain precautions should be taken when using reinforced rubber hoses. For example, only one gas should be used in a hose; the hose should never be patched or repaired; and hot metal should never be placed on the hose.

Torches

The two types of welding torches or welding blowpipes are distinguished by the oxygen pressure required to operate them. The pressure in the injector or low-pressure torch and the pressure in the medium- or equal-pressure torch is controlled by the chambers in the two types of torches and often the difference is not visually apparent (Fig. 25-12).

The injector-type torch can use acetylene pressures of less than 1 psi because of the venturi effect created by oxygen being expelled from the injector tip. However, to maintain this suction, more oxygen pressure is needed than acetylene pressure. Because of the effect of the oxygen rushing through the injector tip, the low acetylene pressure is stable and the mixture of gases is constant.

This feature makes injector-type torches desirable for consumers using low-pressure acetylene generators. The injector torch can also extract more acetylene from a cylinder than can an equal-pressure torch; but since the consumer purchases only the amount of gas needed to recharge a cylinder, this is no great advantage (Fig. 25-13a).

The medium- or equal-pressure welding torch is the more commonly used oxyacetylene torch. The mixing chamber in the equal-pressure torch allows both of the gases to flow together in equal amounts (Fig. 25-13b). The maximum acetylene pressure used on the equal-pressure torch is the ICC limit of 15 lb.

The exact location of either type of blowpipe mixing chamber is determined by the size of the unit or by the whim of the manufacturer. However, a rule of thumb is that smaller torches have the mixing chamber in the removable tip section of the torch and larger torches have the mixing chamber in the blowpipe or torch body.

TORCH WELDING TIPS

Welding tips may or may not have the mixing chamber incorporated within the torch bodies. There are two other major differences in the design of welding tips: their size and their type.

The rated size of welding tips is determined by the diameter of the orifice of the tip (Fig. 25-14). The diameter of the tip opening

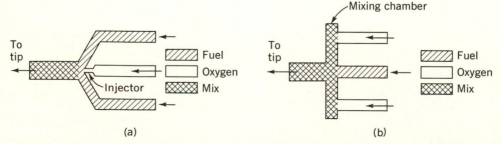

Fig. 25-13. Oxygen-fuel mixing chambers. (a) Injector chamber; (b) equal-pressure chamber.

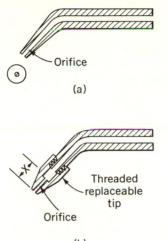

Fig. 25-14. Welding tips. (a) Solid tip; (b) two-piece tip.

or orifice used for welding depends on the thickness of the metal to be welded and the type of metal to be welded.

The selection of the torch tip is determined by whether or not the operator prefers solid- or multiple-piece welding tips. The advantage of the solid-piece tip is that it is lower in initial cost than the multiple-piece tip. However, if the tip is exposed to more than normal wear, the price of replacing it will offset the cheaper original purchase price because the entire tip must be replaced. With the multiple-piece welding tip, it is necessary to replace only a short part at the end of the welding tip (Fig. 25-14b). The overall functioning of both types is identical, and both perform assigned tasks with equal ease.

ACCESSORIES

Accessories for oxyacetylene or oxygen-fuel welding fall into two categories: items for protection and items for operation. The protection items are such things as goggles, gloves, and welding sleeves. The operation items are spark lighters, tip cleaners, gas savers, and any other equipment that aids in the operations to be performed.

Welding goggles protect the welder from ultraviolet and infrared rays emitted from the oxyacetylene flame and the molten weld puddle. Welding goggles also protect the wearer from flying sparks and reduce the glare created by the torch flame and the molten weld puddle.

Welding goggles consist of an adjustable headband, a form-fitted sparkproof frame, a green- or brown-tinted filtered lens, and a clear lens on each side of the colored lens to protect the more expensive filter lens (Fig. 25-15). Lenses come with shade densities that range from 1 to 14, with no. 1 indicating the lightest shade and no. 14 the darkest shade. The average shade intensity for oxyacetylene welding ranges from no. 3 to no. 8, depending on how light-sensitive the welder is. The most commonly used shades are no. 4 and no. 5, the types used for the school laboratory or medium industry, such as construction. Shades that range in intensity from no. 8 to no. 14 are usually used in electric-arc welding.

Welding gloves, sleeves, and jackets may or may not be worn, according to the safety standards of the particular welding facility. However, welding gloves generally are considered a necessary protection from burns. Protective clothing can be made from leather, asbestos, or nonflammable cloth.

The operational equipment that aids in oxyacetylene welding is a necessary part of the total welding system. For example, the spark lighter or striker is the igniter for the

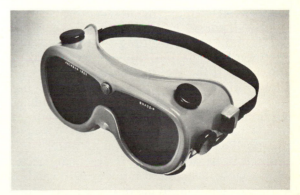

Fig. 25-15. Welding goggles. (*Jackson Products.*)

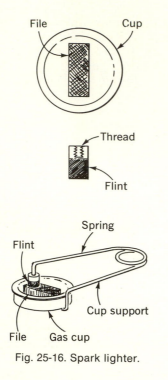

Fig. 25-16. Spark lighter.

oxygen-fuel flame (Fig. 25-16). The striker consists of a cup to catch and hold the gases and a flint and steel to ignite the gases (the same principle used to ignite the powder in flintlock rifles).

The heat and the molten metal that welding tips are exposed to cause a considerable amount of minor damage to the tip. A welding tip should have a clean, smooth, and parallel hole to control the oxygen-fuel flame (Fig. 25-17a). If this passage is dirty, cluttered, or misshapen, the oxygen-fuel flame will be distorted and difficult to use (Fig. 25-17b and c). If a welding tip has become bell mouthed, its end must be resurfaced with a file. If the welding tip has metal particles within the tip passage it must be cleaned with a *tip cleaner,* a wire with a roughened surface and a diameter that corresponds to the diameter of the tip passage (Fig. 25-17d). These wires can be purchased singly or in packaged sets. If tip cleaners are not available, a standard number drill can be used, with caution, to clean the welding tip. Special care must be taken not to ream the

orifice to a larger size nor to ream the orifice out-of-round if a twist drill is used.

To use a tip cleaner properly, the operator must have a minimum of 5 psi oxygen on the working gage, and the oxygen valve on the torch must be open. This will blow the slag and carbon deposits out of the tip when the tip cleaner is extracted from the tip passage. Many times the proper-sized cleaner cannot enter the tip passage and a smaller tip cleaner is used to open the way for the correct-sized cleaner. When the tip is completely clogged, a numbered twist drill may be used to reopen the passage. If the passage cannot be reopened, then the tip should be replaced.

EQUIPMENT SETUP

The correct procedure for setting up the oxyacetylene welding torch must be followed to ensure safe operation. Failure to set up the oxyacetylene torch properly may mean an ex-

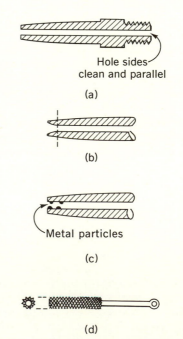

Fig. 25-17. Dirty tips. (a) Correct, clean tip; (b) bell-mouthed tip; (c) metal-splattered tip; (d) tip cleaner.

plosion, resulting in injury to the operator during the setup period. The correct method for assembling and dismantling the oxyacetylene torch consists of the following steps:

1. Secure the cylinders to some object so they cannot fall over (Fig. 25-18). This is of prime importance because if the oxygen cylinder were to fall over with the protector cap removed, the valve could be knocked loose and the oxygen cylinder would become a missile. This reason, however, does not apply to the acetylene cylinder. The acetylene cylinder must be used only in the upright position. The reason it is chained in place is that the acetone which carries the dissolved acetylene would mix with the acetylene gas and contaminate the weld puddle if the cylinder were to fall over.

2. After the oxygen and the fuel-gas cylinders have been secured, unscrew the valve protection caps to expose both the oxygen-cylinder valve and the acetylene-cylinder valve. These valves, especially the valve seats, must be clean. Foreign objects may enter either the oxygen regulator or the acetylene regulator and cause damage. Cloths used to wipe off the oxygen valve and the valve seat must not contain even a trace of grease or oil.

3. Attach the oxygen regulator to the oxygen valve and the acetylene regulator to the acetylene valve. Remember that the oxygen regulator and all oxygen connections are right-hand threads and all gas, acetylene, or fuel connections are left-hand threads. These connections must be tightened with a wrench but should not be excessively tight.

4. Check the diaphragm-adjusting screws to be sure they are in the out position. The screws turn freely in this position. After checking these, open the oxygen cylinder valve all the way. Remember that it is a double valve and must be opened as snugly as it is closed during storage. The acetylene-cylinder valve should then be opened approximately a quarter to a half turn.

5. Blow out the hoses. Both the oxygen hose

(a)

(b)

Fig. 25-18. Torch setup. (a) Secured oxygen-acetylene cylinders; (b) attaching welding blowpipe. (*Union Carbide Corporation—Linde Division.*)

(green or black) and the acetylene hose (red) should be cleaned and checked. To do this, adjust the spring on the oxygen cylinder to approximately 5 lb of working pressure. Do not connect the oxygen hose to the oxygen regulator, however; simply hold it up to the connection and allow the pure oxygen to blow through the hose until all dirt is removed. New hoses are stored with a small amount of talc in the passage to keep the passage free of moisture. The acetylene portion of the hose also has this talc, but acetylene gas should never be used to blow out this hose. Simply hold the acetylene line up to the oxygen line and blow out the new hose in this manner. Once the hoses have been cleaned, connect the green or the black hose to the oxygen regulator and the red hose to the acetylene regulator. Again, remember that all acetylene connections have left-hand threads.

6. Connect the other end of the oxygen hose to the oxygen blowpipe or torch body that is marked OXY and the red hose to the blowpipe valve that is marked ACET or acetylene (Fig. 25-18b).

7. Select the proper tip size for the operation to be performed. If the torch is of the injector design, the acetylene pressure should be set at approximately 1 lb. The number stamped on the welding tip will indicate the setting for the oxygen pressure. If the oxyacetylene torch is the equal-pressure type, the number stamped on the welding tip will be the pressure settings for both the oxygen and the acetylene regulators.

8. Test for leaks. After the equipment has been assembled, always test for leaks by opening the oxygen valve all the way and cracking the acetylene valve a quarter to a half turn; the valves at the torch body are closed. This operation will not put pressure on the system until the pressure-adjusting diaphragm screws have been turned on. It is necessary to put only about 5 to 10 lb of working pressure on the lines to check for leaks. After making a sudsy solution of any commer-

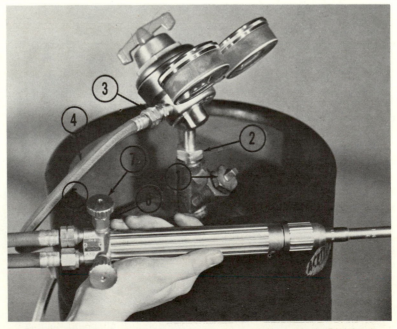

Fig. 25-19. Leak tests. (*Union Carbide Corporation—Linde Division.*)

cial soap that will make suds, take a small brush and paint the soap bubbles over the following connections: (a) the oxygen-cylinder valve, (b) the acetylene-cylinder valve, (c) the oxygen-regulator connections, (d) the acetylene-cylinder regulator connections, (e) all hose connections, and (f) the valves on the torch body. Any leakage may cause damage to the equipment. Figure 25-19 identifies typical connections that need to be checked.

WELDING TECHNIQUE

When welding, an operator can concentrate the heat from the torch either in the weld bead, which is called the *backhand technique,* or ahead of the weld bead or in the weld puddle, which is called the *forehand technique* (Fig. 25-20a). The forehand welding technique usually is used on relatively thin metals. The torch points in the same direction that the weld is being done so that the heat is not flowing into the metal as much as it could. The tip of the torch is held

at approximately a 45° angle, which makes some of the heat deflect away from the metal. Instead of the base metal absorbing all the heat, some of it is reflected off into the atmosphere, making it possible to weld very thin material. The weld bead appearance is characterized by an evenly flowing, rippled design.

The backhand welding technique is one used on heavier or thicker base metals. In this technique, the torch is pointing in the direction opposite to that in which the weld is being done (Fig. 25-20b). The heat is concentrated into the metal so that thicker materials can be welded successfully. Welds with penetrations of approximately ½ in. can be achieved in a single pass with the backhand technique. The bead is characterized by layers that form a much broader based ripple than that of the forehand technique.

The molten puddle is judged continuously by the welder. The characteristics of the molten puddle tell the welder the penetration of the weld and whether any adjustments are necessary in the torch, the torch handling, or the torch movements. The amount of penetration can be determined by the width of the bead. Penetration on thin metal is approximately one-third of the bead width. On heavier metal, with the backhand technique, the width of the puddle indicates for all practical purposes the depth of penetration of the weld bead. Whether a torch adjustment is necessary can be determined by the appearance of the weld bead. If the bead appears scummy, there is too much oxygen. If it has a smooth glossy appearance and if there seems to be a dot floating around the outer edges of the weld puddle, the torch adjustment is good. This so-called *neutral dot* (Fig. 25-21) is a re-

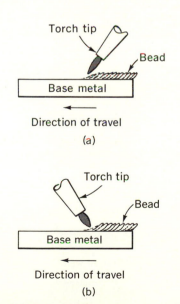

Fig. 25-20. Welding technique. (a) Forehand; (b) backhand.

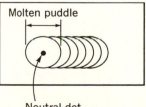

Fig. 25-21. Neutral dot.

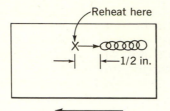

Fig. 25-22. Restarting the puddle.

sult of the oxides present in the weld, and it floats continuously around the outer edges of the weld puddle. Whenever this dot is absent, there is not a neutral flame. Whenever this dot increases in size, there is an over-abundance of carbon present. When this happens, the weld puddle will take on a sooty, dirty, dull appearance, the result of a carburizing flame. The neutral dot is a good thing to watch for when welding with the neutral flame, the most used flame in welding.

The most difficult skill for a welder to master when learning to puddle is stopping and starting at any place desired. To restart the weld puddle or the weld bead, reheat the base metal approximately ½ in. in front of the weld bead and in line with it. Once the metal turns a glossy color and the neutral dot can be seen, the flame can be moved slowly back to the weld zone. Once this weld zone has been reached, the direction of movement should be reversed very quickly. Then the weld can be continued in the direction desired (Fig. 25-22). When the weld zone has been reached, the normal movements must be in-

creased because of the extra heat the metal has absorbed. If the movements are not increased, the bead width will be extra large. If the flame does not come back far enough, there will be a void or a spot in the base metal where penetration will be zero, called *an inclusion.*

Weld Movements

There are as many different weld movements as there are welders. Every person develops his own particular way to move that he finds the easiest after a period of time. Figure 25-23 illustrates six basic ways to move the welding torch. The major point to remember in all of these movements is that the flame tip should not leave the molten puddle and that the welding-torch body should be held with one hand.

The appearance of the finished weld bead gives the welder quite a bit of information. Figure 25-24*a* illustrates the appearance of a weld bead when uneven movements and increased speed of the movement have almost interrupted the weld bead. The operator noticed this error and automatically over-corrected. Figure 25-24*c* illustrates a typical error that most beginners make. This error is caused by not enough heat being pointed to the base metal, or the base metal not being preheated a sufficient amount, or the move-

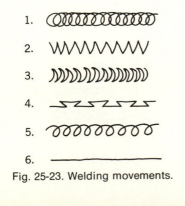

Fig. 25-23. Welding movements.

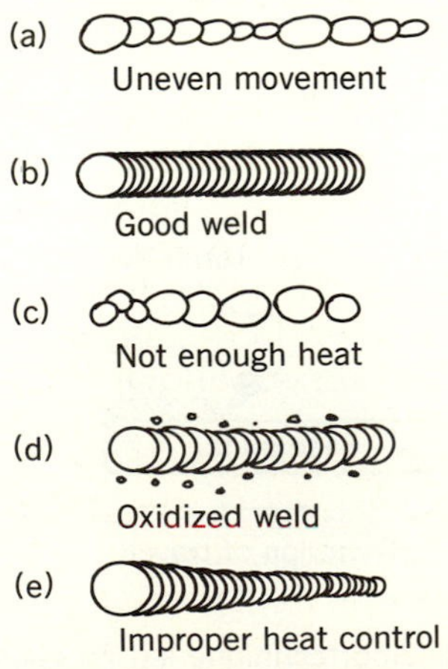

(a) Uneven movement

(b) Good weld

(c) Not enough heat

(d) Oxidized weld

(e) Improper heat control

Fig. 25-24. Weld appearance.

ment being so erratic that a molten puddle cannot be maintained. One thing to be noticed on all these welds is that when the molten puddle solidifies, the neutral dot is no longer visible. It has dissipated into the oxide of the weld zone.

Weld Positions

Oxyacetylene welding or oxygen-fuel welding can be accomplished in any one of four basic positions. These positions include the flat position, indicated by the capital letter F; the horizontal position, H; vertical position, V; and overhead position, O. Of these four positions, the flat and horizontal positions are the most used; and the flat position is the easiest to learn. Many of the movements used in the flat position can be used in the overhead, the vertical, and the horizontal positions. The basic difference in using these movements in the different positions is the rate at which the torch is moved. A slow rate in any position other than the flat position will allow the molten puddle to sag from the weld zone which means that there will be a mass of solidified metal not fused to the base metal but merely overlapping it. Any of these four positions can be welded either by the forehand or the backhand technique, with or without filler rod.

CHEMISTRY OF OXYGEN CUTTING

All metals oxidize when exposed to the oxygen in the atmosphere. In this metallic oxidation, particles of the base metal and the oxygen combine into a sometimes protective coating for the metal. In most ferrous metals, the oxide is a very loose, or porous, coating. Since this looseness allows more of the base metal to be exposed to the atmosphere, more and more of the oxide is formed—the process continues in ferrous material until eventually the whole structure turns into ferrous oxide. An increase in the amount of pure oxygen directed against the metal increases the rapidity of the reaction. Heat also increases

the reaction time, especially in ferrous metals. Many of the metals that have a close oxidation structure, or a tight oxide structure on the outside, such as nickel steel, are considered corrosion-resistant.

When heated to approximately 1600°F or above, ferrous material becomes cherry red. At this temperature, it oxidizes very rapidly when it is brought into contact with a high-pressure stream of pure oxygen. This intense reaction has an extrathermic effect, but it does not provide enough heat to sustain the reaction. Therefore, preheating is necessary in order to sustain the cutting. The principle of the cutting process includes the reaction of the metal to the extreme heat which causes oxides to form and a small amount of metal to liquefy. Both the oxide and the small amount of metal are blown away, exposing more metal to the action of the oxygen which in turn releases a small amount of heat, liquefies a small amount of metal, and also oxidizes a small amount of ferrous metal. The reaction will maintain itself in this way, provided oxygen and a preheat source are present (Fig. 25-25). This process, then, is called *cutting of iron or steel*.

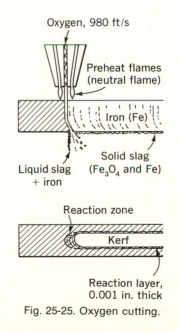

Fig. 25-25. Oxygen cutting.

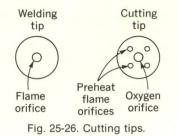

Fig. 25-26. Cutting tips.

Cutting Equipment

The cutting torch is different from the welding torch in two ways. In addition to having the oxygen and the acetylene adjustment valves, the cutting torch has a high-pressure oxygen valve that is activated by a lever, trigger, or button. This high-pressure valve, when pressed, releases a jet of oxygen through the tip. The other difference is that the welding tip has one orifice and a cutting tip has multiple orifices. Cutting tips have preheat orifices and one central orifice that directs the flow of oxygen for the cutting operation (Fig. 25-26).

The oxyacetylene cutting torch uses the same basic components as a welding torch: an oxygen cylinder, an acetylene cylinder, oxygen and acetylene regulators, adequate hosing, and a torch body. But a cutting head attached to the torch body is designed to have preheat orifices in the cutting tip as well as a passage for the high-pressure, pure oxygen. The cutting apparatus may be in a torch designed specifically for cutting, or the proper cutting apparatus may be attached to a standard torch body.

Two types of cutting torches are the premixed and the head-mixed types. In the premixed type, the oxygen and fuel are mixed in the body of the torch. In the head-mixed type, the most widely used type, the oxygen and fuel are mixed just before entering the tip. Torches are further classified as medium-pressure torches, in which acetylene is used in the range of 1 to 15 psi, and low-pressure torches, in which acetylene is 1 psi or less. These two pressure classifications are the same as those used for welding torches.

Whenever a cutting torch removes metal,

it leaves an area called a *kerf*. Studying the kerf helps the operator to determine correct cutting procedures (Fig. 25-27). The markings on the side of the kerf are called drag lines.

The characteristics of a correctly made oxygen cut are drag lines that are vertical and edges that are square. Also, the drag lines should not be too pronounced and should be evenly spaced (Fig. 25-27a). The kerf also helps the operator to identify problems in cutting. For example, preheat flames that are too small for a cut cause bad gouging at the bottom of the cut (Fig. 25-27b). If the preheat flames take too long to melt the top edge of the cut, an excess of slag results (Fig. 25-27c). When the oxygen pressure is too low, the top edge of the cut melts over, which rounds the top edge of the cut (Fig. 25-27d). If the ox-

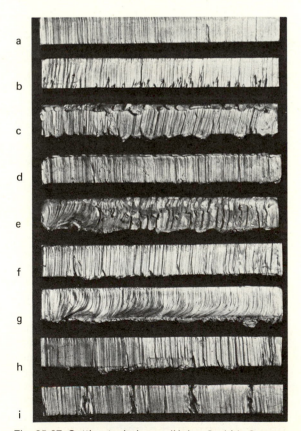

Fig. 25-27. Cutting techniques. (*Union Carbide Corporation—Linde Division.*)

ygen pressure is too high and the tip size too small, the kerf will be irregular and the cut can lose its penetration and fail to go completely through the stock (Fig. 25-27e). The kerf lines indicate if the cutting speed is too slow and if a zigzag motion rather than a straight-line motion is used (Fig. 25-27f). If the cutting speed is too fast, a fast break in the drag lines and an irregular cut will result.

Another indication that the cutting speed is too fast is that a larger amount of slag will collect on one end and the drag or lag lines will change at rapid angles (Fig. 25-27g). When the travel is erratic, zigzag, or wavy, a gouging effect on one end will be created (Fig. 25-27h). Bad gouging also indicates that the cut was lost and had to be restarted (Fig. 25-27i).

QUESTIONS

1. What are the major components of the oxyacetylene welding system?
2. What are the safety devices and how do they work for the acetylene cylinder? How do they work for the oxygen cylinder?
3. Why do oxygen cylinders have special valves?
4. What is the maximum pressure of dissolved acetylene that can be released from a given cylinder?
5. What are the advantages of a two-stage regulator over a single-stage regulator?
6. Why is a fire safety device installed in an oxyacetylene manifold welding system?
7. Why are all fuel lines threaded left-handed?
8. Why should copper lines not be used for acetylene gas?
9. What are the two major types of welding blowpipes? What are their differences?
10. What is the correct procedure for assembling the oxyacetylene welding torch?
11. Explain in detail the leak test for the oxyacetylene system.
12. What are the characteristics of a neutral flame, an oxidizing flame, and a carburizing flame?
13. What is the *safe* working pressure limit of acetylene?
14. What type of oxyacetylene flame should be used to weld carbon steel?
15. What are the basic elements required for combustion?
16. How are acetylene and oxygen stored?
17. What is the maximum temperature attainable with the oxyacetylene flame?
18. What is the function of the secondary combustion envelope?

Gas-Shielded-Arc Welding

In all welding, the best weld is one that has the properties closest to those of the base metal; therefore, the molten puddle must be protected from the atmosphere. The atmospheric oxygen and nitrogen combine readily with molten metal, creating weak weld bonds.

Two welding processes that use inert gases to shield the weld zone are the tungsten-inert-gas (TIG) welding process and the inert-gas consumable-electrode process (MIG).

SHIELDING GAS

The major shielding gases used for both the TIG nonconsumable-electrode and the inert-gas consumable-electrode processes are oxygen, argon, carbon dioxide, and helium or a combination of these four gases. These gases can be classified as either inert gases or chemically reactive gases. Inert gases are stable with their outer electron subshells completely full. Reactive gases, such as carbon dioxide or oxygen, do not have their outer electron shells filled, a characteristic which makes it possible for electrons to combine with other elements in the welding zone, creating impurities.

Using argon results in a deeper penetration pattern than can be achieved with other gases (Fig. 26-1). Welding speed is increased and a required penetration pattern is maintained by mixing argon and helium, capitalizing on the characteristics of each of these inert gases. In this way, the speed permitted by helium can be used with the penetration patterns that result from the use of argon. For welding aluminum, two combinations that can be used are a mixture of 25 percent argon and 75 percent helium or a mixture of 20 percent argon and 80 percent helium. Most nonferrous metals can be welded with either argon or helium or a mixture of both. All ferrous metals can be welded with these gases.

Carbon dioxide is used only for the welding of ferrous metals because of its inexpensiveness. Carbon dioxide costs approximately one-tenth as much as argon or helium and is capable of producing a high-quality weld when used as a shielding gas. The penetration characteristics of carbon dioxide are similar to the penetration characteristics of helium because of the similarities in the weights of these gases. The carbon dioxide that is used for welding must be free of all moisture. Moisture releases hydrogen which will in turn produce porosity in the weld metal. Because carbon dioxide has greater

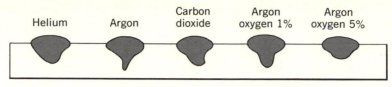

Fig. 26-1. Shielding gas penetration effects.

electrical resistance qualities, the current setting must be 20 to 30 percent higher than that used with argon or helium.

Other inert gases used for gas shielding include nitrogen, oxygen, and hydrogen. When nitrogen is used as a mixing or carrier gas, a very small percentage is used. Oxygen can be used up to 10 percent. A higher percentage of oxygen will yield porosity in the weld bead.

TUNGSTEN-INERT-GAS (TIG)

In TIG welding, the weld zone is shielded from the atmosphere by an inert gas that is ducted directly to the weld zone where it surrounds the tungsten electrode. The two inert gases that are used most often are argon and helium (Fig. 26-2).

The TIG process offers many advantages. TIG welds are stronger, more ductile, and more corrosion-resistant than welds made with ordinary shielded-metal-arc welding. In addition, because no granular flux is required, it is possible to use a wider variety of joint designs than in conventional

shielded-arc welding or stick-electrode welding. The weld bead has no corrosion because flux entrapment cannot occur, and because of the gas fluxing there is little or no postweld cleaning operation. There is also little weld metal splatter or weld sparks that damage the surface of the base metal as in traditional shielded-arc welding.

Fusion welds can be made in nearly all commercial metals. The TIG process lends itself very well to the fusion welding of aluminum and its alloys, stainless steel, magnesium alloys, nickel-based alloys, copper-based alloys, carbon steel, and low-alloy steels. TIG welding can also be used for the combining of dissimilar metals, hard-facing, and the surfacing of metals.

The TIG arc column is similar to that of the standard shielded-arc welding arc column. The electron travel is identical to that in shielded-arc welding (Fig. 26-3). The amount of plasma that is generated in the center of the arc column, however, is thought

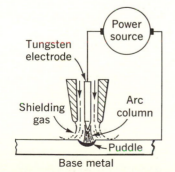

Fig. 26-2. Tungsten inert gas (TIG).

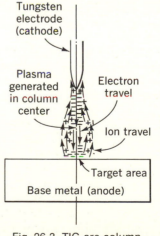

Fig. 26-3. TIG arc column.

to be greater than that generated in the standard shielded-arc stick-electrode welding process because the tungsten electrode has a higher thermionic rating than the mild-steel electrode does. (The thermionic function or emission is the ability of a metal to release its valence electrons.)

There are three basic power supplies used in the TIG welding process. They are a direct-current straight polarity (DCSP) power supply, the direct-current reverse polarity (DCRP) power supply, and the alternating-current high-frequency (ACHF) modified power supply. In the DCSP power supply, the tungsten electrode is negative, the cathode, and the base metal is positive, the anode. The electron flow is from the cathode to the anode. Because of the direction of this flow, approximately two-thirds of the total heat in the arc column, which is approximately 11,000°F, is released in the base metal. The tungsten electrode, then, can be of a very small diameter because the tungsten will not receive the major portion of the heat. It can have a smaller mass to dissipate the heat that it does absorb. The positive ions flow from the base metal to the tungsten electrode. When they impinge on or strike the electrode, a small amount of heat is released. The positive ions strike molecules in the atmosphere, creating an ionization layer of gas or an ionized gas, which protects the major electron flow as in shielded-arc welding. The DCSP power supply does not perform any cleaning action; therefore, the base metal must be clean in order to use DCSP (Fig. 26-4).

In DCRP power supply, the electron flow is from the base metal, or workpiece, to the electrode. Because of this electron flow to the tungsten electrode, approximately two-thirds of the heat generated by the arc column is absorbed by the tungsten electrode; an electrode with a larger mass is required. The minimum diameter of the electrode mass is thought to be ¼ in. so that it can absorb excess heat. The electrons that leave the base metal and are accelerated toward the electrode carry with them some of the oxides that protect the surface of the metal, especially in the case of aluminum. The cleansing of the

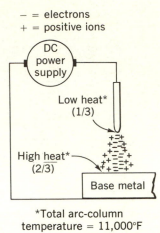

− = electrons
+ = positive ions

*Total arc-column
temperature = 11,000°F

Fig. 26-4. TIG DCSP.

oxide film results from the bombardment of the surface by the positively charged ions. This bombardment is thought to cause an electrolytic dissociation of the surface oxide from the metal, exploding the electrons off the base metal, through the oxide film, toward the anode (Fig. 26-5).

Alternating current is also used as a power supply for inert-gas welding. However, because alternating current is a combination of DCRP and DCSP, the current value is essentially zero at the instant when the current reverses direction. At this point, the arc column is extinguished and must be reignited at the zero amperage point between DCSP and DCRP (Fig. 26-6a).

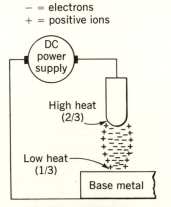

− = electrons
+ = positive ions

Fig. 26-5. TIG DCRP.

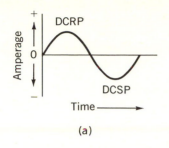

DCRP to DCSP Ratio
can equal 1 to 20

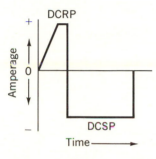

Fig. 26-6. AC cycles. (a) Standard; (b) modified (pulsed).

Even with this extinguishing of the arc column, alternating current can still be used for TIG welding but the arc column that is established will be unstable and erratic. The arc can be stabilized by superimposing by a machine a high-voltage, high-frequency dc cycle. Instead of a cycle running for a given time, like 1 s, there will be, on high frequency, 100 Hz running in this same 1-s period of time minimizing the effective zero point between DCRP and DCSP. The hard-starting characteristic of a standard ac cycle is alleviated and the unstable, erratic arc qualities are corrected. With ACHF, there are better arc-starting capabilities, and longer arc lengths can be maintained without extinguishing the arc column.

In the standard ac cycle, one-half of the heat is absorbed into the tungsten electrode. The ACHF can be further modified by lengthening the DCSP cycle and shortening the DCRP cycle (Fig. 26-6b). This ratio between the DCSP and the DCRP may be as high as 30:1, which means that the tungsten electrode would be a cool-running electrode most of the time and the workpiece would receive two-thirds of the heat. During the short DCRP cycle, the tungsten electrode would heat slightly, but the reverse polarity would have the effect of breaking up the oxides on the surface of the base metal, performing a cleaning action, allowing the straight polarity to perform the major portion of welding. Modified alternating current is usually available with ACHF welding units.

The electron flow, as in shielded-arc welding, determines the penetration patterns of DCSP, DCRP, and ACHF (Fig. 26-7). The penetration of DCSP is narrow and deep because the electrons impinge on the base metal. The electrode is thought of as a cool-running electrode. In DCRP, on the other hand, the electrons flow from the base metal to the electrode and the major portion of heat is absorbed by the electrode; therefore, the weld bead is relatively shallow and wide. The alternating current and the ACHF current combine the characteristics of DCSP and DCRP.

Three kinds of tungsten or tungsten alloys are used for the electrode in TIG welding; pure tungsten, zirconiated tungsten, and thoriated tungsten. Pure tungsten has a melting point of approximately 6170°F and a boiling point of 10,706°F, giving the tungsten electrode a long life. Tungsten is also an excellent thermionic metal; that is, it is a metal that releases electrons extremely well at elevated temperatures. However, slightly modifying tungsten by alloying it improves its thermionic emission. Because there is an easier release of electrons, the arc column starts more easily. Thorium or zirconium are alloyed with the tungsten in small amounts, ranging from 2 percent down to 0.001 percent of the alloying ingredient. Thorium has a melting point of 3182°F.

Fig. 26-7. Base-metal penetration.

Although there is a decrease in the melting point from the pure tungsten, the improved thermionic emission aids in maintaining the life of the electrode.

The mass of the electrode also helps to keep the electrode from melting, as does the cooling effect of the inert gas surrounding the tungsten electrode. The tip of the tungsten electrode is the only part that becomes molten. Generally, a molten droplet is formed at the end of the electrode, especially when using DCRP and alternating current. The initial shape of the tungsten electrode can either aid or hinder the thermionic emission from the tungsten electrode. With DCSP, the tip should be ground to a conical shape (Fig. 26-8). With DCRP, the tip also should be ground into a conical shape but with a blunted end. With alternating current, the tip should be rounded slightly. The current passing through the tungsten electrode and the melting of the tip of the electrode slightly change the shape of the tip. With DCRP, a small ball forms at the end of the electrode, and with alternating current, a large ball forms. However, with DCSP, the tip pretty much maintains its shape.

TUNGSTEN-INERT-GAS (TIG) WELDING EQUIPMENT

The standard inert-gas welding system includes a gas supply, a gas regulator, a power

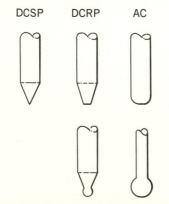

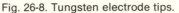

Fig. 26-8. Tungsten electrode tips.

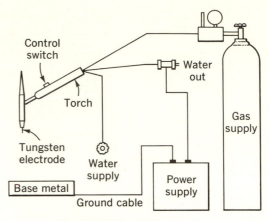

Fig. 26-9. TIG welding system.

supply, and the TIG torch (Fig. 26-9). There is also optional machine equipment that may be purchased in order to use inert gas more economically or to control amperage output.

Any standard shielded-arc welding machine may be used to weld with a TIG torch. However, some machines are more suitable than others for welding certain metals with the TIG welding process. The major machines that are used in TIG welding are: the motor generator, direct current only; the ac transformer; and the rectified ac transformer.

The most used power source for welding with a TIG torch is the rectified transformer with built-in gas timers and built-in water flow circuits that are turned off and on with the control switch that is located on the TIG torch (Fig. 26-10).

There are two basic types of TIG torches: the air-cooled and the water-cooled (Fig. 26-11). The air-cooled torch is operated in the lower amperage range, usually below 200 amperes (A). During the welding process at 200 A or above, a vast amount of heat is liberated. This heat must be dissipated through some medium in order to continue the efficient operation of the TIG welding unit. Special water-cooled torches have been designed to carry away the heat caused by welding. These water-cooled torches can operate successfully up to a maximum of 800 A. These torches are available in sizes that are based on amperage in approximately

Fig. 26-10. TIG welder in operation. (*Miller Electric Manufacturing Co.*)

100-A intervals. There are 200-, 250-, 300-A torches, and torches that range up to a current-carrying capacity of 800 A that are water-cooled. The water is controlled by a water control valve solenoid in the welding machine. When the current starts to flow into the electrode, the water solenoid opens the valve. The water that flows into the torch is clean tap water. The water flows out of the torch into a special connection and into a drain. The cable that carries the water out of the torch into the drain is also the power cable into the TIG torch.

Fig. 26-11. TIG torch. *Note:* Air-cooled and water-cooled look the same. (*Air Reduction Company, Inc.*)

The electrode clamps or collets that hold the tungsten electrode in the TIG torch vary according to electrode size. There is a specific set of electrode collets for every diameter of tungsten electrode, ensuring adequate contact for the clamping of the tungsten electrode. The gas cup or nozzle of the TIG torch is the weakest part of the torch. The gas cups can be either ceramic or metal. The ceramic cups are weaker than the metal cup. Metal gas cups are used for welding at low amperages. When metal gas cups are used at higher amperages, the cup melts and clogs the orifice for the inert gas. At all high amperages and elevated temperatures, ceramic nozzles work satisfactorily. These ceramic nozzles or cups, however, are broken easily because of the intensely hot atmosphere which surrounds them. The cups can also be broken by operator ineptness, as in the case of the operator making a small mistake in manipulation and inadvertently dipping the ceramic nozzle into the molten weld puddle, a mistake which contaminates the weld bead and ruins

Fig. 26-12. TIG regulator. (*Air Reduction Company, Inc.*)

the ceramic nozzle. Nozzles, both metal and ceramic, are fastened to the torch body by a threaded connection.

Special regulators used in the TIG process are standard single-stage regulators with flowmeters attached. The flowmeter is a device calibrated to measure how many cubic feet per hour are flowing through a certain point. The scale is indexed on a glass tube and the cubic-feet-per-hour rate is indicated by reading to the top of a float ball in the glass tube (Figs. 26-12 and 26-13). The

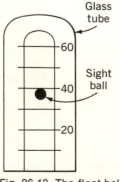

Fig. 26-13. The float ball.

ball in the flowmeter gage in Fig. 26-13 indicates a flow of 40 ft^3/h. Most flowmeters have a preset pressure of 50 psi, the amount of pressure that is fed into the flowmeter. The flow can be adjusted by an orifice control valve. The opening of this valve will increase the flow through the flowmeter tube, causing the ball to rise. One requirement in adjusting a flowmeter is that the torch must be turned on and the gas must be flowing through the torch tip in order to have an accurate adjustment.

The two major welding accessories used in the TIG welding process are the remote-controlled amperage control, which is identical to the remote amperage control used in shielded-arc welding, and the gas-saving device. A gas-saving device is a means to shut off rapidly the gas supply to the torch. It operates on a straight valve technique with a weight placed on a hook. The hook travels downward and then automatically, through a mechanical linkage, shuts off the water line and the gas line to the torch, leaving only the inert gas in the line for postweld waste.

The basic TIG torch movements are the same as those that are used in oxyacetylene welding, and the frequency of the addition of filler metal is also the same as in the oxyacetylene welding technique. The only difference is that filler metal should be added only when the TIG torch is not heating the molten pool; this technique allows only minimum contamination from the tungsten electrode. The ideal way to add filler metal to the weld bead is first to start the weld puddle, allowing a molten weld puddle to develop. Next the TIG torch is moved away from the weld bead just far enough and the arc is lengthened just long enough so that the arc and the gas shielding of the weld bead is maintained. Then the filler metal rod is dipped into the weld puddle for a sufficient length of time to add filler metal and then is removed. The filler metal is moved by manipulating the weld torch (Fig. 26-14).

Many beginning operators of the TIG torch will overcompensate and move the torch too great a distance away from the weld, a mistake which will expose the weld bead to the atmosphere (Fig. 26-15). Mastering the proper technique in order to maintain sufficient shielding gas, however, is a matter of practice. Another common error in welding with TIG torches is having current settings either too high or too low. When the current setting is too high, the bead will resemble the shielded-arc welding bead in mild steel when the current setting is too

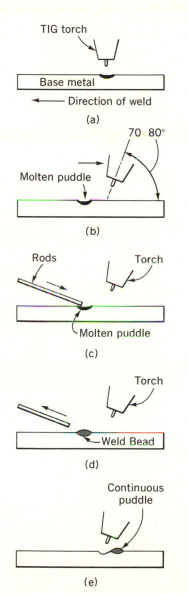

Fig. 26-14. Filler metal manipulation. (a) Start weld puddle; (b) remove torch; (c) add filler metal; (d) remove filler rod; (e) reheat and travel with weld puddle.

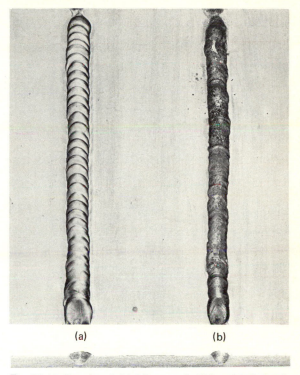

Fig. 26-15. Results of shielding gas in TIG welded aluminum. (a) Sufficient gas; (b) insufficient gas. (*Center for Technology, Kaiser Aluminum and Chemical Corporation.*)

high. If current settings are too low, the bead will be narrow and will pile up on the base metal as in shielded-arc welding mild steel when the current setting is too low (Fig. 26-16). This error can be corrected easily by resetting the amperage on the welding machine.

INERT-GAS CONSUMABLE-ELECTRODE PROCESS (MIG WELDING)

The inert-gas consumable-electrode process, or the MIG process, is a refinement of the TIG process. In the MIG process, the tungsten electrode has been replaced with the consumable electrode. The electrode is driven by a set of drive wheels through the

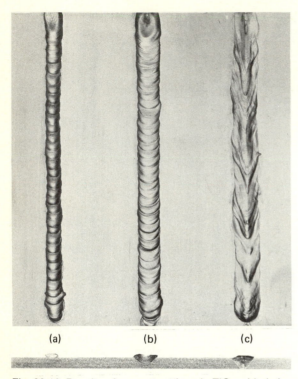

Fig. 26-16. Results of current settings in TIG welded aluminum. (a) Current too low; (b) current correct; (c) current too high. (*Kaiser Aluminum and Chemical Corporation.*)

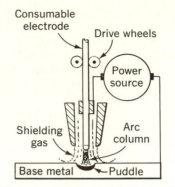

Fig. 26-17. Inert-gas consumable electrode (MIG).

The standard inert-gas consumable-electrode process that just uses a bare-wire electrode and a shielding gas is capable of fusion welding aluminum, magnesium, copper-based metals, nickel-based metals, titanium, carbon steel, and low-alloy steel. The deciding factor in the use of this process is the shielding gas. The shielding gases help to determine the characteristics of the arc column and the penetration of the arc column into the base metal, factors which are true, however, of all three MIG welding processes.

A difference exists in the metals that can be joined by the three different MIG welding processes. The standard processes can join the previously mentioned metals, while the magnetic-flux MIG process lends itself more to the welding of medium- and high-carbon steels. In addition, the magnetic-flux and the flux-cored electrodes can also weld many of

same type of collet that holds a tungsten electrode. In the TIG process, the tungsten electrode acts as the source of the arc column. The consumable electrode in the MIG process acts as the source for the arc column as well as the supply for the filler material (Fig. 26-17).

Three basic processes are employed in the MIG welding process: the bare-wire electrode process (Fig. 26-17), the magnetic-flux process (Fig. 26-18), and the flux-cored electrode process. All three processes use shielding gases. The magnetic-flux and the flux-cored MIG processes, however, yield a slightly different weld bead. The weld bead that is deposited by these two processes has a slag coating as in conventional stick-electrode welding. The standard inert-gas consumable-electrode process does not need any postweld cleaning. Only the magnetic-flux and the flux-cored welding processes need postweld cleaning.

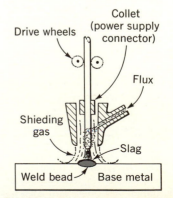

Fig. 26-18. Magnetic flux (MIG).

the metals that a standard consumable-electrode does, except that slag removal is required. The flux components, both with the flux-cored and the magnetic-flux processes, are used to perform the usual functions of flux: to deoxidize the metal, to protect the metal from impurities, and to form a slag that controls postwelding heat treatment. In either the flux-cored or the magnetic-flux MIG process, carbon dioxide is the major shielding gas used.

Metal Transfer

Two basic mechanisms of metal transfer are used in the MIG welding processes: the shorting-arc, or the dip-transfer, method, and the spray-arc method. The difference is based on the reaction of the consumable electrodes to the emf or the potential voltage used to accelerate the electrons from the metal electrode to the base metal.

The short-arc method of metal transfer incorporates a four-step transfer mechanism. In the first stage of the short-arc metal transfer, the end of the electrode, moving at some rate per inch, heats and distorts because of capillary attraction, magnetic influences, and the force of gravity. Because of capillary attraction and electron movement, the metal touches the base metal. At this instant, there is a short-circuiting effect, which lasts just for an instant. During this time, a magnetic field is set up at a 90° angle to the current flow, necking down the metal that has short-circuited. This necking down is called the *pinch effect*. The pinch effect then takes over separating the metal. The ever-moving electrode starts to reheat, beginning another cycle, and the end of the electrode begins to go through the short-circuit interval again.

In spray-arc metal transfer, the densities of both the current and voltage are higher; therefore, more heat energy is injected into the base metal. The process is based on the use of an electrode with a relatively small diameter (generally around $1/16$ in.) and high voltage and current values. For example, a $1/16$-in. steel electrode wire requires approximately 275 A and about 35 to 40 V.

The spray arc with standard steel electrodes operates on a DCRP power supply so that the electron movement is from the base metal to the end of the steel electrode that is being fed into the weld pool. However, the heat-liberation zones in the MIG process are opposite to those of the TIG process. When DCRP is used in the MIG process, more heat is liberated in the base metal than in the end of the electrode because the distance from the electrode to the base metal is much closer, and a larger number of metal ions are mixed into the plasma arc column. These positive ions, attracted to the base metal, strike the base metal in a much hotter condition than the positive metal ions that strike the base metal during the TIG process (Fig. 26-19).

The wire electrode, because of its lower melting temperature, becomes molten at a much lower temperature than the tungsten electrodes. Therefore, the ion flow creates bubbles within the molten mass of the electrode tip. The electrons impinge on this molten mass, which has been dislocated by the small bubbles. The emf then causes the disrupted molten mass to fly off the electrode in metallic particles, creating the spray-arc effect. The higher the emf, the finer the size of the particles.

The distance of the filler metal from the base metal determines the effectiveness of the spray arc. Because of the metal ions and their large mass, the penetration qualities of the spray arc are confined to heavier metals and cannot successfully weld metals as thin

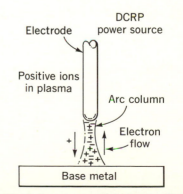

Fig. 26-19. Spray-arc metal transfer (MIG).

as those that can be welded by the short-arc process. The distance of the electrode from the base metal determines the success of the spray arc. An optimum distance is approximately ½ in. from the wire electrode tip to the base metal. When the base metal is farther away than ½ to 1 in. maximum, the arc column becomes erratic and will wander, and the weld bead will be extremely difficult to control. One way to reduce the penetration of the spray arc is to allow the wire to stick out of the wire-feed mechanism far enough so that the wire will be preheated prior to the ignition of the arc column. This preheating will cause the burnoff rate of the electrode to be increased, thus lowering the penetration of the spray arc.

INERT-GAS-METAL-ARC WELDING EQUIPMENT

The basic MIG welding system incorporates an inert-gas supply, regulator, flowmeter, appropriate hoses, welding power supply, wire-feed unit, and, according to the amperage, a water-cooling unit (Fig. 26-20).

The major power supply used in MIG welding is DCRP. The major types of machines used to supply DCRP to the system are the dc generator and the ac rectified transformer. The MIG welding machine must produce either a constant-arc voltage (CAV) or a rising-arc voltage (RAV). The CAV was the first type of voltage-amperage characteristic used in MIG welding machines. The constant-voltage-amperage characteristic gives an operator a great latitude in the arc length without any appreciable change in voltage. The operator first adjusts the arc voltage to a desired level and then the machine maintains that level over an extremely wide range of amperage settings. An RAV or a CAV machine usually has a voltmeter and an ammeter for voltage and amperage adjustment (Fig. 26-21).

The wire-feed units contain all the apparatus that controls the wire feed, the gas flow, and the on-off switch for the voltage and amperage to the MIG gun. Wire-feed units are available that will feed the electrode wire from approximately 200 to 1,000 in. of wire per minute, not to be confused with 1,000 in. of weld metal deposited per minute. Many wire-feed mechanisms that are commercially available have a slow-start nature so that the wire for a part of the first second of welding will feed at a reduced rate to allow the MIG gun operator an easily started weld bead.

There are two basic types of wire-feed mechanisms. The first is the type that is used

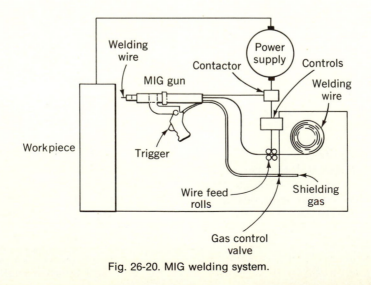

Fig. 26-20. MIG welding system.

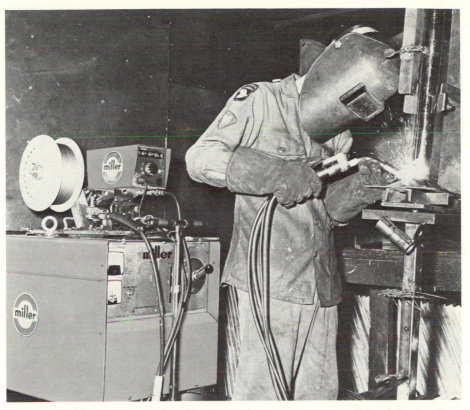

Fig. 26-21. MIG welding with portable control/feeder. (*Miller Electric Manufacturing Co.*)

for standard MIG welding. Another type is used for flux-cored welding. This second type of wire-feed control unit is used also for magnetic-flux MIG welding. This type of wire-feed mechanism has some kind of magnetic-flux reservoir that feeds the flux directly into the MIG gun. Many times that flux container is located on the gun or is piped to the gun.

There are two types of MIG guns: the wire push gun and the wire pull gun (Fig. 26-22). The wire push gun, smaller than the wire pull gun, pushes the wire through the rollers located in the wire-feed mechanism. The wire-feed rolls in the wire push gun also act as a power supply to push and to straighten the wire, delivering it at a specific rate to the MIG gun. The pull gun, on the other hand, pulls the wire from the roll. This **gun** has a set of wire-feed rollers contained within it.

The standard inert-gas regulator flow-meters are used in the same way as they are used in the TIG process. The flowmeters are calibrated according to the type of gas to be used. An argon regulator flowmeter is calibrated differently from a helium flowmeter regulator because of the different densities of the gases, a fact true of all the shielding gases.

The same type of operator protection equipment is used as for the TIG process and the shielded-arc process. The standard leather or cloth welding gloves, long-sleeved shirts, leather sleeves and aprons, and standard welding helmets should be used. Many operators prefer a slightly darker lens shading in the welding helmet than when doing shielded-arc welding. Because of the lack of contaminants in the air surrounding the arc column, the arc column can be seen more easily and this visibility sometimes

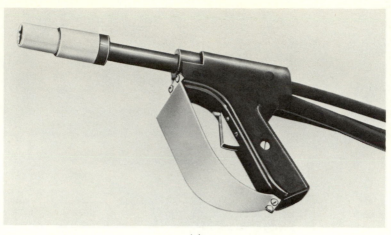

(a)

(b)

Fig. 26-22. MIG welding guns. (a) Air-cooled push gun; (b) air-cooled pull gun. (*Miller Electric Manufacturing Co.*)

leads to eyestrain when a no. 8 or no. 9 lens is used. However, when a no. 10, 11, or 12 lens is used for the MIG welding process, eyestrain is minimized.

MIG WELDING OPERATION

The MIG welding processes are slightly more complex than the TIG welding process because consumable electrodes and a wider range of shielding gases are used. Three variables must be considered before the application of the MIG welding process: the operator-controlled variables, the machine-controlled variables, and the base-metal-controlled variables. These three variables are characteristic of all welding processes but have a more far-reaching inportance in the MIG processes because these have such a wide range of application.

The operator-controlled variables are those to which it is difficult to assign any precise measurement, such as the stick-out of the electrode, the nozzle angle, the angle of the MIG gun, or the wire-feed speed. These variables are controlled in the semiautomatic welding operation by the machine; consequently, they cause some adjustment to the machine-controlled variables.

The amount of stick-out of the electrode is preset on most wire-feed control mechanisms. The wire stick-out determines the amount of penetration of the arc column because the stick-out length controls the current density of the electrode. The longer the stick-out of the electrode, the more resistance it has. As the temperature of the consumable electrode rises, its resistance also rises, placing higher current requirements on the electrode. These current requirements determine the amount of digging action of the electrode. This stick-out rate, then, is controlled by both the current settings and by the wire feed in inches per minute; but mainly the stick-out is controlled by the distance the operator holds the MIG torch from the work, or the tip-to-work distance (Fig. 26-23).

Another operator-controlled variable is

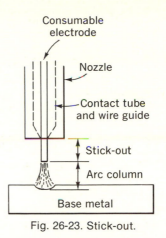

Fig. 26-23. Stick-out.

the angle at which the MIG gun is held to form the weld bead (Fig. 26-24). The three possible angles of an MIG gun are the pulling or trailing angle, which would be comparable to the oxyacetylene method of backhand welding; the neutral position, with the MIG gun held perpendicular to the workpiece; or the pushing position, which resembles the oxyacetylene method of forehand welding. As in oxyacetylene welding, these three techniques determine the penetration of the arc column. However, if the penetration characteristics need to be changed significantly, changing the angle of the MIG welding gun would not be the correct manner in which to manipulate the penetration. The machine variable of amperage or voltage control should be used, or the primary selection of wire size should be reevaluated in order to change the penetration of the arc column.

The last major type of operator control that can be accomplished with the MIG torch is the manipulation patterns that are used by

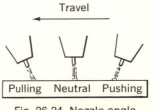

Fig. 26-24. Nozzle angle.

the welder. The most standard manipulation pattern is known as the *drag pattern*, in which the torch is simply moved in a straight line with no oscillation. However, the nozzle should not be allowed to contact the work. Often when materials are welded in other than the flat position, the drag method is not the best manipulation pattern to use. The choice of pattern, however, is often based on the preference of the welder. The whip pattern is often used for out-of-position work, as are the C and the U patterns. These three patterns are especially suitable to weld-puddle manipulation in the horizontal, vertical, and overhead positions. Many times the welder is required to perform a cover pass, such as in pipe work. A lazy eight manipulation pattern can be used to make a cover pass for it is wide and generally will cover approximately three to seven times the width of the normal bead (Fig. 26-25).

The machine-controlled variables include the arc voltage, the welding current, and the travel speed of the weld bead. Although these three variables are controlled by the machine, they are interrelated with the base-metal-controlled variables of the MIG process. The machine variables of arc voltage and welding-current control will determine whether the spray-arc or the short- or pulsed-arc welding system is used. These two controls, the voltage and amperage in combination, determine the optimum travel speed of the weld bead. The amperage used to perform a weld in the MIG processes determines whether or not the metal transfer system is the short arc or the spray arc. The maximum amperage at which the short-circuit effect can take place in the MIG welding system is approximately 250 A. Above this ampere setting, the short-

TABLE 26-1. PULSE OR DCRP MINIMUM CURRENT REQUIREMENTS

ELECTRODE-WIRE SIZE, in.	CURRENT	
	SPRAY ARC, A	SHORT ARC, A
0.030	150	50
0.035 ($^1/_{32}$)	175	75
0.045 ($^3/_{64}$)	200	100
0.0625 ($^1/_{16}$)	275	175
0.09375 ($^3/_{32}$)	350	*

* Short-circuiting is limited to below 250 A.

circuiting effect will not take place. Because of the increased emf, the metal will be removed by a spray effect above approximately 150 A. The point at which this effect occurs is determined by the electrode-wire size plus the voltage-amperage settings on the machine (Table 26-1).

The variables that are selected before the machine variables are those that are determined by the composition of the base metal. The base metal determines the amount and the type of shielding gas that must be used. The base metal also determines the basic type of joint design, the electrode-wire type, and the electrode-wire size that should be used. The type of metal also determines the welding position and the mechanical properties required in the finished weld.

The major shielding gases that are used for the MIG processes are argon, helium, carbon dioxide, and oxygen. Argon is the principal inert gas used to weld nonferrous metals. Helium is used for better control of porosity and better arc stability because of its greater density. The major gases used to MIG weld aluminum are pure argon or a mixture of argon and helium. This mixture may be a combination as high as 25 percent argon and 75 percent helium or a combination of 5 percent helium and 95 percent argon.

The effects of the shielding gas help to remove the surface oxides from the aluminum. When helium is used, it not only helps to remove oxides but it also exhibits a certain amount of porosity control over the weld

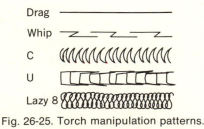

Fig. 26-25. Torch manipulation patterns.

TABLE 26-2. MIG SHIELDING GAS

METAL	GAS	GAS EFFECTS
Aluminum	Argon	Helps to remove surface oxides
	Argon 25%, helium 75%	Oxide removal plus porosity control
Copper	Argon	Reduces sensitivity to surface cracks
	Argon 25%, helium 75%	Counteracts high thermal conductivity
Magnesium	Argon	Helps to remove surface oxides
Nickel	Argon; or argon 50–25%, helium 50–75%	Helps to control base-metal fluidity and provides good wetting
Steel, low-alloy	Argon 98%, oxygen 2%	Eliminates undercutting
	Argon 75%, oxygen 25%	Reduces undercutting
Steel, mild	Carbon dioxide	Low splatter
Steel, stainless	Argon 99–95%, oxygen 1–5%	Oxygen adds to arc stability and reduces undercutting
Titanium	Argon	Improves metal transfer

bead (Table 26-2). When steel and its alloys are welded, carbon dioxide is the chief shielding gas used in the MIG welding process because it has an extremely low cost when compared to the other inert gases, such as argon or helium, and it is capable of producing a sound weld. The major portion of welding is done on mild steel because it is the most used metal in our society. The carbon dioxide gas-metal-arc process is one that requires significantly less operator skill while ensuring proper weld beads. The gas flow in cubic feet per hour depends on the size of the nozzle of the MIG welding torch. Gas flow, however, generally ranges from 8 to 35 ft³/h. Gas flows that range between 15 and 20 ft³/h are the most common.

All the variables have a certain effect on the weld bead, the penetration of the weld bead, and the rate of the deposit of weld material (Table 26-3). Voltage is used to either increase or decrease the width of the weld bead, and amperage is used to increase or decrease the overall size of the weld bead as well as the penetration depth of the weld bead. The size of the weld bead can also be changed by the rate of travel the welder uses to lay down a bead across the work. When the travel speed is decreased, the bead will naturally be larger, as in the case of shielded-arc welding and oxyacetylene welding. The amount that the consumable electrode sticks out of the welding guide and collet affects all the factors that are concerned with the weld bead, the penetration, and the rate of deposit of the weld metal. The stick-out distance is one of the most important distances affecting the weld in MIG welding.

TABLE 26-3. CAUSE-EFFECT WELD VARIABLES

VARIABLE	BEAD				PENETRATION		DEPOSIT RATE	
	SMALLER	LARGER	WIDER	NARROWER	DEEPER	SHALLOWER	FASTER	SLOWER
Voltage			Increase	Decrease				
Amperage	Decrease	Increase			Increase	Decrease		
Travel	Increase	Decrease						
Nozzle angle			Pushing	Pulling	Pulling	Pushing		
Stick-out	Decrease	Increase	Decrease	Increase	Decrease	Increase	Increase	Decrease
Wire size					Decrease	Increase	Increase	Decrease
Wire feed	Decrease	Increase					Increase	Decrease

QUESTIONS

1. What metals can be welded by the MIG process?
2. What types of power supplies can be used for MIG welding?
3. How does the power supply compensate for differences in arc length?
4. What is stick-out?
5. What are the penetration differences between pulling and pushing the MIG gun?
6. What control does the MIG gun operator have over the welding variables?
7. Explain the machine-controlled variables of the MIG process.
8. How is heat liberated in the TIG process and in the MIG process?
9. What is the function of the shielding gases?
10. How do the shielding gases affect the penetration of the arc column?
11. What are the effects of DCRP, DCSP, and alternating current on the deposited weld bead?
12. How do thorium and zirconium affect the tungsten electrode in the TIG process?
13. Why does the preparation of the tip of a TIG electrode vary?
14. How does the standard MIG process differ from the magnetic-flux MIG welding process?
15. What are the major ways that metal is transferred to the inert-gas processes? How do they differ?

27

Submerged-Arc Welding

The submerged-arc welding process, which may be done either automatically or manually, creates an arc column between a bare metallic electrode and the workpiece. The arc, the end of the electrode, and the molten weld pool are submerged in a finely divided granulated powder that contains appropriate deoxidizers, cleansers, and any other necessary fluxing element. The fluxing powder is fed from a hopper that is carried on the welding head. The tube from the hopper spreads the powder in a continuous mound in front of the electrode along the line of the weld. This flux mound is of sufficient depth to submerge completely the arc column so that there is no splatter or smoke, and the weld is shielded from all effects of atmospheric gases. As a result of this protection, the weld beads are exceptionally smooth. The flux adjacent to the arc column melts and floats to the surface of the molten pool; then it solidifies to form a slag on top of the welded metal. The rest of the flux is simply an insulator that can be reclaimed easily. The slag that is formed by the molten flux solidifies and is easy to remove. In fact, in many applications, the slag will crack off by itself as it cools. The unused flux is removed and placed back in the hopper for use the next time (Fig. 27-1).

Granulated flux is a complex, metallic silicate that can be used over a wide range of metals. A typical flux, no. 660, can be used for welding mild steel, low-alloy, high tensile steels, straight chromium, and chromium-nickel steels.

OPERATION

In either automatic or semiautomatic submerged-arc welding, the bare electrode is mechanically fed through an electrical contacting nozzle, or collet. A welding current passes through the collet to the electrode, and the arc is maintained between the base metal and the electrodes. The heat of the arc causes the base metal, the electrode, and the adjacent flux to melt in order to accomplish the tasks of penetrating, filling the crater, and fusing the joint. The electrode is fed into the arc automatically in order to maintain a preset arc voltage and arc length. Direct current supplied by a motor generator welder produces the arc between the electrode and the base metal; however, ac power supplies may be used even though they are not as popular. Use of a dc power supply assures a simplified, positive control of the submerged-arc welding process.

The bare wire electrodes can be pur-

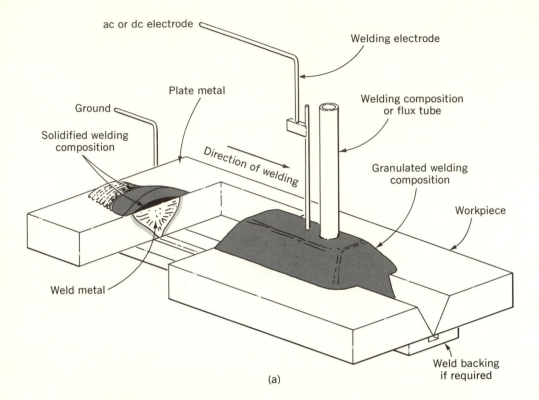

ac or dc electrode

Welding electrode

Plate metal

Ground

Welding composition
or flux tube

Solidified welding
composition

Direction of welding

Granulated welding
composition

Workpiece

Weld metal

Weld backing
if required

(a)

(b)

Fig. 27-1. Submerged-arc process. (a) System; (b) application. (*Lincoln Electric Co.*)

chased either as bare electrodes or with a slight mist of copper coated over the wire to prevent oxidation during the shelf life of the electrode. The coiled electrode comes on a standard reel and is available in diameters ranging from 3/32 to 1/2 in. The most popular electrode is the copper-coated one that has an extended shelf life because its coating prevents rusting. The coating also increases the electrical conductivity of the electrode wire.

The submerged-arc process is characterized by high welding currents. The current density in the electrode is five or six times that used in ordinary manual stick-electrode arc welding. As a result, the melting rate of the electrode, as well as the speed of welding, is much higher than in the manual stick-electrode process. The high current density also results in deep penetration so that plates 5/8-in. thick can be square butt welded without special edge preparation. Currents as high as 1,000 amperes (A) may be used with a 3/16-in. filler wire.

In a sense, the welding wire carries with it a "container" full of molten metal along the weld line. The walls of this container consist of the unmelted flux ahead of the wire, solidified weld metal, slag behind the weld elec-

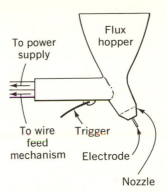

Fig. 27-3. Manual submerged arc. (*Note:* Construction is comparable to that of a MIG nozzle.)

trode, and base metal on either side or below the container. Because of the effect of this container image, base metal as thick as 1½ in. can be welded in a single pass. The use of higher welding currents generally means deeper penetration and greater use of base metal for making many types of welds. Faster welding speeds result, and faster welding speeds minimize distortion and warpage.

The submerged-arc process is also capable of welding fairly thin-gage material. However, because of the greater welding current densities, the electrode many times is pointed or slanted in a particular direction. This wire slant determines the bead appearance. The forward-pointing wire points in the direction of the weld travel and is similar to forehand welding in the oxyacetylene welding process. This position deflects much of the heat of the arc column, yielding a decrease in the penetration, a wider and flatter crown to the bead, and a smaller heat-affected zone. The backward-slanting point does just the opposite and is comparable to the backhand welding technique in the oxyacetylene process. The backward-pointing electrode yields greater penetration, and larger heat-affected zone, and a narrow weld bead (Fig. 27-2).

Submerged-arc welding can be done manually (Fig. 27-3). A small hopper for the granular flux is built into a special electrode holder. The combination electrode feed and cable is attached to the electrode holder. The

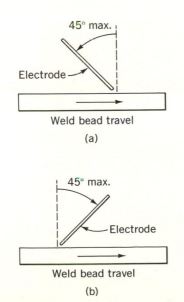

Fig. 27-2. Wire slant. (*a*) Forward point; (*b*) backward point.

operator guides the electrode and is able to make fast welds in places where automatic submerged-arc welding is not suitable, such as on curved lines or irregular joints. Manual submerged-arc welding can be used whenever normal, manual shielded-arc stick-electrode welding is used. The manual and the automatic submerged-arc welding processes are most suited to the flat welding position or the slightly vertical, downhill welding position.

Welds made by the submerged-arc welding process have high strength and ductility with low hydrogen or nitrogen content. This process is suitable for welding low-alloy, high-tensile steels as well as the mild, low-carbon steels. Whatever type of steel is used, the principles governing the mechanism of metal transfer are the same in the submerged-arc process as in the other shielded-arc processes. The voltage requirements of the short arc are fairly low, ranging from 20 to 40 volts (V); 40 V is a sufficient amount of potential for a 1,000-A demand. The submerged-arc process is capable of joining medium-carbon steels, heat-resistant steels, corrosion-resistant steels, and many of the high-strength steels. Also, the process is adaptable to nickel, Monel, Everdur, and many other nonferrous metals.

The submerged-arc welding process has many industrial applications. It is used for fabricating pipe, boiler pressure vessels, railroad tank cars, structural shapes, and practically anything that demands welding in a straight line. The many applications of the submerged-arc welding process have created three general types of equipment: the stationary electrode with the work moving, the electrode mounted on a carriage with the work stationary, and the submerged arc mounted on a self-propelled tractor with the work stationary. The last type, of course, is the manual process, and in this case the special flux-hopper electrode holder is hand-held (Fig. 27-4).

All of the applications of the submerged-arc welding process demand that the heavier sections of the base metal to be welded be prepared in order to ensure optimum penetration. Many times in metal plates that are more than ½ in. thick, the joints are prepared. The major joint designs used are the single V, the single U, and the double V butt joints, with the single V butt joint being the most popular. The square butt joint, fillet joint,

Fig. 27-4. Hand-held submerged-arc welder. (*Lincoln Electric Co.*)

and plug weld joint designs can also be used in the submerged-arc welding process. A major advantage of the submerged-arc welding process is that joint designs can be kept simple, yet the process ensures adequate penetration. An oxygen-fuel cutting process is a satisfactory method to use for preparing a joint, such as a single V; the carbon-arc and the plasma-arc cutting processes are also useful. Generally, in all except the lap- or fillet-type welds, a backing strip is used to support the metal directly beneath the weld zone. If the size of the molten weld pool is large and there is a possibility that the molten metal will sag or if there is a chance that the arc crater will burn through the base metal, the backing strip is used. Usually, the backing plate becomes an integral part of the weld and remains with the weldment.

MULTIPLE-ELECTRODE PROCESS

Submerged-arc welding also may be done with more than one metal electrode. This process is called *twin submerged-arc,* or *twin-arc, welding* (Fig. 27-5). This adaptation changes the weld deposit size considerably. The multiple-electrode, submerged-arc process feeds two electrodes simultaneously, instead of one, into a dual welding head, which permits the use of higher currents. Current demands as high as 1,500 A can be sustained with the multiple-electrode sub-merged-arc process.

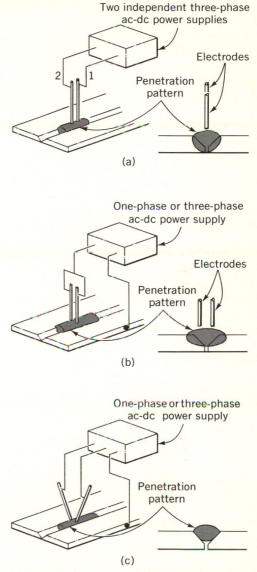

Fig. 27-6. Multiple-electrode submerged arc. (*a*) Multiple power/tandem electrodes; (*b*) single power/parallel electrodes; (*c*) series connection/parallel electrodes.

There are three basic ways that the multiple-electrode process can be achieved (Fig. 27-6). The multiple power supply units with the electrodes in tandem (Fig. 27-6*a*) yield the heaviest, deepest weld-penetration pattern deposits. The electrodes are generally in line with the weld, which creates a deep,

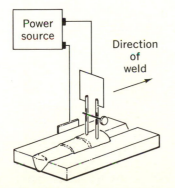

Fig. 27-5. Twin-arc welding.

narrow weld bead. This welding setup is used for heavier, thicker base metals. If a wide bead is required, the head is rotated 90° so that the electrodes are across the weld. The spacing between the electrodes can be varied by lengthening the area between the two electrode holders. The multiple power support can be used with tandem electrodes, but the parallel electrodes usually have a single power supply.

The parallel electrodes (Fig. 27-6b) will not deposit the metal as deeply as tandem electrodes will; however, the weld-pene-

tration pattern can be widened to encompass completely a number of narrow weld beads. The multiple electrodes can also be connected in series so that one electrode is the cathode and the other the anode. The electrodes are parallel to each other across the weld work line. This so-called three o'clock welding yields the least amount of penetration, but permits welding thin-gage metals at a high rate of speed. Because the penetration will be thin, the metal to be welded is usually less than ½ in. thick (Fig. 27-6c).

QUESTIONS

1. What is a submerged arc?
2. How is fluxing powder added in the submerged-arc welding process?
3. What is the function of the flux?
4. Why are the electrodes coated with a copper mist?
5. What are the advantages of the submerged-arc process?
6. What effect does wire slant have on the weld bead?
7. Why is the submerged-arc process generally limited to welding in the flat position?
8. What are the differences between the tandem and parallel applications of the multiple-electrode submerged-arc welding process?
9. How does submerged-arc electrode placement determine the penetration pattern of the weld bead?

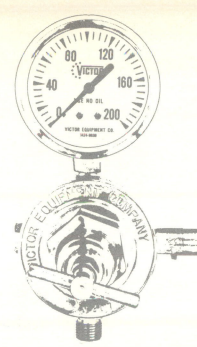

28

Plasma-Arc Welding

The first plasma test device was developed when it was discovered that temperatures as high as 100,000°F could be obtained by making a small vortex of water squeeze through an arc stream in a small channel.

THE PLASMA ARC

Any high-current arc is comprised of plasma, which is nothing more than an ionized conducting gas. The plasma gas is forced through the torch, surrounding the cathode. The main function of the plasma gas is to shield the body of the torch from the extreme heat of the cathode. Any gas or mixture of gases that does not attack the tungsten or the copper cathode can be used; argon and argon mixtures are most commonly used.

The plasma arc, or jet, has a controlled composition and can cut any metal since it is primarily a melting process. Plasma-jet energy is virtually unlimited. The greater the power used, the greater the temperature for melting the metal. The design of the plasma-arc torch constricts the arc force through a small opening and, at the same time, bombards the arc stream with gas particles, causing multiple collisions of electrons

within the particles; consequently, the energy released depends on the amount of electric energy induced into the system (Fig. 28-1).

Many plasma-jet torches have a temperature capability of approximately 60,000°F. Theoretically, the temperature range for other types of plasma-jet torches extends into the thermonuclear range. The arbitrary temperature of 200,000°F separates thermal plasma from thermonuclear plasma. As a comparison, oxyacetylene welding is limited to the maximum temperature of the chemical reaction, or to approximately 6500°F. The ordinary electric arc, because of its diffuseness, can attain a maximum temperature of approximately 20,000°F. The maximum temperature achieved by the ordinary welding electric arc is thought to be approximately 10,000°F.

Plasma arc consists of an electronic arc, plasma gas, and gases used to shield the jet column. The plasma gas does not provide enough shielding protection because its low pressure must be maintained to prevent turbulence around the area of the cut or the weld. If there were high pressure in the plasma column, it would cause a displacement of the molten metal in the weld bead or in the kerf of the cut. Therefore, supplementary shielding gases must be supplied for this purpose.

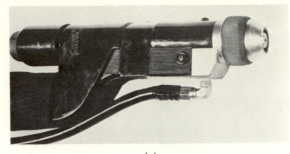

(a)

(b)

Fig. 28-1. Mechanized plasma-arc welding components. (a) Plasma torch; (b) Remote current and gas control. (*Union Carbide Corporation—Linde Division.*)

EQUIPMENT

The equipment necessary for plasma-arc welding includes a conventional dc power supply with a drooping volt ampere output and with 70 open-line volts. This type of power supply is suitable for most applications in which argon or argon mixtures are used.

When hydrogen exceeds the amount of argon by 5 percent, two power supplies must be connected in series to obtain the necessary open voltage for igniting the arc or the jet stream. Both rectifiers and motor generators can be used for the power source, although rectifiers are preferred because they produce better arc stability as the machine warms up to an operating temperature.

The two main types of torches for

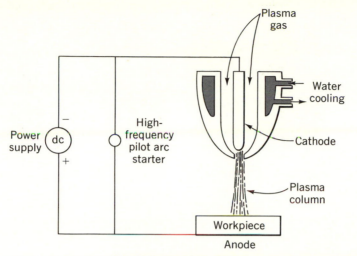

Fig. 28-2. Transferred arc.

welding and cutting with plasma arc are the transferred arc and the nontransferred arc. The *transferred-arc plasma-jet torch* is similar to the TIG torch, except that it has a water-cooled nozzle between the electrode and the work. This nozzle constricts the arc, increasing its pressure. The plasma, because of the collision of gas molecules with high-energy electrons, is then swept out through the nozzle, forming the main current path between the electrode and the workpiece (Fig. 28-2). The transferred arc is generated between the tungsten electrode, which is the cathode, and the workpiece, which is the anode. The second type of plasma jet torch, the nontransferred arc torch, extends the arc from the electrode to the end of the nozzle (Fig. 28-3). This type of plasma jet is completely independent of the workpiece, with the power supply contained within the equipment.

The arc force in the transferred-arc torch is directed away from the plasma torch and into the workpiece; thus the arc is capable of heating the workpiece to a higher temperature than that produced with the nontransferred arc. In the nontransferred-arc torch, the arc force generated from the electrode is absorbed in the water-cooled nozzle, making the nontransferred-arc torch more adaptable

to metal spraying and welding. The transferred-arc torch is more adaptable to melting or cutting metal.

The *gas-tungsten-arc cutting process*, also called the *plasma-jet process*, is started simply by striking an arc between the tungsten electrode in the torch and the surface to be cut. A pilot arc circuit that connects the torch nozzle to the ground by a current-limiting resistor makes the arc easier to start. This starting unit disconnects itself once the arc is started. The electrodes in the metallic nozzle of the torch usually are cooled with water. The electrodes and the arc-constricting nozzles are responsible for about 5 per-

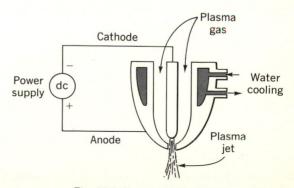

Fig. 28-3. Nontransferred arc.

cent of the input energy being used as heat and for the remainder of the energy entering the plasma column. The plasma gases used for the cutting of nonferrous metals and stainless steels are a mixture of argon and hydrogen, with 100 percent argon being used to start the cut and approximately 25 percent hydrogen added to the argon after the cut has been started.

The plasma-arc cutting process has been applied with tremendous results to the cutting of carbon steels, aluminum, stainless steels, Inconel, Monel, many of the hard-to-cut steels, and other metals. When carbon steel is cut with the plasma arc, dross-free cuts with smooth surfaces, sharp edges, and almost square faces can result.

Cutting aluminum has proven to be a successful application of this process. When aluminum is cut with the arc, a mixture of 65 percent argon and 35 percent hydrogen is used. The amount of material that can be cut in a designated period of time by the plasma arc exceeds that of any other methods for cutting aluminum. High-quality, dross-free cuts can be produced in aluminum up to 5 in. thick. Because of its successful application to the cutting of aluminum, new concepts in both manual and automatic cutting of aluminum have come into use. The plasma jet has been adapted for cutting risers on castings, manholes in tank shells, and heavy bulky items that are impossible to cut by means of a shear or saw. Its ability to cut intricate contours aids in reducing operating costs in the metalworking industry (Fig. 28-4).

In 1958, a major breakthrough was made in plasma-jet cutting. At that time, the plasma jet was developed to cut stainless steel economically, its most common use today. In the current applications of this process, the plasma causes virtually no distortion; distortion may exist in the chemical flame cutting process. The corrosion resistance of stainless steel is not affected by the plasma jet except for a microscopically thin layer of metal on

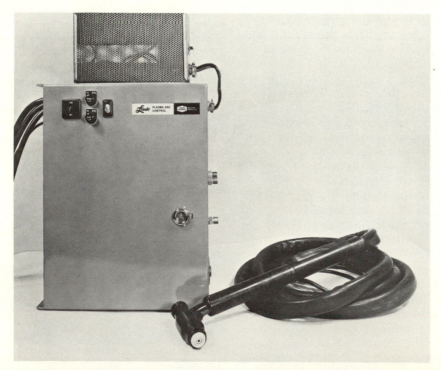

Fig. 28-4. Manual plasma-arc cutting torch. (*Union Carbide Corporation—Linde Division.*)

the surface of the cut. In shape cutting, cuts can be started at any point on the workpiece because of the ability of the torch to cut stainless steel up to 2 in. thick.

The newest application of the plasma arc is in welding. In the welding process a nontransferred-arc torch is used that has electrical circuits similar to those used in the plasma-arc cutting process, and a power supply with a high-frequency pilot-arc starter is used. The electrode used for stainless steel welding and most other metals is a straight-polarity tungsten electrode. When aluminum is welded, reverse polarity is used with a water-cooled copper electrode.

The plasma-arc welding process is used in aerospace applications, and in the welding of reactive metals and thin materials. It is capable of welding stainless steel, titanium, maraging steel, and high-carbon steel. The plasma-jet torch that has been designed for welding has one extra passage within the nozzle, providing a passageway for the shielding gas during the welding operation. The plasma gas itself does not sufficiently protect the metal of the weld bead. The gases used for this shield are the same as those used in the TIG welding process: argon, helium, and carbon dioxide, or mixtures of these gases.

OPERATION

In the welding process, plasma gas, shielding gas, and water to cool the nozzle are piped to the lower portion of the torch. By changing the tip of the nozzle of the torch, the shape of the weld can be varied. The penetration of the weld and type of metal that can be welded are influenced greatly by the size and type of tip used. Practically all welding done with plasma arc is done mechanically because the process requires great stability and speed. The high temperature of the jet stream further limits manual application of this process.

The actual process of welding with the plasma jet is done with what is called the

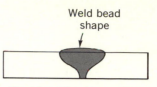
Fig. 28-5. Wineglass effect.

keyhole method. The jet column burns a small hole through the material that is to be welded. As the torch progresses along the material, the hole progresses also; however, it is filled up by the molten metal as the torch passes. Welding with this method automatically ensures 100 percent penetration. Because the plasma jet strikes the surface of the metal, a larger area is melted at the surface, resulting in a unique cross-sectional weld bead design called the *wineglass design* (Fig. 28-5).

The nontransferred-arc plasma-jet torch is also used for the spraying of metals, especially those metals that have a melting point above 600°F. The metals to be sprayed are injected into the plasma-jet stream either approximately where the shielding gas is injected into it or just outside the nozzle (Fig. 28-6). The wire or powder can be injected into the plasma stream, which is hot enough to melt any of the metals and blast them out into the jet stream at sonic velocities, forcing the now-molten metal onto the part to be sprayed. The filler materials that can be plasma-arc jet sprayed are: ceramics, some of the nonferrous metals, all of the ferrous

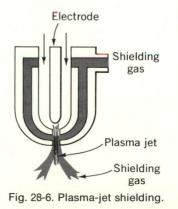
Fig. 28-6. Plasma-jet shielding.

metals (including tungsten and tungsten carbides), and metals that range in hardness up through vanadium and the vanadium carbides. The feed rate for metal spraying depends on the fusion point of the filler material used. Aluminum can be sprayed from approximately $1/10$ to $7\frac{1}{2}$ lb/h, while tungsten can be sprayed from $1\frac{1}{2}$ to 25 lb/h. Generally, when spraying, the plasma gun is held 2 to 6 in. from the workpiece. Most of the filler materials have a deposit rate of around 60 to 75 percent. With aluminum oxide, the rate is approximately 85 percent.

There are several dangers connected with use of a plasma jet. More electrical equipment is used, increasing potential electrical hazards considerably. Also, ultraviolet and infrared radiation is present, requiring the use of welding tinted lenses from no. 9 to no. 12. The ultraviolet and infrared radiation sometimes is so intense that it can cause violent sunburning, even through clothing. Also common to this process is a high-pitched noise, so that the operator must wear ear plugs. The noise ranges around 100 decibels (dB) if it is unrestricted. This noise level must be reduced to 80 dB in order to prevent damage to the inner ear.

QUESTIONS

1. What is the keyhole method of welding?
2. What is the difference between a plasma gas and a shielding gas?
3. What are the two basic types of plasma torches? What are their characteristics and applications?
4. What is the difference between thermal plasma and thermonuclear plasma?
5. How does the heat generated by the plasma jet compare with the heat generated by the electric arc and by the oxyacetylene flame?
6. Why does the nozzle of the plasma torch not melt?
7. What is the most common use of the plasma torch?
8. What are the operational hazards in using the plasma-jet torch?

29

Resistance Welding

Electrical resistance can best be explained as opposition to electric current as the current flows through a wire. This resistance is measured in units called *ohms*. Resistance has been used for a long time as a source of heat generation for welding (Fig. 29-1). In resistance welding, two factors perform the welding application: the resistance heating of the two pieces to be joined and the forging pressure exerted joining the two pieces of metal.

The resistance welding machine is cycled so that the needed heat is produced at a time which coincides with the exertion of pressure by the electrodes on the surfaces of the metal pieces to be joined. The approach or the squeezing time is the first stage in the common four-period resistance welding cycle. This squeeze stage takes place when the electrodes are clamped onto the pieces to be welded. The next stage is the heating stage or the weld time, which occurs when an area in the two pieces of metal is brought up to welding temperature. This stage is indicated by S in Fig. 29-2. After the metal has reached the fusion point, the current is shut off and additional pressure is applied by the electrodes. This pressure is held until the metal is cooled; then the machine automatically shuts itself off. This pause begins a new cycle.

Welding time usually is controlled by the machine, but the operator can set the machine to a desired cycle time by means of a rheostat in the primary winding. The welding time commonly runs from 3 to 120 Hz with a 60-Hz current or standard current; 120 Hz will yield approximately a 2-s welding time cycle. The four-period cycle is used because hardenable alloys are prone to cracking when one surge of current and uncontrolled cooling is employed for welding. However, with a controlled approach to the welding, forging, and cooling cycle in the machine, hardenable alloys can be spot-welded with a high degree of success.

Spot-welding and butt welding are the two chief methods of applying heat energy and mechanical force in resistance welding.

SPOT-WELDING

One of the most common pieces of welding equipment found in industry and in school shops, especially when relatively light-gage metal is used, is the spot-welder. It is characterized by low cost, speed, and dependability, making it a common electrical resistance welding process.

The three basic electrode tip de-

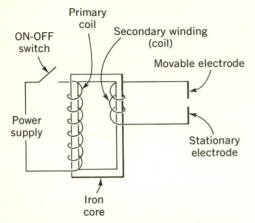

Fig. 29-1. Typical resistance welder.

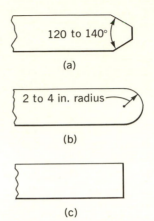

Fig. 29-3. Tip design. (a) Pointed electrode; (b) domed electrode; (c) flat electrode.

signs—pointed, domed, and flat—are used according to the weld desired (Fig. 29-3). Pointed electrodes are the most widely used. They are used for ferrous materials. Domed electrodes are designed to withstand heavier current loads and more mechanical force, which make them applicable to nonferrous metals. Flat electrodes are used when spot-welding deformation is not wanted or when the spot-weld should be inconspicuous. Usually one flat electrode is used with one domed electrode.

Process

The diameter of the electrode determines the diameter of the fusion zone of the weld spot (Fig. 29-4). The diameter of the fusion zone will be 0.01 in. plus twice the thickness of the thinnest member being spot-welded; however, this preset weld fusion size is chosen according to the application; that is, a sheet metal shop would determine the optimum sizes for their spot-welding needs, but an automotive body shop might require different electrode sizes. The amount of lap that is required for a good spot-weld depends on the size of the fusion weld. Usually spot-welding is limited to metals that range in thickness

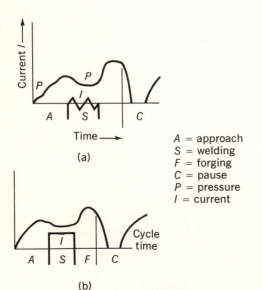

A = approach
S = welding
F = forging
C = pause
P = pressure
I = current

Fig. 29-2. Four-period resistance welding. (a) ac; (b) dc.

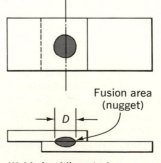

Weld size (diameter) = 0.10 in. + 2 × thickness of thinnest member

Fig. 29-4. Fusion spot weld.

from 0.03 to 0.188 in. The lap joint is twice the diameter of the spot-weld plus ⅛ in. for alignment. However, if the two pieces to be spot-welded are held in a fixture, the ⅛ in. for spot alignment can be eliminated. If the spot-weld is made too close to the edge of the metal, the metal will become overheated, and cracking will result around the weld. Spot-welding too close to the edge of a lap joint causes the metal to explode from its surface.

As the current passes through one electrode and the work to the other electrode, a small area is heated. The temperature of this weld zone is approximately 1500 to 1700°F. Because of this flow of current from one electrode to the other, the heat mark shows a tendency to pull toward the center. After the weld is completed, it is allowed to cool, producing a fine, strong weld. During this complete weld cycle, the welding time can be as short as 0.01 s, or it can be as long as 5 s. The amount of discoloration and burning or weakening of the base material is related to the length of the weld cycle.

SEAM WELDING

The equipment used for seam welding utilizes the same principles as any of the resistance welding processes. Seam welding uses a two-step transformer with a primary and secondary winding. The secondary winding is hooked to the horns or arms that support the electrodes. The horns are movable and can apply pressure to the work, as in spot-welding. However, the electrodes are wheel-shaped and can be rotated. These copper wheels carry the current to the pieces to be welded. As they rotate, ignitron and thyratron tubes are used to switch the current on and off through the rollers. This switching of the current produces a continuous or overlapped spot-weld, which is called a *seam weld* (Fig. 29-5).

Basically, two types of welds can be formed in seam welding with the individual nuggets: the stitch weld and the roll weld

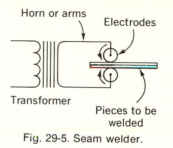

Fig. 29-5. Seam welder.

(Fig. 29-6). The *stitch weld* is made by turning the current on the rolls off and on quickly enough so that a continuous fusion zone is maintained. The fusion zone will not be parallel but will be in the shape of each overlapped bead. The *roll weld* occurs when the current to the copper-rolled electrodes is turned off and on intermittently, causing individual nuggets to be formed.

Stitch welding is used more for joints for use with liquid or gas, while roll welding is used for simple joining of two pieces of metal. The roll weld will not be watertight, liquidtight, or gastight.

PROJECTION WELDING

Projection welding uses the same equipment as spot-welding. The only difference is that the electrodes used are flat on the ends and

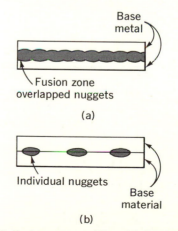

Fig. 29-6. Fusion seam welding. (*a*) Stitch; (*b*) roll.

slightly larger in diameter than the flat electrodes used in spot-welding. Successful projection welding depends greatly on the surface preparation of the pieces to be welded. Projections, small deformations that will touch the surface of the material to be welded, are made on the weld areas. One of the main advantages of these projected points is that welding areas can be located easily, which makes projection welding a high-production welding technique (Fig. 29-7). As the current flows through the two parts to be welded, the projected points are the main contact areas. Wherever a point or a projection touches the metal, a weld nugget will start. These weld points soon reach the plastic state, and the force applied by the electrodes finishes the weld nugget. The cycle time is the same as the spot-weld cycle time. As the points reach their plastic state, the metal is compressed so that the finished weld is similar to the spot-weld with the exception of the small indentations created by the projections.

An adaptation of the projection welding method is metal-fiber welding, which uses a metal fiber rather than a projection point. This metal fiber may be composed of various metals, such as any brazing metal or any metal that can be used for a filler material, but generally it is a felt material. Tiny elements of the filler metal are used to produce a thin sheet of felt metal cloth. This cloth is placed between two pieces of metal which are projection welded in the usual manner. The metal fiber used in the filler material makes it possible to weld dissimilar metals, such as copper to stainless steel, stainless steel to a ferrous material, and copper to brass. The metal-fiber welding process is more expensive than the projection welding technique.

BUTT WELDING

Welding two pieces of metal together with a butt weld can be done by many resistance welding processes. The butt weld consists of joining two pieces of metal together either on face or on edge. Some of the major types of resistance butt welding are: flash welding, upset welding, stud welding, foil butt welding, high-frequency welding, and percussion welding.

Flash Welding

Flash welding is the resistance welding process that received its name from the arc or flash that is created between the two pieces of metal to be welded. Metal to be welded is clamped into specially designed electrodes that have one stationary platen and two movable platens. As the current is turned on, the two pieces of clamped metal are brought into close proximity. As the metals move closer, their near or slight contact causes an arcing. This arcing immediately raises the temperature of the metal particles to a welding temperature. The arc stream then projects incandescent particles of metal. At this point, the current is turned off and the movable platen presses the molten areas together to form a fusion weld (Fig. 29-8).

Stud Welding

Stud welding is similar to flash welding and metal-arc welding. Stud welding incorpo-

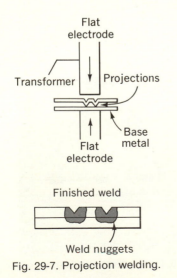

Fig. 29-7. Projection welding.

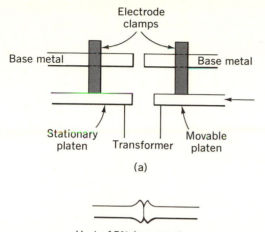

Fig. 29-8. Flash welding. (a) System; (b) finished weld joint.

rates a method of drawing an arc between the stud and the surface of the metal. Then the two molten surfaces are brought into contact with each other under pressure.

The same methods are used to operate both the portable and the stationary welding equipment. The equipment required for stud welding consists of a stud welding gun (Fig. 29-9), a device to control the time of the cur-

rent flow, a source of dc welding current (usually 300-, 400-, or 600-A dc current), and studs and ferrules. The Nelson and the Phillips stud guns are most commonly used in the United States. Both stud guns weigh approximately 5 lb and resemble a pistol with an oversized barrel. The frame is made from fabric-reinforced bakelite, with the welding leads and control circuits entering the gun through the pistol grip. A pushbutton switch or trigger is located in the handle for starting the welding cycle.

The mechanism of the gun has a copper coil that is cast integrally with the frame of the gun. Inside this heavy copper coil is an armature, connected through linkages to the stud chuck or holding device. When the trigger is pulled, a slight lateral shift of the armature sets up the necessary arc gap, establishing the flow of welding current. After a predetermined, preset elapsed time, the current is interrupted. Then a spring in the gun barrel moves the stud into the weld pool to complete the weld.

The control unit used consists of a high-speed relay and timer. The timer is adjusted to the desired number of cycles to be used, with the cycles based on 60 Hz. The time interval will vary from 3 to 45 Hz, depending on the size of the stud to be welded.

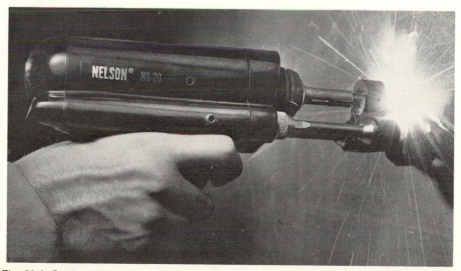

Fig. 29-9. Stud welding gun. (*Nelson Stud Welding—A United-Carr Division of TRW, Inc.*)

Both types of stud welding equipment commonly used in this country operate on the same principles. The cyc-arc equipment operates by drawing an arc between the stud and the base metal to which it is being welded. The current is set at a predetermined rate and the stud is lowered into a molten pool formed in the base metal by the arc stream. The gun is removed and the fusion weld takes place between the stud and the base metal.

The Phillips stud welding process uses a timing device that is activated by a cartridge placed on the end of the stud. The cartridge, which is a semiconductor, starts the arc between the stud and the base metal. While

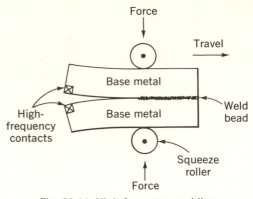

Fig. 29-11. High-frequency welding.

the welding is taking place, that part of the cartridge connected to the stud fuses away and releases the stud, which then is pressed into the molten weld puddle.

The size of the generator used depends on the size of the stud to be welded, and the circumstances under which the welding is done. Direct-current generators from 300 to 600 A that recover their peak voltage from 1 to 2 Hz are the most desirable for good stud welding performance. The ac generator is not used widely because its use is restricted to the flat welding position, which limits the application of the studs considerably.

Ferrules used are either ceramic or porcelain. They perform several functions. The ferrule serves to concentrate the heat of the arc in the weld zone, to act as a dam by confining the molten metal to an area, to protect the operator from the harmful effect of the rays of the arc, to prevent overheating of the base metal, and to protect the weld puddle from contamination. Any stud may be used, provided it can be welded by the generator available. Most commercially available studs come with a ferrule. Some of the many types of studs include the straight, female, bent, and threaded.

The stud welding cycle involves several steps (Fig. 29-10). The stud is placed in the chuck of the gun and the ferrule is slipped into the position over the stud. Then the gun is placed in the proper position against the surface of the base metal to be welded. The trigger is pushed causing the stud to be re-

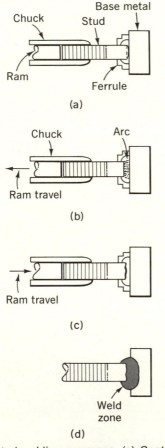

Fig. 29-10. Stud welding sequence. (a) Contact stage; (b) arc stage; (c) forge stage; (d) finished stud (ferrule removed).

Fig. 29-12. High-frequency welder. (*AMF-Thermatool Company.*)

tracted automatically from contact with the base metal by a solenoid coil inside the gun. This action causes an electric arc to be established between the stud and the base metal. The arc melts the base metal and part of the stud. The arc is then automatically shut off by the timer, deenergizing the solenoid coil, which releases the main spring. The spring drives the stud into the molten pool of the base metal, resulting in a fusion weld between the stud and the base metal.

High-Frequency Resistance Welding

The phenomenon of high-frequency current which causes it to flow at or near the surface of a conductor and not through the entire thickness of a conductor makes it possible to resistance weld extremely thin pieces of material, as thin as 0.004 in. Another phenomenon of high-frequency current is the *proximity effect* (the current follows a path of low conductance rather than low resistance) which means that the effective resistance of the metal being welded is much higher with high-frequency current than standard 60-Hz current. Therefore, the amperage requirement for a given amount of calorie release or heat release is but a fraction of that needed for standard resistance welding. This characteristic, coupled with the fact that the low-inductance path is the one that is closest to the conductor of the circuit, determines the design of the high-frequency resistance welding machine.

Supplied to the high-frequency contacts

placed on the base metal is 450,000 Hz of ac power. Because of the extremely fast cycling, the conductor of the current assumes the shape of a V between the conductors (Fig. 29-11). The V path acts as a return conductor for the low inductance, which causes the surfaces of the two pieces of base metal to be heated. At the point of the V, there are two rollers which force the metals together, slightly upsetting the base metal and causing the weld to take place. Materials can be joined that range from 0.004 to 0.012 in. thick at welding speeds from approximately 200 to 1,000 ft/min. The high-frequency resistance welding process (Fig. 29-12) can be used to join copper and its alloys, nickel and its alloys, aluminum, and many types of steels. The process is used mostly for the welding of tubing, especially with a butt weld or a butt seam weld.

QUESTIONS

1. What is resistance welding?
2. What are the two cycles in resistance welding?
3. How is seam welding an application of spot-welding?
4. What are the advantages of a pointed electrode?
5. What is a nugget?
6. How is the size of a resistance spot-weld determined?
7. What are the advantages of a stitch weld over a roll resistance weld?
8. Why is projection spot-welding a higher production output welding method than standard spot-welding?
9. What are the advantages of metal-fiber spot-welding over projection spot-welding?
10. How do flash welding and upset (resistance butt) welding compare?
11. What are the four stages in the stud welding cycle?
12. What is the proximity effect?

30

Metal Spraying

Flame spraying is a general term used for several different methods of applying a metallic coating to a base metal. The four different processes are: wire metallizing, thermospray, plasma-arc spray, and electric-arc spray.

The original credit for flame spraying goes to M. U. Schoop, a Swiss engineer who first patented the process of flame spraying in 1902. The first commercial recognition of flame spraying came some years later. Originally, the process was developed to build up worn parts that were expensive to replace. Most of the processes of flame spraying create a strong chemical bond between the filler material and the base metal. The filler material is in the form of either a wire or pulverized metal that is used as a powder. Both types of filler material are melted by means of some type of fuel or electric arc and are forced into the base metal with tremendous momentum. As the metallic particles are propelled through the air, oxides are picked up from the atmosphere. The minute particles and oxides are splattered on the metal, forming an oxide bond between the particles. As the particles hit, they spread out and interlock with other particles, forming a tight mechanical bond. In some cases, point-to-point fusion takes place, depending on the process and the filler material used.

The bonding that takes place is essentially mechanical, however. Both adhesion and cohesion take place in order to ensure bonding (Fig. 30-1). Adhesion of the sprayed metal globules takes place when these atomized particles force themselves into the cracks and tears of a properly prepared surface. Cohesion takes place when the oxide surfaces and even the pure liquid metal particles fuse together into the prepared surfaces.

The compression strength is low when the coating is compared with the original material, or the base metal. The applied material could be compared to a sintered powdered metal because of the grainy appearance and the strength of the bond between the particles.

Several applications of thermal, or flame, spraying in use today include the coating of the metal to increase its resistance to corrosion and oxidation and the hard surfacing of metal to increase its wearability. A hard surface can be applied up to 0.001 in. thick. Any coating thicker than 0.001 in. has a tendency to flake off. When worn parts are built up, as much as ¼ in. can be applied successfully. Hard surfacing usually is applied to pump shafts; large, slow-moving shafts; and, in some cases, large pistons, such as diesel pistons that can be built back up to a standard size.

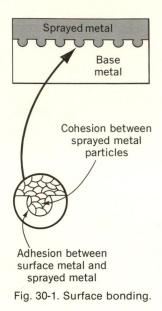

Fig. 30-1. Surface bonding.

Heat derived from an oxygen-fuel source is used for metals with melting points under 5000°F. For filler materials with melting points greater than 5000°F, metal-spraying equipment with the plasma or electric arc is used. Because little heat is necessary on the workpiece, metal spraying can be used on wood, plastic, and other soft materials. The air stream that helps carry the metal particles from the metal-spraying device to the base metal also has a cooling effect on the base metal, and this cooling helps prevent the base metal from melting. With this advantage, metal spraying can be used in making molds for mass production of small parts and molds for foundry work as well as for the plastics industry.

SURFACE PREPARATION

When a surface preparation for metal spraying is selected, attention must first be given to the shape of the base metal. The choice of surface preparation depends on whether the surface of the base metal is flat or round, and whether a hard, smooth, wear-resistance surface or a soft, bearing-like sur-

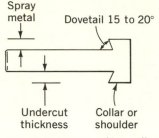

Fig. 30-2. Undercut/dovetail.

face is required. The seven processes used to increase bonding qualities between sprayed metal and the base metal are undercutting, rough threading, grit blasting, using self-bonding materials, electric bonding, studding, and sanding or grinding (Figs. 30-2 and 30-3).

Before any of these methods can be utilized, it is necessary to clean the metal to be sprayed of dirt, oil, oxides, and any other impurities that may weaken the bond between the sprayed metal and the base metal. Cleaning is done before the surface preparation so that contamination does not take place when the base metal is being prepared for the bonding metal. Usually oil-free solvents are employed. In the case of porous metals (such as in metal castings), oil may be removed by heating the casting to a temperature that will vaporize the oil. Oxide coating may be removed by a mechanical method, provided that the metal surface is sprayed within a reasonably short time after the mechanical preparation has been used.

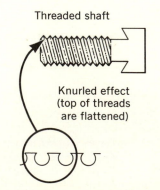

Fig. 30-3. Dovetail grooves (rough threading).

WIRE METALLIZING

The wire metallizing process was one of the first metal-spraying processes used in the United States, starting as early as the 1920s. The equipment used in a metallizing system includes the following (Fig. 30-4a):

1. An air compressor with a capacity of at least 30 ft³/min
2. A standard oxygen cylinder
3. A standard acetylene cylinder with regulators
4. A flow meter
5. An air-pressure control
6. A wire straightening and feeding device for the gun
7. The gun itself

The gun feeds metal wire into an oxygen-fuel flame, which is encased in a stream of compressed air that forms an air envelope around the outside of the flame and the liquid metal. The compressed air cools the metal and helps to accelerate it on its path to the base metal. As the wire is melted by the high temperatures, it is atomized by compressed air and blown onto the base metal. Among the several fuels used to melt the wire are acetylene, which can achieve temperatures up to 5660°F, and methylacetylene propadiene, which attains temperatures of 5300°F; hydrogen propane also is used extensively for the softer metals, such as zinc, lead, aluminum, and tin.

The size of the gun varies depending on the manufacturer, but it usually weighs from 3 to 6 lb for the normally operated gun and up to 10 lb for the machine-mounted gun. A gun is often mounted on a lathe or some other mechanism so that it can travel evenly, thus producing a more even surface (Fig. 30-4b).

The wires used range in size from a no. 2 Brown and Sharpe up to 3/16-in.-diameter wire. For easy use, the wires can be purchased in rolls. Wire can also be purchased in lengths from 3 to 8 ft, especially if the wire type is too rigid to coil. The amount of filler material deposited on the base metal de-

pends on the type of wire used and the size of the wire. Depending on its diameter, steel wire can be sprayed at a rate of 17 in./lb and zinc wire at approximately 55 lb/h. Lead wire can be applied at about 100 lb/h.

There are two parts to a wire metallizing unit. The first part is a power unit which is used to feed the wire at the desired speed through the nozzle. Most power units use a high-speed air-driven turbine to feed the wire. The turbine operates through a series of gears that reduce the speed of the turbine to a slow rate. This speed is adjusted by increasing or decreasing the speed of the turbine or by restricting its air intake. The wire is then fed into the oxygen-fuel chamber. Another type of wire feed consists of a variable, dc electric motor, which is bulkier and used primarily for mounted spray units. The second component of the wire metallizing gun is a gas head, which has a wire nozzle, and an air cap, which controls the fuel gas, oxygen, and compressed air mixtures (Fig. 30-5). Usually 10 psi of acetylene and 16 psi of oxygen are sufficient to complete the spraying operations. Compressed air must be kept at a constant 35 psi.

Several nozzles are available for a variety of jobs. Extension tubes can be used for spraying metal inside cylinders of small diameters. Broad flat nozzles can be used to produce a fan-shaped spray for large areas. The metal particles that are sprayed are extremely small and range in size from 0.0001- to 0.0015-in. diameter when sprayed from the optimum distance of a minimum of 4 in. to a maximum of 10 in. When spraying metals from these minimum and maximum distances, approximately 95 percent of the metal sprayed will adhere to the prepared base metal.

The two critical adjustments when using the gun involve the wire feed and the neutral flame. A slightly carburizing flame is acceptable; however, an oxidizing flame will cause the wire to oxidize too much and will prevent some of the metal particles from adhering properly to the base metal. When the wire travels too fast, the wire will not atomize properly. When it travels too slowly, oxida-

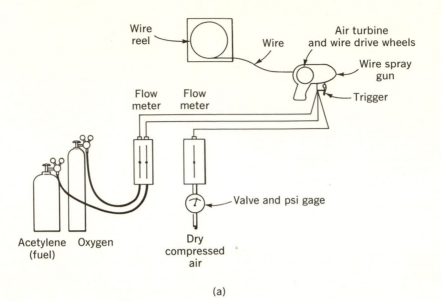

(a)

(b)

Fig. 30-4. Wire metal spraying. (a) System; (b) lathe-mounted wire spray (*Metallizing Company of America*).

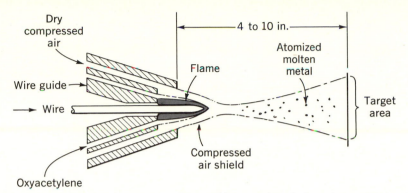

Fig. 30-5. Flame, wire, and air jet nozzle. (*Note:* A luminous white cone is a distinct characteristic of a balanced oxyacetylene flame).

tion takes place or the wire may fuse to the nozzle, causing failure of the gun.

THERMOSPRAY

The thermospray process is similar to the wire metallizing process, except that a powder is used instead of a wire and this process can be used for hard-facing. The thermospray process does not involve as much equipment as does the metallizing process. The thermospray system includes an oxygen supply and a fuel supply with regulators for each, a flowmeter, and a thermospray gun (Fig. 30-6).

The thermospray guns that are manufactured in the United States operate on the venturi principle; that is, they employ a neutral oxygen-fuel flame that uses the oxygen as an aspirating gas to draw the powder into the flame. The powder is then melted outside the body of the gun and forced onto the metal by the action of the aspirating gas (Fig. 30-7). The spray distance ranges from 4 to 10 in. Approximately 95 percent of the sprayed powder will strike the base metal at these distances. The thermospray powder either may be gravity fed into the aspirating chamber or it may be fed by an electrical vibrating mechanism attached to the chamber so that the passageways are kept full of powder while each chamber has powder in it.

The sizes of the powder particles used in the thermospray process fall into three groups ranging from 100- to 150-mesh size. However, up to 325 mesh is used for special jobs. The first group of particles fuses from 1800 to 2500°F and consists of nickel-silicon-boron alloys or nickel-chromium-silicon-boron alloys. The second group fuses from 1920 to 2080°F and consists of cobalt-chromium-silicon-boron alloys. The last group fuses from 1950 to 2050°F, and are the tungsten-carbide composites. These various materials may be applied to almost all irons, nickels, coppers, and copper alloys. Often, when materials are applied to austenitic stainless steels or other high-temperature alloys, preheating precedes the application of the metals. The base metal must be between 400 and 900°F to compensate for the expansion that takes place. When metals that contract a great deal are sprayed, additional filler material must be added to make up for shrinkage. Sometimes as much as 20 percent filler material must be added.

A fusion process follows the application of the metal powder. This fusion process usually is done with oxyacetylene or oxygen fuel, using a neutral or reducing flame. Heat is applied first to the area adjacent to the sprayed deposit until the area is a dull red. Then the torch is moved slowly toward the sprayed coating until the complete surface has been fused.

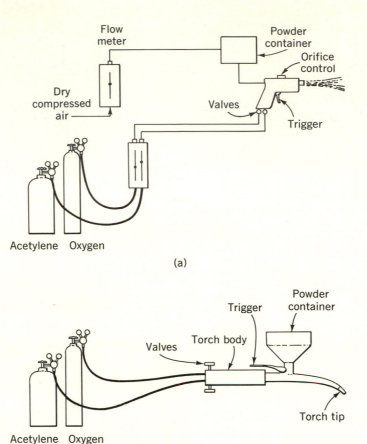

Fig. 30-6. Metal powder spray system. (a) Pressure system; (b) nonpressure system.

PLASMA-ARC SPRAY

When higher fusion points (above 5000°F) must be reached, the plasma-arc spraying process usually is used (Fig. 30-8). The plasma torch is an untransferred-arc type that is independent of the material to be sprayed because it has a contained heat source. The only difference between a plasma-arc torch that is used for cutting and welding and one that is used for spraying is the addition of a device that injects powder into the arc stream. The electric arc travels from a tungsten cathode to a copper anode on the front of the gun. Gas enters the torch and is expanded by the arc, resulting in a plasma jet, which is forced out of the nozzle at velocities that may

reach as high as 20,000 ft/s. Powdered metal is metered into this plasma stream just as it leaves the expansion cavity in the front of the gun. Then the filler metal is carried to the base metal in a liquid state, actually melting in the air and not in the gun because of the high temperatures of the plasma arc. Because of the high temperature created inside the gun, cooling is mandatory and is accomplished by circulating 50- to 100-lb water pressure through the gun at a flow of 3 to 5 gal/min. On some models the tungsten electrode is water-cooled. The water must be clean, pure water in order to prevent corrosion inside the gun. Many times the plasma-arc spray gun maintains temperatures of 30,000°F.

There are several fuels used for plasma-

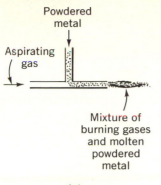

(a)

(b)

(c)

Fig. 30-7. Powder spray. (a) The venturi principle (the aspirating gas may be a mixture of oxygen, fuel, or compressed air, depending on the manufacturer of the spray equipment); (b) the powder spray gun (*Metallizing Company of America*); (c) a powder spraying application (*Metallizing Company of America*).

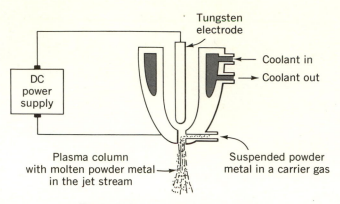

Fig. 30-8. Plasma-arc spray process.

arc spraying, mainly either monotomic or diatomic gases. Argon is a monotomic gas used for spraying carbides. Helium is useful as an auxiliary gas. An auxiliary gas sometimes is injected with the plasma gas to produce certain burning characteristics. Of the diatomic gases, nitrogen is used most frequently because it is inexpensive, has a high spraying speed, and an efficient deposit rate.

The electrical power supply for plasma spraying must have a 100 percent duty cycle, with ranges of 14 to 100 kilowatts (kW). The average unit demands 28 to 40 kW with 220 V, 60 Hz, three-phase power. All controls are located on the control console with none on the gun. The various controls on the consoles are: the plasma-gas control, the power-current control, the stop-start high-frequency control, the secondary-gas control, and the powder-gas control. The current level is adjusted with a rheostat after the gas and powder speeds have been set.

The filler materials are made of ceramics, some of the nonferrous metals, all the ferrous metals, and even those metals that range in hardness through tungsten carbide, vanadium, and vanadium carbides. The feed rate depends on the fusion point of the filler materials used. The feed rate for aluminum ranges from 0.10 up to 7.5 lb/h, while tungsten can be deposited from approximately 1.5 to 25 lb/h. The plasma-arc gun is held from 2 to 6 in. from the workpiece to ensure the largest percentage of filler material deposited.

Most filler materials will deposit from 60 to 75 percent at this distance. The actual technique of spraying with the thermospray, or the powder spray, is identical to that used with oxyacetylene fuel, with the exception that the powder fuses to the base metal instantly.

There are several dangers when any plasma-jet device is used. These devices have a high noise level, ranging around 100 decibels (dB). This noise level must be lowered to a maximum of 80 dB to prevent damage to the inner ear. There is also intense ultraviolet and infrared radiation, which may cause sunburn, making it mandatory that eyes be protected; usually from a no. 9 to no. 12 eye lens is used.

ELECTRIC-ARC SPRAY

The electric-arc spraying process was first invented in 1938, but it was not used commercially in the United States until 1964. This process utilizes two electrical guides through which two wires pass forming an arc as they make contact at the center in front of the gun. The arc formed by the two electrodes as they meet produces sufficient heat to melt the wire. Compressed air sprays the metal onto the workpiece in the form of fine particles of metal (Figs. 30-9 and 30-10). The ends of the wire make and break contact at the rate of 100

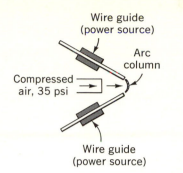

Fig. 30-9. Electric-arc metal spray.

times per second, causing pulsating action that is so fast it seems as if there is one solid stream of filler material. This filler material is then forced by air pressure onto the base metal. The air pressure should be held at a constant 35 psi.

Either a motor generator or a solid-state power source can be used to supply power to the arc spray gun. Both units should be able to supply from 50 to 650 amperes (A). Sometimes the newer solid-state power supply will yield a higher deposit rate. The electric spray gun sprays much faster than other types

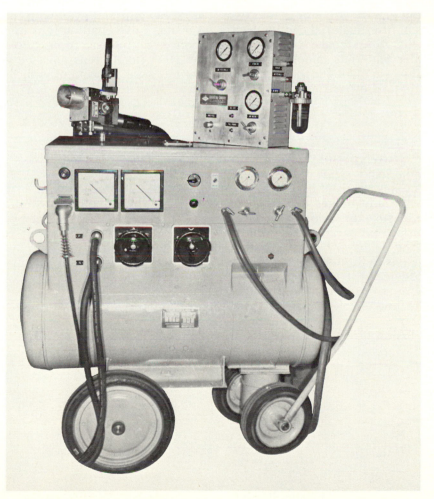

Fig. 30-10. Electric-arc metal spray unit. (*Metallizing Company of America.*)

of spray guns because of the high temperatures created by the arc. Sometimes the travel speed will reach 200 ft/min with deposits of 0.005 to 0.010 in. per pass. The distance from the workpiece to the spray gun should be maintained at approximately 10 to 12 in. This distance will yield the optimum metal deposit.

The cost of operating the electric spray gun is small because electric power is used. At $0.02 per kilowatt, the 360-A unit can be operated for $0.25 per hour, and electricity for a 650-A unit costs only $0.56 per hour. The plasma gun in some cases has an operating cost of $25 per hour, making the electric spray gun much cheaper to operate. Another advantage of the electric-arc gun is that two different types of filler material can be used: one type for the cathode and one for the anode. The filler materials, meeting in the arc zone, produce a homogeneous mixture that is blown onto the base metal. For example, stainless steel wire could be used on one side in one wire guide, and aluminum bronze could be used in the other guide. These materials would then intermingle and be accelerated onto the base metal, resulting in a long-wearing surface with a desirable bearing surface.

The electric-arc spray process is not as hazardous to use as the plasma-arc process, but it has more hazards than either of the oxyacetylene flame spraying processes. The hazards are created because of the high speed at which the work must be done. This high speed increases the fumes, dust, and odors around the work. There is usually a protective shield on the front of the electric-arc spray gun, but even with this shield a no. 4 or no. 5 eye-shading lens must be used. If there is no built-in protective shield, then a no. 10 or no. 12 lens must be used. Noise is not too great a problem with the electric-arc spray process.

QUESTIONS

1. Explain the two types of surface bonding in metal flame spraying.
2. What are the major types of metal-spraying devices?
3. What fuel gases are used in the chemical types of metal flame spraying?
4. What are the advantages of using the electric-arc spray method over using the plasma-arc spray method?
5. Why is surface preparation important?
6. What are the major surface preparation methods?
7. What happens to the wire or powder when it enters the flame of metal-spraying devices?
8. How is wire used for flame spraying stored?
9. What is the function of compressed air in the wire metallizing process, the thermospray process, and the arc process?
10. Why is a fusion process sometimes applied after the spraying process?

Part Six

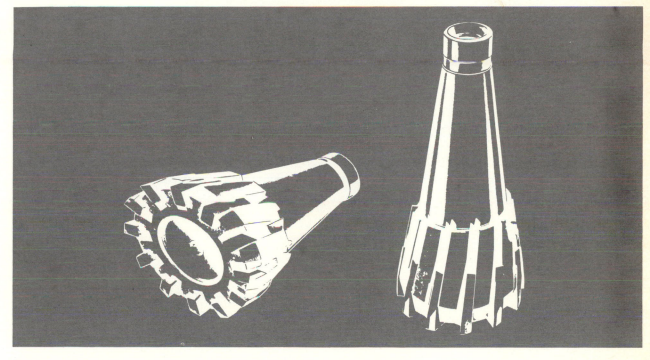

Machine Tools

31

Sawing, Drilling, and Grinding

Although different machine tools perform the operations of sawing, drilling, and grinding, these operations do have a single unifying theory—the cutting action. For example, when a drill press is used, the twist drill has a cutting edge; when a saw is used, the saw blade has cutting edges or teeth; and in grinding, each abrasive grain presents a cutting edge to the metal.

The cutting action is a simple one. Essentially the metal is being forcibly ruptured. In all cutting actions, the metal in a cutting edge first comes in contact with the metal being cut. As a result, the unstressed grains of the metal placed under localized stress rotate away from the stress of the cutting edge. As they continue to rotate, the grains elongate and a weak frontal area is set up by the crystals, allowing them to fracture (Fig. 31-1).

Sawing, drilling, and grinding are different methods of performing this same basic action. Sawing presents more than one tooth during the cutting, but each tooth removes metal the same way. In drilling, two cutting lips of the drill are working simultaneously, removing the metal. In grinding, the many abrasive edges on the grinding wheel are performing the same task as single cutting edges. Each of these three types of cutting can remove large amounts of metal.

SAWING

At the heart of any sawing operation is the blade. The blade is the only part of the metal-cutting saw that comes into contact with the work, and blades that are not in good condition will not yield a good cut even though an expensive machine tool is used to hold the blade. Blades come in three types: regular tooth, hook tooth, and skip tooth (Fig. 31-2). The regular tooth, the type most generally used, presents a straight cutting edge to the work. The hook tooth and the skip tooth are used primarily for softer metals or for deep cuts in thick sections. The hook tooth and the skip tooth are ideal for cutting materials such as aluminum because they have enough clearance between teeth to carry a large metal deposit away from the saw cut.

The set of the hacksaw blade or a band-saw blade is the amount of clearance between the kerf of the saw and the blade thickness (Fig. 31-3a). The reason the saw blades have set in them is to keep the body of the saw blade from rubbing against the kerf, causing heat to develop. Heat would take the temper out of the saw blade or cause the blade to bind in the saw cut. Currently, blades are available in three sets: the raker, the wavy, and the alternate or straight sets

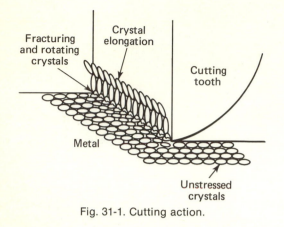

Fig. 31-1. Cutting action.

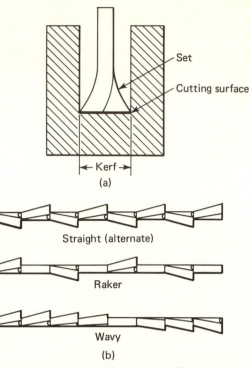

Fig. 31-3. Set types.

(Fig. 31-3*b*). The raker set, the most common, is used for most metal-cutting operations. Most machine saws use raker sets. The teeth are bent so that one tooth is bent to the left, the next tooth is not bent, and the third tooth is bent to the right. This pattern is repeated the full length of the saw blade.

In the wavy set, a group of teeth are bent to the left and then a group of teeth are bent to the right, creating a wavelike appearance to the teeth. Wavy set saws are general-purpose saws, but they usually are employed when cutting structural shapes of low-carbon steel. In the alternate or straight set pattern, one tooth is bent to the left, the next to the right, and the next to the left. This pattern is repeated for the full length of the saw blade. Although the alternate set can be used for cutting nonferrous metals and plastics, it is seldom used in metalworking. It is used most in the meat cutting industry and in woodworking.

Besides the set and the shape of the tooth, a third important factor in blade characteristics is the pitch. The *pitch* of a blade refers to the number of points in 1 in. For example, a blade with a pitch of 5 points would have four teeth within a 1 in. span. The pitch for general use is 18 points. This general-use blade is used for cutting ferrous as well as nonferrous metals. However, different pitches are used for different applications. Although a pitch of 18 is the general-use pitch for all cutting, if heavy, thick sections are to be cut, more tooth clearance is needed

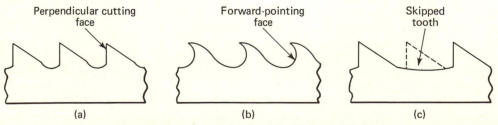

Fig. 31-2. Blade types. (*a*) Regular; (*b*) hook; (*c*) skip.

PITCH	STOCK
14	Cold-rolled steel
	Hot-rolled steel
	Structural steel
	Cast iron
18 (general use)	Aluminum
	Cast iron
	Steel
24	Brass
	Copper
	Sheet metal
	Thin stock
32	Thin-wall tubing
	Sheet metal (16 gage or thinner)

Pitch = 5 points

|← 1 in. →|

Fig. 31-4. Pitch selection.

to carry away cut metal debris. Consequently, many companies order a blade with a pitch of 14 to do standard heavy cutting. Thin materials require a higher number of points per inch. Figure 31-4 lists the recommended pitches to use with different metals.

The two major requirements in blade selection are that two or more teeth be in contact with the material that is being cut and that the teeth have adequate clearance

to carry away the chip that is cut from the workpiece (Fig. 31-5a).

Procedures

The procedures for sawing are the same whether the material is to be cut with a hand hacksaw, a power hacksaw, or a vertical or horizontal band saw. The first step should always be to secure the material to be cut. With power saws, the machine should always be turned on to be sure it is running correctly before the material is secured. In power machines, the blade should move toward the stationary jaw of the holding device. The blade should never move away from the jaw.

Clamping round or square materials into the clamping device offers few problems because these shapes present a common face. However, some structural shapes (such as the channel, plate, or angle) present a problem. Channels and angles should always be turned so that their toes are pointed downward. Plate should always be cut in a horizontal rather than in a vertical position (Fig. 31-5b).

The introduction of the saw to the material should always be done easily whether the saw is a hand-held hacksaw, a power saw, or a band saw. The first touch of the blade to the metal should be done lightly. The full weight of the machine should not be allowed to make the first few cuts in the metal. Always introduce the blade with a light touch, then as the cut starts to progress, more

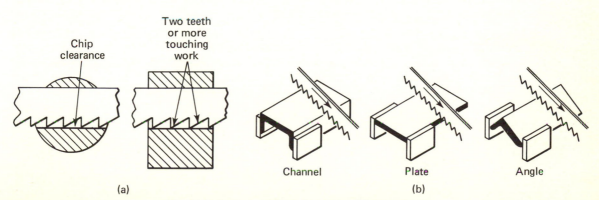

Fig. 31-5. Sawing. (a) Requirements; (b) procedures.

TABLE 31-1. WORK DAMAGE

ERROR	Blade Dullness	Blade Speed	Blade Tension	Feed, Heavy	Feed, Light	Pitch	Saw Guides	Tooth Shape
	CAUSE							
Blade dulls too quickly		X		X				X
Kerf wanders	X		X	X			X	
Rough finish	X	X	X	X		X	X	X
Teeth breaking				X		X		X
Teeth clogging		X				X		X

(a)

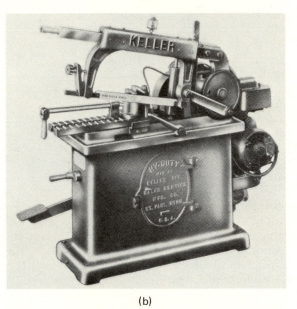

(b)

Fig. 31-6. Hacksaws. (a) Hand (*Stanley Tools*); (b) Power (*Sales Service Manufacturing Company—Keller Division*).

force can be applied to the back of the blade. If the blade in a band saw, for example, is allowed to contact the work metal with the full weight of the band saw behind it, teeth may be broken from the blade, or the blade may be bent or in some other manner destroyed, ruining both the saw blade and the piece being cut. Table 31-1 identifies other causes of work damage.

Equipment

Saws for metalworking are either hacksaws or band saws. Hacksaws have a back and forth motion; band saws travel in a circle in only one direction.

The most common hacksaws are the hand hacksaw and the power hacksaw (Fig. 31-6a and b). All hacksaws are controlled by the length of the stroke, the speed of the stroke, and the amount of pressure applied on the blade during the stroke. These three things are difficult to control when hand hacksawing an object. The most common mistakes when hand hacksawing are applying too much pressure on the blade, taking short fast strokes, and not raising the blade on the return stroke.

It is wise to try to approximate the characteristics of power hacksawing when hand hacksawing. Forty strokes per minute is usually the maximum number of strokes in power hacksaws. A larger number of strokes results in the blade's rubbing instead of taking a good cut. Also, power hacksaws make long, slow, steady strokes under a controlled amount of pressure. Ideally, hand hacksawing should be done in the same manner. The power hacksaw also raises the blade on the rear stroke, lowers the blade, and then takes the power, or the metal removal, stroke. In hand hacksawing these procedures should always be kept in mind. The blades used for hand hacksawing are basically the same as those used in power hacksawing with the exception that power hacksaw blades are thicker and longer. The tooth type as well as the set are identical.

Band saws are available either as vertical saws or as horizontal saws. The saw blades for both types are supported by two wheels to which heavy, hard rubber layers have been cemented. The saw blade travels on this tire. This tire accomplishes two things. First, the tire is convex so that the saw blade rides at its highest point, which is the center of the tire; and the layer of rubber protects the saw blade teeth. The blade in both the vertical and horizontal band saws is always placed so that the cutting edge travels toward the drive wheel or the stationary part of the vice of the saw. While both the vertical and horizontal band saws can be equipped with wet cutting coolant, usually only the horizontal machine has a coolant pumping system that pumps a coolant to remove metal-cutting debris and to maintain an even, cool temperature in the workpiece. The vertical band saw, also called the contour band saw, often has a dry cutting attachment, an attachment that forces air into the cutting zone, clearing the chips from the zone and cooling the work slightly (Fig. 31-7).

All band-saw sizes are determined by the thickness of the metal that they can cut. For example, the maximum thickness of a vertical band saw may be 16 in. with a capacity of handling a piece that is 12 in. wide. The machine would be classified as a 16-in. band saw because this is the thickest piece of metal that can be placed through the cutting opening. Many band saws have built-in speed controls to vary the speed of the saw blade passing the work. Those machines that do have built-in variable-control band-saw speeds usually have mounted on them a chart that identifies the metal to be cut, the ideal cutting speed of the saw blade, and the simple adjustments and rheostat settings that can be used.

Band saw blade material comes in 100-, 200-, or 500-ft rolls. The formula to follow for measuring the blades for length is half the diameter of the bottom drive wheel, plus half the diameter of the top drive wheel, plus twice the distance between the centers of the drive wheels. It is general manufacturing practice to make both drive wheels the same size so a simplified formula for determining band-saw blade length is:

$$l = 2x + \pi D$$

where l = band-saw length
x = distance between the centers of the drive wheels
D = diameter of the drive wheel

As an option on most vertical band saws, a welder is available. These welders have alignment guides plus a separate grinder for preparing the blades. The blades are prepared so that they can be butted together and placed in the welder attachment to be flash welded. After they have been flash welded, the excess metal is ground from the sides and the back of the plate until the blade can be passed through a built-in sizing mechanism and then annealed. The flash welder usually has an annealing cycle built within the unit so that the band-saw blades can be welded and annealed right on the band-saw machine.

DRILLING

Drilling machines may be simple hand-held portable drill motors or complex numerically controlled turret drills capable of performing many operations. All of these machines have one thing in common: They are designed only to support the drill. The drill does all of the cutting action; the machine is only for the control of the drill. The accuracy of the drill or cutting edges determines the basic accuracy of the machine.

The two-fluted drill, the most-used drill, is responsible for about 85 percent of all drilling (Fig. 31-8). The main parts of this twist drill are its two cutting lips, or edges, and the dead center, the end of the web of the drill. The dead center is available either with a chisel point or a spiral point. The chisel point, or dead center-type, drill is currently the most popular. All twist drills have cutting

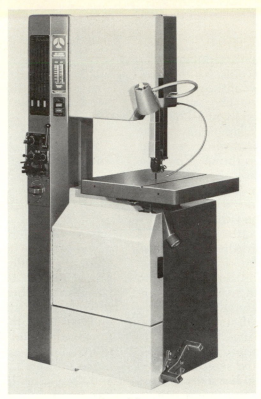

(a)

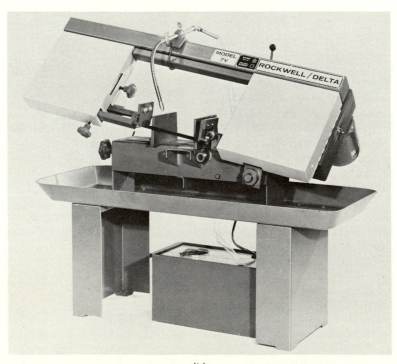

(b)

Fig. 31-7. Band saws. (a) Vertical; (b) horizontal. (*Rockwell International—Power Tool Division.*)

lips supported by the dead center. The dead center has two or more margins. Their function is to provide body clearance for the drill so that only a small amount of friction and heat is created. If the whole body of the drill were to rub against the sidewall of the drilled hole, the drill would bind and ruin the work, the drill, and possibly even the drilling machine.

When drills are reground, the web needs to be checked; for as the web travels toward the shank of the drill or the far end of the drill, it thickens, increasing the dead center area. The dead center of a drill does no cutting and provides only friction.

The major styles of drill shanks used in metalworking are the straight shank, used with the standard Jacobs chucking devices, and the tapered shanks. Tapered shanks usually have Morse or Jarno tapers. The Morse taper is approximately ⅝ in./ft and the Jarno taper is 0.60 in./ft. The sizes of tapers are designated by number. For example, a no. 2 Morse taper is larger than a no. 1, and a no. 3 Morse taper is larger than a no. 2. The same system is also true of Jarno tapers.

Drill Sizes

Twist drills are available according to three separate classifications: letter, number, and decimal. Letter and number drills are small drills and are available in sets. Decimal drills are also available in sets. The standard letter drill set has 26 drills ranging from A to Z, where an A drill has a 0.234-in. diameter and a Z drill has a 0.413-in. diameter. The number drill standard set ranges from no. 1, which has a 0.2280-in. diameter, slightly smaller than an A drill, to a no. 60 drill, which has a 0.040-in. diameter. The secondary number set ranges from a no. 61 to a no. 80 drill, which has a 0.0135-in. diameter. While drills are available in both letter and number classifications, they are also available in decimal equivalent. Twist drills also are available in a fractional set. The basic fractional set begins with a $\frac{1}{16}$-in.-diameter drill and proceeds by sixteenths up to a ½-in. drill. Drills can also be purchased individually in deci-

mal sizes. A drill is measured accurately by a micrometer caliper, measuring from margin to margin.

When twist drills are ordered, three things must be identified:

1. What kind of steel it will be made of, whether carbon or high speed
2. The shape of the shank of the drill, either straight or one of the taper types depending on the type of equipment
3. The diameter of the drill

Given these three things, any drill manufacturer could send a standard two-fluted twist drill. If any other type of drill is desired, the type must be stated. For example, if a deep-hole drill or an oil-hole drill is desired, more information would be needed to order one, and certainly the type of drill would have to be specified.

Drill Clearance Angles

Three angles ground into the cutting face of a drill are: the dead center angle, the lip angle, and the rake angle (Fig. 31-8). The general-

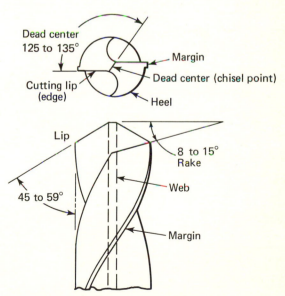

Fig. 31-8. Drill clearance angle. (*Note:* General purpose—125° dead center, 59° lip angle, 12° rake.)

purpose two-fluted drill angles, unless otherwise specified from the factory, have a 125° dead center angle, a 59 or 118° lip angle, and a 12° rake angle, or clearance angle. These angles are considered standard.

Drill clearance angles differ according to the type of material being drilled. For example, if wood, plastic, or other soft materials are cut, a sharper point with a higher clearance is necessary. If harder than normal metals are cut, a blunter clearance angle is needed. These clearance angles are ground into the twist drill in three ways: by hand with a pedestal grinder, with a special drill grinding attachment on the pedestal grinder, or by a special drill grinder.

Cutting Speed

The revolutions per minute (r/min) of a drill and the recommended cutting speed for the material being cut are factors used in determining the cutting speed of a drill. Table 31-2 identifies cutting speeds of selected metals. A cutting speed of 100 ft/min has generally been accepted as a standard speed for all materials. The basic procedure for determining drill r/min is to identify the cutting speed of the material to be cut and to multiply it by 12 in. The result is the cutting speed in feet per minute. This figure is divided by the circumference of the drill in inches. The circumference, of course, is π times the diameter. Therefore,

$$r/min = \frac{CS \times 12}{\pi \times D}$$

where CS = cutting speed
  D = diameter of drill

TABLE 31-2. CUTTING SPEED OF SELECTED METALS

METAL	ft/min
Aluminum	200
Brass	200
Cast iron	80
Cast steel	40
Machine steel	100
Tool steel	60

For example, if machine steel were chosen and a ½-in.-diameter hole were indicated by the blueprints, the first step would be to refer to a table of cutting speeds (Table 31-2) and find that the cutting speed of machine steel is 100 ft/min. Then,

$$r/min = \frac{100 \times 4}{\frac{1}{2}}$$
$$= 100 \times 4 \times 2$$
$$= 800$$

Drill presses are adjusted in two ways: by a variable speed control attached in conjunction with the tachometer to the drill spindle, or by the more common method of a cone pulley arrangement. When the belt is changed in a pulley-controlled speed device on a drill press, the smaller pulley on the spindle side always runs faster than the larger pulleys on the spindle side (Fig. 31-9). The major parts of the drill press, besides the cone pulleys, the spindle, and the electric motor, include the base, column, table, switch, and the feed handle (Fig. 31-10).

Drill Press Types

The most-used types of drill presses are the bench drill press, the floor drill press, and the regular or sensitive-feed press. The sensitive-feed drill press is one that allows the operator to "feel" the drill cutting into the workpiece. The regular drill press transmits the force from the feed

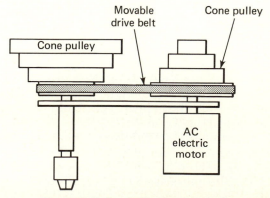

Fig. 31-9. Drill spindle speed control.

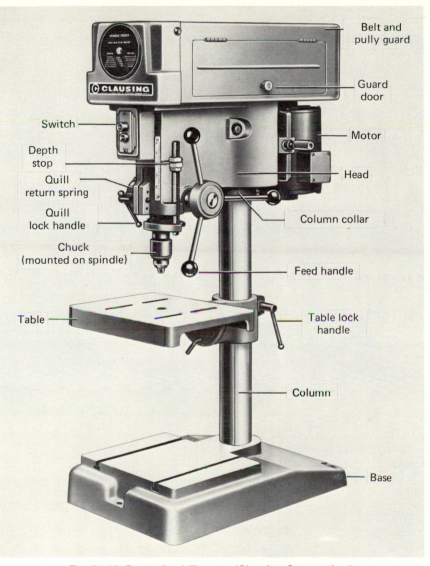

Fig. 31-10. Parts of a drill press. (*Clausing Corporation.*)

handle to the spindle by means of a set of gears. Other types of drill presses are ganged drill presses, a number of drill presses mounted on one table; the multiple drill press, a number of spindles mounted in one machine; the radial arm drill press, similar to the radial arm saw in flexibility of operation; and the turret drill press, like a multiple-head drill press but capable of performing only one operation at a time. The multiple drill press can perform more than one drilling operation at the same time (Fig. 31-11).

The drill press is well suited to numerical control devices for many of its drilling functions. Such functions as countersinking, boring, reaming, spot-facing, and counterboring can be accomplished without further attachments to the drilling machine (Fig. 31-12). Countersinks are used for recessing screw heads and bolt heads, and for

(a)

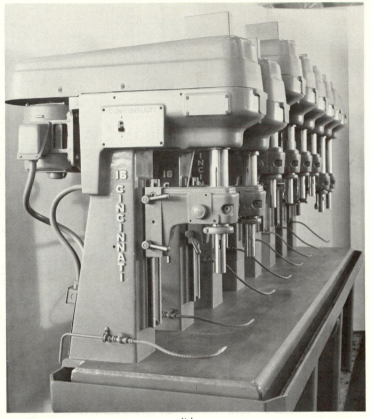

(b)

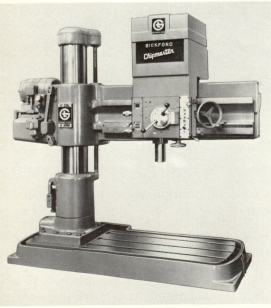

(c)

Fig. 31-11. Drill press types. (a) Bench (*Clausing Corporation*); (b) ganged (*Cincinnati Lathe and Tool*); (c) radial (*Giddings and Lewis—Bickford Machine Company*).

deburring holes. They are available in 60, 82, 90, 100, 110, and 120° angle sizes.

Reaming produces a smooth finish in a hole and it is also used to true holes for roundness. Reamers have a series of parallel cutting blades and are used as a second operation after drilling. Reamers should always be rotated against the cutting faces and never rotated in a direction opposite to the cutting face. Although reamers are available in a number of different shapes and sizes, all reamers perform the same operation. Often, reaming is done in the drill press setup with the reamer rotated by hand.

Spot-facing is a means of supplying a shoulder or a bearing surface for the head of a

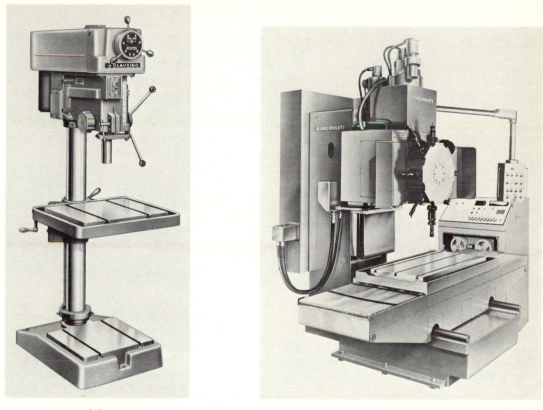

(d)   (e)

Fig. 31-11 (*cont.*). (*d*) Floor (*Clausing Corporation*), (*e*) turret (*Cincinnati Lathe and Tool*).

bolt. Spot-facing is accomplished with a device that cuts at a 90° angle to the side of the drilled hole. Incorporated within the spot-facing device, which fits into the drill chuck, is a pilot. This pilot helps to align the cutting edge of the spot-facer to the predrilled hole.

Boring is another drilling function that can be accomplished without the use of any attachments except for the boring bar itself. The boring bar uses a single-point tool, such as a lathe tool, to perform the cutting action. Boring trues the drilled hole, but it generally

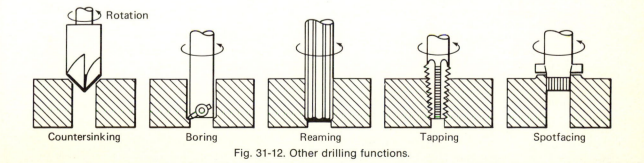

Countersinking   Boring   Reaming   Tapping   Spotfacing
Fig. 31-12. Other drilling functions.

is not considered a major function of the drilling machine.

Tapping requires an attachment that is placed on the drill chuck and the spindles of the drilling machine. The tapping attachment is basically a gear reduction mechanism that lowers the revolutions of the spindle so that the tap can be used. Tapping speed is important because if the speed is too fast, threads will be rolled out of the tapped hole. Drill presses with automatic feed must have the feed controlled to such a point that the tapping action will stop and reverse. The tap must be fed out of the hole as well as fed in. Generally, the feed on drill presses that have feed mechanisms is too slow for use with tapping attachments. Standard drill feeds are determined by the revolution of the drill spindle, and generally range from 0.001 in. of travel per revolution for small drills to 0.025 in. for large drills, such as a 1½-in. drill. These speed rates are far too slow for tapping. Many drills with tapping mechanisms built into them have an accelerated feed-rate mechanism enabling control of the feed rate over a larger range of speed.

Holding Devices

Because the drill rotates at a high r/min, a holding device should always be used. The basic types of holding devices are: the step block, the vise, the V block, and the angle plate (Fig. 31-13). The basic step block uses a slotted drill table in which a T bolt is inserted. The step block holds a strap to the workpiece which in turn puts pressure on the workpiece and holds the face of the workpiece parallel to and against the worktable.

Drill vises are very popular, but they are items that are easily misused. When work is clamped into a drill vise that previously has been clamped onto the drill table, parallels should always be used. The *parallel* is made up of hardened ground pieces of metal whose sides are parallel. They are used in sets of two or more. A workpiece is clamped correctly into the vise by placing the workpiece on parallels and then clamping it into the vice. Correct clamping can be tested by checking to see if the parallels can be moved after the workpiece has been tightened into the vise. They should not be movable. The parallels protect the vise by not allowing the hole to be drilled in the way of the drill vise.

The V block is another popular method of clamping work on a drill table. The blocks demand a drill table that has slotted ways for T bolts. T bolts are inserted into the ways; the V block is placed in the appropriate location; the work, usually round or irregular parts, is placed in the V and a strap then holds the part to the V block, which is, in turn, held to the surface of the drill table.

Coolant

As with all machine tool cutting, a cutting fluid should be provided for both cooling and lubricating the workpiece and the tool. A liquid coolant is the most effective in controlling the heat at the cutting edge—heat which is transmitted to the workpiece and to the body of the drill. Good characteristics of cooling fluids are that they reduce cutting friction while improving the cutting action, wash away all of the chips that are formed, and cool both the workpiece and the tool. Table 31-3 identifies cutting fluids for selected metals.

TABLE 31-3. CUTTING FLUID FOR SELECTED METALS

METAL	FLUID
Aluminum	Kerosene
	Kerosene/lard oil
	Soluble oil
Copper base	Dry
	Kerosene
	Lard oil
	Mineral oil
Iron, cast	Dry
	Soluble oil
Iron, malleable	Dry
	Soda water
Steel	Lard oil
	Mineral oil
	Soluble oil
	Sulfurized oil

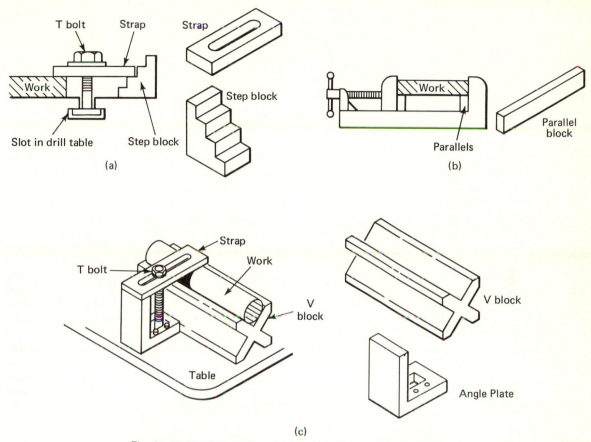

Fig. 31-13. Holding devices. (a) Step block; (b) vise; (c) V block.

GRINDING

Grinding is a process of cutting a material with a multipoint cutting tool composed of abrasive particles bound together, such as those found on the grinding wheel. The abrasive grains are extremely hard and irregularly shaped so that each grain makes up one or more cutting edge. Since the grinding wheel is composed of many such small cutting edges, it can make very fine cuts (Fig. 31-14). Also close tolerances can be obtained by abrasive grinding. Tolerances range within 0.0005 to 0.0001 in. These close tolerances enable the grinding wheel to do both the sizing, or rough cutting, and the finish cutting operations.

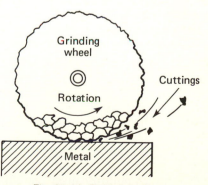

Fig. 31-14. Cutting action.

Abrasives

For a material to be classified as an abrasive, it must be hard material that can cut or abrade other materials. There are two types of abrasives: natural and synthetic or artificial. The natural abrasives are not as uniform nor do they have a wear quality that is as even as the artificial abrasives. Artificial abrasives are manufactured.

NATURAL ABRASIVES. The most common natural abrasives are emory, corundum, quartz sand, and diamonds. Emory and corundum are made with large amounts of crystalline variation. As a consequence of this lack of uniformity, corundum and emory do not make good grinding wheel materials. Quartz, with a Mohs' hardness rating of 7, is used in the abrasive industry for abrasive coatings (such as on sand paper), but it is not used for grinding wheels.

Diamonds that are used as abrasives are off-colored and not suited for use as gemstones and jewelry. They are crushed into small particles and are bound together to form grinding wheels. This type of grinding wheel is used to sharpen carbide and ceramic tools. The diamond is the hardest of all natural materials, 8,200 on the Knoop hardness scale, with a Mohs' rating of 10, the maximum possible.

ARTIFICIAL ABRASIVES. The first artificial abrasive fabricated was silicon carbide. Silicon carbide is made by fusing coke and sand in extremely high temperatures. The resultant crystal rates next to the diamond in hardness, with a rating of 9.5 on the Mohs' scale.

Aluminum oxide is another artificial abrasive developed a few years after silicon carbide was fabricated. It is formed by fusing bauxite, iron filings, and coke. Aluminum oxide crystals are not as hard as silicon carbide crystals, but they are tougher, making aluminum oxide a more general-purpose abrasive.

Recently, ceramic material abrasives have been replacing both aluminum oxide and corundum. A ceramic abrasive wheel has 300 percent more life than aluminum oxide or corundum counterparts. For example, it is possible for a ceramic grinding wheel to remove 154 lb of stainless steel with only a 2-lb loss of abrasive material; while a conventional wheel can remove only 45 lb of stainless steel before the wheel is worn out.

Material Hardness

In the abrasive industry, the Mohs' scale has been used for many years to determine the degree of hardness of abrasive particles. The basis for the Mohs' scale is that a no. 2 scale item will scratch a no. 1 item but not a no. 3 item, and so on up the scale to no. 10. However, this scale is not a very accurate method of testing hardness; consequently Knoop's scale was devised. The Knoop tester pushes a diamond penetrating point into the material. The amount of force required to penetrate the material is then recorded. The Knoop scale runs from 0 to 10,000. The diamond on the Mohs' scale rates 10; the Knoop rating is 8200. The Knoop scale is also a scale that more correctly defines the distance between the metals. For example, on Table 31-4 notice in particular the distance between the scales in ranking corundum and the diamond.

Grain Size

Abrasive grains are divided into U.S. standard sieve sizes. The size of the abrasive particles is designated by the number which corresponds to the number of meshes or sieves that the particles pass through. The commercial standard grain sizes for abrasives are broken down into classes. The standard grains that fit through screens 6 to 24 are designated as coarse. Grains that fit through sieves 30 through 60 are rated as medium, and grains that fit through sieves 70 to 230 are fine (Table 31-5). The size of the abrasives bonded to the grinding wheel controls the surface finish of the piece being cut. The grain size also determines the amount of metal removed per revolution. Small grains are capable of carrying away only small amounts of metal per revolution; while large or coarse grains can carry away a great deal of metal per revolution of the grinding wheel.

TABLE 31-4. KNOOP AND MOHS' HARDNESS SCALES COMPARED

MATERIAL	KNOOP	MOHS'
Talc	12.3	1
Gypsum	61	2
Calcite	141	3
Fluorite	181	4
Apatite	483	5
Feldspar-orthoclase	621	6
Quartz	788	7
Topaz	1,190	8
Corundum	2,200	9
Diamond	8,200	10

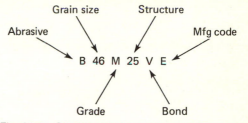

Fig. 31-15. Sample markings on a grinding tool.

Abrasive Bonds

A grinding wheel or any abrasive tool is formed by using some type of bonding material to hold the grains together in the desired shape. The bond material holds the grains in shape, allows them to flow freely, and also allows the grinding wheel to be flexible. The type of bond used determines the amount of force needed to dislodge the abrasive particles from the wheel. The rate at which the abrasive particles are dislodged determines the grinding life of the wheel. The major types of abrasive bonds used are: vitrified, sodium silicate, shellac, rubber, and glass fiber.

Vitrified bonds, the most commonly used bonds, are made of clays and other natural ingredients. The abrasive particles are coated with wet clays and then formed into a wheel. After the grinding wheel has been formed, it is placed in a kiln and fired. The vitrified wheels are unaffected by oil, water, and temperature. They have operating speeds that range from between 5,500 and 6,500 surface ft/min.

In order to identify bonds and the grade of the bond, the abrasive industry uses letters of the alphabet to represent the hardness and softness of the bonding material. A soft bonding material is one that releases its abrasive grains from the wheel readily. The letter designations are E through G for very soft, H through K for soft, L through O for medium, P through S for hard, and T through Z for very hard. A very hard bonding agent is one that does not give up its abrasive particles easily.

A method has been devised by manufacturers of abrasives (and accepted by the Grinding Wheel Manufacturers Association) so that important characteristics can be determined by the markings on the grinding tool itself. There are six characteristics to be identified: the abrasive, the grain size, the grain grade, the structure, the bond, and the manufacturer's special coding. In Fig. 31-15 one such set of identifications is given: B designates the type of abrasive; 46 represents the grain size; M represents the grade; 25 represents the structure; V designates the type of bonding material; and finally, the E is a special letter code of the manufacturer.

TABLE 31-5. GRAIN SIZE CATEGORIES

COARSE	MEDIUM	FINE	FLOUR
6	30	70	240
24	60	230	600

GRINDING MACHINES

A basic type of grinding machines is the bench or pedestal grinder. It has a grinding wheel and a tool rest, and the work is hand-

Fig. 31-16. Bench grinder. (*Powermatic.*)

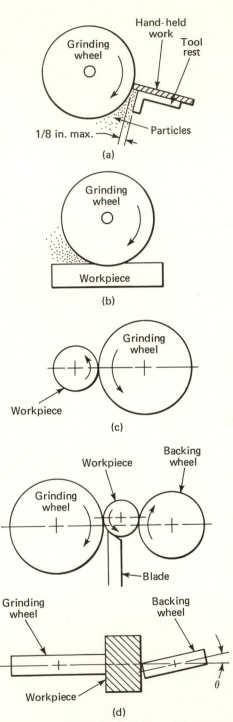

Fig. 31-17. Types of machine grinders. (*a*) Grinder; (*b*) surface grinder; (*c*) cylindrical grinder; (*d*) centerless grinder.

held (Fig. 31-16). With this grinder it is important to allow only ⅛ in. maximum between the inside edge of the tool rest and the grinding wheel. A great deal of skill is necessary for efficient operation of this machine, and its use requires much practice (Fig. 31-17*a*).

A second type of grinding machine is a surface grinder (Fig. 31-17*b*). Surface grinders have a machine table to which the work is fastened so that the work is passed under the rotating grinding wheel. The surface grinder can produce accuracy up to 0.000001 in. when correct procedures are used. Not all surface grinders achieve this high degree of accuracy. Basic surface grinders have automatic features that control not only the traversing back and forth of the worktable but also the feed of the grinding wheel in specific thousandths of an inch per stroke of the worktable. Surface grinders come in two basic styles: a vertical surface grinder and a horizontal surface grinder. The only difference between these machines is the direction in which the grinding wheel runs, either vertically or horizontally. The vertical and horizontal classifications, then, refer to the position of the spindle to the worktable (Fig. 31-18).

The cylindrical grinder has the workpiece mounted between centers and rotates it in the opposite direction to the grinding wheel (Figs. 31-17*c* and 31-19). The cylindrical grinder can perform two basic types of grinding actions: traverse grinding and

Fig. 31-18. Horizontal surface grinder. (*Clausing Company.*)

plunge grinding. In traverse grinding, the grinding wheel makes one cut completely across the workpiece; in plunge grinding, the wheel grinds continuously in one position on the workpiece but does not move or traverse the workpiece. In plunge grinding, the workpiece is fed into the grinding wheel. The workpiece is mounted on a machine table that goes in the x, y, and z directions, and its movement is controlled by automatic feeds. The grinding wheel is mounted on a stationary spindle. On a universal cylindrical grinder, both the grinding wheel and the worktable can be rotated, a characteristic which can generate various combinations of compound angles.

Centerless grinding is an adaptation of cylindrical grinding. The workpiece centers are removed and are replaced by a backing or regulating wheel and a support blade (Fig.

31-17d). The grinding wheel rotates clockwise while the workpiece rotates counterclockwise. The workpiece is reinforced by the backing wheel, which is also rotating in a clockwise direction. This combination makes it possible to grind work without the benefit of a center; consequently it is called centerless grinding. The function of the blade is to support the work during the operation. The center of the workpiece is always above the centerline of the grinding wheel and the backing wheel. The work support blade is always positioned to ensure this height differential (Fig. 31-20). The work is fed between the grinding wheel and the backing wheel by placing a forward-pointing angle on the backing or regulating wheel. Any amount of forward rotation of this wheel results in the work's moving in the direction that the wheel is pointing (Figs. 31-17d and 31-20b).

TRUING

Grinding wheels are trued, or dressed, by three separate types of mechanisms. One is a mechanical wheel dresser which is composed of a series of hand-held metal disks. Another is a diamond-pointed dresser, and the third is a diamond-impregnated grinding stick. Grinding wheels should always be trued and dressed. *Truing* refers to correcting any out-of-round conditions of the revolving wheel. *Dressing* refers to forming, smoothing, and cleaning the grinding wheel. These two operations should be done each time a wheel is put on a spindle, or any time the grinding wheel becomes dull, glazed, or loaded with metal.

The basic procedure used with hand-held devices (such as the grinding stick or the mechanical wheel dresser) is to rest them against the tool rest and move them back and forth across the full face of the grinding wheel. Diamond-pointed grinders, on the other hand, should not be hand-held but should be placed in a truing fixture so that the machine's movements are used to true and dress the grinding wheel correctly.

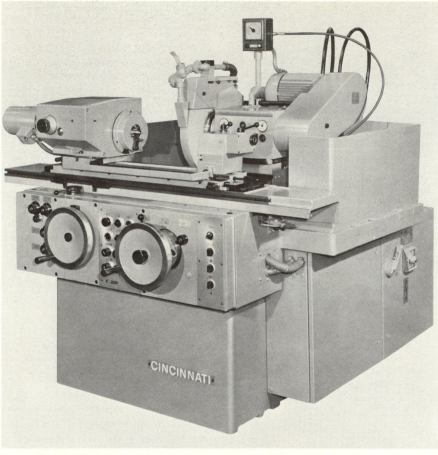

Fig. 31-19. Cylindrical grinding machine. (*Cincinnati Milacron Company.*)

Usually a special fixture fits on the worktable of the grinding machine that can be manipulated by the adjusting handwheels. When a diamond-point grinder attachment is being used, care should always be taken not to take too large a cut at one time. A good cut with a diamond-point tool should be only 0.001 or 0.002 in. (Fig. 31-21).

QUESTIONS

1. Explain the cutting action of sawing, grinding, and drilling.
2. What are the major types of blades for saws?
3. What is kerf?
4. Explain the difference between raker, straight, and wave set.
5. What is pitch and what is its significance?
6. What major reasons cause the kerf to wander?
7. What are the two major classifications of saws?
8. What is the formula for figuring band-saw length?

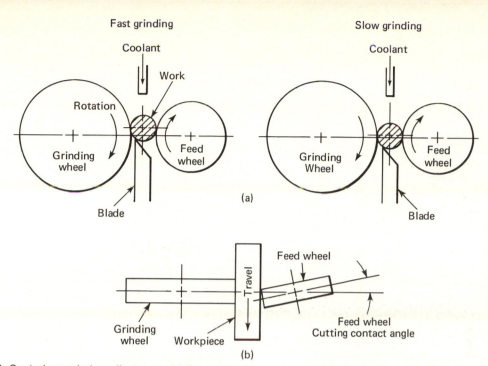

Fast grinding

Slow grinding

(a)

(b)

Fig. 31-20. Centerless grinder adjustment. (a) Blade adjustment—side view (*note:* the workpiece is held above the centerline for fast grinding and slightly to the side of the centerline for slow grinding); (b) regulating, or feed, wheel adjustment—top view (*note:* the cutting contact angle is 5 to 6° for rough grinding a workpiece and 5′ to 2° for finish grinding; roughing metal removal 0.005 to 0.008 in., finishing metal removal 0.0015 to 0.003 in.).

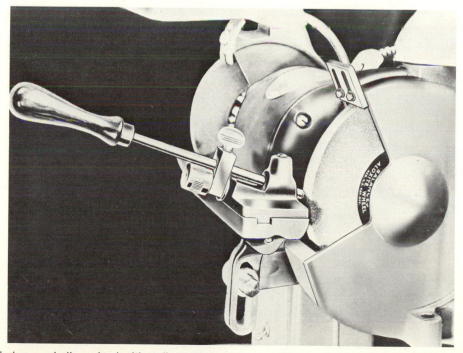

Fig. 31-21. Truing a grinding wheel with a diamond-point dresser. (*Rockwell International—Power Tool Division.*)

9. What are the major styles of drill shanks?
10. What is the function of a margin in a two-fluted drill?
11. What are the two major types of tapers used in tapering shapes?
12. What are the three major classifications of drill size?
13. What is the general-purpose lip angle for a two-fluted twist drill?
14. What is the cutting speed for machine steel?
15. Determine the r/min for machine steel with a ¾-in.-diameter drill.
16. Identify five different drill press types.
17. What is the difference between countersinking and counterboring?
18. What is the difference between reaming and boring?
19. What basic holding devices are used for securing work on the drill press table?
20. What cutting fluid should be used when drilling cast iron?
21. Why is a grinding wheel thought to be a multiple cutting tool?
22. Explain the difference between the Knoop and the Mohs' hardness scales.
23. What is the range of sieve sizes that designate abrasives with medium-grain size?
24. What are the major types of machine grinders?
25. Explain how a centerless grinder can grind stock.
26. How are grinding wheels dressed?

32

The Lathe

The engine lathe originally was designed to cut threads and to do cylindrical turning. Although these functions are still major operations performed by the lathe, it has become more versatile in performing other operations, such as boring, drilling, and faceplate turning (Fig. 32-1).

PARTS OF THE LATHE

The parts of a lathe are classified into three categories: the motor to rotate the work, the devices to hold the work, and the devices to control the cutting. All of these parts are held in close alignment by the lathe bed, also known as *the ways*. The ways of the lathe are made of steel that has been heat treated and has been honed and ground to a close accuracy. The flatness, or parallelism, of the lathe ways determines the accuracy of the cutting performed by the lathe. If the ways have been twisted or otherwise knocked out of alignment, the accuracy of the lathe will suffer. The headstock, the cross slide, and the tailstock are fitted to the ways of the lathe bed.

The *headstock* contains the driving apparatus that rotates the work. The *tailstock* supports the work at the other end of the

lathe, and the *cross slide* provides a platform on which to mount the cutting tool (Fig. 32-2). These three parts and the lathe bed are used to identify the size of a lathe. The size of the lathe is determined by the swing of the largest item, or how large an item can be rotated by the headstock with a small amount of clearance between the lathe bed and the work. A second measurement for identifying the size of a lathe is the length of the ways. Two other sizes given to identify lathes, although the amount of swing and the length of the ways are the primary measurements used, are the maximum length between the headstock center and the tailstock center, and the maximum swing when the cross slide is pulled up to the headstock. Actually, this action cuts down the true maximum swing since the cross slide raises above the lathe ways (Fig. 32-2).

The headstock contains the driving mechanisms. One is the cone pulley, located in the headstock, with a drive motor located in the cabinet beneath the headstock. The other is a gear head lathe. The gear head lathe also has a motor incorporated in the cabinet below the headstock, but it also has a system of gears that transmits the necessary turning to the head stock spindle. The total function of either type of drive mechanism is to control the spindle speed, or r/min, of the

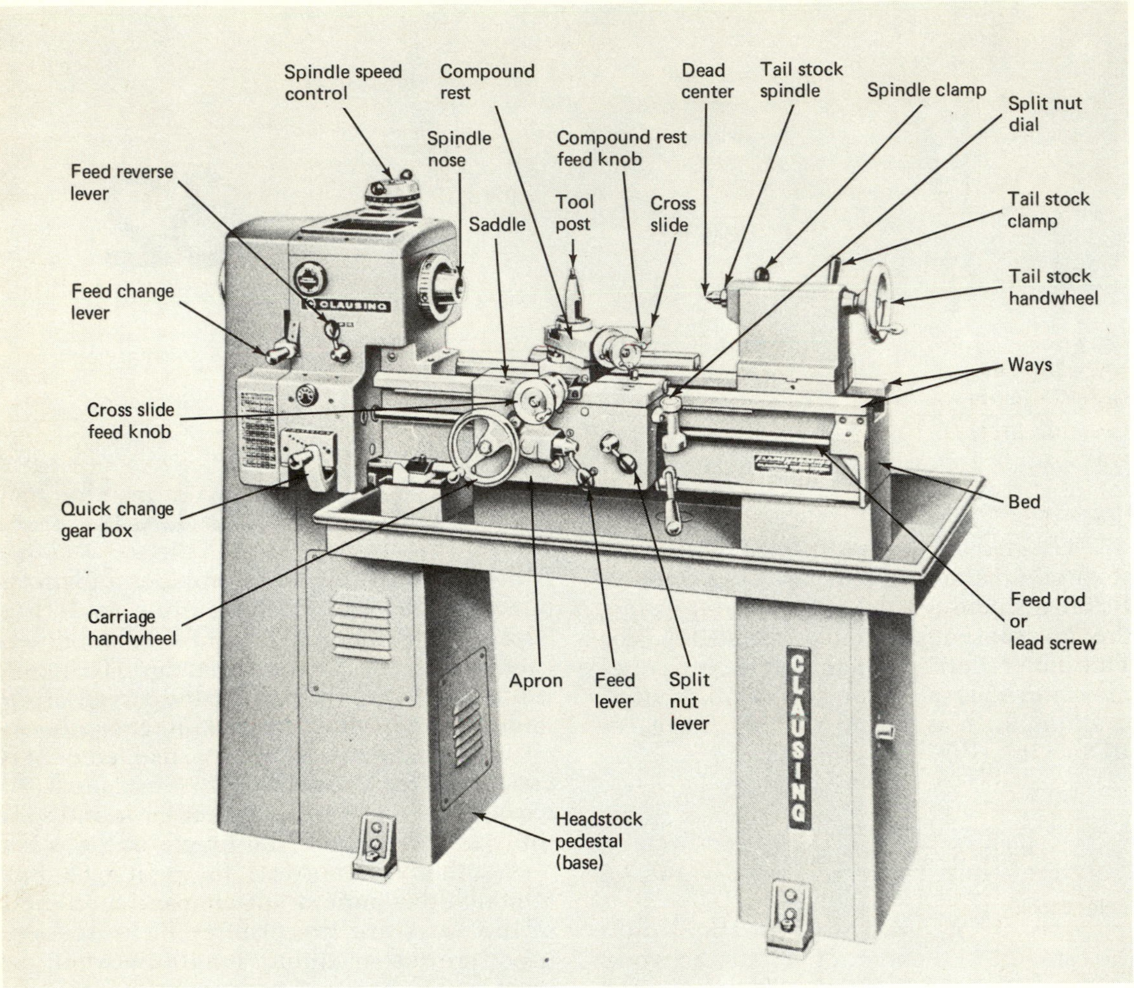

Fig. 32-1. The engine lathe. (*Clausing Corporation.*)

headstock. All work-holding devices are attached to the headstock spindle.

The most common types of connectors for attaching work-holding devices to the headstock spindle are: a threaded headstock spindle, a cam lock headstock spindle, and a long key headstock spindle (Fig. 32-3). Headstock spindles also have a hole going through their centers in which the live center is placed. This hole makes it possible to remove the live center easily with a knockout bar or to provide a passage for the work through the headstock into the cutting area (Fig. 32-4).

The function of the tailstock is to hold various tools either to support the work or to machine the work. The work is supported basically by the use of a dead center (known by that name because it does not rotate). A live center is also available. It is a ball-bearing center that allows the body of the center to fit into the tailstock and allows the center to rotate while the body remains stationary. Live centers are more costly than dead centers. The tailstock also holds drilling chucks so that the work can rotate while the drill remains stationary, holds reamers, and holds

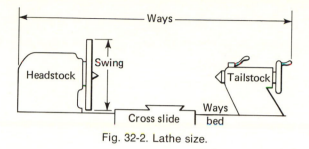

Fig. 32-2. Lathe size.

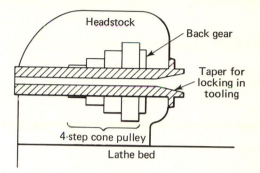

Fig. 32-4. Headstock spindle hole.

taps or dies for threading. The tailstock is fastened to the ways of the lathe by a clamping bolt. This clamping bolt makes it possible for the tailstock to be moved up or down the ways of the bed to accommodate various lengths of work between the headstock and the tailstock.

The lathe carriage, between the headstock and the tailstock, rests on the lathe bed. Its only function is to control the rigidity and the direction of the cutting tool movement. The lathe carriage has a compound rest

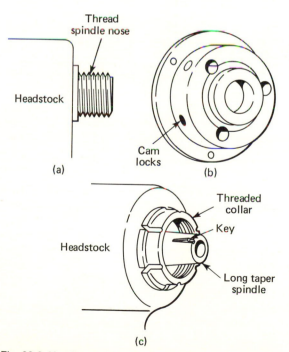

Fig. 32-3. Headstock spindle connections. (a) Threaded; (b) cam lock; (c) long taper key. (*South Bend Lathe.*)

mounted to the tool post. The basic controls located on the compound rest include the feed knob and the compound rest knob. The compound feed knob moves the compound rest across the saddle, and the compound rest knob moves only the tool post on the compound rest (Fig. 32-5).

Also located on the top of the carriage is a carriage lock. When this nut is tightened down, the total carriage is locked into one position on the lathe bed. The other operating mechanisms are the automatic feed friction clutch, which is used for general turning; the half-nut lever, which is used only for chasing threads; and the feed-change lever. The feed-change lever transmits power from the apron handwheel and reroutes it into the cross-feed knob, making it possible for the half-nut lever to control the lathe in two directions, either parallel to or perpendicular to the lathe bed.

LATHE TYPES

While lathes have become more complicated and their functions more complex, all lathes have headstocks, ways, tailstocks, and tool-holding and controlling apparatus located on some type of carriage. These basic parts are essential for the cutting operation of a lathe. Some lathes used most include the tool run lathe, the tracer lathe, the numerical control (N/C) lathe, and the turret lathe.

Lathes also are classified according to the operation they perform in the production

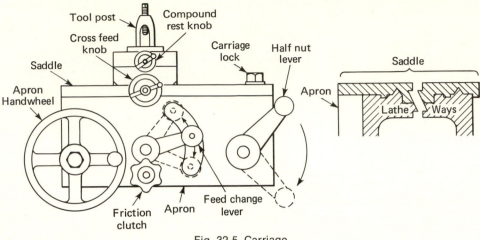

Fig. 32-5. Carriage.

line, such as a first-operation lathe, a second-operation lathe, or a third-operation lathe. The operation number refers to the number of times the part has been machined. For example, a second-operation lathe performs the second machine tool operation on a part in a production line series of possibly 100 operations. The part, having already gone through one machining sequence, has been transferred to a second-operation lathe that has been set up for one particular cut or series of cuts. At the end of the operation performed by the second-operation lathe, the part may go to another machine tool for further operations.

CUTTING TOOL

The cutting tool is the most important part of the whole lathe. The cutting tool determines the accuracy and the smoothness of the cut. It does all the work of the lathe. Whenever possible, the cutting tool should be used to cut in the direction of the headstock because the headstock is stationary and securely fastened to the ways, while the tailstock is movable and may slip, ruining the work. The primary method for the cutting action to take place is to rotate the work onto the cutting tool; the

cutting tool then travels at a controlled rate toward the headstock, creating the cut. Figure 32-6 illustrates a typical setup where the work is swung between centers.

The cutting action of the lathe tool can generate three types of chips depending on the material being cut, the speed of the cut, and the condition of the cutting tool. The three types are: the continuous chip, the continuous chip with built-up edge, and the discontinuous chip (Fig. 32-7).

Usually aluminum and free-machining steel form continuous chips. The *continuous chip* is a continuous rolled ribbon of metal (Fig. 32-7*a*). The continuous chip can be

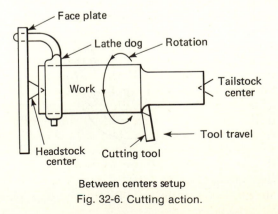

Between centers setup
Fig. 32-6. Cutting action.

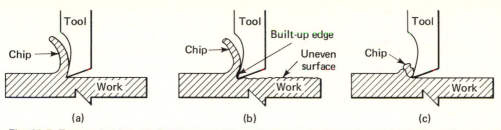

Fig. 32-7. Types of chips. (a) Continuous; (b) continuous with built-up edge; (c) discontinuous.

formed because the metal becomes heated as the tool cuts through it and as a result the metal work hardens. Consequently, only those metals that work harden are capable of creating a continuous chip. The work-hardened area strikes the cutting tool and rolls away from the tool. This rolling effect creates a continuous circular ribbon chip. Any change in the tool speed across the work will change the work-hardening effect and cause the chip to break and to restart in a different form of continuous chip. A continuous chip generally is associated with a smooth, accurate surface. Of course, the accuracy of the surface depends on the cutting edge of the tool. If the cutting edge is not smooth and accurate itself, the surface formed as the continuous chip is removed from the metal will not be smooth and accurate.

As the ductility of the metal becomes lower (as in medium-carbon steel, tool steels, and alloy steels), the continuous chip is still formed by the cutting tool. In these materials the heat created in the chip work hardens the chip to such a point that internal stress is locked into the chip, causing the chip to break. At the same time, because more energy is used by the cutting tool to cut the metal, more heat is created so that the part of the metal welds itself to the cutting tool, building up an additional edge on the tool. This *continuous chip with built-up edge* then dulls the keen cutting edge of the tool and causes a rough surface. The only way to correct this defect is to remove the tool, stop the lathe, and hone the built-up edge from the cutting tool. Often an edge can be stopped from building up on the cutting tool

by decreasing the traverse speed of the cutting tool. The chip that results from a cutting tool with a built-up edge may be an intermittent continuous ribbon. A continuous ribbon will flow from the cutting tool, but it will break abruptly. It may even break into numbers of short pieces of ribbon. The ribbon itself will be brittle because of the extreme work-hardening effects on the metal.

The *discontinuous chip* is associated with cast irons and some of the copper-based metals, such as bronze. Instead of forming a continuous chip, the chip is in the form of a flake of metal. This flake, also called a *segmental chip*, is associated with all of the brittle metals. Because brittle metal is being cut and because a small amount of shattering will result from the formation of these segmented flakes of metal, tool wear is high. The tool wear can be controlled to a certain extent by using a smaller rake angle on the cutting tool as well as by lowering the cutting speed.

LATHE TOOL BITS

If a product is to be machined accurately and efficiently, the correct type and shape of lathe tool bit must be applied properly. The bit must have a well-supported cutting edge that is ground for the specific operation to be performed; it must be set up to the work; and it must have a keen, smooth, and then honed edge. These factors determine the quality and the accuracy of machined parts. Almost all lathe tool bits are ground by hand by the lathe operator. Therefore, a knowledge of the angles and clearances used is essential to the operator. The same cutting tool, the tool bit, can be used for machine tools other than the lathe, for instance, milling machines, planers, and shapers.

The form of the tool bit is always shown from the top view. The general form determines the basic function of the tool bit (see Fig. 32-10). After the form has been selected, there are six angles that must be considered when grinding and forming a tool bit: the angle of keenness, the side clearance angle, the side-rake angle, the back-rake angle, the front clearance angle, and the cutting-edge angle.

The *angle of keenness* is controlled by the hardness of the material being cut. Soft materials usually are cut to a 68° angle of keenness, while hard materials are cut with an angle of keenness that ranges up to 90°. The cutting edge must have support in order to remain stationary and vibration free. The harder the material that the tool bit is cutting, the greater the energy that must be expanded to force the tool along the surface to be cut, creating more and more pressure. The cutting edge, while it must be sharp and keen, must also have material backing it up in order to support it. The angle of keenness provides the support area for the cutting edge (Fig. 32-8).

The *side clearance angle* prevents the tool below the cutting edge from rubbing against the work creating friction. The angle of the side clearance ranges from 3 to 10°, according to the hardness of the material being cut. Softer materials require more clearance than harder materials (Fig. 32-9).

The *side-rake angle* and the side clearance angle determine the angle of keenness.

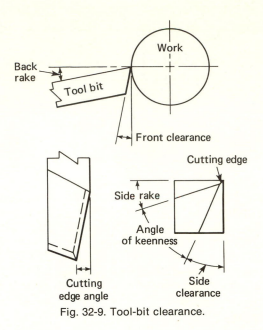

Fig. 32-9. Tool-bit clearance.

The angle of keenness and the side clearance angle always add up to a total of 90°.

The *back-rake angle* makes it possible for only one point, or the furthest point, of the tool to cut the workpiece. This angle is easily misunderstood by the novice because 16½° of the back-rake angle is produced by the toolholder that fits into the tool post. The angle of the toolholder should always be taken into consideration when a back rake is ground because the true back rake will be different from the grinding back rake by the 16½° angle of the standard toolholder. In most instances, charts give the true rake of a tool. For example, when brass is cut, it should be cut with a back rake of 0°, which means that the cutting tool itself must be ground to a *negative angle* of 16½° so that when the tool is placed in a toolholder, the back rake will be 0°.

The *front clearance angle* is determined in the same manner as the side clearance and is governed by the hardness of the material to be cut. The angle ranges from 3 to 10°. The major item to remember when grinding the front clearance on a tool bit is that the front clearance angle determines the amount of

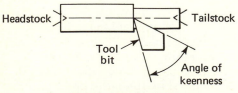

Fig. 32-8. Angle of keenness.

TABLE 32-1. TOOL ANGLES FOR HIGH-SPEED STEEL CUTTERS

MATERIAL TO BE CUT	BACK RAKE ANGLE, °	SIDE RAKE ANGLE, °	FRONT CLEARANCE ANGLE, °	SIDE CLEARANCE ANGLE, °
Bronze	0–5	0–5	8	8
Hard bronze	5–10	0–5	8	12
Copper	10–14	20–25	12	14
Aluminum	10–30	15–18	10	8
Cast iron	3–5	5–10	8	8
STEEL (ANNEALED)				
Cold-finished, screw stock	16	22	8	8
Medium-hard plain carbon	12–15	14–16	8	8
Tough high carbon	5–8	10–12	8	8
Nickel alloy	12–15	14–16	10	13
Nickel-chromium and chrome-molybdenum alloys	10	12	8	10
Chrome vanadium	8	12	8	10
Stainless	16	10	8	10
NONMETALS				
Molded plastic	0	0	12	8
Cast plastic	5	0	14	10
Laminated plastic	16	10	15	10
Hard rubber	5	0	20	15

support that the point of the cutting tool has. Too large an angle for a front clearance results in a weakened point on the cutting tool, causing it to break or fracture easily.

The *cutting-edge angle* is a function of the basic form of the cutting tool and is dictated by the special cut that the tool is supposed to make. This angle is measured on a plane parallel to the shank of the tool. For example, a right-hand turning tool for machine steel should have a cutting-edge angle of approximately 50° (Fig. 32-9). Table 32-1 identifies tool angles for high-speed cutters. When the tool-bit material itself is not high-speed steel, other clearance angles are necessary. Lathe tool bits, whether they are made from high-speed steel, stellite, tungsten carbide, tantalum carbide, or some of the more exotic ceramic materials, will all have different clearance angles recommended by the manufacturer.

Some of the most common lathe tool forms include the right-hand turning, the round nose, the right-hand facing, the threading, the cutoff, and the general-purpose right-hand tool (Fig. 32-10). Each tool form is ground, usually on the tool blank, for one specific purpose. The tool blank is formed with a 16° angle on each end so that excess grinding will not have to be done by the lathe operator. The tool blanks generally are ground on each end. Tool blanks range in size from ⅛ to 1 in.²

When a lathe bit is ground, only the face of the grinding wheel should be used, never the side of the grinding wheel. The clearance angles needed on the tool bit can be varied simply by raising the tool bit above the center of the grinding bit to increase the angle of attack of the tool bit to the grinding wheel (Fig. 32-11). Tool-bit grinding is an art that requires considerable practice in order

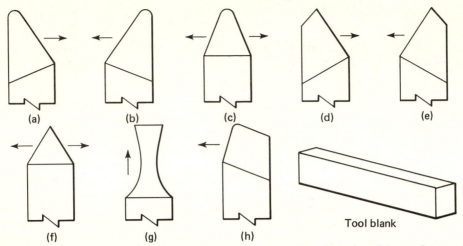

Fig. 32-10. Common lathe tool forms. (a) Left-hand turning; (b) right-hand turning; (c) round nose; (d) left-hand facing; (e) right-hand facing; (f) threading; (g) cutoff; (h) general-purpose right-hand.

to produce correct clearance angles and bit forms consistently.

The most critical factor in developing an effective technique of tool grinding is holding the tool at the proper angle while dressing the full width of the grinding wheel. The most common mistake is changing the angle of attack of the tool bit to the grinding wheel while sweeping across the face of the grinding wheel. This error results in a tool bit that is not hollow-ground and one that has a rough, dull cutting edge which cannot be honed (Fig. 32-12).

SPEEDS AND FEEDS

All materials have a best cutting speed. Table 32-2 identifies some of the average speeds for selected metals. These speeds, however, should be regarded as averages within a range of speed, meant only as starting points for setting the machines. For example, a cutting speed for the rough cutting of aluminum is approximately 200 surface ft/min, and a speed for rough cutting machine steel is approximately 90 surface

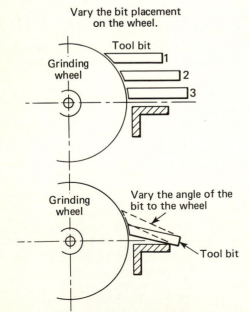

Fig. 32-11. Grinding a lathe tool bit.

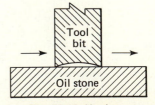

Fig. 32-12. Honing.

TABLE 32-2. AVERAGE CUTTING SPEEDS FOR SELECTED METALS

METAL	ROUGHING CUT	FINISH CUT
Aluminum	200	300
Brass	150	200
Bronze	90	100
Cast iron	60	30
Steel, machine	90	125
Steel, tool	50	75

ft/min. However, the condition of the tool, the temper of the metal, and the size and capability of the engine lathe can change these cutting speeds radically. Consequently, the average cutting speeds are only used as starting points for figuring out the maximum cut that can be taken.

Most lathe operators seldom take a maximum cut but use slower cutting speeds. Cutting speed itself is expressed in surface feet. It is controlled by the r/min of the headstock spindle that holds the workpiece, and the diameter of the workpiece in inches. The cutting speed and the diameter of the work then determine the r/min of the spindle chuck. The basic formula for figuring r/min spindle speed is:

$$r/min = \frac{CS \times 4}{D}$$

where CS = cutting speed
D = diameter of the work

Table 32-3 lists precomputed spindle r/min based on cutting speeds and diameters of workpieces.

A second variable that must be controlled when cutting materials is the feed of the tool bit across the work. *Feed* is the speed at which the carriage travels along the bed. It is expressed in thousandths of an inch of travel per revolution of the workpiece. Basic rules control both the cutting speed and the feed. The harder metals require slower surface ft/min, slower feeds, and smaller depths of cut than do softer metals. Roughing cuts require slower surface ft/min, faster feeds, and greater depths of cut when compared to finishing cuts. Finishing cuts require faster surface ft/min and less depth of cut. Table 32-4 identifies ranges of feed for selected metals. Remembering that finishing cuts require slower feeds and roughing cuts require faster feeds is a helpful general rule.

HOLDING DEVICES

There are many methods used for holding work in a lathe; however, four basic methods are used more than any others. They are: swinging the work between centers, the three-jaw chuck, the four-jaw independent chuck, and the collet (Fig. 32-13).

The standard procedure for swinging work between centers is first to mount a live center and a faceplate on the lathe spindle

TABLE 32-3. CUTTING SPEEDS, r/min

DIAMETER OF WORKPIECE, in.	15 ft/min	20 ft/min	30 ft/min	40 ft/min	50 ft/min	65 ft/min	70 ft/min	80 ft/min	90 ft/min	100 ft/min
¼	229	306	459	611	764	993	1,070	1,222	1,375	1,582
½	115	153	229	306	437	497	535	611	688	764
1	57.3	76.4	115	153	191	248	267	306	344	382
1¼	45.8	61.1	91.7	122	153	181	194	222	250	278
2	28.7	38.2	57.3	76.4	95.5	124	134	153	172	191
2½	22.9	30.6	45.8	68.8	76.4	99.3	107	122	138	153
3	19.1	25.5	38.2	50.9	63.7	82.7	89.1	102	115	127
4	14.3	19.1	28.7	38.2	47.7	62.1	66.8	76.4	85.9	95.5
5	11.5	15.3	22.9	30.6	38.2	49.7	53.5	61.1	68.8	76.4

TABLE 32-4. HIGH-SPEED LATHE BIT FEED RANGES

METAL	FEED RANGE		
	FINISH ←————→		ROUGH
Aluminum	0.005	0.012	0.030
Copper-based	0.003	0.012	0.025
Cast iron	0.005	0.012	0.025
Steel, machine	0.003	0.010	0.020
Steel, tool	0.003	0.010	0.020

and a dead center in the tailstock. With a center drill, a hole is predrilled in the center of the stock at each end, but the hole is only deep enough for two-thirds of the center drill to penetrate the surface of the stock. Lubricant is placed only in the dead center end of the workpiece. The faceplate lathe dog is attached to the faceplate end of the workpiece, and the predrilled workpiece is inserted between the headstock and the tailstock center, and then the tailstock center is snugged into the work.

The three-jaw chuck is used for most general-purpose work because it can grasp any regular or round shape in its jaws and the jaws will close evenly. The mechanism works in the same manner as a three-jaw drill chuck. Because the three-jaw lathe chuck automatically aligns work to within 0.001 to 0.002 in., it is used consistently by job shops. One restriction when using a three-jaw chuck is that once the work is placed in the chuck, all turning operations should be accomplished before removing the work. When the

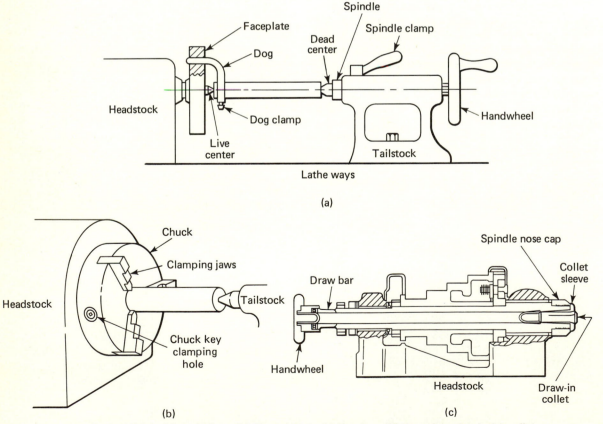

Fig. 32-13. Work-holding devices. (a) Faceplate and lathe dog; (b) three-jaw chuck; (c) collet.

work is taken out, it may not be aligned properly if it is put back into the chuck again.

The four-jaw chuck has four independent jaws. Each jaw must be adjusted by the lathe operator. Four-jaw chucks require some setup time because the piece being placed in the jaw is not aligned automatically and each jaw must be tightened or loosened by the lathe operator until the workpiece is centered, a feat that requires a great deal of practice before the skill is mastered and also requires secondary tools. The secondary tool used most often for aligning material with a four-jaw chuck is a dial indicator with a magnetic base. The magnetic base is attached to the compound rest of the lathe, and the dial indicator is then placed on the work. Work that is irregularly shaped or could not be fastened in a lathe for other reasons can be held by a four-jaw chuck.

The collet method of securing stock is used when bar stock is fed through the spindle in the lathe. Collets are available in a range of sizes. The sizes begin with a $1/16$-in. collet and proceed in increments of $1/64$ in. up to the spindle opening of the lathe. Collets are machined so that when they are drawn into the headstock spindle, they tighten down on the work, thus holding it securely on the centerline of the headstock spindle. Collets are available in a wide variety of shapes: round, hexagonal, octagonal, or square; and they come in many special order forms.

OPERATION

After the correct stock for turning has been selected and the lathe tool bit has been ground to the correct shape and clearance angle, the next step is to fasten the work onto the lathe. For example, round stock can be mounted directly into a three-jaw chuck. A drill and a drill chuck can be placed in the tailstock, and the stock center then can be drilled. The next step is to mount the stock the correct distance from the three-jaw chuck to the tailstock, lubricate the center drill hole, and clamp the tailstock in dead center place.

After this is done, the lathe tool bit should be positioned. The correct position for the lathe tool is with its point from 0 to 5° above the centerline of the stock. An easy way to determine if the tool bit is located at the center or above or below the workpiece is to place a 6-in. machinist's rule between the tool bit and the workpiece and then move the compound rest knob until the tool bit securely holds the machinist's rule to the workpiece. The angle of the machinist's rule will indicate whether or not the tool bit is at the center point, below it, or above it (Fig. 32-14). If the machinist's rule moves toward the tool bit, the tool bit is below the center of the workpiece. If the machinist's rule tips away from the operator, the tool-bit point is then above the workpiece. The height of the tool bit should be 0 to 5° above the workpiece for all machining.

In threading and internal boring, the tool point should be located exactly at dead center of the workpiece. When facing and cutoff tools are used, and when some nonferrous metals are cut, the tool point should also be at dead center. All other cutting should be done with the tool point a few degrees above the center of the workpiece.

The next step in the operation of straight cutting is to bring the tool piece up by hand to touch the workpiece. This step should be done before turning the machine on. The cutter bit should just barely scratch the work surface so that the position of the tool is indexed and the depth of a cut can be measured without guessing. It is poor practice to deter-

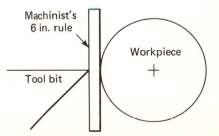

Fig. 32-14. Locating the tool bit.

mine the depth of cut by touching the tool to the workpiece while the workpiece is rotating. After the initial starting point has been determined, the next step is to determine the depth of cut and then engage the automatic friction clutch. Regular turning should not be done with the half-nut lever. The half-nut lever should only be used when chasing threads.

Some of the more complex operations accomplished on the engine lathe include cutting threads, taper turning, internal thread cutting, boring, and knurling.

Threading

The original purpose of the lathe was to cut threads. The lathe can cut any thread shape. Because of the large number of thread shapes, the National Screw Thread Commission has established basic forms for threads. The most used of these basic forms are the unified national, the square, and the acme threads (Fig. 32-15). The unified national is the thread used most throughout the world. It is basically a 60° thread with a round or flat crest and a round root.

At one time the square thread was used to transmit power but because square threads are difficult to cut, the acme thread is quickly replacing them. The unified national thread is available in coarse, fine, or extra fine classifications, known as UNC, for coarse; UNF, for fine; and UNEF, for extra fine. All threads are available in classes of fit. The four basic classes are Class I, a loose fit of the nut to the bolt; Class II, a free fit; Class III, a medium fit; and Class IV, a snug fit.

There are two methods for forming either internal or external threads on the lathe: by the use of taps and dies (Fig. 32-16) or by chasing threads (Fig. 32-17). Using a tap or a die is much simpler than cutting threads with a single-point tool. Taps and dies are used by drilling the correct size hole and then setting the correct feed per revolution by using the charts mounted directly on the feed-change gear box on the lathe. These charts apply to die cutting, tap cutting, and chasing threads.

After this step has been accomplished, the tapped hole can be started with a starting tap. Starting taps have five to seven threads ground back with a long taper, making it easier to start a hole. Often instead of using a starting tap, a plug tap is used to act as a starting tap. The plug tap can reach further into the hole and form larger threads at the bottom of the hole because only three to five threads are tapered back by grinding. A bottoming tap has one-half to one thread ground back, a characteristic which allows the forming of full threads almost to the bottom of any bored hole. Whatever tapping is used, a coolant should be used to cool the tap and the workpiece and to help in removing chips. The coolant fluid should be used in large amounts.

Chasing threads is another method for cutting threads on a lathe. The procedure for cutting threads with this method is the same as the procedure used for tapping threads, except that the final cutting is done with a single-point tool. The single-point tool must be in the shape of the thread. For example, if a 60° tool is used, the tool must be positioned perpendicular to the work as well as at the vertical center of the work. This positioning can be accomplished by using a center gage (Fig. 32-17a). Before the bit is set perpendic-

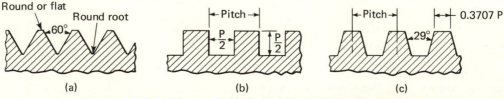

Fig. 32-15. Thread forms. (a) Unified national; (b) square; (c) acme.

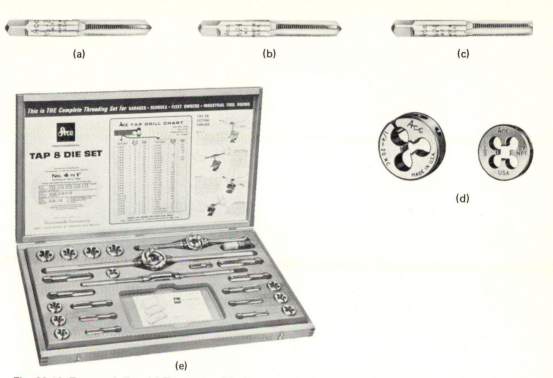

Fig. 32-16. Taps and dies. (*a*) Taper tap; (*b*) plug tap; (*c*) bottoming tap; (*d*) dies; (*e*) tap and die set.

ular to the work, the compound rest on the lathe must be set at 29°. This 29° mark is a special mark; many lathes have a large index mark identifying this point.

After the feedrate has been set, the tool has been set correctly to the work, and the thread is cutting correctly into the work, then the tool is brought up just to touch or scratch the surface of the workpiece. The tool is then backed off and the lathe turned on. When threading, the half-nut lever on the apron is always used because it maintains a positive control on the lathe lead screw. The half-nut clamps directly to this lead screw. Also con-

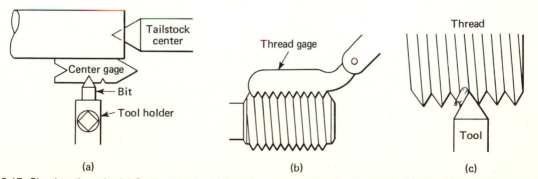

Fig. 32-17. Chasing threads. (*a*) Setting the tool bit (*note:* compound rest set at 29°); (*b*) checking the feed; (*c*) feed control (*note:* use the compound rest knob for depth of cut).

nected to the lead screw is a thread indicator. The thread dial indicator points out when the half-nut lever should be engaged to start the cutting tool at the correct time with reference to the lead screw.

Even-numbered threads are made with the lead screw closed at any or each eighth revolution index point. For odd-numbered threads, the half-nut is closed at any quarter revolution or numbered line. For threads such as 10½, 11½, or any thread with ½ revolution, the half-nut is closed at any odd-numbered line. Threads involving ¼ thread per inch, such as 6¾, should always be started at the original starting point before the half-nut lever is engaged.

When the threading tool bit has been brought up to touch the work, and the half-nut has been engaged at its proper place, the tool should traverse the full area of the workpiece, making only a light cut. At this point a check should always be made. The lathe is stopped; the tool is not backed out; and the threads are checked for accuracy to see if there are the correct number of points. This check can be made with a thread gage or simply by counting the number of threads in 1 in.

After the check, the next step is to loosen the micrometer collar on the cross-feed knob and set the collar at zero. Then the same step is performed with the compound rest knob micrometer collar. The lathe is started and the compound rest knob is fed to determine the depth of the cut, which may range from 0.003 to 0.015 in. Since the cutting is being done from both sides, 0.030 in. of material will be removed if the depth of the cut is 0.015 in. The half-nut lever should be engaged at the right time and the tool should be allowed to traverse the workpiece at the end of the cut. The half-nut lever is released and the cross-feed knob is backed out. The cutting tool is repositioned by moving the apron handwheel to the original starting position. The cross-feed knob is turned back to zero, making sure that all the excess cross-feed slack is taken out. The compound rest knob is fed in for another cut; and then, at the appropriate time, the half-nut lever is engaged. This process is repeated until the full depth of cut for the thread has been taken. Many times it will take as many as four or five cuts to reach the correct depth. A thread should never be chased in one deep cut.

QUESTIONS

1. How are lathe sizes determined?
2. Identify the major headstock spindle connections.
3. Why does the headstock spindle hole go completely through the headstock?
4. Identify the major operator controls on the apron.
5. What is a lathe dog?
6. Why should all cuts be toward the headstock?
7. Compare and contrast the three basic types of chips.
8. Explain the angle of keenness.
9. Identify and explain the six basic angles for tool bits.
10. What are two ways to grind clearance angles on a grinding wheel?
11. Explain how to hone a lathe tool bit.
12. What is the speed for rough cutting cast iron and for making a finishing cut of cast iron?
13. Determine the correct spindle r/min if the cutting speed for machine steel is 90 and the diameter of the workpiece is 3 in.
14. Explain feed.
15. Why are three-jaw chucks used more often than four-jaw chucks?

16. Explain one method of determining the height of the location of the tool bit to the workpiece.
17. What is the difference between a square thread and an acme thread?
18. What are the differences between starting, plug, and bottoming taps?
19. Explain how to chase a thread on an engine lathe with a single-point tool.

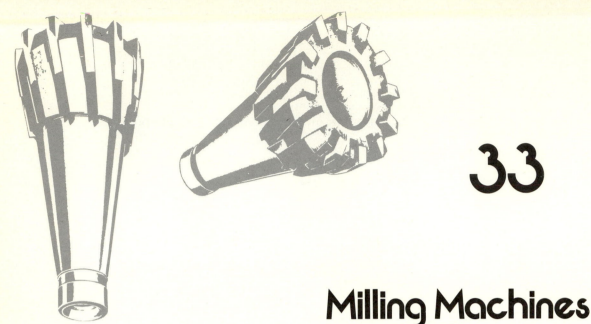

Milling Machines

33

Milling machines are now used for the production of almost every item manufactured. In the last century, when its first major use occurred, the milling machine was used for cutting gears, mainly for clocks.

Current milling machines are divided into two groups: the knee-and-column group and the bed type (Fig. 33-1). There are other types of milling machines with special characteristics but these are special machines that have been constructed to perform specific functions. The knee-and-column and the bed types are used more than any other machines, and of these two, the knee-and-column type is used more.

The worktable on the knee-and-column machine is supported by a knee. The knee, which is a casting, slides up and down on a column. The knee-and-column milling machines are made in horizontal- and vertical-spindle machines, as well as plain or universal table machines. The knee-and-column milling machines frequently used in tool and die manufacturing lend themselves to an easy setup for a wide variety of work.

A milling machine is classified according to the type of worktable it has. It can be a plain milling machine or a universal milling machine. On a plain milling machine, the worktable can be controlled along three axes. The vertical feed can be adjusted by raising or lowering the table; the traverse feed occurs when the table is moved toward or away from the column; and a longitudinal adjustment is made when the table is moved parallel to the column. The plain milling machines are efficient for either short or long production runs, and they have a wide range of usefulness, particularly in those toolrooms that do not have work requiring the use of the universal milling machine.

The universal milling machine is basically the same as the plain milling machine but it has one additional advantage: the worktable can be swiveled on a horizontal plane. The universal milling machine is so named because it is the most flexible of all milling machines. Because of the universal table movement, the milling machine is capable of producing spur gears, spiral gears, helix gears, cams, twist drills, milling machine cutters, and an infinite variety of other manufactured goods.

The position of the spindle that holds the cutter is also a designation for classifying milling machines. The two categories are the vertical-spindle milling machine and the horizontal-spindle milling machine. The major controls on each machine are the same and the only difference is whether the spindle is held in a vertical or a horizontal position (Figs. 33-2 and 33-3). The spindle of

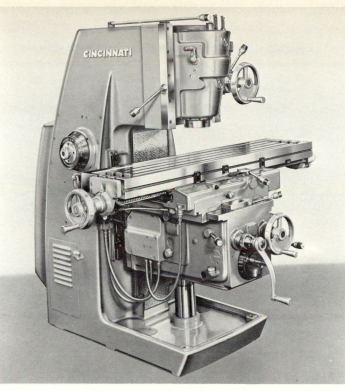

(a)

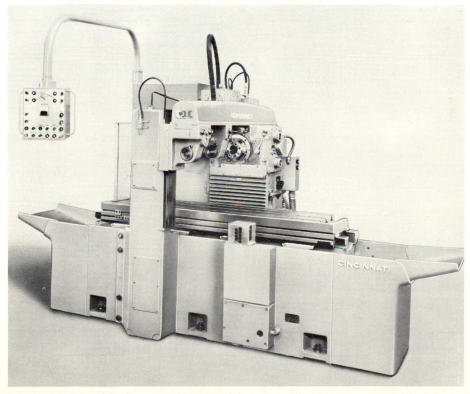

(b)

Fig. 33-1. Milling machines. (a) Knee and column; (b) bed. (*Cincinnati Milacron Company.*)

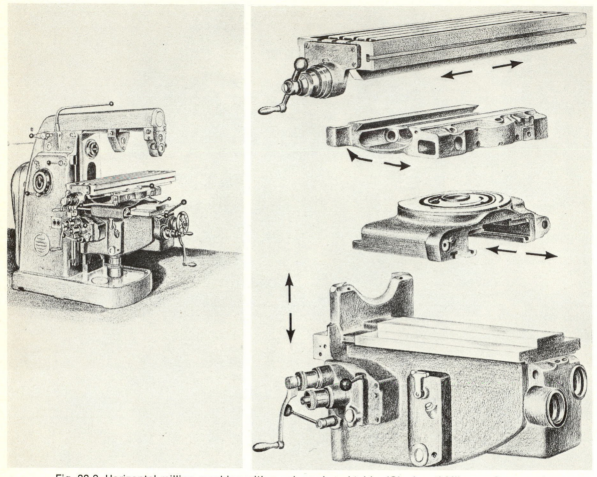

Fig. 33-2. Horizontal milling machine with a universal worktable. (*Cincinnati Milacron Company.*)

the horizontal milling machine is horizontal to the worktable, and the spindle of the vertical milling machine is at a right angle to the surface of the worktable. The vertical milling machine can raise or lower the cutter by an adjustment on the spindle head. The horizontal milling machine cannot. If a great deal of face mill work or end mill work must be done, the vertical milling machine is better adapted to do this work than the horizontal milling machine.

The need for more control over the milling operation has led to a new generation of milling machines, now considered machining centers, that are capable of performing drilling, reaming, boring, milling, and many other machine operations. These machining centers can perform the more complicated operations demanded by the production of more complex products and larger numbers of products. Advancements made in the field of numerical control have also prompted the development of machining centers (Fig. 33-4).

MACHINE SIZE

Because of the wide variety of milling machines available, milling machines are identified by the longitudinal travel of the

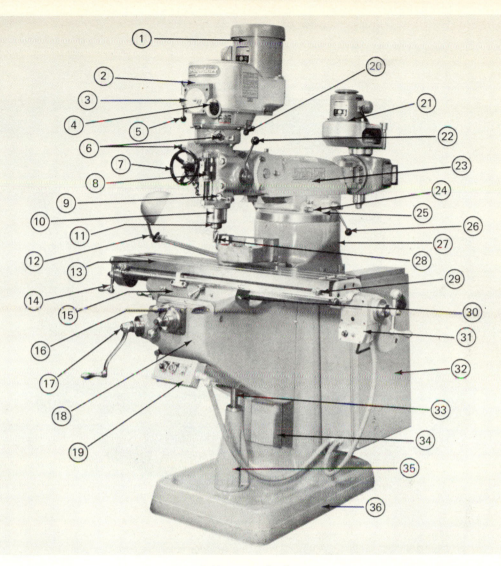

Bridgeport series 1
vertical turret miller

1 - 1-1/2 H.P. motor
2 - Variable speed milling, drilling and boring head
3 - Speed selection dial
4 - Speed selection handwheel
5 - Spindle brake
6 - Power downfeed levers
7 - Manual fine downfeed control
8 - Quill depth stop (adjustable)
9 - Quill lock
10 - Quill
11 - Spindle
12 - Work light
13 - Table
14 - Table crank
15 - Saddle
16 - Cross feed (saddle) crank
17 - Knee crank
18 - Knee
19 - Operator control panel
20 - Hi/Lo speed range lever
21 - Head mounted on rear of ram
22 - Quill downfeed lever
23 - V ram
24 - Turret swivel lock nut
25 - Turret
26 - Ram movement lever
27 - Column
28 - Tooling
29 - Adjustable table stop (2)
30 - Way grease fittings (8)
31 - Power table feed
32 - Electrical cabinet
33 - Knee elevating screw
34 - Column V-ways
35 - Pedestal
36 - Base

Fig. 33-3. Vertical milling machine. (*Bridgeport Machine Tool Company.*)

Fig. 33-4. N/C machining center. (*Pratt and Whitney Machine Tool Company.*)

worktable in inches (Table 33-1), as well as the horsepower of the drive motor, the model, and the type. A standard for the longitudinal travel of the worktable has been adopted by the manufacturers of milling machines. The table travel has been identified by number; for example, a no. 4 milling machine has a longitudinal table travel of approximately 42 in., plus or minus an inch or so. The horsepower rating of the main drive motor can be either a single-speed motor or, as in most instances, a two-speed motor. When a two-speed motor is involved, the higher horsepower (hp) is always stated first and the lower horsepower second; for example, a no. 3 milling machine with a 20/10 hp motor.

A third designation of milling machines, the model, is not standardized. Each manufacturing firm has different symbols or meanings for all of its models of milling machines. The last category in the identification of milling machines is the milling machine type, referring to whether the milling machine is a bed type, a knee-and-column type, a horizontal milling machine, a vertical milling machine, or a special milling machine. An example of what a milling machine identi-

TABLE 33-1. STANDARD MILLING
MACHINE SIZE

*TABLE 33-1. STANDARD MILLING
MACHINE SIZE*

NUMBER	LONGITUDINAL TABLE TRAVEL, in.
1	22
2	28
3	34
4	42
5	50
6	60

Example identification series: 50/20 hp no. 5 HL.

fication series would look like is presented at the bottom of Table 33-1.

CUTTERS

Cutters for milling machines are divided into three specific groups: facing cutters, peripheral or slab cutters, and form cutters. Facing cutters are designed so that they can machine large flat surfaces (Fig. 33-5). Peripheral cutters are designed to cut on the periphery of the cutters; they are also used for large flat surfaces (Fig. 33-6). Form cutters are designed to impart a specific form to the machine part (Fig. 33-7).

Generally, milling cutters are not sharpened or converted, as are lathe tools; but rather they are purchased from manufacturers of milling machine cutters in predetermined shapes and sizes. Consequently, hundreds of shapes and sizes are available. The two basic types of cutters generally ordered are the solid cutter or the insert tooth cutter. Solid cutters are made of high-speed steel or other alloy metals; and insert tooth cutters have ceramic, tungsten, or some other exotic materials used as inserts for the cutting teeth.

A cutter becomes dull after it has been used for a significant length of time. Many job shops send the milling machine cutter out for resharpening to a company that specializes in sharpening cutters. If the cutter is not

expensive, it is simply replaced with a new cutter and not resharpened at all.

Milling cutters can do conventional or climb milling (Fig. 33-8). The direction of the cutting teeth of the cutter combined with the direction of the table feed controls which type of milling is done. Conventional milling, or up milling, compensates for the backlash of the table feed mechanisms. The cutting tool rotates against the feed mechanism that moves the worktable, placing tension on the lead screw. The lead screw activates the feed table and keeps all slack out of it. Conventional milling can be performed chatter-free; but climb milling, or down milling, will result in tool chatter because the tool is rotating in the same direction as the worktable is moving.

Because the milling cutter in conventional milling is always feeding from the milled work toward the unmachined area of the workpiece, the cutting edge always has cleaned machined material to cut. This characteristic, and the fact that it cuts from the interior of the workpiece to the exterior, makes conventional cutting ideal for machining forgings and the cast irons, both of which have tenacious skins.

Climb milling, on the other hand, also has some distinct advantages. It is used especially when there are irregular pieces because the downward pressure created by the cutting edge moving down on the workpiece presses the workpiece onto the worktable and helps to hold the workpiece in alignment against the worktable. Climb milling produces a higher quality machined surface than conventional cutting. Also, climb milling increases tool life, decreasing the production cost of a particular item. The major disadvantage of climb milling is that backlash is uncontrolled so that the milling machine must be of sufficient size and have backlash compensators built into it.

Cutters are held in vertical milling machine spindles by collets or by drill chucks. Installation of cutters is simple in vertical machines, but this is not true of horizontal milling machines. Horizontal milling machines require that the cutter be mounted on

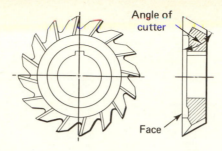

Angle of cutter

Face

(a)

(b)

Fig. 33-5. Selected facing cutters. (a) Principle; (b) application. (*Cincinnati Milacron Company.*)

(a) (b)

Fig. 33-6. Selected peripheral cutters. (a) Slabbing; (b) combination of ganged cutters. (*Cincinnati Milacron Company.*)

an arbor with the arbor mounted into the spindle. Arbors are available in A, B, and C types (Fig. 33-9). Style A and B arbors depend on the design of the milling machine itself, while style C arbor can be used on both types of arbor setups. The style A arbor has a bearing surface on the end furthest from the spindle, and style B has a movable bearing sleeve that is keyed to the arbor but can be placed at any distance from the spindle. The style B arbor is a stronger arbor than style A.

SPEEDS AND FEEDS

A milling machine differs from a lathe in the speed at which it can remove or cut materials. Table 33-2 identifies some of the

average cutting speeds for selected metals when high-speed steel cutters are used. If carbide-tip cutters are used, for example, the feeds and cutting speeds can be more than doubled. The type of metal of the cutting tool determines the cutting speed of the metal workpiece. The cutting speed is expressed in inches per minute (in./min). For example, aluminum has a cutting speed of 750 in./min. This speed is an average within a range of speeds for cutting aluminum and is meant to be only a starting point for the setting of the machines.

The milling machines should be set so that the largest amount of metal can be removed while leaving an adequate surface finish. When aluminum is cut, for example, the cutting speed can be started at 750 in./min, and then this speed is increased until the surface finish of the part starts to become impaired. Then the cutting speed is backed off slightly so that a good surface remains with the highest cut. The chief point to remember when determining a cutting speed is to always reduce the cutting speed for hard materials, abrasive materials, high-alloyed materials, or for deep milling cuts. Conversely, the speeds should always be increased for soft materials, finer finishes, fragile workpieces, and fragile holding setups in lathes. It is standard practice always to start with the

TABLE 33-2. AVERAGE CUTTING SPEEDS WITH HIGH-SPEED STEEL CUTTERS FOR SELECTED METALS

METAL	CUTTING SPEED, in./min
Aluminum	750
Brass	450
Cast iron	50
Steel, machine	210
Steel, tool	120

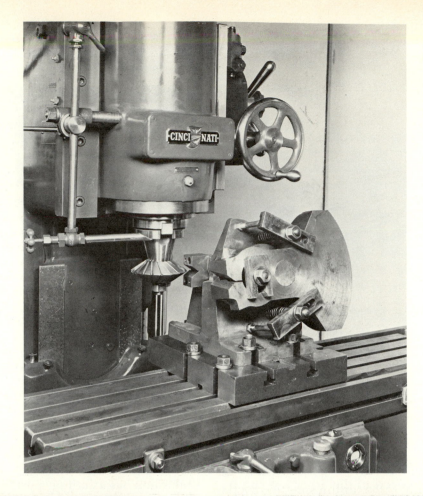

Fig. 33-7. Selected form cutters. (*Cincinnati Milacron Company.*)

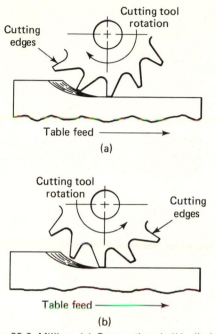

Fig. 33-8. Milling. (a) Conventional; (b) climb.

In the abbreviated formula for r/min, π has been divided into 12 to roughly represent 4; therefore, the abbreviated formula for r/min is

$$r/min = \frac{CS \times 4}{D}$$

The results of this abbreviated formula produce an accurate enough r/min spindle estimate because milling machines have various spindle speed selections and the specific r/min resulting from the formula may or may not be one of these selections. The spindle speed closest to the figure derived from the formula should be selected, even though it may be a slightly higher or lower speed.

As an example of how to use the formulas, if a product is made of aluminum and aluminum has a cutting speed of 750 in./min, and the cutter that has been selected by the operator is 5 in. in diameter, the r/min would equal 750 times 4, divided by 6, which equals 500 r/min for the spindle speed.

The milling machine cutter has more than one tooth that revolves against the work. Because of the multiple teeth, it is necessary to determine how much material is removed with one tooth in order to determine the feed requirement. Various types of cutters can remove different amounts of metal. First, the type of metal must be known; second, the type or shape of the cutter must be known. Table 33-3 identifies average high-speed steel tool feeds with a per tooth removal rate of material. For example, a side cutter will remove 0.015 in. of aluminum per tooth per revolution. Therefore, the formula for deter-

average cutting speed and then compensate accordingly.

The spindle r/min, or the spindle speed, of the milling machine is computed according to the cutting speed and the diameter of the cutter used to do the cut. The basic formula for r/min of the spindle is:

$$r/min = \frac{12CS}{\pi D}$$

where CS = cutting speed
$\quad\quad$ D = diameter of cutter

TABLE 33-3. AVERAGE HIGH-SPEED STEEL TOOL FEED (PER TOOTH)

METAL	END MILL	FACE MILL	FORM MILL	SAW	SHELL END MILL	SIDE	SLAB
Aluminum	0.016	0.028	0.008	0.008	0.020	0.015	0.012
Brass	0.011	0.020	0.007	0.005	0.016	0.012	0.009
Cast iron	0.007	0.012	0.005	0.002	0.009	0.007	0.005
Steel, machine	0.007	0.014	0.005	0.004	0.011	0.008	0.006
Steel, tool	0.005	0.008	0.004	0.002	0.006	0.005	0.003

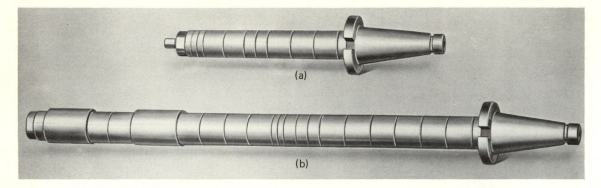

(a)

(b)

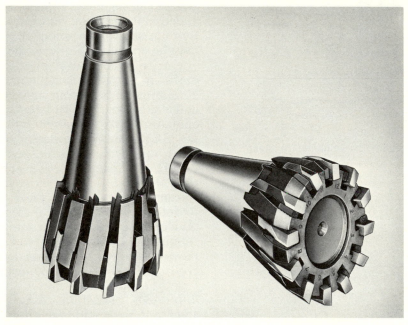

(c)

Fig. 33-9. Milling arbors. (a) A style; (b) B style; (c) C style (with facing cutter). (*Cincinnati Milacron Company.*)

mining feed is feed is equal to the feed per tooth times the number of teeth times the number of revolutions, or r/min. Therefore the rate for removing aluminum with a side mill is 0.015 times 16 teeth (in this particular side cutter) times 500 r/min. Feed would be equal to 120 in./min. Again, this figure is an estimate and the feed setting that most closely approximates 120 in./min should be set on the milling machine regardless of whether it is above or below the setting that results from the r/min formula.

CUTTING FLUIDS

Cutting fluids are more essential in milling machines than on the engine lathe because a larger amount of metal is removed by the cutting action. The cutting fluids should always be directed over the cutter so that the cutter delivers the cutting fluid to the work. In this way the fluid cools the cutting tool, flushes the chips out of the cutting tool teeth, and lubricates the cutting tool. The fluid also goes

TABLE 33-4. CUTTING FLUIDS FOR SELECTED METALS

METAL	FLUID
Aluminum	Kerosene
	Kerosene/lard oil
	Soluble oil
Copper based	Dry
	Kerosene
	Lard oil
	Mineral oil
Iron, cast	Dry
	Soluble oil
Iron, malleable	Dry
	Soda water
Steel	Lard oil
	Mineral oil
	Soluble oil
	Sulfurized oil

to the work to flush the chips from it and to cool it. Table 33-4 identifies cutting fluids for selected metals.

OPERATION

Before any work is done, the operator must choose the type of cutter to use. The operator must also decide on the rigidity of the work-holding device and the speed and feed settings on the milling machine itself. The final decision of whether or not to use a plain mill or a facing mill depends on the finish desired on the workpiece. The face milling cutter gives a better finish than the plain mill, but the facing mill does not perform the cutting operation as quickly. After the milling cutter has been selected and the arbor installed in the spindle, the spindle speed and the feed are computed and the machine is set.

The next step is to secure the workpiece to the table. The most popular work-holding attachment is the vice. The vice is bolted to the T slots on the worktable and work is simply fastened in the vice. Other types of holding devices are the same as those used in drill press work, with such holding devices as T bolts, parallel bars, step blocks, and jacks. After the work has been properly secured and checked, the cutter is lowered to within ½ in. of touching the work. One method of determining the distance between the cutter and the workpiece is to place a piece of paper on top of the work, engage the spindle so that the cutter revolves, and slowly bring the cutting tool into contact with the piece of paper (Fig. 33-10). As the cutting tool touches the piece of paper, it will pull it off the workpiece. Since a piece of paper is approximately 0.003 in. thick, the operator knows that the cutting tool is approximately 0.003 in. from the workpiece. The distance between the cutter and the workpiece is readjusted to the thickness of the piece of paper.

The major adjustments available on the knee-and-column machine are those that adjust or position the worktable in relation to the cutter by moving the worktable either longitudinally, traversely, or vertically. Each of these movements can be accomplished with either a feed handle or a handwheel. Cross-feed movement of the table is achieved by turning the handle C in Fig. 33-11. Longitudinal movement is accomplished by turning either the table control handwheel L, or the feed control L_1. The vertical movement of the table is adjusted by the hand crank V or by a vertical feed mechanism V_1 that usually is located on the left-hand side of the vertical hand crank.

Milling machines also have position-locking clamps that are located on the table,

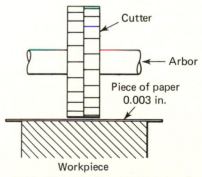

Fig. 33-10. Setting tool height.

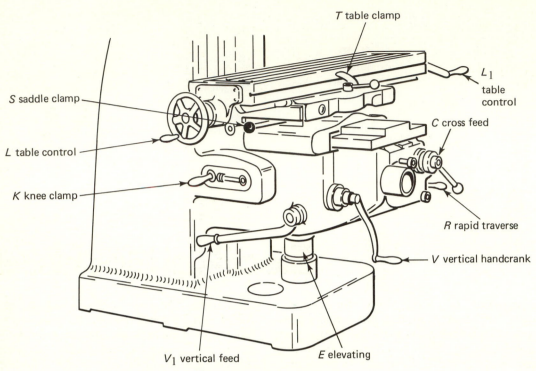

Fig. 33-11. Operator controls.

saddle, and knee. These clamps ensure that the table position will not change. For example, after the vertical height of the table has been established, the table is locked by the vertical clamping device so that the table will not vibrate or travel in any direction, thus ensuring the correct height of the cut or the correct depth of the cut.

QUESTIONS

1. What are the basic types of milling machines?
2. Compare and contrast the plain worktable and the universal worktable.
3. How are milling machines classified?
4. What are up milling and down milling?
5. How are milling cutters sharpened?
6. How does conventional milling compensate for backlash?
7. What are the advantages of climb milling?
8. Explain the formula for determining spindle r/min.
9. What are the functions of cutting fluids?
10. How is the workpiece held on the milling machine worktable?

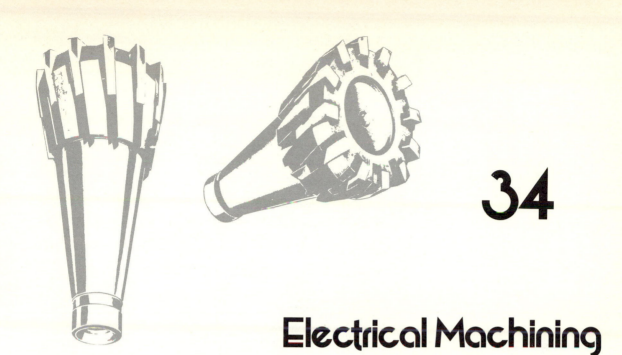

Electrical Machining

34

The demand by technology for lighter, stronger, and harder metals has caused machine tool manufacturers to derive new forms of metal cutting. The electrical machining processes are typical of the advances in machine tool development. The basic electrical processes now include electrical discharge machining, electrical chemical machining, and electrochemical grinding. These new processes have existed in theory for many years. However they have been used on a production basis for only a little more than 10 years.

ELECTRICAL DISCHARGE MACHINING

Electrical discharge machining (EDM) removes or shapes metal by electrical discharges between the cutting tool, or electrode, and an electroconductive workpiece in the presence of a dielectric fluid. This process is now the most widely used method of removing metal without the use of mechanical cutting force. Although the EDM method was once considered an exotic machining process, it is now relatively commonplace. In fact, the EDM process has become the standard method used for many complex

machining operations. The rapid growth of EDM can be attributed to its faster removal rates, closer tolerances, smoother surface finishes, and longer tool life than were possible before EDM equipment and production techniques.

The growth of electrical discharge machining as a machining process is linked directly to the ability to control precisely electric spark discharges. These discharges are capable of cutting carbides and refractory metals as easily as they cut low-carbon steel. Fully hardened heat-treated steels and even the superalloys seem to machine faster with EDM than the softer metals. The close control over sparking makes it possible to produce close tolerances, holes at any angle, and produce deep slots and cavities of unusual shapes that would have been impossible or extremely costly to produce before by other machining methods. Electrical discharge machining is being used widely by both large and small manufacturers for the production of dies and permanent molds. Its use often permits the production of better parts, dies, and molds at a lower cost and with a greater design flexibility because the tool does not touch the workpiece. Because there are no cutting forces generated, it is possible for fragile or thin parts to be machined. Other major advantages of EDM are that its finished cut is free of burrs and that surface finishes of 2 to 4 μin. are possible.

The most widely accepted theory of the operation of EDM is that it is controlled erosion caused by the melting of the metal, coupled with a small amount of vaporization of the metal. Within the electric spark, minute particles of metal are melted and ejected from the workpiece. These small particles are cooled by the dielectric fluid and forced between the workpiece and the tool, flushing them from the work area. The extreme heat may reach as high as 10,000°F and is caused by several things. The first of these is the large number of electrons that are trapped in each spark, a number that ranges in the billions. The release of the stored energy from this large number of electrons coupled with the large number of sparks, as many as 10,000 to 30,000 sparks per second, generate the

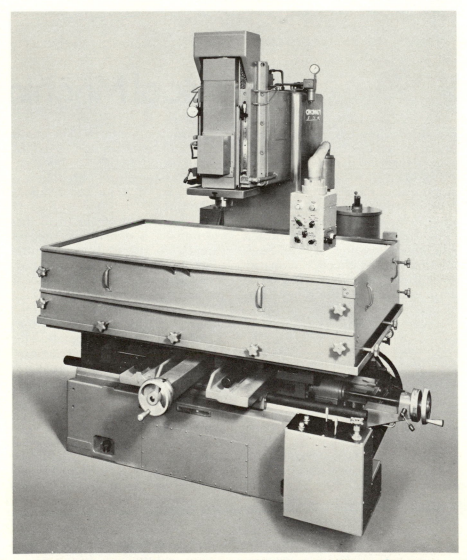

Fig. 34-1. Electrical Discharge Machine (EDM). (*Cincinnati Milacron Company.*)

high heat which literally explodes small particles of metal from the surface.

The rate at which metal is removed from the workpiece depends on what materials the tool and the workpiece are made of as well as the amount of electric power delivered to the tool. Electric power delivered at the gap between the tool and the workpiece is measured in amperes (A). A rule of thumb is that a 20-A current is capable of removing steel at the rate of 1 in./h. The amperage on most electrical discharge machines ranges from ½ to 300 A. The pulse rate, or number of sparks, on most commercial machines ranges from 200 to 30,000 pulses per second. Some experimental machines are capable of delivering well over ¼ million pulses per second. The metal-removal rate is controlled by varying the pulse rate and the amount of electric energy delivered to the electrode or tool (Fig. 34-1).

Operation

After the workpiece has been clamped into place and hooked to the power supply, the tool is lowered until sparks begin to flow between the tool-electrode and the work. This occurs at a distance that is usually preset; it is known as the *overcut distance*. The overcut distance is usually 0.001 in. Voltage between the tool and the work builds up across this gap even though the gap is filled with the dielectric fluid. An intense electric field is developed along the closest path between the tool and the workpiece, and the dielectric fluid ionizes, causing a discharge of power. The energy of this discharge vaporizes and decomposes the dielectric surrounding the path of the electrical conduction. As conduction continues, the diameter of the discharge area expands so that the current increases (Fig. 34-2).

Small areas on the tool as well as areas on the work surface become hot. The rise in temperature continues until the metal is above melting point and small molten metal pools are formed. A crater is then produced by each electrical discharge. The voltage during the spark, or the discharge, is con-

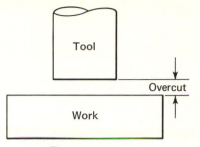

Fig. 34-2. Overcut.

stant, and the size of the crater is proportional to the amount of the charge that is transferred between the tool and the work. For maximum stock removal rates, there should be a minimum time between each charge. A minimum time will minimize the amount of heat dissipated from the work surface into the interior of the workpiece (Fig. 34-3).

High amounts of energy with large discharge capacitors produce a rough surface finish which is created by the large craters formed. A smoother finish is obtained by using a smaller spark or discharge, which creates smaller craters and results in a smoother finish. For fast production and high rates of metal removal, higher amperages are required. The more power, the faster the metal-removal rates. In general, high metal-removal rates are associated with high amperages, low frequency, and minimum gap voltage; finishing cuts or low removal rates are accomplished by low amperages, high frequencies, and the highest possible gap voltage (Fig. 34-4). Many metalworking firms increase production by cutting a part at a high amperage and low pulse rate for the rough cut, and then follow with a finish cut that uses low amperage with a high pulse rate.

Power Supply

A basic element in electrical discharge machining is a pulsating dc discharge. This pulsating discharge does the cutting by melting and vaporizing the metal. This discharge is controlled by three types of power supplies: the relaxation type, the rotary impulse supply,

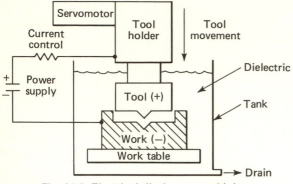

Fig. 34-3. Electrical discharge machining.

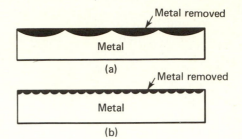

Fig. 34-4. EDM removal rates (a) High amperage/low pulse rate; (b) low amperage/high pulse rate.

and the solid-state pulsing power supply. Of the three, the solid-state pulser type is used most.

The relaxation power supply, or the capacitor power supply, the first type used for EDM metal removal, is simple in construction, low in cost, and capable of a high-energy output. The power supply, however, has several limitations that are inherent to this system: low stock removal rates and high electrode wear. Also, the relaxation-type power supply has extremely poor controls to handle and limit cutting rates adequately.

Rotary impulse generators are also used in electrical discharge machining as power supplies. They are reliable and simple in construction, but like the relaxation type, they have serious limitations because of their fixed frequencies across the overcut and their inability to be adjusted. Another serious limitation is that the rotary impulse generator cannot be controlled enough to produce a finished surface.

The most advanced electrical discharge machine tool uses pulsed energy, solid-state circuitry for power supplies. Pulsed systems do not have the limitations of the other power supply systems. Solid-state switching devices pulse extremely fast. The solid-state energy systems are versatile and allow almost exact control over the machining process. A distinct advantage is that metal-removal rates can be adjusted and varied according to the desired results. Even electrode wear can be controlled and, under special sets of conditions, can be eliminated. Another advantage of the solid-state systems is that the overcut can be controlled to a much smaller distance than with other systems (Fig. 34-4).

Tooling

The electrode, or tools, are subject to the same electroerosion processes that remove metal from the workpieces. Erosion, or wear of the tooling electrodes, however, is much slower than the erosion of the workpiece because all of the energy from the individual discharges is directed toward and dissipated in the workpiece. Most of the wear of the tooling electrodes occurs at their corners where the electrical discharges are concentrated.

Tool wear is often expressed as a wear ratio of the amount of metal removed from the workpiece to the amount of electrode tooling material removed. The rate of electrode erosion depends on the materials from which the tool and the workpieces are made, as well as the amount of energy used, and the servomotor feed rate.

Tooling materials that have high melting points are the most desirable. The materials should also have good or excellent electrical conductivity. Selection of a particular tooling electrode material depends primarily on the specific application and the material being machined. Some tooling materials (such as electrodes of stainless steel) have low wear rates, but are expensive and difficult to machine to the required form. Others have faster wear rates, but they may be cast from existing cavities using inexpensive material. Yellow brass has been a standard tooling material for use with electrical discharge machines because of its good machinability and relatively low cost. Other materials used for electrotooling include copper, tungsten carbide, silver-tungsten, chromium, plated materials, and some of the hard zinc alloys. The wear ratio for a copper tungsten electrode is about four times the ratio obtained with a brass tool. The copper tungsten tip makes possible proportionately longer electrode life. Since the tooling costs can amount to 80 percent or more of the cost for using the EDM machines, careful consideration should be given to the price, machinability, and wear rate of the tooling material.

Dielectric Fluid

Fluids used for EDM serve several functions. The fluid acts as an integral part of the discharge between the tool electrode and the workpiece. Iron elements in uncharged molecules of the fluid are largely responsible for initiation of the discharge and for providing the conductive ionized path for the discharge. The bulk of the fluid serves to confine the path of the ionized channel. Thus both the amount of energy transferred and the size of the crater produced are influenced by the type of dielectric fluid used.

The dielectric also is used for flushing eroded particles out of the discharge area. This step is accomplished by forcing the fluid through hollow tools or through holes in the workpiece between the tool and the work or by vibrating the tool. Poor flushing will slow down cutting speeds and cut down on accuracy, increasing both the amount of machining necessary and the cost. Hole cutting coolant is forced down through a hollow tool. Another way adequate tooling is provided for is by cutting holes in the workpiece for the coolant to flow through. Generally, the coolant holes are incorporated into the finished product (such as holes used for ejector pins). When the holes are cut in the workpiece for flushing, they are either classified as up

flushing or down flushing holes. *Up flushing* refers to the pressure being supplied where the fluid passes through the workpiece toward the electrode tool. *Down flushing* occurs when the fluid passes by the electrode and then through the workpiece. Down flushing usually is accomplished by a vacuum that draws the fluid through.

The flow of clean fluid displaces the fluid that has been contaminated with eroded particles. Eroded particles can cause bridging or arcing between the electrode and the work. The clean fluid prevents these effects. Metallic debris resulting from the erosion may cause unwanted metal removal since each tiny particle can act as an electrode. Because of this arcing problem, holes become tapered. However, proper flushing of the holes during machining will control or eliminate taper.

A large EDM machine operating at full capacity is capable of producing 300-A units, creating as much as 14,000 Btu/h, enough heat to heat adequately a three-bedroom, full-sized house. The heat is created by two sources, the large amount of amperage and also an ultrasonic effect that occurs in the discharge zone during machining. This heat must be removed in order for the accuracy of the workpiece to be maintained. The dielectric fluid acts as a heat-transfer medium for both the workpiece and the tool, thereby controlling the dimensional accuracy of the workpiece.

EDM uses hydrocarbon oils ranging from kerosene through lubricating oils, as well as other petroleum distillate fractions. More expensive silicone-based oils are used for special applications as are triethylene and glycol water solutions.

ELECTROCHEMICAL MACHINING

Electrochemical machining (ECM) is basically an electroplating process except that the metal that should adhere to the plate is not allowed to adhere to the workpiece but instead is carried away by the electrolyte. ECM removes the surface atoms of a metal one layer at a time. The metal that dissolves removes the anode metal at a very high rate. Another name for the ECM process is *zero force machining*. The words *zero force* denote that the ECM process machines metal without placing any type of pressure or stress on the workpiece. In other words there is no pushing, tearing, or cutting of the metal as with the standard machine tool processes. Instead, ECM steadily erodes the workpiece until a proper amount of metal is removed.

Michael Faraday's law explains the basic electrochemical action. A positive electrode (the anode) and a negative electrode (the cathode) are separated by an electrolyte and are energized by low-voltage direct current. When the current flows, electrons are moved from the anode to the cathode, with ions moving also from the anode to the cathode. In

the ECM process, the ion-rich electrolyte does not allow any of the removed metallic debris to attach itself to the cathode but rather carries it away. The charged particles leave the anode and pass through the electrolyte; then the electrolyte forces the particles away. Erosion takes place at the anode until it is formed exactly into the shape of the cathode with clean, burr-free edges.

ECM is highly efficient when the workpiece becomes more complex or as the production runs become longer. It readily competes with the conventional processes of cutting, especially with superalloys, refractory metals, and those metals whose hardnesses range above 42 on the Rockwell C scale. Often it is one of the few ways that some of the exotic alloys can be machined on any economical, high-production basis. The time needed to machine a part by ECM in re-

Fig. 34-5. Electrochemical machine. (*Chem Form, a division of KMS Industries.*)

cent years has dropped from hours to minutes. For example, ECM is used to machine gas turbine aircraft engine components because it leaves a surface finish that ranges in accuracy from 2 to 60 μin. Also during the machining process, it does not change the metal metallurgically while producing a burr-free finished product (Fig. 34-5).

Operation

After an electrode or hollow tool has been ground into a final shape, it is placed in a toolholder which is negatively charged. The workpiece is mounted on the positively charged worktable, and the electrolyte is then pumped into the sealed tank. As the electrolyte pump is turned on, it moves the fluid between the tool and the workpiece, forcing it out between this gap. The combination of electric energy and chemical energy then starts removing atoms from the surface in the immediate area between the tool and the workpiece. As the atoms are freed, the

high-pressure fluid washes them away. The heat generated as a result of the direct current is dissipated by the electrolyte, which also acts as a coolant (Fig. 34-6).

Metal Removal

The metal removal rate is about 1 in.^{3} of metal/min for each 10,000 A of current. Current densities on the machines range from 500 to 5,000 A psi. The rate of electrolyte flow in a typical project is 100 gal/min through a 0.015-in. gap, resulting in the high-current density that is made possible by the extremely high electrolyte flow. Removal rates at 1,000 A psi will be about ¾ lb aluminum/h, or 0.126 in.^{3} of aluminum/min, as shown in Table 34-1.

There are two types of machines: spe-

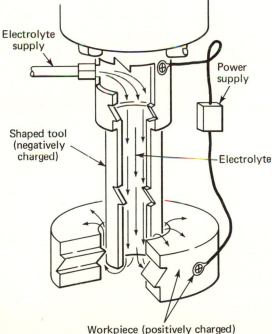

Fig. 34-6. Electrolyte supply.

TABLE 34-1. REMOVAL RATES OF SELECTED METALS

METAL	VALENCE	DENSITY, lb/in.³	REMOVAL RATES AT 1,000 A/in.² lb/1,000 A-h	in.³/min
Aluminum	3	0.098	0.74	0.126
Antimony	3	0.239	3.33	0.232
	5		2.00	0.139
Arsenic	3	0.207	2.05	0.165
	5		1.23	0.099
Beryllium	2	0.067	0.37	0.092
Chromium	2	0.260	2.14	0.137
	3		1.43	0.092
	6		0.71	0.046
Copper	1	0.324	5.22	0.268
	2		2.61	0.134
Gold	1	0.698	16.22	0.387
	3		5.40	0.129
Iron	2	0.248	2.30	0.135
	3		1.53	0.090
Manganese	2	0.270	2.26	0.139
	4		1.13	0.070
	6		0.75	0.047
	7		0.55	0.040
Molybdenum	3	0.369	2.63	0.119
	4		1.97	0.090
	6		1.32	0.060
Nickel	2	0.322	2.41	0.129
	3		1.61	0.083

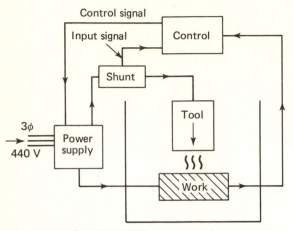

Fig. 34-7. ECM power supply.

cific and general purpose. They are either vertical metal removal machines or horizontal metal removal machines. Machine readings are designated by the amount of metal removed, by the size of the worktable, or by the ampere rating. The smallest units are rated from 50 to 100 A, and the highest are 20,000 A or above. General purpose machines enjoy several advantages over specific purpose units: general purpose machines cost less and require little maintenance (Fig. 34-7).

Tooling

As in conventional cutting, the dimensional accuracy in the surface finish of a machined part is directly proportional to the cutting conditions and the accuracy of the tool. One major difference between ECM and conventional cutting tools is that surface defects, such as nicks and scratches, on the ECM tool will be transferred to the workpiece.

Also, a good ECM tool must be electrically conductive. It should be capable of being machined to the desired shape with relative ease and must be capable of being repaired easily if a short circuit occurs. ECM tools must also have a large enough cross-sectional area to conduct current of sufficient quantities without burning out. The tools must not corrode, become distorted, vibrate, or erode when exposed to high-pressure corrosive electrolytes.

The major design feature that must be remembered is that the workpiece will conform exactly to the shape of the ECM tool so that the tool must be designed and machined carefully in order to reproduce the opposite of itself. Also, the tool must be designed to control the flow of electrolyte carefully because the flow pattern of the electrolyte determines the accuracy of the ECM process.

Electrolyte System

The *electrolyte* is a fluid material which conducts current. Generally, the electrolyte is made of water that is mixed with salt, mineral acid, caustic soda, or caustic potash. The strength of the electrolyte solution greatly affects the metal-removal rates. If the solution is a weak solution, the metal-removal rate will be low. Also, excessive heat builds in the electrolyte solution and causes harm to the workpiece. The electrolyte must be kept at a precise temperature and must have a uniform flow rate and a constant pressure.

The electrolyte system (Fig. 34-8) has pumps, heaters, thermostats, pressure gages, and flowmeters built into the system to control all of these variables. The temperature, usually controlled within $\pm 2°F$, is usually from 95 to 140°F. Pumps and valves control the pressure, which is maintained from between 200 to 300 psi within the system. The flow rates can range from as little as 50 gal/min up to 250 gal/min.

All of the electrolyte controls enter the cutting gap and become contaminated with metallic debris. Consequently, filters must be built into the system to remove these particles and to clean the electrolyte chemically so that it can be recycled. The electrolyte can be thought of as the actual cutting tool, and the electrode tool can be thought of as the object that shapes the electrolyte cutting tool. Therefore the electrolyte controls the surface finish as well as the shape of the tool. Because the electrolyte is the basic tool used in ECM, and because fluid acts in specific ways,

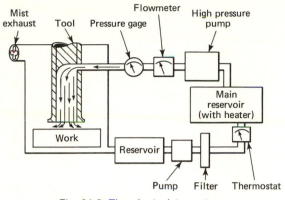

Fig. 34-8. The electrolyte system.

ELECTROCHEMICAL GRINDING

Electrochemical grinding, also called electrolytic grinding, combines standard wheel grinding with an electrochemical action, as in ECM. The abrasive action of the grinding wheel removes less than 10 percent of the metal while 90 percent of the metal is removed by anodic dissolution, or deplating, as in ECM.

Electrolytic grinding requires a flow of direct current between the wheel of the machine and the workpiece in the presence of an electrolyte (Fig. 34-10). The low voltage is applied between the grinding wheel and the workpiece, or the machine table. The electrolyte solution passes through the workpiece and the rotating metallic-impregnated grinding wheel, causing an electrochemical reaction, or deplating, which removes the surface atoms from the workpiece. The electrolyte fluid washes the metallic debris away into the storage tank. The electrolyte then passes through a filtering system and is pumped

it is extremely difficult to machine sharp corners. Fluid does not respond to sharp corners but to flowing shapes (Fig. 34-9).

A surface finish of 30 to 40 μin. can be obtained by the ECM process. A surface finish of 400 μin. can be machined in special cases. The finish of the surface is controlled by the velocity of the electrolyte, and the metal-removal rates vary with the velocity of the electrolyte flow. If this flow goes below a minimum amount, a short will occur in the system, damaging both the electrode and the workpiece.

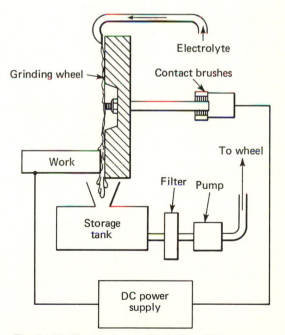

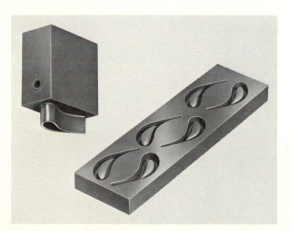

Fig. 34-9. Parts machined by ECM. (*Cincinnati Milacron Company.*)

Fig. 34-10. Electrochemical grinding (EG) system.

again under pressure to the grinding wheel. Again, as in ECM, the current is set up in a direction so that the work is the anode, or positive terminal, and the grinding wheel is the cathode, or the negative terminal. Under these conditions, the work surface is removed through the precisely controlled decomposition of atoms.

Current requirements for electrochemical grinding range from 500 to 1,200 A/in.^{3} of metal. The current flows from the dc source through the workpiece, to the electrolyte, to the grinding wheel, and back to the dc source. The metallic-impregnated grinding wheel must be insulated so that the dc supply is unimpaired because most electrolytic grinding requires an external motor to drive the grinding wheel. This motor has to be insulated from the dc deplating power supply (Fig. 34-11). The dc power supply to the grinding wheel is controlled by automatic voltage and current controls that should provide optimum conditions for the particular piece being ground. The optimum level is determined by the condition of the wheel and the work, the size of the work, the type of material, and the type of electrolyte. Sparking should always be controlled. A voltage adjustment usually is incorporated to minimize sparking. The object is to use the highest possible voltage while keeping sparking to a minimum. The voltage requirements for

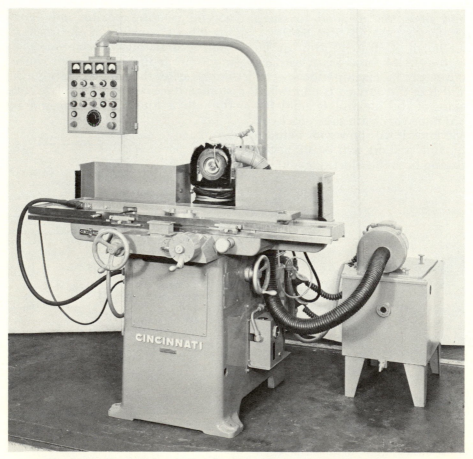

Fig. 34-11. Electrolytic grinding machine. (*Cincinnati Milacron Company.*)

electrolytic grinding range from only 6 up to 20 volts (V), with 20 V referred to as high voltage.

Operation

The actual removal of the stock is accomplished because the electrolyte is ionized during the electrochemical process. The ions combine with the workpiece to form an outside film. The spark that occurs between the wheel and the workpiece removes the ionic layer of metal oxide, and the electrolyte washes the oxide away. The electrolyte then acts as a coolant, as well as an electrical conductive solution. The grinding wheel, when operated, throws off a spray of electrolyte. The spray carries away the debris and then is collected and returned to the supply tank where it goes through filtering systems before it is recirculated under pressure to the workpiece (Fig. 34-10). As in ECM machines, no heat is generated during the grinding operation, making it possible to grind metal in much the same way as in the ECM process. EG grinders are capable of cylindrical grinding, form grinding, plunge grinding, traverse grinding, and surface grinding depending on the design of the particular electrolytic grinding machine.

QUESTIONS

1. Explain the principles of operation for electrical discharge machinery.
2. How do amperage and pulse rate affect EDM removal rates?
3. What are the advantages of the solid-state pulser over the relaxation and rotary pulsers?
4. What is overcut?
5. What is a dielectric?
6. What is an electrolyte?
7. How does ECM compare to electroplating?
8. How fast can the ECM control signal shut down the three-phase, 440 power supply?
9. Why is the control of the ECM electrolyte system important?
10. Explain the electrolytic grinding system.

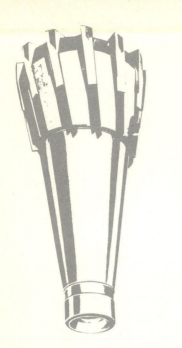

35

Numerical Control

A current trend in manufacturing is higher machine productivity at lower cost with closer product tolerances. These results can be achieved with numerical control. Numerical control minimizes human error and maximizes precision. It also makes it possible to turn out large numbers of items with narrow tolerances. Numerical control (N/C), an automation system that is highly adaptable and flexible, can make one basic tool, such as a milling machine, perform all the operations of the machine in any order desired, producing a finished product.

Numerical control regulates production systems by using numbers. The actual process involves numbers that are translated into electronic impulses. These impulses then control the workings of various machine tools. Common machine tools that use numerical control are the lathe, punch press, planer, shaper, and milling machine. Figure 35-1 is an example of an N/C vertical mill. Often N/C metalworking machines do not have handwheels for a machine operator but simply have drive motors to perform all the functions of a skilled operator. It is common practice to have a skilled operator in attendance to control the N/C machine. Numerical control can be attached to almost any type of machine, but the controls will be the same so that N/C equipment can be classified ac-

cording to the control system used and the type of command on the machine.

CONTROL SYSTEMS

Machines are controlled numerically by open-loop control systems (Fig. 35-2) and closed-loop control systems (Fig. 35-3). The open-loop system, a forerunner of the closed-loop system, uses a tape reader to send out discrete electrical signals to a motor control unit that drives a dc servomotor which in turn moves either the machine table or the toolholder. Since the amount of movement cannot be checked in the open-loop system, the closed-loop system was developed.

In the closed-loop system, the movement is sensed by a transducer, which feeds back an electrical impulse either into a motor control unit or into the tape reader (Fig. 35-3). The basic function of the transducer, or feedback device, is to convert any linear or rotational movement into an electrical signal and send it back to the motor control unit or the tape reader.

The two types of transducers used are the analog and the digital. The analog transducer is a synchronous motor device, producing a continuous signal that is propor-

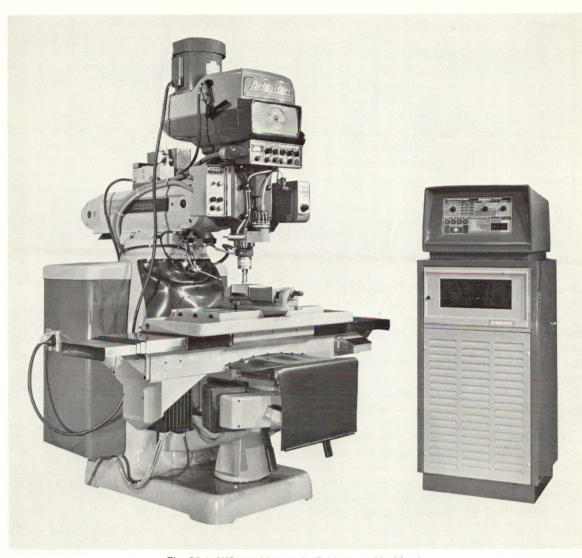

Fig. 35-1. N/C machine tool. (*Bridgeport Machine.*)

tional to the rotation of a lead screw, as for example, on a machine of a vertical mill. The digital transducer puts out an individual signal which identifies the position of the lead screw. The major thing the transducer does is to provide a feedback signal which is then compared to the original move command so that any error of the movement can be identified. Many times the motor control unit instructs the servomotor to move again to correct the error in the original movement. This total system is sometimes referred to as feedback.

THE N/C INDEXING SYSTEM

Tape-controlled machines are referred to as two-, three-, four-, or five-axis controlled ma-

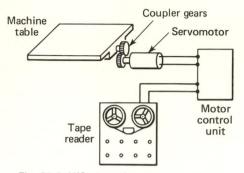

Fig. 35-2. N/C control system, open loop.

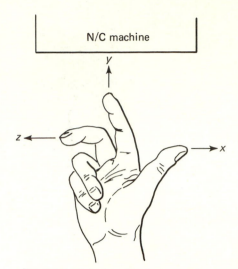

Fig. 35-4. Right-hand indexing system.

chines. The basis for all N/C indexing systems, regardless of the number of axes, is the Cartesian coordinate system. The Cartesian coordinate system, or the x, y, and z system, refers to the location of the tool in relation to the machine table. It does not matter whether the tool moves or the table moves; the indexing system (established by the Electronic Industries Association) remains the same. This system indexes N/C machines so that by holding the palm of the right hand upward and by following the hand diagram in Fig. 35-4, the x, y, and z coordinates are established.

The Cartesian coordinate system is used as either a two- or a three-axis system. Many N/C machines are identified as three-axis machines, but they operate numerically only with the x and y axes. The third axis, the z axis, is controlled by stops or by some means

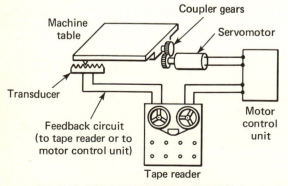

Fig. 35-3. N/C control system, closed loop.

other than an N/C tape. These machines are only two-axis machines. True three-axis N/C machine tools are capable of being programmed in all three axes.

The Cartesian coordinate system always has an index point, an origin point, which is referred to in the two-axis system as x, y, or point (0,0). In a three-axis system, it is called x, y, z, designated as (0,0,0). If the point (3,3) is to be located, the x as the first number would be 3, and the y would be 3 also (Fig. 35-5). The Cartesian coordinate system is also broken up into quadrants, so that in quadrant I, the x and y numbers are always positive. In quadrant II, the x is always negative, and the y is always positive. In quadrant III, both the x and the y are negative, and in quadrant IV, the x is positive and the y is negative. Many N/C machines are programmed to run only in quadrant I. However, some manufacturers have machines that are programmed to run in other quadrants (Fig. 35-5).

The location of the origin when compared to the machine table if it is a movable table, or to the toolholder if the toolholder is movable, must be known for this identifies the numbers that will be used in programming for parts. For example, in Fig. 35-6 the

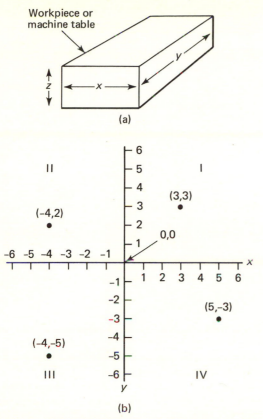

Fig. 35-5. Indexing systems. (a) Three-axis: x, y, and z; (b) two-axis (top view): x and y.

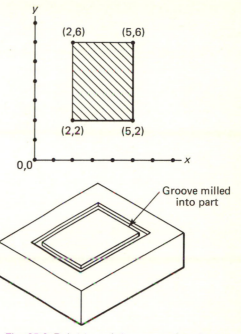

Fig. 35-6. Point-to-point command system.

part is located by the points (2,2), (5,2), (5,6), (2,6). If these numbers were programmed to perform their function, the groove to be milled might be cut in the wrong place if the origin (0,0) were not known. If the program identifies the (2,2) line as the origin, the part would be machined incorrectly. The origin location on a particular N/C machine must be known. Many machines have movable origins that can reestablish different numbers on a coordinate system.

COMMAND SYSTEMS

All N/C machines obey one of two types of command: the point-to-point command or the continuous, or contour, command. The point-to-point system is also called the numerical positioning control system (NPC), and the contour system is known as the numerical contouring control system (NCC).

The NPC command system is used to perform such simple tasks as straight milling, drilling, or welding. For the example in Fig. 35-6, milling a groove into a part, the point-to-point system would work well. In a vertical mill if the tool were to start at rest at the origin, or (0,0), it would be a comparatively small task to order the tool to go to point (2,2), and then to proceed to point (5,2) and to change direction to (5,6) and to (2,6) and then back to the (2,2). Following these points would mill a groove in the path if the tool were set at a cutting depth. If a two-axis NPC machine were used, a tool stop location would be required in the z axis.

One characteristic of point-to-point N/C machine tools is that the manner in which the cutter moves from the origin to the first cut is not specified and the path for the tool to take in order to arrive at the specific point is unimportant. Also, the move from the origin to the first specified point is done as rapidly as possible, usually at a rate of over 100 in./min. This rate reduces the cost factor by reducing the time required to use N/C machines.

A disadvantage of NPC systems is that extensive programming is required to cut lines that are not parallel to the x, y, or z axis, such as in cutting a curve (Fig. 35-7). In Fig. 35-7, if a curve originates at point (2,6) and then goes to (3,5), (4,4), and (5,2), four tape instructions would be required to perform this one task. The curve would be cut in short straight lines. If more accuracy were demanded, a series of intermediate tape instructions would be required in order to program the tool correctly. Often when NPC equipment is used to construct a radius, over 100 tape commands may be required, making the NPC command system best suited for less complicated tasks, such as drilling, tapping, boring, straight-line milling, and punching operations.

The NCC command system does not require the number of commands that the NPC system does. The contour milling system relies more on algebraic formulas or mathematical functions. For example, all circles are described as $x^2 + y^2 = r^2$, where r is the radius. The radius determines the size of the circle, so that if a radius and a formula were programmed into a tape, the continuous command system coupled to a machine tool could reproduce a circle to any specified depth (Fig. 35-8). The NCC system can also produce lines that are not parallel to the x or the y coordinate system.

For example, any line may fit the formula $x = ay$, where a is a multiplying factor of y. If a is 3, whenever the tool rests at x, it would also rest at 3, or at point (1,3). The tool can be advanced two spaces in a positive x direction so that x is equal to 3 and y would then equal 9. So the Cartesian coordinates would be (3,9) describing all points between (1,3) and (3,9) in a connecting straight line. When programming a continuous command system, it is important to remember both the beginning position of the tool and the end position of the tool, for the tool path is controlled by the equation covering direction and the length between the beginning and the ending points.

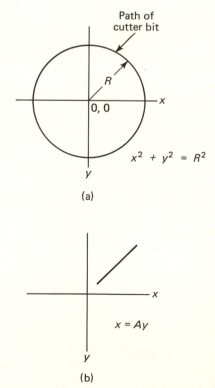

(a)

(b)

Fig. 35-8. Continuous command system (NCC). (a) Circle; (b) line.

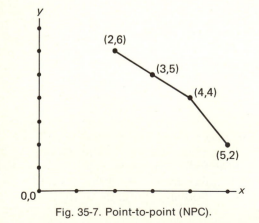

Fig. 35-7. Point-to-point (NPC).

CODING CONTROL

Numerical machine coding systems usually are placed on standard 80-hole punched cards, magnetic tape, or punched tape. In the beginning, the N/C input was done on punched cards. However, punched cards had some serious disadvantages. Atmospheric changes and dirt on the cards greatly affected their accuracy. Also the handling and storage of punched cards were critical. If a deck of punched cards were scrambled, the N/C program would be scrambled. Most manufacturers quickly created either magnetic tape or punched tapes in order to code N/C programs.

A magnetic tape for input into N/C machines is used when the N/C machine is used in conjunction with a computer. The standard tape is ½ in. wide, and the information is stored on the magnetic tape approximately in the same manner as with the punched tape. The major disadvantage of the magnetic tape is that expensive tape readers and control systems must be used with it. The cost of the magnetic tape reader is much more than the cost of a punched tape reader. Also, as is true in all magnetic tape uses, information can be erased accidentally if the magnetic tape is exposed to a magnetic field. A further disadvantage to magnetic tape is that it takes a special reader to check the tape for error in the N/C program because nothing visible appears on the tape.

The punched tape approach is used most often for controlling N/C machines. While punched tape does have some disadvantages, its advantages far outweigh them. For example, no reading device is necessary when checking errors in the programmed control. Errors in the program can be deleted by simply punching one more hole in specific locations. The storage, as with magnetic tapes, is simple and the cost for standard Electronics Industries Association (EIA) standardized tape is low. The punched tape has been standardized to a 1-in. 8-channel tape capable of producing most of the necessary information used in all manufacturing. The system that converts Cartesian coordinate system numbers to the tape is called the *binary-coded decimal system*.

BINARY-CODED DECIMAL SYSTEM

The binary-coded decimal system (BCD) has been adopted by the N/C industry for the tape input into machines. This system combines the binary system and the decimal system. Values are assigned to each of the available 8 channels, making it possible to reproduce any given combination of numbers. For example, in Table 35-1, channel 1 is assigned the numerical value of 1; channel 2, the value of 2; channel 3, the value of 4; channel 4, the value of 8; and channel 6, the value of 0. With these five channels, it is possible to generate any specific number. For example, if 6 is punched on the tape, the channel 3 and channel 2 holes are punched out, since $4 + 2 = 6$. Channel 5 in the coding system is used for a parity check or an error check. The *parity check*, a simple test, ensures that all holes punched across one row add up to an odd number. In other words, the parity check establishes that an even number of holes plus the parity check hole creates an odd number. If there is an even number of holes across one row, the program has an error which will be indicated by the tape reader. Channel 6 and channel 7 are also used for alphabetical symbols to spell out words. A combination of channel 6 and 7 makes it possible to identify the complete alphabet A through Z when they are coupled

TABLE 35-1. BINARY-CODED DECIMAL SYSTEM (BCD)

Channel 1	Value of 2^0 or 1
Channel 2	Value of 2^1 or 2
Channel 3	Value of 2^2 or 4
Channel 4	Value of 2^3 or 8
Channel 5	Parity check
Channel 6	Value of 0
Channel 7	"X"
Channel 8	End of block

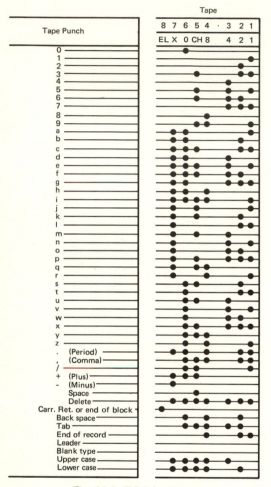

Fig. 35-9. EIA 1-in. tape.

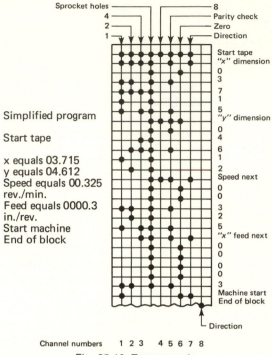

Simplified program

Start tape

x equals 03.715
y equals 04.612
Speed equals 00.325
rev./min.
Feed equals 0000.3
in./rev.
Start machine
End of block

Fig. 35-10. Tape sample.

with channels 1, 2, 3, and 4. A hole punched in channel 8 indicates the end of a block of information (Fig. 35-9).

A simple N/C program on a vertical mill would start a tape on x- and y-axis dimensions and would contain the r/min of the tool, the feed of the tool in inches per revolution (in./rev), and the order to start the machine. This information would constitute one sentence or one block of information (Fig. 35-10). The standard tape would have a series of holes punched that would indicate this information. The example in Fig. 37-10 contains this simplified program as well as a

parity check for the program. The check, located in column 5, is always punched so that an odd number of holes appear in the tape. The punch mark in channel 8, designating the end of this particular program sentence, indicates that there is a whole language system unique to numerical control. Some of the major terms used are: bit, tab, block, end of block, and program. *Bit* is N/C terminology for either *binary digit* or words (Table 35-2).

TABLE 35-2. N/C TERMINOLOGY

N/C TERM	MEANING
Block	Sentence
End of block	Complete sentence
Numbers	Numbers
Bit	Word
Word	Word
Tab	Spacing
Program	Story

TAPE FORMAT

Tape format can have as few as three or four words or an unlimited number of words. Usually a tape format will be set by the manufacturer of the machine tool. A basic format is a five-word format that will include the sequence, the function, x and y dimensioning words, and miscellaneous words that control the tool change. A basic three-dimensional format will have a sequence word, a function word, an x dimension word, a y dimension word, a z dimension word, and a miscellaneous word statement. This statement will then be followed by an EOB (end of block), and the next N/C statement, composed of the same number of words, will follow. Some of the basic types of tape formats are: the fixed sequential format, tab ignore format, tape tab sequential format, word address format, word address tab ignore format, and the word address computer control format.

Computer Formats

The various tape formats proved incapable of handling the development of more complex programs so computers were coupled to multiaxis N/C machines, enabling them to form complicated cutting procedures. One of the most used computer-assisted N/C programs is the Automatic Programmed Tools System (APT). The APT system requires a fairly large computer. Although there are a number of other systems, all the computer-assisted programs function basically in the same manner. The APT system is one that uses geometric forms and English terminology to program the machine tool. A very simple statement, such as "Go to x 0.0500," is one part of a sentence and is all that is needed for the operation to be performed.

A special feature of computer-controlled programs is their ability to check out tape errors prior to the printout of the program. Because any mistake in programming can lead to a large-scale error, it is vital that the computer-controlled machines have the ability to check out the accuracy of their programs. For example, in the APT program the control of the machine may be such that if there is an error message (such as a given circle and a given line do not intersect as desired), the computer read-out will not only indicate the error but will also indicate the corrective action that must be programmed into the machine. Also, the computer will stop the machine tool when the error is detected and will not proceed until directed to do so.

When the computer is programmed, the viewpoint of the tool is considered the essential function so that the program is written as if the programmer were sitting at the very point of the cutting tool. In fact, when writing the program, the programmer must remain tool-oriented because directions are given from a starting point in the APT program in relation to the tool, such as *go up; go down; go lft* (which means left), and *go fwd* (which means forward). In the APT program, as in the case of all computer programs, a programming guide identifies the key words and directions. All the programmer must do is determine the direction which yields a key word. The programmer then needs only to put a length dimension to this key word to program the computer.

QUESTIONS

1. What is the difference between an open-loop and a closed-loop control system?
2. What is the standard EIA right-hand indexing system?
3. Identify and explain the Cartesian coordinate system as used with N/C tools.
4. Explain the point-to-point NPC command system.
5. Explain the NCC command system.

6. Compare and contrast punched card, magnetic tape, and punched tape input systems.
7. Explain parity check.
8. What is a bit?
9. Why are computers used in conjunction with N/C machines?

Index